When Women Wrote Hollywood

ALSO BY ROSANNE WELCH
AND FROM MCFARLAND

Why The Monkees *Matter: Teenagers, Television
and American Pop Culture* (2016)

When Women Wrote Hollywood

Essays on Female Screenwriters in the Early Film Industry

Edited by ROSANNE WELCH
Foreword by Cari Beauchamp

McFarland & Company, Inc., Publishers
Jefferson, North Carolina

LIBRARY OF CONGRESS CATALOGUING-IN-PUBLICATION DATA

Names: Welch, Rosanne, editor.
Title: When women wrote Hollywood : essays on female screenwriters in the early film industry / edited by Rosanne Welch ; foreword by Cari Beauchamp.
Description: Jefferson, North Carolina : McFarland & Company, Inc., Publishers, 2018 | Includes bibliographical references and index.
Identifiers: LCCN 2018020609 | ISBN 9781476668871 (softcover : acid free paper) ∞
Subjects: LCSH: Women in the motion picture industry—California—Los Angeles. | Women screenwriters—California—Los Angeles—Biography.
Classification: LCC PN1995.9.W6 W48 2018 | DDC 812/.03—dc23
LC record available at https://lccn.loc.gov/2018020609

ISBN (print) 978-1-4766-6887-1
ISBN (ebook) 978-1-4766-3277-3

BRITISH LIBRARY CATALOGUING DATA ARE AVAILABLE

© 2018 Rosanne Welch. All rights reserved

No part of this book may be reproduced or transmitted in any form or by any means, electronic or mechanical, including photocopying or recording, or by any information storage and retrieval system, without permission in writing from the publisher.

Front cover: Jane Murfin at RKO Pictures, 1934 (Academy of Motion Picture Arts and Sciences' Margaret Herrick Library); background photograph by Brycia James Kiewlak (iStock)

Printed in the United States of America

McFarland & Company, Inc., Publishers
Box 611, Jefferson, North Carolina 28640
www.mcfarlandpub.com

Table of Contents

Acknowledgments — vii

Foreword: Finding Frances Marion
  CARI BEAUCHAMP — 1

Introduction
  ROSANNE WELCH — 5

Adela Rogers St. Johns: Survival of the Feisty
  SARAH AMBLE WHORTON — 11

Jeanie Macpherson: A Life Unknown
  AMELIA PHILLIPS — 20

Anita Loos: A Girl Like Her
  TONI ANITA HULL — 35

The Nature and Genius of Alice Guy Blaché
  KHANISHA FOSTER — 47

"You'd better learn to hold your liquor": Bess Meredyth and a Career in Early Hollywood
  SYDNEY HAVEN — 56

The Best Revenge Is Outliving Them All: The Life and Heartbreak of Frederica Sagor Maas
  MIKAYLA DANIELS — 63

Silent Screenwriter, Producer and Director: Marion Fairfax
  SARAH PHILLIPS — 69

Smart Girl in Charge: Eve Unsell
  LAURA KIRK — 80

The Glorious Ms. Glyn
  AMY L. BANKS — 88

Fearless and Fierce: June Mathis
  LAUREN ELIZABETH SMITH — 95

Table of Contents

Writing Around Lois Weber
  CHASE THOMPSON 104

Gene Gauntier: Ascending by Drowning
  YASSER OMAR SHAHIN 112

Lorna Moon: A Woman of a Certain Influence
  ELIZABETH DWYER 117

Clara Beranger: The Unseen Laborer
  AMANDA R. STOCKWELL 125

Ida May Park: Prolific Pioneer
  JACKIE PEREZ 133

Frances Goodrich and Albert Hackett: The Most Beloved Couple in Hollywood
  JULIE BERKOBIEN 140

In Defense of Lillian Hellman
  KELLEY C. ZINGE 150

The Intimately Unknowable Dorothy Parker: A Study of Her Life and Art
  ELIZABETH DWYER 157

Joan Harrison: Redefining Femininity in Film Noir and Hollywood
  CHELSEA ANDES 166

The Six Degrees of Sarah Y. Mason and Victor Heerman
  PAMELA L. SCOTT 175

Zoë Akins: A Quiet Rebellion
  SARAH AMBLE WHORTON 183

Marriage of Words: Bella and Sam Spewack
  LAURA KIRK 192

The Forgettable Ms. Murfin
  AMY L. BANKS 200

A Team in Passionate Action: Ruth Gordon and Garson Kanin
  ROSANNE WELCH 205

About the Contributors 217

Index 219

Acknowledgments

I am very grateful to Ken Lazebnik, director of the Stephens College MFA in TV and screenwriting, for inviting me along on an adventure that brought me into contact with this dedicated cohort. Their deep interest in keeping the names and work of these early female screenwriters alive makes me optimistic that soon many more students will be introduced to such pioneering women film writers.

I also want to thank my husband, Douglas, and my son, Joseph, for their support when I am often so focused on a deadline that I seem to be in another world during dinner discussions—and my mother, Mary, who initiated all the library visits I mention in the Introduction, as they were the beginnings of my love of reading and writing ... and history.

Foreword

Finding Frances Marion

CARI BEAUCHAMP

From copyright records, we know that almost half of all films made before 1925 were written by women, yet too often their names are found only in the footnotes of Hollywood histories. Women such as Anita Loos, June Mathis and Jeanie Macpherson are not familiar to us today, yet Loos catapulted Douglas Fairbanks to stardom by creating his athletic comedies before going on to write such classics as *Gentlemen Prefer Blondes* and half a dozen films for Jean Harlow; Mathis mentored Rudolph Valentino and starred him in her *Four Horsemen of the Apocalypse*; and Macpherson acted and directed before going on to write most of Cecil B. DeMille's most successful and iconic epics. They and dozens of other fascinating women were highly paid, powerful players at studios that churned out films at the rate of one a month.

While *Photoplay* mused that "Strangely enough, women outrank men as continuity writers," it wasn't strange to the women. They had always found sanctuary in writing; it was accomplished in private and provided a creative vent when little was expected or accepted of a woman outside the home. For some, a virtue was derived from oppression; with so little expected of them, they were free to accomplish much. These early female screenwriters were drawn to a business that, for a time, welcomed and nurtured women, and they flocked to Hollywood to share their talents and fuel their financial independence in the decades before they even had the right to vote. With few people taking moviemaking seriously as a business, the doors were wide open.

For more than 20 years, no writer was more sought after than Frances Marion. With her versatile pen and a caustic wit, she was a leading participant in one of the most creative eras for women in American history. She is credited with writing more than 300 scripts covering every conceivable genre, and she also directed and produced half a dozen films. As a government correspondent recording the contributions of women during World War I, she was the first Allied woman to cross the Rhine. When Frances was elected vice president and only woman on the first board of directors of the Screen Writers Guild, she was dropped from the MGM payroll. MGM production chief Irving Thalberg claimed unions were only for plumbers, but she told him that she was doing it for the writers who made 50 dollars a week and did not receive credit for the films they wrote. (Within a year they "agreed to disagree" about the guild and Thalberg brought her back to MGM at more than $100,000 a year because he needed her to adapt *The Good Earth*.)

Foreword: Finding Frances Marion

Whatever studio she was working with, Frances credited her friendships with other women as the key to her success and happiness. She began as a protégé of the director Lois Weber (whose story you will read in one of these essays) in 1914 and soon became close friends with Mary Pickford for whom she would write a dozen films including *Poor Little Rich Girl*, *Stella Maris* and *M'liss*. In the early '20s, Frances initiated what she called "hen parties" at her home on Angelo Drive. In casual clothes and little make up, a dozen or more women gathered for dinner and often retreated to the basement theater to watch movies they had made years before, and according to Frances, "laugh until our sides hurt."

At MGM, Frances was depended upon to write for their biggest stars including Greta Garbo, Lillian Gish and Marion Davies. Behind the camera, Frances knew she could count on Ida Koverman, President Hoover's former assistant who became Louis B. Mayer's gatekeeper, to debrief her on the boss's moods and needs. And then there was Kate Corbaley, the head of the MGM story department, who conspired with Marion to sell the scripts of other female friends to the studio. Frances always looked out for friends down on their luck such as Marie Dressler, ZaSu Pitts and Hedda Hopper, by writing parts for them and making sure they were cast. The production process was very different from today: Thalberg would approve Frances's script, together they would go over the cast actors, and only then would the production head check and see which director was available the weeks they intended to shoot the film.

After Thalberg's death in 1936, Frances said screenwriting became "like writing in the sand with the wind machine going," and she turned to writing short stories, novels and the first textbook on writing for film. Frances painted, sculpted, spoke several languages fluently, and played "concert caliber" piano. Throughout her life she continued to write, which she claimed was "the refuge of the shy," and shunned publicity; she was uncomfortable as a heroine, but she refused to be a victim.

I only learned this and more when I became frustrated, irritated and eventually inspired by the fact that I could find so little on the women whose names I recognized from the credits of films I loved. I began what soon became a mission to excavate their stories, culminating in my book, *Without Lying Down: Frances Marion and the Powerful Women of Early Hollywood*. I originally envisioned a social/cultural history of a group of women who were also friends, but Frances Marion quickly skyrocketed to the top. From 1915 through 1935, she was the highest paid screenwriter—male or female—and remains the only woman to win two Academy Awards for Best Original Screenplay (*The Big House* in 1930 and *The Champ* in 1932). As the acclaimed journalist and screenwriter Adela Rogers St. Johns (another writer you will meet in one of these essays) said, "Frances was the senior all of us sophomores wanted to be."

Much remains to be learned about and from these impressive, accomplished women. In a few cases, they wrote autobiographies, but none are particularly forthcoming and they often focused more on their colleagues than on themselves. Most of them did not maintain archives, let alone save their papers or memorabilia via more private family collections. I have Frances's long time secretary, Martha Lorah, to thank for taking material out of the dumpster when Frances was blithely tossing it out in preparation for a move.

I was recently asked by a filmmaker friend to help him locate impressive gravesites of important women of early Hollywood. In pondering the question, I realized that while Cecil B. DeMille and other male producers and directors had large mausoleums, statues or monuments, Lois Weber, Frances Marion and many others had been cremated (Frances specifically requested her ashes be spread over a rose garden, but the family scattered them over her father's ranch in northern California). It occurred to me these women died the way they lived, taking their work seriously but not themselves. Most were secure in their own skins, if not as confident in their skills as they should have been. Their work was important to them, but they were not pulled into its vortex; they valued their families and friends with equal passion. As Frances put it, her two sons "come first, then it is a photo-finish between my work and my friends."

I know the challenges I faced in unearthing information about Frances and her colleagues and much of what I did discover would be impossible to find today. So many of the friends and relatives who knew these women are no longer with us. However, other information is at our fingertips like never before as research has changed dramatically over the past 20 years. Newspapers and magazines have been digitized and an article from the *New York Times* is now available in minutes without ever leaving my desk, whereas finding such a small yet necessary item used to require a drive to the downtown library and hours spent squinting at microfilm. Sites such as the Media History Digital Library provide instant access to magazines such as *Photoplay* and industry periodicals such as *Film Daily*. However, fledgling researchers and writers, please beware of sites such as Wikipedia whose idea of fact checking is finding the information somewhere else on the Internet. Solid research still requires venturing to libraries such as the Academy's Margaret Herrick, New York's Performing Arts Library and the Library of Congress in Washington, D.C. Local historical societies, libraries and courthouses often have gems to be revealed. For the most part, material comes in bits and pieces, but I keep hearing about families who discover stashes of letters, papers and home movies, and the Academy is constantly enlarging its collections.

My journey to learn about these women and share it with others has been rewarding in many ways, and one of those is my participation with Stephens College, the second oldest women's college in America. Their MFA program in television and screenwriting not only acknowledges the need for more women screenwriters, but is also actually doing something about it. And best of all, they are doing it right. Their innovative low residency, mentor-based program encourages energetic, multi-faceted participants who would find the demands of a full time college program difficult, if not impossible. These are the writers who often have the most interesting stories to tell.

The Stephens' curriculum also respects and values the history of film, with a focus on the craft of screenwriting. I don't want to think about the number of times I have spoken at what are considered the finest film programs in the country to be greeted by students who have never heard the names of Frances Marion or Anita Loos or seen a movie made before 1960, much less 1939. That won't happen with Stephens' graduates. The students I work with already have the passion, and in this program they are learning the history of filmmaking, the art of screenwriting and the realities of the film business. That combination of knowledge and experience is exactly what is sorely underrepresented in Hollywood today.

This volume of essays on women screenwriters brings new research and information to the existing scholarship and I hope it inspires further investigation. Some essays focus on singular aspects of a subject's life and others use broad strokes, but all provide building blocks for future scholars. I have recently read several book proposals that claim spectacular conclusions that simply are not justified. I understand the need for academics to publish something new and marketing departments that want to herald spectacular findings. Of course we can and should put the spotlight on these women individually, but we have to resist the temptation to remove them from their larger community of filmmakers or make any single accomplishment so much greater than the others. The truth is we all build on each other's work—both as scholars and as filmmakers—and that is how it should be.

One of the important lessons I have learned is how little difference there is between the women of early Hollywood and those of us today. Seeking acceptance and approval from a primarily male power structure is familiar to most women, as is the search for professional fulfillment while meeting the needs of children and husbands. That these universal challenges have always been with us was illustrated to me when I read a 1915 interview with the writer Mary Roberts Rinehart. She admitted to hiding in the bathroom to finish a story and when asked how she managed to be so prolific with the inherent interruptions of her household, she said it wasn't the interruptions as much as it was working "in fear of interruption." Exactly. It occurred to me, trying to finish a book with two young boys in the house, to put a sign on my door saying "It better be an artery," but of course I didn't. Somehow knowing that Mary and so many others had faced the same obstacles and conquered them gave me a new sense of serenity. Once we realize we are links in a chain, we never feel alone, and that is liberating and empowering. Movie making, like a full life, takes a village. Now more than ever we need that community to succeed, both personally and professionally. Hopefully, we can be inspired by and exemplify Frances Marion's admonition: "I owe my greatest success to women ... I have found that it has always been one of my own sex who has given me a helping hand when I needed it."

Cari Beauchamp is the author of Without Lying Down *about women screenwriters in early Hollywood. She is a* Vanity Fair *contributor, appears on Turner Classic Movies and is the only person twice named an Academy Film Scholar. She is the resident scholar for the Mary Pickford Foundation and is on the Center for the Study of Women in Television and Film's advisory board.*

Introduction

Rosanne Welch

When I was first asked to create a history course for a new MFA in TV and screenwriting focused on the mission of bringing more female voices and female-centric stories to Hollywood, I made two decisions. One, I would focus on *screenwriting* history, not the more generic and more traditional *film* history because film history translates into the history of directors. Students clearly had had enough exposure to the auteur theory in their earlier degree programs. They could name directors by the bushel, but could barely list the screenwriters they knew with the fingers of one hand. In listing their own favorite films they often knew which directors to associate with them, but rarely which writers. So, *screenwriting* history it would be. Two, I decided we had to start at the very beginning, when women ran Hollywood. No other course I had ever taken or been asked to teach had focused on these women, some of whom I had been reading about since the summers of my childhood in Cleveland, Ohio. Back then, I walked to the local library branch once a week to collect a stack of memoirs by women like Anita Loos and Adela Rogers St. Johns, who I had seen interviewed on *The Merv Griffin Show*. Or women like Mary Pickford who, by founding United Artists with Douglas Fairbanks, Charlie Chaplin and D.W. Griffith, became one of the first female studio executives and later helped found the Academy of Motion Picture Arts and Sciences. These women's memoirs introduced me to the names of movie moguls like Louis B. Mayer or Jack Warner, who make up most of the history courses I later found in academia.

Armed with this knowledge, I was saddened to find that most film history courses, and their accompanying textbooks, glossed over these women with a paragraph if they mentioned them at all. Since I was often the only person in the room who mentioned these female screenwriters and producers, I conceived a course that would begin with these women who wrote Hollywood into existence and culminate in research by each graduate student into the life and career of one particular female screenwriter. That is what you find here. A collection of *her*stories about how these women lived, loved and created the cinematic stories that gave their audiences new ideas about life and love.

These essays cover the gamut of under-represented screenwriters from early silent films to early talkies, with the exception of the woman who was the highest paid writer, male or female, of the era—Frances Marion. See Cari Beauchamp's groundbreaking *Without Lying Down: Frances Marion and the Powerful Women of Early Hollywood*. Also, if you want to learn more about the women writers of early Hollywood, read works by the women themselves wherever you find them scattered on the web or in archives all over the country. That is how I found them all originally, through their own writings in my beloved local library. It is why I shared their stories with these students and why they, in turn, wanted so deeply to share what they discovered with a wider audience than one college course could provide. If we do not study these women, if we do not read their work and understand their contributions to screenwriting, we are compliant in their historical erasure.

These MFA candidates found research in huge archives such as the Margaret Herrick Library of the Academy of Motion Picture Arts and Sciences and in tiny tidbits in hometown newspapers scanned into digital copies for the information age. The goal was to provide a clearinghouse of information on which other future historians could continue to build so that future scholars can find new facts, and even contradict some of those found here, as is the way of history—and *her*story.

Each of the 24 essays in this volume concerns itself with a female screenwriter, the themes of her writing and the trajectory of her career. The volume opens with "Adela Rogers St. Johns: Survival of the Feisty" by Sarah Amble Whorton. Whorton introduces readers to former journalist turned screenwriter turned "Mother Confessor" to her colleagues in Hollywood and concludes that St. Johns' success came from humanizing her subjects whether they be fact or fiction. St. Johns understood the real challenge in Hollywood was to survive. Whorton understands that St. Johns is one of the lucky women who lived long enough to be a historian of this earlier period and therefore assure her own place in its telling.

The essay that follows chronicles a true survivor whose name is not even as well known as St. Johns because this woman never wrote about herself. In "Jeanie Macpherson: A Life Unknown," Amelia Phillips digs deep into the backstory of Jeanie Macpherson, who acted in over 147 films and wrote 54 financially successful films. She was a pilot in her spare time when she had any, but whenever her films are mentioned they are completely credited to their director, Cecil B. DeMille. Phillips discovers that Macpherson wrote the bulk of his financial successes, and when they stopped working together, his movies failed. Phillips also discovers one of the most difficult issues in researching these women: the fact that few left records, so their place in history came from interviews with the men they had worked with. Sadly, those men often cared more for their own legacies than those of their female colleagues.

One of the most enduring female legends of the silent era appears in the third essay, written by Toni Anita Hull. In writing "Anita Loos: A Girl Like Her," Hull faced a different task than her fellow essayists, as Loos lived to the age of 92 and told her own story in several well received memoirs. Distilling down the truth from the legend of the author of *Gentlemen Prefer Blondes* proved a formidable task, but in focusing on what Loos' work tells us, Hull found a writer who was a master at satirizing sex and love and was capable of writing rich, multi-faceted females who drove the action in their films.

The fourth essay is about a true pioneer long left out of film history books, though today she is being more and more recognized as one of the first writers and directors to use the new medium of film to tell narrative stories rather than merely document daily life. In "The Nature and Genius of Alice Guy Blaché," Khanisha Foster grants the genius title to a woman who began as a secretary to Léon Gaumont and became the first woman in the world to open her own film studio. Responsible for writing, acting, producing, and directing more than 1,000 films in the era of the one-reeler, Foster posits much of Blaché's genius may have been in the doing of things.

Another pioneer of sorts appears in "'You'd better learn to hold your liquor': Bess Meredyth and a Career in Early Hollywood" by Sydney Haven. Meredyth's ability to survive the transition from silent films to sound kept her career thriving, as did her ability to do whatever it took to turn around troubled productions such as *Ben-Hur* (1924), which ran over budget while filming in Rome. In that instance, Meredyth even had to smuggle film cans out of the country in her hatbox. To find out why, read Haven's essay.

A similar fate found Frederica Sagor Maas, but she did not go soft into that good oblivion. When she was 99, Maas published a scathing memoir of her time in Hollywood, which provided much of the fodder for "The Best Revenge Is Outliving Them All: The Life and Heartbreak of Frederica Sagor Maas" by Mikayla Daniels. From Maas' own telling, and corroborated by various histories of the Writers Guild of America, many writers often worked on screenplays for which they received no formal credits. While a salary is useful, credits create career longevity. For this and many reasons, Maas' most clear credit comes from *The Shocking Miss Pilgrim* (1947), which arrived too late to boost her career.

The next essay presents a woman more successful, yet, again, unknown today. In "Silent Screenwriter, Producer and Director: Marion Fairfax" Sarah Phillips confronts an issue facing many who want to study the women of this era. From the origins of Fairfax's career in the silent era through her mysterious disappearance from the Hollywood scene after the advent of talkies, there is little information available on her work as an actress, playwright and screenwriter, and the information that is available is not consistently correct. Thanks to a treasure trove of telegrams and letters in the archives, Phillips creates a portrait of an everywoman who effortlessly moved from writing for stage to writing for screen and founded Marion Fairfax Productions in 1921.

Laura Kirk resurrects a formerly prominent woman in "Smart Girl in Charge: Eve Unsell," noting that even while running her own self-named studio, her male colleagues and local reporters still referred to Unsell by the diminutive "girl" when reporting on her many, many successes. Kirk does not shy away from controversy in her coverage of Unsell either. She openly discusses Unsell's work in what were then called "yellow peril" pictures, films that exploited a fear posed to the West by intermarriage with Asian peoples. Kirk concludes that Unsell, like her many peers, owed her success to her education, reputation, skill, work ethic, and independence fired directly in the face of gender inequity.

On a sunnier note, Amy L. Banks' essay, "The Glorious Ms. Glyn," gives thanks to Elinor Glyn for her studies in sensuality that live on in any number of female stars considered sexual icons today, those who possess the "It" that Glyn defined for all time in her film of the same name starring Clara Bow. Banks also finds a woman who wrote to keep her family financially afloat, something true about many women, not only writers, who lived through the shaky beginnings of the 20th century.

In the next essay, Lauren Elizabeth Smith claims June Mathis to be both "Fearless and Fierce" and finds that one of the characteristics that set Mathis apart from other writers and filmmakers of her time was her determination to study the art of filmmaking, not only for the art's sake, but also for the artist's sake. When she moved from stage acting to screenwriting, Mathis buried herself in literature, reading everything from Shakespeare to de Maupassant, and such influence can be seen in her classics *The Four Horsemen of the Apocalypse* (1921), *Camille* (1921) and *Blood and Sand* (1922).

Fierce in her own way is a fair description of a female writer-director who Chase Thompson believes deserves to take her place among the much more lauded male directors of her day. In "Writing Around Lois Weber," Thompson discusses the historian's issue of access. Many of Weber's films have not survived to be transferred to modern screening technology, making her impact on film history more difficult to process. Only recently have historians and researchers begun to truly see the impact Weber posed on the silent era of film despite her receiving 118 writing credits, 137 directing credits, 102 acting credits, and 19 producing credits.

In a sadly similar fashion, Yasser Omar Shahin attempts to revive more of the story of early film pioneer Gene Gauntier, though his title, "Ascending by Drowning" references the one story most repeated in histories of the silent era. So excited to enter the burgeoning business of show, Gauntier took her first acting job even though it required her to swim when she could not. Eventually, she wrote and produced films in Ireland, England, Scotland, Germany, Italy, and Egypt, and filmed the first story of the Christ, *From the Manger to the Cross*, in Palestine in 1912.

The perils of international filming were apparently nothing compared to the perils of surviving the societal pressure of the early 1900s, even in a town dubbed "Sin Town." In "Lorna Moon: A Woman of a Certain Influence," Elizabeth Dwyer finds reason to quote the oft-said warning that well-behaved women seldom make history. It is true that Moon's name never reached the fame to match that of the father of her illegitimate son, William C. de Mille, despite being a novelist and short story writer with titles such as *Doorways in Drumorty* (1925) and *Dark Star* (1929). Dwyer posits that Moon's audacity not only carried her far and wide, but also provided consistent fuel for her various writings.

Continuing the awkward de Mille family tree, "Clara Beranger: The Unseen Laborer" by Amanda R. Stockwell covers the life a journalist, playwright and screenwriter in her own right, who is nevertheless relegated to history books as the wife of William C. de Mille or as one of the founding lecturers at the incipient film degree program at the University of Southern California. While her work in higher education makes her unique among the writers in this collection, previous focus on that misses the fact that Beranger amassed 79 screenplays across her career.

In the following essay by Jackie Perez, we see the recurring concept of the kind of continuous work required by these women to gain and maintain their success in Hollywood. "Ida May Park: Prolific Pioneer" highlights the aforementioned issue of women notable enough to have some of their work survive, but not notable enough for many history books or archives to chronicle her career. Park wrote approximately 500 scenarios and 50 features, and had a successful career as a director with fourteen films.

Perhaps the most well-known woman with the most well-preserved work in this collection appears in Julie Berkobien's "Frances Goodrich and Albert Hackett: The Most Beloved Couple in Hollywood." In collaboration with her husband for over 50 years, Goodrich churned out classics such as *The Thin Man*, *It's a Wonderful Life* and the Pulitzer Prize–winning *The Diary of Anne Frank*. Due to their longevity they also became chroniclers of the early Hollywood era, and thanks to their efforts, many of these other women are remembered when Goodrich and Hackett are remembered.

Likewise, "In Defense of Lillian Hellman" by Kelley C. Zinge discusses the work of the other best-known female screenwriter and another woman who can thank longevity and the writing of memoirs for her continued fame. With plays turned into films such as *The Children's Hour* and *The Little Foxes*, and with her heartfelt testimony against testifying for the HUAC during the Blacklist era, Lillian Hellman cemented her place in film history textbooks.

The essay on Hellman is followed by her confidante in New York City, "The Intimately Unknowable Dorothy Parker: A Study of Her Life and Art" by Elizabeth Dwyer. Though Parker's work in poetry and short stories is widely known, like F. Scott Fitzgerald, she, too, dabbled in Hollywood. *A Star Is Born*, her most successful screenplay, proved more successful than anything by Fitzgerald, yet his name appears in more screenwriting histories than her name.

Though Joan Harrison's name tends to appear in textbooks, it is often overshadowed by the director with whom she worked most often, Alfred Hitchcock. In "Joan Harrison: Redefining Femininity in Film Noir and Hollywood," Chelsea Andes reports that they worked together during what is considered Hitchcock's most artistic period, and after they stopped working together, none of his films found the same critical and financial success. In order to maintain more control over her films, Harrison later became a producer.

For her essay on one of the earliest writing teams, Pamela L. Scott resorted to "The Six Degrees of Sarah Y. Mason and Victor Heerman." Though earning an early Academy Award for adapting the Louisa May Alcott novel *Little Women* into a screenplay, the married couple has rarely been mentioned in history texts. If mentioned, it is Heerman who receives attention due to his later directing career in connection with the Marx Brothers. Then, too, Heerman gave an oral history wherein he took most of the credit for their writing work together, though Mason's list of solo writing credits far outweighs his. But when men write history they do tend to focus on the achievements of ... men.

With "Zoë Akins: A Quiet Rebellion," Sarah Amble Whorton delves into the various works of the Pulitzer Prize–winning author of poetry, novels, plays, and movies. Whorton finds a writer concerned with contemplating a question that many faced in the beginning of the 20th century—how the modern woman can discover her true self within the social, political, and financial restraints remaining from a bygone era.

Laura Kirk offers a portrait of another pair of married screenwriters for whom writing and politics served as the glue that sometimes outlasted love in "Marriage of Words: Bella and Sam Spewack." Kirk finds the Spewacks conquered Hollywood as a team during a turbulent time when their peers were being sacrificed by producers to a government blacklist fueled by fear of Communism, and that the Spewacks were more of a writing partnership than romantic pair in some ways.

Amy L. Banks reminds us of "The Forgettable Ms. Murfin," a study of Jane Murfin, who earned an Academy Award nomination for Best Story for *What Price Hollywood?* (which she co-wrote with Adela Rogers St. Johns in 1932). Banks finds that when writer-director Murfin co-directed her dog-actor (and personal pet) Strongheart, she created the first canine screen star. In a final irony, while Murfin's name nearly never appears in textbooks, Strongheart dog food was available in stores until at least 2002.

The final essay comes from your editor and covers one of the more well-known women in this collection, Ruth Gordon, though she is known more as an Academy Award–winning actress (for *Rosemary's Baby*) than as a screenwriter, and that is a mistake. Together with her husband Garson Kanin, Gordon created the most iconic film abut marriage, *Adam's Rib*, a film that cemented Katharine Hepburn in American cinematic history as a feminist, which this essay argues comes from Gordon's writing more than Hepburn's acting ability. The essay also argues for Gordon's name to be among these prominent female screenwriters since three of the four films she co-wrote with Kanin earned Academy Award nominations for Best Original Screenplay.

Across this Introduction, as you will find across this collection, the reader will encounter recurring phrases such as "despite" and "forgotten," a fact that could create pessimists of anyone hoping to study these women further. That is not the purpose of this collection. Instead, let those words serve as a call to action for other historians to continue the search and build on these stories so that someday soon all textbooks will include the work of these women alongside the work of the many already far too famous men.

A final note on the essays: while each focuses on one female screenwriter, readers will find how many ways their lives intersected, how much networking they fostered as they championed each other's careers across the eras. This is not always the case in reading the memoirs of male moguls who tend to see their success as their proper inheritance from the world. These women saw the value in each other, which is perhaps the greatest lesson of their lives and of presenting them all together in this collection.

Editorial Note

Historians have found working with women difficult, as their last names often change across their lifetimes. Also, in writing about married writing couples, how can one use a surname when it is shared by two? Students were instructed to use the female's surname throughout and the male's first name in those cases, though it is not yet a widespread idea in academia.

Similarly, most of academia still follows the auteur theory and claims the author of the film is the director, using (usually his) name at the head of citations in the Works Cited page. As this is a collection of essays about screenwriters, the editor has chosen to claim the writers as the authors of their films, thereby adjusting the citations accordingly in the style currently being used by the *Journal of Screenwriting*: "*Little Miss Sunshine* (2006), Wr: Michael Arndt, Dirs: Jonathan Dayton and Valerie Faris, USA 101 mins."

Adela Rogers St. Johns
Survival of the Feisty

Sarah Amble Whorton

In the memoir *Love, Laughter, and Tears: My Hollywood Story*, Adela Rogers St. Johns writes, "Once, when Joan Crawford and I were doing a tea-talk television show, our hostess, I think it was Virginia Graham, was stressing our enduring success in our chosen fields and Joan leaned over and put her hand on my arm and said, "You know what's remarkable about Adela and me? We *survived*. We did indeed" (33). Due to sharp journalistic skills and strong storytelling prowess, St. Johns rocketed to fame during early Hollywood. She knew the right people and infiltrated the most exclusive circles. Her eyes were always open, searching for the next story. St. Johns' impact as a writer is evident, yet some historians assign her a passive role. "[St. Johns] both reported on Hollywood and fictionalized the lives of the stars she covered; thus her significance was as an observer of Hollywood rather than as a participant in it" (Morey "Adela Rogers St. Johns"). On the surface, St. Johns seems to report just the facts; who arrived at what party, sporting this year's designer gown. Dig deeper though, and St. Johns' careful guidance is clear. She humanizes her subjects, particularly female movie stars. St. Johns understood the real challenge in Hollywood was to survive.

Adela Rogers was born on May 20, 1894, to Earl and Harriet Rogers. The marriage was unhappy and the couple divorced when Adela was eight years old. Adela admired her father and chose to live with him full time. Earl Rogers is considered one of the greatest criminal defense attorneys to ever practice, only losing three of his seventy-seven cases. He was the first to use visual aids and forensic science in a trial. Some say the fictional lawyer Perry Mason is based on Rogers, although author Erle Stanley Gardner never confirmed this assumption. Earl Rogers kept his daughter close, meaning St. Johns grew up in courtrooms. She attended school sporadically and claimed her real education came from the people her father worked with: "criminals, police officers, reporters and pickpockets."

St. Johns' life and work were shaped by her father. They were similar in many ways. For example, St. Johns inherited Earl Rogers' reputation for proving guidance during crisis. "Get me Earl Rogers" was a common phrase uttered in holding cells. Likewise, St. Johns advised studio executives and movie stars. The common phrase was "Adela will know what to do." When police arrested silent film actress Mabel Normand for the murder of director William Desmond Taylor, Normand called St. Johns. "I was in Chicago when

I heard Mabel's voice saying over the phone, "Please come home. I have to tell you ... you have to tell me what to do...," writes St. Johns (*LLT* 60). Before consulting a lawyer, Normand consulted St. Johns.

Earl Rogers and Adela Rogers St. Johns' relationship was far from perfect. St. Johns reflected later in her life, "Woman's work as a listener is never done.... I thought I'd spent too much of my life listening for some damn man—for my father and now for my husband" (*The Honeycomb* 70–71). Earl Rogers was a sensible man, encouraging plainness over frills. As a young girl, full of self-doubt, St. Johns never received confidence from her father. She writes, "...my father had informed me most kindly that my only claims to beauty were my *eyes* which he said were Killarney blue and put in with a sooty finger" (*LLT* 35). St. Johns continues, "But—without *bosoms*, with only *eyes* and *ankles*, a girl could be forlorn" (36). This sparse reality taught St. Johns to cultivate brains over beauty. She developed her strengths and set her steely gaze onto her career.

One unmistakable benefit of being Earl Rogers' daughter was the breadth of connections available to St. Johns. An introduction to publisher William Randolph Hearst provided St. Johns with employment opportunities throughout her lifetime. At 18, she began working as a reporter at the Hearst owned *San Francisco Examiner* and, soon, moved to the *Los Angeles Herald*. At first, St. Johns was assigned to the hotel beat. Slowly, she began covering sports, city politics, and crime. Reporting was St. Johns' first love. She said, "Newspaper work is the most exciting thing in the world to me, it's where I live. I would do it for nothing" (Steiner 89). Being a "girl reporter" was not easy. Popular opinion believed journalism was not a woman's job. "In the late 19th and early 20th centuries, most editors and publishers justified this assertion by citing the job's physical difficulty and dangerousness. Others emphasized woman's (dis)abilities, that is, women's inability to be logical and accurate" (Steiner 91). St. Johns worked hard and won the reputation as "tough, hard newspaper woman" (Pace "Adela R. St. Johns").

Writer Adela Rogers St. Johns, circa 1927. Adela Rogers St. Johns was known alternately as "The World's Greatest Girl Reporter," or "The Mother Confessor of Hollywood" (courtesy Cari Beauchamp).

St. Johns' influence as a reporter went beyond the front page. Legendary film critic Pauline Kael asserts St. Johns inspired the prototype of female reporters in film. Kael writes, "...just as the movies about lady fliers were almost all based on Amelia Earhart, the criminal-mouthpiece movies on William Fallon, and the gossip-column movies on Walter Winchell, the movies about girl reporters were almost all based on the most highly publicized girl reporter—Hearst's Adela Rogers St. Johns" (*Raising Kane-I*). St. Johns' carbon copy arrived on screen in *His Girl Friday*

(1940). Kael continues, "…Rosalind Russell [as Hildy Johnson] was so obviously playing Adela Rogers St. Johns that she was dressed in an imitation of the St. Johns girl-reporter striped suit." Wardrobe was not the only connection between the real woman and her on-screen equivalent.

In a few short years, St. Johns had achieved name recognition in her chosen career, but her home life required a drastic change. St. Johns left the newspaper, citing personal reasons. "Unhappy with her childcare arrangement, Rogers St. Johns decided to accept the *Photoplay* job, primarily because it allowed her to work from home" (Steiner 89–90). It is easy to imagine St. Johns reciting Hildy Johnson's famous line in *His Girl Friday*, "And that my friends, is my farewell to the newspaper game. I'm gonna be a woman, not a news-getting machine. I'm gonna have babies and take care of them. Give 'em cod liver and watch their teeth grow." Like her fictional counterpart, St. Johns returned to reporting whenever the opportunity arose.

At *Photoplay* magazine, St. Johns quickly became known as Mother Confessor of Hollywood. St. Johns recounts her quick rise to celebrity columnist,

> Thus it seemed all right back there in the Roaring Twenties for Adela Rogers St. Johns to become Mother Confessor of Hollywood though she was only in *her* twenties and thirties. Often and often after she went to live and work spang-bang in the middle of it, she felt herself too young and inexperienced for so momentous and dangerous a position. For soon with all this beauty and genius and sex and love-of-life boiling in one little pot things began to happen that even Shakespeare had hardly thought of. But there she was *when* the elevator went up and there she stayed [*LLT* 12].

When interviewing Hollywood stars, St. Johns saw beyond the glamour. She knew the extravagant woman on the red carpet was not that different from the average woman. Both fight to make a living and that battle is worthy of recognition. When covering Gloria Swanson's premiere for her newest picture, St. Johns wrote,

> It wasn't the new manner, the poise, and presence and culture that Gloria has acquired that made the audience to the highest seat in the gallery rise and cheer her madly. It wasn't Madame la Marquise that they were greeting. It was little Gloria Swanson, whom they'd known since she was a bathing girl on a comedy lot…. For the grit, the sheer determination, the genius, the force and fire were all melted together into a sweetness that I, at least, have never seen before in Gloria's face [*Photoplay*].

For St. Johns, Swanson's newest movie was irrelevant and, in some ways, her performance in that film was irrelevant. Swanson had survived another day and that journey was the real accomplishment to highlight.

St. Johns applied those same standards to the unemployed women of Los Angeles. In 1931, Hearst hired St. Johns to write sixteen articles for the *Los Angeles Examiner*, exposing the unemployment epidemic and inadequate charitable response to that crisis. St. Johns went undercover to truly experience the landscape. In the beginning, St. Johns plays a role, making reference to her costume. "The mere fact that I wore old clothes, a pair of horn-rimmed glasses, a hat of the fashion made famous by Maria Dressler as Min, and was without benefit of make-up couldn't so deeply alter things. I was still ME" (December 20, 1931). Quickly, the articles focused on working class citizens. St. Johns' ability to gain her subject's trust reveals the double standard of poverty. She interviewed a woman named Ruby, "When you're poor, you got to be good. The rich can do what they like. They got their own souls to look after. When you're poor; the whole darn world looks after yours for you. If you're not "worthy," you don't get help from anybody" (December 22, 1931). St. Johns highlights the additional strain placed on women. "Remember, we're a silk stocking and lip rouge nation. It's been bred and trained into us. As women, by the greatest advertising campaigns in the world, we have been sold the idea of beauty, of grooming, of cleanliness. It hurts so to feel yourself slipping below the tide. Down and out, unemployed, hungry, we are still women" (December 25, 1931). The series brought St. Johns fame and immense satisfaction. It also brought reform to the charitable agencies interacting with the unemployed men and women of Los Angeles. "It had been an eye-opening experience for [St. Johns] and her readers and now she was able to say after finding "entrenched horror and neglect," attitudes started to change and agencies were improving their services" (Beauchamp 282). St. Johns' words sparked change. The assertion that St. Johns' only contribution to society was as a passive observer seems null and void.

St. Johns' natural curiosity, investigative abilities, and storytelling techniques collide in her fictional work. In 1918, her first short story, *The Black Cat*, was published. That same year, she received her first writing credit in motion pictures, *Old Love for New*. St. Johns' last screen credit occurs posthumously in 1991. During that span, she mostly received "story by" credits, with her novels and short stories being adapted for film. St. Johns' work shines brightest when she examines her personal experiences. Those movies instantly connected with audiences, often resulting in St. Johns' most popular films.

St. Johns' first notable collaboration in cinema was with actress Dorothy Davenport, who lost her husband, Wallace Reid, to drug addiction. Davenport formed a production company with the sole purpose of creating social conscience films. In 1924, St. Johns' short story, *Broken Laws*, was adapted into a film of the same name. Marion Jackson and Bradley King wrote the screenplay about a spoiled boy standing trial for vehicular manslaughter and his mother's resolve to provide parental discipline. The public's acceptance of *Broken Laws* allowed Davenport to move forward with her next film.

Davenport's most well known work as a producer and director is *Red Kimono (1925)*, although her contribution remains uncredited. Again, St. Johns provided the source material, this time, with Dorothy Arzner adapting the story for screen. The film centers on an innocent, young woman tricked into prostitution by a handsome, older man. The critics were not kind to the resulting product. The *New York Times* review stated, "There have been a number of wretched pictures on Broadway during the last year, but none seem to have quite reached the low level of *The Red Kimono*, a production evidently intended to cause weeping, wailing and gnashing of teeth" (Hall "Red Kimono"). The poor critical reception was the least of Davenport's troubles. The court case that followed the film's release gained national attention. St. Johns' source material was based on the actual trial of Gabrielle Darley. St. Johns covered the case as a crime reporter, but had failed to change the woman's name when converting the story into a "fictional" piece. The real Darley, who had created a new life for herself, sued Davenport for privacy violation and won. Davenport, suddenly penniless, folded her company, and returned to acting. St. Johns remained unscathed by the scandal and continued to work steadily in Hollywood.

St. Johns' background as a reporter shows up in at least two films. *Back in Circulation* (1937) is based on her short story *Angle Shooter*, published in *Cosmopolitan Magazine*. The official synopsis reads, "A fast-moving newspaper reporter senses a story when she spots a recent widow partying in a nightclub." Warren Duff receives the screenplay credit while Seton I. Miller's dialogue contribution is uncredited. A copy of *Back in Circulation* currently resides in the Library of Congress. For *Miss Fane's Baby Is Stole*n (1934), St.

Johns switches from her usual role and writes the adaptation of Rupert Hughes's play. The review by the *New York Times* is favorable. "...the subject is dealt with in an intelligent, restrained, and provocative fashion (Hall "Miss Fane's Baby Is Stolen"). St. Johns' name is never mentioned in the article. When St. Johns' work is adapted, the success of the film is attributed to the screenwriter. When St. Johns is the screenwriter, the success of the film is attributed to the author of the source material.

Courtroom dramas quickly became St. Johns' specialty. Those formative years spent in her father's office paid off. Some examples include her "story by" credit on *Marked Cards* (1918) and her adaptation of *Smart Woman* (1948). St. Johns' exploration of her relationship with Earl Rogers arrives on screen in more obvious interpretations. Her novel, *Free Soul*, became a film in 1931. In the movie, an alcoholic defense attorney defends his daughter's ex-boyfriend on the charge of murder. The thin veil of fiction does not disguise the source material, growing tension between a father and daughter. In the film, Stephen Ashe, the defense attorney, exclaims to his daughter, "I've had to drink as I've had to breathe, and you know it!" Later, Jan Ashe, the daughter, confides in her suitor, "I just don't want to get married, Dwight. I don't want life to settle down around me like a pan of sour dough. I don't want it one little bit." The film received positive attention from critics and the industry. Norma Shearer was nominated for an Academy Award for Best Actress (1930). Clarence Brown, the director of *Free Soul*, received a nomination for Best Directing. Lionel Barrymore won the Academy Award for Best Actor for his performance in *Free Soul*. Subsequent versions include *The Girl Who Had Everything* (1953) and *Final Verdict* (1991). *Free Soul* is an early indicator that St. Johns excelled at memoir based writing.

St. Johns' feminist beliefs are on display in her portrayal of strong women. Her characters wrestle with the expectations of the "modern" life. *Lady of the Night* (1925) was converted to screen by Alice D.G. Miller, using St. Johns' short story as the foundation. Norma Shearer plays two roles, the well-educated Florence Banning and the reform school graduate Molly Helmer. Molly, now a prostitute, yearns for the respectability Florence receives automatically based on her standing within society. Complications ensue. The film performed well during the original run and continues to find audiences. A recent reviewer writes, "Humanity, social concern and a deep sensitivity—spiked with wit and a total command of visual storytelling..." (LaSalle "Film Review"). The author contributes the picture's success to Monta Bell, the director, and never mentions writers St. Johns or Miller. The reviewer continues, "*Lady of the Night* was made at a time when Americans were questioning an old morality and women were assuming freedoms they'd never had." In the film, Miss Carr, Florence's aunt, is appalled by the activities of her niece. Miss Carr exclaims, "In my day, girls didn't go to dances with strange young men alone." Florence Banning replies, "You never married did you, Auntie?" *Lady of the Night* features two interesting and complex women. Those roles were written by two interesting and complex women, yet the male director receives the praise.

The Single Standard (1929), based on St. Johns' novel, explores the modern woman's desire for equality. Weary of societal views regarding female fidelity, a socialite, played by Greta Garbo, decides to acquire lovers like a man. Each man involved with the socialite becomes possessive. After one lover kills himself, the socialite marries the millionaire suitor and bears his children. Another example, *That Brennan Girl* (1946), includes the additional responsibilities of war time love affairs. A young woman with no resources is at risk for being declared an "unfit" mother. Her husband is killed in action and her own mother refuses to help. The woman is alone and aid is not available. The rigged system only offers punishment and the mother loses her child. She works to recover her baby, but is only successful once a man, willing to marry her, pleads for the child's safe return. St. Johns knew how to write candy-coated social awareness films. Each movie offers dramatic conflict and the expected happy ending. Hidden at the core is St. Johns' point of view that women could not fully succeed in a society bound by antiquated gender roles.

St. Johns lived by the adage "no woman could drive three mules." She reflected "that work and friends had lasted a lifetime, but husbands had been the first to go" (Beauchamp 356). St. Johns' own life was wrought with marital difficulties, divorcing three times. Her job as a reporter was usually at the center of the dissolution. She would often leave at a moment's notice to cover a story for the newspaper, leaving her husband in charge of childcare. Her fictional stories place couples at the cusp of divorce, desperately clinging to their idea of marriage. The characters in *Children of Divorce* (1927) have grown up in broken homes and are determined not to repeat the mistakes of their parents. They marry the wrong people and live unhappily. Despite their best efforts, staying in the marriage does not equal success. Kitty Flanders declares, "You'd make a marvelous second husband, but you are too much of a luxury for a poor girl's first husband." A similar plot can be found in *I Want a Divorce* (1940). In this scenario, the McNallys' mend their relationship after witnessing a client's nasty divorce. In *Animal Kingdom* (1932), the characters build marriages on the idea of respectability, but soon find the title to be an empty shell. Before their wedding day, Tom Collier confides to his fiancée, "Oh, heaven help us both. Just this one marriage please. You know I haven't been very good about marriage. I was exposed to a very bad case of it as a baby. We must make a grand go of it." Later, Tom realizes his mistress means more to him than his marriage. His mistress responds, "Well, it's true that side of it was never so much to us, not in comparison, not … well, not after those first crazy months. But I…I thought that was natural. I was even glad. Glad that it was all our needs that held us together. So closely. Not a claim. Never a claim, but so closely." Perhaps, St. Johns hoped these stories would help her children find their own path to happiness.

St. Johns' strongest work occurs when she turns her pen toward the film industry. It was a world she knew intimately, particularly the destructive nature of fame. In *Love, Laughter and Tears*, St. Johns describes how quickly adoration becomes hatred: "Yet [Mabel Normand's] former worshippers, who had placed her on the highest pedestal, dragged her down like a pack of hyenas…. Drug addict, drunkard, wanton—they shrieked at her. Poor, sick, heartbroken, bewildered little clown, she wasn't any of those things ever" (66–67). The printed word allowed St. Johns to explore these themes without naming people or destroying reputations. In *The Honeycomb*, St. Johns claims fiction "was the only way in which you could print the truth" (136). St. Johns' novel, *The Skyrocket*, provides a unique perspective on the world of show business. A waitress becomes a movie star after she marries a wealthy playboy. Her happiness quickly fades as she loses her husband and her career. St. Johns' book was published the same year as Frances Marion's novel, *Minnie Flynn*. The simultaneous release was not coincidental. Both women witnessed Hollywood's transformation into a cold, heartless machine. The framework of a novel allowed the women to operate independently of the industry and to express their true feelings: "Often penned by women with first-hand experience in the movies, these novels view cinema's lack of sound as implicated in the broader forms of silence surrounding women in Hollywood" (Gautreau 229). Both books sought to warn women, particularly those dreaming of sudden fame, to look beyond the glamour. "The insight of *The Skyrocket* is that the problems of Hollywood are collective rather than individual, that the film industry creates an environment in which it is difficult to live sanely..." (Morey "Adela Rogers St. Johns"). Both Marion and St. Johns could attest to the living conditions among the rich and famous being members of that elite club themselves.

The Skyrocket features opposing female characters. Sharon is a foolish young woman dreaming of a life beyond her waitressing job. Nadine is a successful actress married to the studio executive who guided her career. Sharon envies Nadine's life without realizing the hefty price Nadine has paid for her success. In the novel, Nadine says, "I know what I owe the man who made me. At least, I married him.... It all has its price, always, doesn't it, mama?" (252). Nadine is trapped in a loveless marriage but must remain silent for the sake of her career. To use St. Johns' adage, those two mules, marriage and career, were interconnected. Separation would mean sacrificing both personal and professional relationships.

Despite the warnings, Sharon repeats Nadine's mistakes. Sharon allows a sleazy director, William Dvorak, to develop her career. Before Sharon can sign her film contract, Dvorak places parameters on the deal. "Will you let me dictate every move of your life?" (131). Sharon, without hesitation, agrees to Dvorak's proposal and Dvorak wastes no time taking control. "[Sharon] was in a formative stage, off screen, where her personality was strangely missing. The old Sharon was gone ... in her work, the new individuality was being molded. But off the screen, she had as yet evolved no positive personality to take place of the old" (149). Sharon has sacrificed her individuality, and she has done it willingly. Soon, the public is only interested in Sharon, the image, not Sharon, the human being. In one of the final scenes, fans claw at each other, hoping to get a glimpse of the starlet: "While early Hollywood welcomed fans for the sake of selling itself, the same fans in this scene are at war with one another as they each seek the same product: Sharon. None of them will ever acquire her, of course, because she has turned into one of the industry's promotional fictions" (Gautreau 245). Quickly, Sharon's sweet success turns bitter. After the lights are dimmed and the red carpet is rolled up, Sharon has nothing.

Despite the tragedies contained inside *The Skyrocket*, the novel only increased the public's appetite for Hollywood stories. The first cinematic version, *The Skyrocket* (1926), was directed by Marshall Neilan and written by Benjamin Glazer. It was a soft adaptation, focusing on the glamour of show business. The next version, *What Price Hollywood?* (1932), was directed by George Cukor. The writers involved were Jane Murfin, Gene Fowler, Rowland Brown, and Ben Markson. St. Johns shared a story credit with Louis Stevens. This adaptation made fundamental changes to the plot. The villain is now an alcoholic director while the hero is the sensitive studio executive. The actress still dreams of fame and allows the men around her to determine her fate. This time, she ends up happily married.

Audiences, critics, and industry insiders welcomed *What Price Hollywood?* The review in *Variety* reads, "Director George Cukor tells it interestingly. The story by Adela Rogers St. Johns has its exaggerations, but they can sneak under the line as theatrical license" ("What Price Hollywood?"). Not quite praise for St. Johns but, at least, her name is mentioned. During the film's warm reception, David O. Selznick took credit for the idea, claiming he commissioned St. Johns to write the "true" Hollywood story. St. Johns and Jane Murfin were nominated for an Academy Award for Best Story, but they lost to

Frances Marion for *The Champ* (1931). Another incarnation of *The Skyrocket* is *A Star Is Born*, made in 1937 and remade in 1954, and 1976.

St. Johns' latter years were formed by tragedy. She struggled with alcoholism and depression. St. Johns' oldest son, Bill, died in World War II, leaving her heartbroken. Frances Marion, an ever true and loyal friend, created a clay bust of Bill for St. Johns. St. Johns was touched by the gift and displayed it with great pride. St. Johns kept busy with several projects including nudging Margaret Tante Burk to co-founded Round Table West with Marilyn Hudson. Inspired by New York's Algonquin Round Table, the club hosted over 2,500 Pulitzer Prize winners, first-time authors, and Hollywood movie stars. The audience tended to be women of a certain age and attendance was steady. St. Johns also began writing memoirs: *Honeycomb* in 1969, *Some Are Born Great* in 1974 and *Love, Laughters, and Tears: My Hollywood Story* in 1978. The books provide wonderful anecdotes of a by-gone era. St. Johns, contemplating her legacy, writes, "Today, I am The Old Woman of the Sea, Mother Confessor turned custodian of the Legends of Hollywood from first to last. If you live longer than practically anybody you find you have a debt to the past…" (*LLT* 19).

In 1970, President Richard M. Nixon awarded Adela Rogers St. Johns the Presidential Medal of Freedom. In Nixon's introduction, he said,

> "Reporter, feature writer, author,"—and incidentally while it is not here in the citation, she also was once a sports reporter, the first woman sports reporter—she has enhanced every field she has entered. Beginning her career when women reporters were few, she has brought entertainment and information to millions with the energy, vigor and grace characteristic of both her style and her personality. Demonstrating an exceptional ability to reveal the human story behind the news, she has brought to her writing an excitement and warmth that for many years have earned her the high esteem of her profession and of her public.

As a boy, Nixon delivered groceries to St. Johns. As a president, Nixon presented her a medal. St. Johns responded with one of her favorite baseball stories,

> Out in St. Louis the other day, one of your good friends, Mr. Red Schoendienst said the only thing in the world that you can give a pitcher is confidence. Mr. Nixon has given it to me tonight, and I think to the press all over the United States, great confidence. It has been a wonderful thing to think that we who have worked in it so long have earned such a reward. I think it is going to make all the press and the women of the press feel that they are going to survive. I thank you very much.

St. Johns knew how to survive. Her unorthodox childhood prepared her for an unorthodox life. She thrived in two cutthroat industries during a time when a woman's place was only in the home. St. Johns earned the trust of her peers. She accessed the most privileged circles and she took notes. Yet, St. Johns never lost sight of the person behind the label of "movie star" or "unemployed woman." She paid equal tribute to the struggles and to the triumphs. On the final page of *Love, Laughter, and Tears*, St. Johns reflects on a life well-lived,

> I have to realize now how many of those who lived these legends, these beautiful yesterdays I've tried to recall for you, have gone through that door called death…. They were never afraid of it. They were willing to *love* deeply, to laugh *all* of their laughter, to weep *all* of their tears…. So I look forward to seeing them again, these my old friends, in that Tavern at the End of the Road where we shall all meet someday. Until then, I can say to them with my whole heart—and maybe now that you know them too you can say it with me—*Thanks for the memories* [342].

WORKS CITED

Beauchamp, Cari. *Without Lying Down: Frances Marion and the Powerful Women of Early Hollywood.* Berkeley: University of California Press, 1998.
Gautreau, J. "'Movie Plots Pushed into Prose': The Extra Girl, Will Hays, and the Novel of Silent Hollywood." *Adaptation* 7.3 (2014): 229–52.
Hall, Mordaunt. "Miss Fane's Baby Is Stolen (1934)." *New York Times*, 20 Jan. 1934. Web. 13 Oct. 2015.
_____. "Red Kimono (1925)." *New York Times*, 3 Feb. 1926. Web. 1 Dec. 2015.
Johns, Adela. *The Honeycomb.* Garden City, NY: Doubleday, 1969.
Johns, Adela Rogers. "How Jobless, Hungry Girls Live." *Los Angeles Examiner*. 20 Dec. 1931.
_____. "How Jobless, Hungry Girls Live." *Los Angeles Examiner*. 22 Dec. 1931.
_____. "How Jobless, Hungry Girls Live." *Los Angeles Examiner*. 25 Dec. 1931.
_____. *Love, Laughter, and Tears: My Hollywood Story.* Garden City, NY: Doubleday, 1978.
_____. *The Skyrocket.* New York: A.L. Burt, 1925.
Kael, Pauline. "Raising Kane-I." *The New Yorker.* 20 Feb. 1971.
LaSalle, Mick. "Film Review—A Hauntingly Lovely 'Lady'/Norma Shearer Plays Dual Role in 1925 Silent Masterpiece." *SFGate.* Web. 18 Nov. 2015.
Morey, Anne. "Adela Rogers St. Johns." In Jane Gaines, Radha Vatsal, and Monica Dall'Asta, eds. *Women Film Pioneers Project.* Center for Digital Research and Scholarship. New York: Columbia University Libraries, 2013. Web. September 27, 2013.
Nixon, Richard. "Remarks on Presenting the Presidential Medal of Freedom to Eight Journalists." April 22, 1970. Online by Gerhard Peters and John T. Woolley, *The American Presidency Project.*
Pace, Eric. "Adela R. St. Johns, 94, Journalist, Novelist, Teacher and Scriptwriter." *New York Times*, 10 Aug. 1988. Web. 20 Oct. 2015.
Photoplay Magazine. Internet Archive. Web. 14 Oct. 2015.
Steiner, Linda. "Stories of Quitting." American Journalism: 89–116.
"What Price Hollywood?" Variety. 1932. Web. 1 Nov. 2015.

Jeanie Macpherson
A Life Unknown
Amelia Phillips

Jeanie Macpherson was born into a family of wealth and distinction on May 18, 1887, in Boston, Massachusetts. She died on August 26, 1946, in Los Angeles, CA, of cervical cancer. During her 59 years of life, she worked successfully first as an actress with D.W. Griffith and the Edison Company, then as a writer/director/actress for Universal Studios, and finally as a writer for Cecil B. DeMille. She acted in over 147 films, wrote 54 films, most of them financial successes, and directed a handful. She was a pilot in her spare time, when she had any. She never married and never had children, but she was one of Cecil B. DeMille's three long-standing mistresses, his other two being his secretary of more than 39 years, Gladys Rossum, and actress Julia Faye. These women built DeMille, working closely with him for all the years that he produced and directed.

All of this can be ascertained from a few-hours-long Google search. Beyond that, there is little to nothing on Jeanie Macpherson. Even scratching the surface of Macpherson's life is difficult. Tracking her is difficult just based on her many pseudonyms: Jeanie MacPherson, Jeannie MacPherson, Jeannie Macpherson, Jeane McPherson, Jeanie McPherson, Jeanie Mac Pherson, and Jeanne McPherson. IMDb also notes J. DuRocher MacPherson and L. du Rocher Macpherson as pseudonyms. Variations of the male "Rocher" are listed as the author of plays on which the films *Evidence* and *Washington Melodrama* are based. There is no evidence tying these pseudonyms to Macpherson elsewhere, however this may mean that she wrote plays under an altogether different name. Furthermore, multiple sources vary on her year of birth, from 1881–1888, but 1887 would put her at 59 when she died, the common age reported in the obituaries. However, the *LA Times* notes her age at death to be 60. She may have been as old as 65. Thus, the woman who wrote *The Ten Commandments* (1923) and *The King of Kings* (1927), along with dozens of other of DeMille's blockbusters, is largely unknown. The records that do exist on her life contradict each other. In this essay, differing accounts will be culled and interviews and biographical facts will then be applied to the themes of Macpherson's films. Together, this information will create a cohesive image of a woman who literally created a career out of nothing but grit and determination.

In her book titled, *The First One Hundred Noted Men and Women of the Screen* (1920), historian Caroline Lowrey writes that Macpherson, "received her early education in Paris, finishing her studies at the famous Kenwood Institute, Chicago" (110). The *LA*

Writer Jeanie Macpherson on set, circa 1920. Macpherson's family traveled in highly literary circles. After a dinner party where he argued with someone, Oscar Wilde supposedly sent Macpherson's mother his cuff with the note, "What do you think of this as a title for my new play: 'A Woman of No Importance.'" The cuff became a family heirloom (courtesy Cari Beauchamp).

Times' Lee Shipley supports this by stating, "Most of her girlhood was spent in Paris … in a girls' school in the Faubourg St. Germain" (A4). A 1916 article in *Photoplay* by Alice Martin concurs, stating that Macpherson was born in Boston, "and her family one of the most prominent and proper in that area of prized propriety. When she was but a child Miss MacPherson went to Paris and entered Mlle. De Facq's school" (95–97). Despite all the corroborating evidence, an encyclopedic entry on Macpherson by historian Denise Lowe states, "She was raised in upper-class society in Boston. However, before she could leave for Paris to be educated abroad her family went bankrupt and she had to find work to help support the family" (340). Thus, the discrepancies begin. Of course, it is plausible that Macpherson never made it to Paris, but instead had to take care of the family. However, it seems unlikely that Macpherson felt *show business* was the best way to raise money for a family in need. More likely is that Macpherson did, in fact, make it to Paris, that she did learn to write and surround herself with culture while there, and that she left after some time for either personal or financial reasons. Still, culture and the arts were in Macpherson's blood. She is named after the Scotch Joan of Arc, her mother's family lineage can be traced back to Louis XV in France, her grandfather owned and published Detroit's *Evening Journal*, and her stepfather was Henry O'Neil, a successful grain trader in Chicago known as The Barley King (Lowrey 110). Lee Shipley, a columnist for the *LA Times* in the 1940s, reports that Macpherson's mother knew Oscar Wilde as a young girl and had one of his cufflinks (A4). Macpherson was no stranger to the arts and elite society.

Moreover, her family had a flair for the dramatics. Most sources report that Macpherson was born to Evangeline Tomlinson and John Sinclair Macpherson (1). However, historian Lowrey lists Macpherson's mother as Claire O'Neil in a source from 1920 (110). The following research is based off of 115-year-old newspaper articles. Further and more thorough research involving birth records and family genealogy should be conducted to verify the claim that Evangeline Claire, Evangeline Tomlinson, Claire O'Neil and Evangeline Claire Tomlinson O'Neil are all the same person, and that they are indeed all Macpherson's mother. Birth records for Evangeline Claire are unknown, though she was probably born in Paris, France around 1860. This discrepancy in names, Evangeline Tomlinson versus Claire O'Neil, was confusing at first, until further research revealed the truth. Macpherson by all accounts was raised in the lap of luxury, and that can be attributed to the wealth of Henry O'Neil, her stepfather, who made a good deal of money in the barley trade. Tomlinson was her mother's maiden name and O'Neil was her stepfather's name. However, the "Claire" is still unexplained. The name change may be a sign of Macpherson's mother's aspirations for a grander life than she was born into. An article in *The Jeweler's Circular* in 1899 writes:

> The hearing of Mrs. O'Neil, wife of Henry O'Neil, of Chicago, a well known plunger ["gambler"], known at one time as the "Barley King," by her maiden name, Evangeline Claire, of Chicago, charged with having swindled different firms of over $30,000 in jewels and dresses, resumed to-day…. Mr. Markey, representing Mrs. O'Neil, remarked the goods of his client were bought on running account. Some were bought in Paris, some in Baltimore, in fact, everywhere she had traveled [19].

From this 1899 article, it seems Macpherson's mother dropped her first name, took her middle name, and married a rich, older man. It is also evident that Claire O'Neil was a thief with expensive taste. Five days after the previous article was published, a subsequent article writes that the Michigan-born Chicagoan Claire O'Neil was caught in Montreal, Canada after returning from a trip to Paris with, "over $8,000 worth of lace, linens, jewelry, and silver ware. The silver ware was just as delivered from the stores, but the purchaser had engraved the family monogram deeply into every piece, making it practically worthless except for the melting pot" (*Jewelers' Circular* 19). To engrave stolen goods with the family monogram is a special kind of thief, one that fully buys into the façade of grandeur. "Barley King O'Neil Returns" from *The Minneapolis Journal* on June 10, 1902, defends the accusations of theft and estimates the cost of goods to be as high as $150,000, to 4.2 million dollars today. Regardless of the cost of the goods, Macpherson's family was embroiled in a theft that caught the interest of the nation's newspapers. One source did note Jeanie Macpherson's past: the 2011 book, *Bringing Up Oscar: The Story of the Men and Women Who Founded the Academy*, by D. A. Pawlek who writes:

> Once a wealthy man, O'Neill lost his fortune in bad barley investments just before the turn of the century. He claimed that he owed $500,000 to various debtors, but had only $5,000 in assets.... The extravagant Evangeline was not about to pay up so she took Jeanie and fled to Montreal. There, she checked into the swanky Windsor Hotel. Her plan was to board a Dominion Line steamer headed to Liverpool ... via first class passage ... however, Evangeline was arrested [Chapter 3].

Yet, no article, press release, biography, letter, or other information from Macpherson's time mentions this fact. Macpherson most likely was not proud of this history, yet her hidden family history greatly informed her writing.

Jeanie Macpherson was about 13 years old when her family was embroiled in scandal. Though sources conflict on Macpherson's schooling, Pawlek notes that by 1901 the family's credit issues were resolved and Macpherson was in school in Paris (3). It is possible that young woman found herself called back to the United States due to financial issues. Her family's money may have been tied up in the scandal, hence the reason for the encyclopedic article wrongly stating that Macpherson never made it to France due to bankruptcy. More likely she finished high school in Paris and then went to arts school in Chicago at the Kenwood Institute to study opera and dance. Two articles make light of the reason for her return, with Shipley stating it was because her grandmother was appalled that she did not know American history and so brought her home (A4). Macpherson herself was quoted, "In Paris.... I wrote poetry, French poetry, very bad indeed. But friends assured me my center of song rested below my brain, so I went to Chicago to become a grand opera singer" (Martin 95–96). Regardless of the reason, Macpherson was back stateside. Lowe notes that she worked in the Chicago Opera House for a few years before moving to New York, but that is not supported elsewhere.

After graduation in Chicago, Jeanie made her way to New York City and acted in plays on Broadway to little success. Shipley in the *LA Times* article from 1942 notes that when Macpherson wanted to work on Broadway, "She wore the managers out until one gave her a job. It was a bit part in a road show doing one-night stands. One season cured her" (A4). Here begins the characterization of Macpherson as a fierce young woman who "never had been afraid of anything" (Shipley A4). In a 1916 *Photoplay* interview, she states that she was cast in *Caesar and Cleopatra* and followed that with a season in "Strongheart" (Martin 96). After that, she went back to opera, spent one season as Tita in *Havana* on Broadway, and as she states, "wrapped my vocal ambitions in a sheaf of cancelled checks and tucked them away for memoirs" (Martin 96). With a description like that, it was no surprise that she leaned towards writing.

In 1908, Macpherson decided to act in movies. A friend made the suggestion to her, and she went on the hunt for a studio. Finally, a friend, possibly the same friend, told her of Griffith and his work at Biograph Studios. The resounding mythology around the start of Macpherson's film career is that she, with immeasurable pluck, simply walked into Griffith's office and waited for him for days on end. Finally, the assistant asked about her. "I told him my stage experience. He ignored it, scorned it. 'We want to know what you can do before a camera,' he said. I said: 'If you get me on my Scotch day, I can't do anything, but if you get me on my French day, I can do 'wop' parts" (Martin 96). Griffith called her the very next day. Macpherson's known credits with pictures directed by D.W. Griffith begin in 1908, and this coincides with her personal scrapbook of publicity and personal photographs. Macpherson's striking features suited her well for silent films, and she often played "exotic" and emotional parts, hence the politically incorrect "wop" remark in her interview. She worked consistently with Griffith and Biograph for over two years, but by 1911 she was also acting for the Edison company, not mentioned in the numerous articles about Macpherson. At Edison, she met Oscar Apfel and watched as he moved out West to be with Jesse Lasky and Cecil B. DeMille. Of note, Macpherson's scrapbook features many pictures of her in films from both the Edison Company and Biograph that are not listed on IMDb. Of course, this is common for the time period, when actors were seen more as props than as artists. They were interchangeable and lowly paid, not deserving of credit so proper lists were not kept. Additionally, many films from this time are simply lost. Therefore, to state the actual number of films that Macpherson acted in is impossible, but it is certainly higher than the 147 listed on IMDb.

By 1912, Macpherson had left Biograph and Edison and moved West. She began working with Universal where she began as an actress, but eventually stepped into the role of director. In 1913, she wrote, directed, helped produce, and starred in her own film, *Tarantula*. The stills of the film are breathtaking, with Macpherson's dark eyes piercing through the photographs. One picture features Macpherson in a peasant blouse with her red, curly hair in a bandana, lips parted, climbing a rocky mountainside with cacti in the background. She sensuously crawls to a large tarantula, nearly touching it. *Tarantula* was such a financial success that Macpherson won her own department filming two-reelers for Universal. She wrote, directed, acted, and oversaw an entire team of artists, creating at least six films for Universal. "She literally made herself up with her left hand while writing a scene with her right" (Paramount press release). However, Macpherson only worked with Universal for a short while. According to Martin, she quickly suffered from "nervous prostration" (96).

Her rest and relaxation was brief, however, and she quickly made contact with DeMille. Again, the lore around Macpherson's first encounter with DeMille is thick: Macpherson was set to direct a film in the San Fernando Valley, but when she arrived, DeMille was already filming. She returned to her boss at Universal with her tail between her legs and he admonished her for taking too long with the shooting. The very next day she "flounced to the old Lasky barn to see [DeMille]. She had an appointment but when she entered the barn DeMille was writing and kept her waiting. 'Where I came from,' said Miss Macpherson, 'a gentleman would ask a lady to have a seat.' Said DeMille: 'Maybe you're right. Have a seat'" (Shipley A4). So began a 30-year working relationship. The fact that DeMille most likely already knew Macpherson from her acting and writing career clouds the veracity of this story, yet what rings true is Macpherson's strength and gumption. Also making this story hard to believe was Macpherson's stature in Hollywood at the time, beyond just being a known actress. Yes, she ran her own department at Universal, but she was also a suffragette and elected as police judge of the brand new Universal

City on the Oak Crest ranch of the Universal Film Company ("Doings at Los Angeles"). What resonates from this story is the fact that Macpherson matched DeMille on their "first" encounter; but it was not without cause. Macpherson herself repeatedly notes in press releases and interviews that DeMille was notoriously hard to please, requesting endless drafts of scripts, but that, "He will take advice from anyone—if it's right. He won't take it from anyone if it's wrong" (Shipley A4). Over the years, Macpherson was one of the few people who was able to appease "Mr. Hard to Please."

At first, DeMille cast Macpherson in a handful of films, but finally in 1915 he demanded that she only write. She accepted the challenge and became his primary scenarist. They jumped studios together, starting with Artcraft, which transformed into the Famous Players–Lasky in 1917, finally absorbed by Paramount, which officially named itself Paramount Famous Lasky Corporation in 1927. Also in 1927, she became one of three women, along with Mary Pickford and Bess Meredyth, and thirty-three men to form the Academy of Motion Picture Arts and Sciences. However, in 1928 the studios took a hard hit and it was rumored that DeMille would slow down. Valeria Belleti, a secretary at Paramount, writes in a letter that Pathé bought DeMille and the "Demille crowd is being let out and I presume the Pathé people will bring their own crowd." Despite this, DeMille put on a strong front and plowed through, creating seven pictures during the economic downturn, including *The Godless Girl* (1929) and *Dynamite* (1929) ("No Let-Down Planned" 7). Neither *The Godless Girl* nor *Dynamite* were financial successes despite being thematically rich and insightful, but the *Godless Girl* (1929) marks DeMille's last silent film and, as such, it was doomed from the beginning.

In 1930, Macpherson and DeMille split for any number of reasons. It may have been financial since after the crash of the stock market, Hollywood was in flux. It may have been over the size of her paycheck or a rumored controversy with writer Josephine Lovett ("Jeanie Macpherson is definitely"). DeMille changed studios once again and may not have been allowed to work with Macpherson by contract. However, it also may have been that 1930 marked the end of the sexual part of their relationship. Thus, in 1930, Macpherson made a move to MGM and with them she wrote the comedy *Fra Diavolo* (1933) (*The Devil's Brother* in the United States) for Laurel and Hardy, directed by Hal Roach. *Fra Diavolo*'s (1933) success buoyed the studio (Stafford 4). From 1930 to 1934, Macpherson was a contracted writer with MGM. She submitted regular synopses but does not have another produced film on record with MGM besides *The Devil's Brother* (1933). Most likely, as a contracted writer, she is uncredited on a number of scripts with the studio, as was customary for the time.

In 1934, DeMille and Macpherson began to work together again, but this time Macpherson chose to do more on the research side. With a team of twelve under her, she meticulously researched *Cleopatra* (1934) to the point that "If Cleopatra herself had visited the set, she would have felt right at home" (Pawlek Ch. 19). Following the success of *Cleopatra* (1934), the two worked together on five more films—*The Plainsman* (1936), *The Buccaneer* (1938), *Union Pacific* (1939), *Reap the Wild Wind* (1942) and *Unconquered* (1947). For these films, Macpherson is either head researcher, contributor, or wrote the original adaptation while others wrote the screenplay. She is not listed as a sole writer after 1930. Of note, *Unconquered* (1947) was released one year after Macpherson died. DeMille requested Macpherson have a stronger hand in the production, but just months after he requested her help, Macpherson died from cancer.

After her death, DeMille wrote and directed only four films, a marked deceleration from his earlier years with Macpherson. He stepped back from filmmaking and his role transitioned to movie-maker in name and money only. On her own, Macpherson had written six films for Universal and a box office hit for MGM. With DeMille, she is listed as the only writer on *The Ten Commandments* (1927) and *The King of Kings* (1923), two films that essentially created DeMille's legendary status. Macpherson is credited on over half of all of DeMille's films. Though she may not have written all of DeMille's box office hits, her name is attached to all of them. This proves that Macpherson was a writer, researcher and artist in her own right, with or without DeMille, and without her, DeMille slowed down remarkably.

Thus, DeMille's quote from a 1957 interview is especially disheartening: "She was not a good writer. She would bring in wonderful ideas but she could not carry a story all the way through in writing. Her name is on many things because she wrote with me. I carried the story and she would bring me many, many ideas. You'll find her name on a lot of scripts" (Gaines 3). Possibly, DeMille was a cranky old man in 1957, and the fact that he would pass away just two years after this interview clouded his attitude on this particular day. Or perhaps DeMille genuinely thought he did all of the work on the films himself. Yet, he obviously valued Macpherson, evidenced by the fact that he requested her input time and again for thirty years. Not only did he respect her, he seemed to love and appreciate her. When Macpherson was dying, he visited her at the hospital, "held her hand and told her they would surely meet in the next world. She murmured that they would" (DeMille). While healthy, Macpherson was always by his side, with an office attached to DeMille's and a ranch called Paradise Ranch where she resided full time and he stayed on the weekends.

Additionally, Macpherson was no lightweight at Paramount. In 1928, she was the highest paid scenarist at Famous Players–Laskey, making $1000 a week (Gaines "Famous Players Laskey Corporation payroll"). Valeria Belletti notes her excitement at working with Macpherson directly after being hired. In a personal letter on December 21, 1927, upon being called in to work for Macpherson, Belletti writes, "I never dreamed I'd step into DeMille's which is such a big studio and be assigned to such an important person so soon." Belletti worked for hours on end transcribing Macpherson's words, even when the rest of the studio had been sent home. True, Macpherson's drafts were edited by DeMille, but never was there a question as to who wrote the scripts. Macpherson was the writer and she was a talented, sensitive artist. To insinuate otherwise is simply inaccurate and incendiary.

To insult Macpherson's legacy is especially egregious when one considers her work ethic. As mentioned, Macpherson drove herself to exhaustion while working with Universal, and she chose to work with DeMille in order to *slow down*, yet Belletti worked late with Macpherson on countless evenings, even over the holidays. Macpherson's work ethic was notorious. Daniel A. Lord, the official advisor for the Catholic Church during the production of *The King of Kings*, stated, "Jeanie Macpherson was the scenarist, swiftly killing herself with an intensity of work and a passion for precise detail that kept her on a sixteen-hour-a-day schedule during the long months of production … she had no time for anything—friendship, correspondence, hobbies, or care for her health" (Birchard Ch. 51) In a Paramount press release from the 1930s, she offers advice to young writers, especially female writers:

> Don't expect favors. Be prepared to work 24 hours a day. Don't make the mistake of thinking that woman's traditional fragility and delicacy should relieve you of any responsibilities. If some one tells

you you, "Write like a plumber," accept it as the truth and profit by it. Don't attract attention to yourself by your dress. And above all don't be satisfied with just ordinary work. If you're not the best in your line you might as well quit before you start.

Surely, this inner drive is in line with the mythology surrounding Macpherson's beginnings—to hound her future employers until they had no choice but to hire her. She continues, "Any girl who thinks that the studios of Hollywood offer a lazy, romantic, way of making a living, if she aspires to creative success, is doomed to disappointment and failure. ... The bromide about perspiration and not inspiration making for genius is truer in this work than in any other" (Paramount press release Whitmore). She goes on to discuss how many times she had to re-write her first script, six times, and how each time she accepted the challenge with enjoyment. Macpherson, in a press release from around 1940 muses, "When a great number of us start to work ... we ask ourselves subconsciously, 'What can Hollywood give me?' instead of 'What can I give Hollywood'" (Paramount press release Chatfield). This prescient missive reminds a modern reader of John F. Kennedy's inauguration speech, but in the '40s it was a novel idea, especially for women. Jeanie Macpherson was sitting in a head office encouraging women of the day to work harder than men in order to move up in the world. She never spoke of marriage, of men, of children, or of her relationship with DeMille. Not once in any interview did she complain about the workload or the toll it took on her personal life and, most notably, on her health.

Jeanie Macpherson pushed her way into Hollywood with powerful male directors and spoke her mind in order to gain attention, but she also was excellent at her art and moved up in the ranks for that reason. She was not just a workhorse. She was a craftswoman. In 1917, she wrote "Development of Photodramatic Writing." In it she noted:

> We have found out it isn't necessary for a photodrama to have only one dramatic scene, but each scene must be a drama in itself. The whole picture must be made up of a series of small dramas. This makes the completed drama a mosaic of little ones. Scenes that have no dramatic value in them, or say nothing, must be eliminated. So the scenario writer must bear in mind at all times not what he can put into a picture, but what he can leave out. If each scene has a why and a wherefore and an excuse for being, then you get a perfect continuity.... If the writer will take a simple single theme, then work up the detail, decorate it with embroidery and lace, every little bit different from the last, but have each bit of trimming pertain directly to the main theme, he will have a much better story [Sargent 269].

Macpherson's direct notes for all writers still hold true today. Each scene must be a microdrama with a reason for existence, and the entire story must not be muddled with multiple themes, but held strong with one theme upon which the writer skillfully builds. To write a script in this manner would be a feat, but Macpherson did it multiple times throughout her lifetime. As her long hours show, it was not easy. But she was a woman with a goal—to produce excellent work. Her craft carried her from the silent films deep into the "talkies." Had she lived past the young age of 59, she would have continued to work, as she showed no sign of slowing down. However, her work in the industry may have morphed from writer into something more, as it was beginning to do in the 1940s. It is not unreasonable to imagine her in the role of producer and mentor had she not passed away so young.

Occasionally Macpherson did have time for relaxation, but even those times were used as learning experiences. A *Moving Picture World* blurb from 1919 cites her dinner in honor of Adolph Zukor and states that Mary Pickford, Douglas Fairbanks, Mary Miles Minter,

Charles Ray, Edgar Selwyn, and John Flynn, among others, attended ("Writers Give Dinner for Zukor"). Evidently she had these dinners regularly. However, twenty years after the fact, she discussed her famous dinners and how important it was to only have one person. "Two or more celebrities cramp each other. The success of the party depends not on the number of celebrities, or popular or beautiful people, but the number of 'human mirrors' in which the one who is famous, popular or beautiful can shine" (Paramount press release Hebert). This tongue-in-cheek response seemingly snubs the celebrity of Hollywood, and this makes sense. Macpherson kept out of the spotlight as much as possible, and though that makes cataloguing her life difficult, it also makes her all the more likable.

In terms of writing, Macpherson saw stories from a different angle than DeMille, which is why she complimented him so well. She saw the human side and fearlessly brought her real life into her writing. To start, when Macpherson was not writing historical or Biblical dramas for DeMille, she was writing stories that seemed to be ripped from her own life. Macpherson's films come into clarity when one realizes that her mother was caught smuggling jewels, silverware and lace worth thousands if not hundreds of thousands of dollars when Macpherson was just a young girl. Macpherson was raised in a household that struggled for money, caught in the conundrum of keeping up the façade of turn-of-the-century socialites. Macpherson's mother lusted after a life that was just out of reach, and her stepfather went bankrupt through bad business gambles while funding his wife's luxurious lifestyle. Her real father played little to no part in her life. Thus, the drama of *The Cheat* (1915), *The Whispering Chorus* (1918), *Male and Female* (1919), *Adam's Rib* (1923), and even *The Devil's Brother* (1933) center on the sin of living an aspirational life.

In *The Cheat* (1915), a young wife, frustrated that her stock-trader husband works too much, decides to spend all day shopping, spending, and donating money that her husband has not yet made in order to keep up appearances. When she promises to give $10,000 to a charity, she refuses to acknowledge that she does not have the money despite the fact that she believes her husband's deal has gone bad. Instead of consulting with her husband, she takes the money from a Burmese ivory baron whom she has been flirting with heavily. In exchange, he wants her, literally. She does not take the trade seriously, but the next day she realizes she must pay. On the way to what she thinks will be her rape, it turns out her husband made the money back. He writes her a check, and she tries to give it to the Burmese millionaire, but he refuses it, still wanting sex. A tussle ensues and she shoots the Burmese man. Her husband finds the man shot and takes the blame. In the end, the Burmese man survives, the husband goes to court, but when she confesses that she did it in self-defense, both husband and wife are released.

This film is especially interesting because it is the clearest example of a woman frittering away her husband's money and the dangers therein. Her husband must take the fall for her, much like Henry O'Neil did for Evangeline Claire. Also of interest, the Burmese character is actually played by an Asian actor, something extremely rare in the silent film era. This detail may have been due to Cecil B. DeMille's desire for authenticity in the details in his scripts, but it is a breath of fresh of air and seems to speak to Macpherson's realism. Yes, the Burmese character is lecherous and villainous, but he is well rounded enough that the audience understands, even if slightly, his point of view. Furthermore, he is not just a stereotypical prop; he plays a large part in the story. All of his workers, furthermore, are played by Asian actors.

In *The Whispering Chorus* (1918), a husband's obsession with a certain level of economic success ends with him penniless, homeless, and unrecognizable, while his wife, who was happy with life as it was, remarries the richest man in town. When Macpherson writes, "Hell is paved with good intentions," it feels as if she is speaking from her own experiences. Possibly, Macpherson felt for her mother and her poor life choices. This film, as well, used actual Asian actors instead of having white actors play Asian. The 1919 film, *Male and Female* with Gloria Swanson, is one of DeMille's extravagant films that, seemingly for no reason other than to show decadence and lions pawing at Swanson, travels in time to Babylonia. The themes of the film, however, hold true to Macpherson's heart. An aristocratic woman has no patience for her butler and acts like a brat until the family is shipwrecked and has to survive on a stranded island. At first, Swanson's character continues to reject the butler until the butler, with more practical knowledge than the spoiled aristocrats, becomes the leader of the group. Swanson's character falls in love with him. Just as she is about to marry him, a ship comes to save them, and the family returns to England. Everyone falls back into his or her social rank, and now it is unrespectable for Swanson to marry the butler. He insists they mustn't marry and settles for the maid. The final shots of the film reveal the butler living happily with the maid in America, forging a new life freed from the bonds of aristocracy and classism, while Swanson's character is alone and unhappy. This film is the biggest admonishment of elitism and the coveting of riches. There is no redemption for Swanson's character, possibly a reflection of Macpherson's mother. Swanson's character pretended to be more important than she was (no one should be above love) and so she cannot be forgiven.

With the lack of redemption of Swanson's character, we tread into the territory of Macpherson's disdain for weakness. Though Macpherson seemed to reject coveting wealth, she found that pardonable. What she could not excuse was weakness and laziness. Swanson's character was lazy and refused to work, and so she ended up alone. In *The Cheat* (1915), though the woman covets money, she is not lazy. She worked hard for that money, and was willing to sacrifice her own body! Thus, she comes out of the picture unscathed. Yet, in *The Whispering Chorus* (1918), more than coveting a higher lifestyle, the main character refused to work hard for it. He wanted a quick solution and so he essentially stole from his boss. It is no wonder that he ends up poor, alone, and eventually put to death for his crime of ineptitude. In *Don't Change Your Husband* (1919), Gloria Swanson again plays the leading lady but this time as a woman who feels slighted by a husband who works too hard and ignores her. When she trades her husband in for a young flirt, she realizes her life is worse off than before. In the end, she learned her lesson: Don't change your husband. Though this script feels dashed off and written solely for the sake of the studio, it is in line with Macpherson's themes of hard work being the most important thing.

Yet, Macpherson's personal life comes into her writing in even more startling ways. In perhaps the most honest reflection of her own past financial struggles, Macpherson writes the following sequences in *Adam's Rib* (1923): a main character who is a wheat broker from Chicago has to sacrifice all to get the woman he loves out of trouble (reminiscent of her stepfather), and an insolent woman who smuggles a rare feather from a bird of paradise into the country is saved by love (reminiscent of her mother). This is a comedy and has some very amusing moments, but the hearts of the characters are ripped straight from Macpherson's life. In one potent line, the paleontologist calls the main woman who smuggled the feather an "inexcusable impertinent product of the Movies—Women

Suffrage—and the War! And you don't belong in a Museum, except for the purposes of research!" (Macpherson *Adam's Rib*). Not only was Macpherson a suffragette—she ran for county office of Universal City—but one can only imagine how many times she had been called "impertinent." Again, Macpherson writes from her life and the result is a humorous yet realistic look at society.

In line with Macpherson's realistic portrayal of society is her portrayal of women. Not only were all of Macpherson's female characters impertinent, they were fully-formed and human. Some would argue that in *The Cheat* (1915), the wife is a weak woman who has broken into impurity and needs saving. Yet, in reality this is a strong woman who makes very strong, independent choices, including fighting off a dangerous man. Though her husband saves her, her character cannot be described as weak. In *Joan the Woman* (1916), Macpherson insisted on creating Joan of Arc as a real woman with flaws, hence the title. After all, Macpherson was named after her (Lowrey 110), and so she owed it to the original Joan of Arc. Even Gloria Swanson in *Male and Female* (1919) was a woman with wants and desires, not merely an object of other's desire. All of Macpherson's women had an inner strength, and all of Macpherson's films featured women. In *The Godless Girl* (1929), a young female atheist falls in love with a Christian and is thrown into a violent, corrupt juvenile detention facility that literally burns to the ground. The woman is the one who sees that religion is poisonous and she provides the man with the strength he needs to save the girls in the facility. Furthermore, the male Christian's "brassbound ideology leads him to attempt the conversion of the Godless Society by force, leading directly to the death of one of his classmates" (Birchard ch. 52).

In *The Godless Girl* (1929), we see Macpherson's antifundamentalist traits. She did not rely on the stories of the Bible but she expanded upon them and found their humanity. It was DeMille who time and again urged Macpherson to emphasize the benefits of religion. Macpherson, on the other hand, wanted to make her stories character-based, as evidenced by her humanizing Joan of Arc in *Joan the Woman* (1916). Joan died a martyr but not as an indestructible saint. In *The King of Kings* (1927), "the film portrayed Mary Magdalene as a woman who was not evil but misguided, and Jesus as a virile and strong man" (Foreman 257). Again with Magdalene, a woman whom the Bible is quick to demonize, Macpherson works to create a natural woman with human, relatable, flaws. In *The Little American* (1917), the nearly defeated Mary Pickford stumbles into a bombed-out church in France during World War I. As she lugs her near-death Austrian lover into the church, the walls fall around her, but she huddles under the Cross. Jesus on the Cross survives the explosions and creates a beautiful image for the film. Again, it is not clear if this is DeMille's or Macpherson's touch. Either way, the emphasis is on Pickford's strength. She finds a quick and beautiful respite in the church, but it is not the crux of the film.

To focus more on *The Little American* (1917) provides a particularly striking example of the strength of women. Mary Pickford, playing counter to her "America's Sweetheart" little girl type, portrays an unexpected hero as a woman who falls in love with an Austrian general during World War I. She decides to stay with him despite the fact that her life is in danger, and when the war comes to her home she stays to nurse the wounded. The Austrian army invades, but she refuses to budge, eventually putting her own life on the line in order to save the women in her home and the soldiers who need her help. She stands up to sexual advances, she gives up her wealth and comfort, and in the end she nearly loses her love, but she never gives up the fight for love and strength. It is a powerful representation of the force of one woman. She is complex and conflicted as she questions her lover's government and profession, a rendering that it seems only a woman could maneuver.

The final theme in Macpherson's works is that of the complexity of love, something she surely struggled with in her own life. Many of Macpherson's films feature violent sexual exchanges—for example in *The Cheat* (1915) and *Dynamite* (1929). Macpherson's women are forever caught in a world that attempts to overpower them, despite their own strength. Most notably, it's difficult to count how many of Macpherson's characters are caught in a sexual affair with married men. Never is this portrayal more realistic than in *Dynamite* (1929), where wife and mistress literally stand across from each other and bargain over the price of a second-hand husband. A deleted scene revealed the women sitting across from each other, silently sizing each other up, a moment most likely ripped from her own experiences with DeMille's actual wife who tolerated his affairs but did not love them (Birchard ch. 46). The fact is, Macpherson was not just a mistress. She was an equal. Close in age to DeMille, she was able to stand up to him and challenge him the way no other in the industry could. It is rumored that Macpherson did not tolerate the reality of his other mistresses well, either.

When it came to affairs, Macpherson managed to legitimize them in a number of her scripts. The disdain Macpherson had for "lazy" women who did not work to keep the interest of their men comes through in an interview she conducted in 1918 for *Picture-Play Magazine* with journalist Media Mistley. When she speaks about her idea of affairs, Macpherson notes,

> Well, then, if you imply the trading of old wives for new ones, I should say the arrangement is occasionally a very satisfactory one, as divorce records prove.... Of course, I don't believe that an old wife who has helped a man to succeed should be turned in like a secondhand car.... But a wife who has simply failed to do her part ... that is a different matter [252].

In *Old Wives for New* (1918), as one would suspect based on Macpherson's comments, the current wife is overweight, does not take care of herself, nags her husband, and compulsively eats. Yet, Macpherson still offers the woman a little compassion, and the audience's heart breaks in moments of her quiet solitude, when she cries after being insulted by her husband and eats bonbons alone in bed. However, according to Macpherson, "He had given her every chance, and she had utterly failed" (Mistley 253). Macpherson notes that marriages must be built on mental as well as physical attraction and that, "Such love ... is usually found only in the cases of those who are mated perfectly in every way" (Mistley 254). Reading this interview, it is impossible to not imagine Macpherson is reflecting on her own situation. She is quick to dismiss a lazy wife, but notes that wives who help their men succeed are worthwhile, even if they have ceased to be attractive. Possibly this was how she tolerated DeMille's ever-tolerant wife. Again, we see Macpherson's disdain for laziness, but we also see a softer, sadder side. Perhaps Macpherson felt she was perfectly suited for DeMille in every way, as they were able to meet mentally and physically, and yet he was to remain married to the woman who was beside him from the beginning.

In *Dynamite* (1929), all of Macpherson's themes come to the forefront. This film tells the story of a young woman, Cynthia, who must marry in order to inherit her family's business. She bristles at the thought of marrying for anything but love. Instead, she wants to marry her lover—the problem is he is already married. In the film treatment,

Macpherson writes, "His wife refuses her consent!" Here we see a female character with power, a sense of humor, and a good deal of impertinence, and once again she is involved in an affair. Cynthia pays a man on death row, Derk, $10,000 to marry, but when he is released from prison at the last minute, he arrives at her house. In line with Macpherson's themes, Cynthia is rich and seems to only care about money. Derk arrives at Cynthia's house to give her back the money, but Cynthia thinks he is there to consummate the marriage and they fight. He violently kisses her but then points out how terrible she is being to him. She ends up calling herself cheap and worthless and he leaves. Once again, a strong woman is nearly overpowered sexually by an even stronger man, and the woman suffers through an attack of conscience. After a change of heart, Cynthia arrives in Derk's small mining town and takes on the challenge of being his wife. She learns simple tasks required in small-town life and she teaches him about art and culture. Again, here we see Macpherson's theme about the benefits of a simple life and hard work. Macpherson was able to walk between two worlds, rich and poor, because of the multi-faceted life she lived and the struggles she had to endure. In the end, Cynthia falls in love with Derk and chooses him over the rich socialite, despite the fact that the socialite literally sacrifices his life for her. The theme of coveting money and a necessary redemption found only through hard work resounds strongly throughout this piece.

Thus, Macpherson's films depict honest, realistic women and men. They struggle with their desire for wealth, engage in illicit affairs, and are funny, strong, and even self-hating at times. Still, Macpherson was part of the studio system and often her endings feel like an insincere afterthought, as in *Don't Change Your Husband* (1919), where the woman happily ends up with her rich husband after trading him in for a poor philanderer. In *The Cheat* (1915), the main characters end up walking out of court, living happily ever after, despite the fact that the entire film seemed to be setting them up for mutual destruction. The redemption is not earned and feels tacked on in an effort to remain positive. Yet, the characters themselves are not studio clichés. However, many scholars of the silent film era would disagree. Donna R. Casella writes that Macpherson was bound by the confines of the studio and thus "focused on traditional patterns of right and wrong in domestic and social settings.…Women are either the voice of expected moral behavior or struggling with men who threaten their purity, their piety" (227). Casella is focusing on a small number of Macpherson's films, and wholly ignoring her representation of Mary Magdalene, Joan of Arc, or even Gloria Swanson's character in *Male and Female* (1919). In each of these films, the women are not threatened by men's sexuality and are not shown as pure icons relegated to the bedroom and kitchen. Furthermore, while Casella cites the main female character in *The Cheat* (1915) as a woman who should not be tarnished, that representation of the character fails to acknowledge that the woman had tarnished herself from the beginning. That woman was a flirt, a spend thrift, and an absolutely frivolous human. She worried for the safety of her husband and her home, but she was by all accounts flawed and not simply part of the cult of domesticity. When she was freed from trouble, it was by her own strength of admission. Never does the film show her being a "good" homemaker.

Another scholar that misrepresents the work of Jeanie Macpherson and other female screenwriters from the silent era is Anthony Slide. Though Mr. Slide is an accomplished archivist, he makes sweeping statements about the low number of women in silent film that is hard to verify and discredits other researchers, namely Cari Beauchamp, without consulting Beauchamp's numbers that directly contradict his. Even he acknowledges that most films were not archived from the beginning of the film industry. Yet, he persists in belittling the contribution of female writers in an effort to reach for the "truth." When he states that Alice Guy Blaché "should have accepted responsibility for her life and her career. She made the wrong move in leaving the United States" (Slide 120), it appears he has an axe to grind against women filmmakers. He claims to respect them, but from this reader's perspective, his tone is clearly attempting to keep women in their place. Had he taken a closer look at women like Jeanie Macpherson he would have learned that there is no "place" for women other than the one they rightfully worked for with their extraordinary talents and drive to succeed.

Jeanie Macpherson is just one of the severely under-recognized women in the film industry. When she died in 1946, her obituary was given substantial space in the *LA Times*, but still most people did not know her name. Though it is difficult to succinctly summarize these women's lives due to the spotty archiving from the beginning of Hollywood, the records are there and worth inspecting. Jeanie Macpherson was born into wealth and the arts but experienced extreme hardship with the bankruptcy of her family due to her mother's covetous lifestyle, and she spent her entire lifetime making up for that fact. Her films, at a time when melodramatic, quickly-dashed-off work reigned supreme, shine with honesty and heart. She spoke from her heart, drew from her life, and her characters and films reflect that fact. Thus, her films remain potent and topical. Love, lust, envy, fear, inner strength—these themes will never go out of fashion. It is this researcher's hope that the lessons learned from Macpherson—to work hard, practice one's craft, and write from one's personal truth—reach young writer's ears today.

Works Cited

"'Barley King' O'Neil Returns." *The Minneapolis Journal* 10 June 1902: 3. *Chronicling America: Historic American Newspapers*. Library of Congress. Accessed 8 Dec. 2015.

Birchard, Richard S. *Cecil B DeMille's Hollywood*. Lexington: University Press of Kentucky, 2004. Accessed 7 Dec. 2015.

Casella, Donna. "Feminism and the Female Author: The Not So Silent Career of the Woman Scenarist in Hollywood—1896–1930." *Quarterly Review of Film & Video* 23.3 (2006): 217–235. *Film & Television Literature Index with Full Text*. Accessed 1 Nov. 2015.

Curbow, Dave. "Jeanie Macpherson." www.imdb.com. Accessed 5 Dec. 2015.

de Mille, Richard. *My Secret Mother*. New York: Farrar, Straus & Giroux, 1998.

"Doings at Los Angeles: Universal City Elects Officers." 14 June 1913. Special collections, Margaret Herrick Library, Academy of Motion Picture Arts and Sciences.

Foreman, Alexa L. "Macpherson, Jeanie." *St. James Women Filmmakers Encyclopedia* (1999): 255–258. *Film & Television Literature Index with Full Text*. Accessed 1 Nov. 2015.

Gaines, Jane. "Jeanie Macpherson." *Women Film Pioneers Project*. Center for Digital Research and Scholarship, New York, 27 Sept. 2013. wfpp.cdrs.columbia.edu/pioneer/ccp-jeanie-macpherson/. Accessed 9 Dec. 2015.

"Jeanie Macpherson Is Definitely Out of Cecil B. DeMille Company." 3 Sept. 1930. Special collections, Margaret Herrick Library, Academy of Motion Picture Arts and Sciences.

Jeanie MacPherson photograph album, special collections. Margaret Herrick Library, Academy of Motion Picture Arts and Sciences.

The Jewelers' Circular and Horological Review. Vol. 39. Jewelers' Circular Publishing Company, 1899. 19. New York Public Library. Digitized 18 June 2008. Accessed 8 Dec. 2015.

Lowe, Denise. "Macpherson, Jeanie (1887 Boston, MA—1946 Hollywood, CA)." *Encyclopedic Dictionary of Women in Early American Films, 1895–1930* (2005): 340–343. *Film & Television Literature Index with Full Text*.

Lowrey, Carolyn. *The First One Hundred Noted Men and Women of the Screen*. New York: Moffat, Yard & Co., 1920.

Macpherson, Jeanie. Dynamite synopsis. Special collections, Margaret Herrick Library, Academy of Motion Picture Arts and Sciences.

Martin, Alice. "From 'Wop' Parts to Bossing the Job." *Photoplay*. October 1916: 95–97. Academy Library Archives.

Mistley, Media. "What I Think of 'Old Wives for New.'" Editorial. *Picture-Play Magazine,* Aug. 1918: 251–54. Media History Digital Library.

"No Let-Down Planned for DeMille Units." *LA Times (1923-Current).* 5 Sept. 1927. ProQuest Historical Newspapers: Los Angeles Times, 7. Accessed 1 Nov. 2015.

Paramount press release, Chatfield. Special collections. Margaret Herrick Library, Academy of Motion Picture Arts and Sciences.

Paramount press release, Cooper. Special collections, Margaret Herrick Library, Academy of Motion Picture Arts and Sciences.

Paramount press release, Hebert. Special collections, Margaret Herrick Library, Academy of Motion Picture Arts and Sciences.

Paramount press release, Whitmore. Special collections, Margaret Herrick Library, Academy of Motion Picture Arts and Sciences.

Pawlek, Debra Ann. *Bringing Up Oscar: The Story of the Men and Women Who Founded the Academy.* New York: Pegasus Books, 2011.

Sargent, Epes Winthrop, and Jeanie Macpherson. "A Screenwriting Sampler from the Moving World." *Film History* 9.3 (1997): 269–276. *Film & Television Literature Index with Full Text.*

Shipley, Lee. "Lee Side o' L.A." *ProQuest Historical Newspapers: Los Angeles Times.* 6 March 1942: A4.

Slide, Anthony. "Early Women Filmmakers: The Real Numbers." *Film History* 24.1 (2012): 114–121. *Film & Television Literature Index with Full Text.* Accessed 1 Nov. 2015.

Stafford, Jeff. "The Devil's Brother." TCM.com. Turner Classic Movies. Accessed 9 Dec. 2015.

Valeria Belletti letter to Irma. Belletti Box 1, 13 March 1928. Special collections, Margaret Herrick Library, Academy of Motion Picture Arts and Sciences.

"Writer Gives Dinner for Zukor." *Moving Picture World.* 1 Feb. 1919. Special collections, Margaret Herrick Library, Academy of Motion Picture Arts and Sciences.

Anita Loos
A Girl Like Her

TONI ANITA HULL

Best known for writing *Gentlemen Prefer Blondes*, Anita Loos is a great American author, playwright, and screenwriter. In the silent era, Loos shaped the integral role that intertitles played, and is known for her title work for some of the most acclaimed movies of the day. She was a master of satirizing sex and love, and was capable of writing rich, multi-faceted females who drove the action in their films. Growing up with a philandering father who she so adored, marrying a codependent hypochondriac, and loving the man who would never love her back would heavily influence her writing no matter the medium.

Loos was born as Corrine Anita Loos on April 26, 1888. However, when she died, newspapers speculated that she was anywhere from seventy-nine to ninety-one years of age. In fact, the *New York Times* originally printed that she was born in 1893, making her eighty-eight at the time of her death. Today, Wikipedia states that she was born in 1889. Clearly, Loos was always stretching the truth a bit and keeping people guessing as to what was fact and what was fiction. As her full-page obituary in the *New York Times* put so perfectly, "An excellent anecdotalist, Miss Loos seldom permitted precise facts to spoil a good story" (Alden "Anita Loos..."). It would be a gross understatement to say that it has been interesting to piece together her story.

Loos was born in Sisson, California, which is now known as Mount Shasta, to R. Beers and Minnie Ellen and the family relocated to San Francisco four year later. Loos was the middle child of three. Older brother, Clifford, a doctor, would go on to implement a prepaid health services plan that we know today as a health maintenance organization or an HMO. Sadly, younger sister, Gladys died after complications with peritonitis at the tender age of eight. Loos, who was only two years Gladys' senior, claimed, "I knew that Gladys was going to die, because while we sat waiting for a phone call I picked up a copy of *Life*, which in those days was a humorous weekly, and when I opened it my gaze lighted on a joke concerning death" (Loos, *A Girl Like I* 37).

Loos would often refer to her mother as an "earthbound angel" as Minnie turned a blind eye to Beers' continued interest in other women and never complained. Loos claims to have known about her father's infidelities at an early age. She often recounts the story of one of Beers' beauties showing up to their home asking Minnie to divorce him. "But instead of treating the beauty with disdain, my mother was actually sympathetic. She

Writer Anita Loos working at Biograph in 1916. Though she knew she wanted to write from an early age, Loos started out as a child actress, appearing in the American premiere of Ibsen's *A Doll's House* as one of Nora's children (courtesy Cari Beauchamp).

explained the she had suffered for years because of other women's infatuation with her Harry..." (Loos, *A Girl Like I* 23). Despite Beer's behavior, Loos adored her father and they shared an affinity with one another that distinguished them from the rest of the family. Able to see past her father's tragic flaw Loos didn't blame Beers for the fact that women were so drawn to his charm. She enjoyed traipsing about the Barbary Coast with her father and getting to know his cronies, which she claims included Harry Houdini, Jack London, and Wallace and Will Irwin, to name a few (Loos, *A Girl Like I* 37).

Beers introduced both Loos and Gladys to the stage a young age. Loos was a natural comedian from the beginning, "At a very early age she found her forte—she had a talent to amuse" (Beauchamp and Loos 9). Off-stage, Loos was a cheeky young girl, even once cracking a joke to a director to save her mother from embarrassment because Minnie had put her and Gladys in yellow tights: "While the director was loudly criticizing my mother, I piped up to suggest he insert a line of dialogue saying that, owing to the persecutions of the Roman Emperor, we Christian children contracted jaundice" (Loos, *A Girl Like I* 32). She was writing zesty one-liners even then.

Loos had quite the stage career as a young child, and was often the family's sole breadwinner. Directed by the great David Belasco in a production of *May Blossom* at the Alcazar Theatre, she would later use this connection to him lure an actress from him for one of her own plays. She was also in the American premiere of Ibsen's *A Doll's House*, in which she played one of Nora's children. When the family moved to San Diego in 1903, Loos joined a theatre stock company which her father managed. Loos could have continued to act, and would have made a nice career out of it; however, her passion was elsewhere.

When he managed his stock company, Beers would run short films between acts; this is where Loos discovered a taste for writing. She wrote a script, took the Biograph address from a film canister, and sent off her work. A few weeks later, she received a letter stating they had accepted her scenario. *The New York Hat* starred Mary Pickford, Lionel Barrymore, and Lillian Gish is a delightful piece. This simple story of a girl, her hat, and a kind minister displays one of Loos' many skills: her natural ability for narratives that appeal to the human condition. After selling her first scenario, Loos penned a vaudeville skit, *The Ink Well*, which went on to have a successful run in San Francisco. Now twenty-four (although as she grew older, this age changed), Loos earned her own money as professional writer though she claims she was first published at age eight in a children's magazine of the time entitled *St. Nicholas* where she wrote ad copy for F.P.C Wax: "The best thing I've seen, said the Man from Mars/Since I left my abode from among the stars/Is something my own world sadly lacks/The earth's greatest boon F.P.C Wax" (Loos, *A Girl Like I* 33). For winning this contest, Loos earned $5 that she "lent" to her father, knowing that she would never see the money again. This loan offers an insight into Loos, "Although unaware, I was beginning to sense the thrill a girl can feel in handing money to a man" (Loos, *A Girl Like I* 23). This speaks volumes to her relationship with her second husband, John Emerson, in which she yearned for control and gave him everything. On the other hand, it is the total opposite philosophy of her most famous character, Lorelei Lee.

Loos' unique fascination of men, women, sex, and relationships would ultimately characterize her writing and profoundly affect her personal life. Her attraction to how men operated started early on with her Uncle Horace, who was by all definitions, a conman. She recalls learning her first important lesson about the opposite sex from Uncle Horace. He tried to give Loos a kiss, and although Loos was fond of Horace, she refused. Uncle Horace, who had been more casual around her, was now interested and intrigued by the seven-year-old Loos and bought her a diamond ring. At seven years old, Loos witnessed human behavior: you are always attracted to something you cannot truly have. Years later, when spending the summer at the Hotel del Coronado, Loos had to choose between two beaus, a Detroiter and a Senator's son. A duel between the two ensued, but Loos was terribly unimpressed as she had written this same scene in a slapstick farce and in her own words: "Therein lay my tragedy: I was generally going to laugh away romance" (Loos, *A Girl Like I* 67). But Loos would make her own discovery about sex. She was taught to keep her mouth shut about her literary career because either men didn't believe her or being an author meant she was no longer a girl. This harsh reality followed Loos until she had Emerson committed to an institution as he was always threatened by her success. It is anecdotes like these that Loos chooses to write about in her autobiography, *A Girl Like I* and it is these moments that create the foundation of her writing.

After *The New York Hat*, Loos continued to sell scenarios to Biograph such as *A Girl Like Mother, Saved by Soup, The Little Liar* among many. According to an interview in *Everybody's Magazine* in 1917, Loos would "write 200 scenarios before she ever saw the inside of a studio" (Schmidt 623). Loos finally met D.W. Griffith in January 1914. Her mother accompanied Loos and he mistook Minnie for the scenario authoress. After Griffith's initial shock that the childlike Loos was the actual writer, he took Loos and Minnie to the set of *Judith of Bethulia* and then onto lunch. At lunch, Loos and Griffith engaged in a heated discussion about literature and her audacity and knowledge captivated Griffith. Bored with the theater and her life in San Diego, Loos had finally found the place where she belonged. "I can't say I fell in love with Griffith that day over a sandwich in a corner drugstore, but our session provided the sort of cerebral excitement that makes the bohemias of the world, the Greenwich Villages, and Sohos and Left Banks, so much more sexy than any other place" (Loos, *A Girl Like I* 81). Another account of the latter meeting appears in Marc Norman's *What Happens Next*. Norman's spinning of this anecdote plays out as if little Loos fell madly in love with Griffith finding the "cerebral excitement" forever erotic. I would absolutely dispute this ridiculous speculation. Loos and Griffith shared a mutual admiration and respect for one another for the several years they worked together and beyond. He trusted her with one of his greatest works. Unfortunately, Minnie still wasn't having her child in the movies. After Griffith made an attempt to cast Loos in a scene of *Judith of Bethulia*, Minnie put Loos on a train back to San Diego.

As the summer of 1914 came to a close, Loos finally found the courage to send Griffith another script after running out on him earlier in the year. *Only a Fireman's Bride* was received with delight and elicited an open invitation from Griffith to return to the studio. As Minnie was skeptical of the movie biz, Loos saw marriage as her only way out of San Diego and back to Hollywood, so she found herself a beau, Frank Pallama: "Poor little Freddy (or was is Frankie?) had been hanging around in the background while I stalked more notable prey" (Loos, *A Girl Like I* 84). The day before the wedding to Frank, Loos saw the stupidity of her plan and wanted out. Nonetheless, Minnie wouldn't have it because she had already ordered the cake.

Loos went through with the ceremony and claims her marriage lasted one awful night at the Hotel del Coronado. The tale that Loos devised goes something like this: The day after the wedding, Loos sent Frankie out for some hairpins. While he was out, she rushed back to Minnie and said she was leaving Frankie. Relieved Minnie and Loos boarded a train to Los Angeles and Loos was back at Griffith's studio the following day. The idea that it all happened within forty-eight hours is a bit of a stretch as this sounds like the perfect outline to a hilarious scenario. "In reality, her marriage to Frank last several months. However, when she did return home, her mother's attitude was primarily one of relief. Now that her daughter had been respectably deflowered, Minnie saw no reason to further impede Anita's moving to Los Angeles" (Beauchamp and Loos 39). Nevertheless, Minnie still accompanied her daughter.

At Biograph, Frank Woods, or "Daddy" as everyone called him because of his paternal manner and his mop of white hair, hired Loos. She worked for $50 a week and wrote stories for their stars as needed, and earned extra for any script accepted. It seems Loos was the first staff writer that movies ever saw. Her first year was spent writing scenarios for its secondary units, but she could not wait for the day she could work with Griffith. Ironically, Emerson would pave the way for her to do so.

Now in partnership with Thomas Ince and Mack Sennett at Triangle Films, Griffith hired John Emerson, Broadway actor turned director, to direct a film version of the play, *The Conspiracy*, which turned out to be underwhelming. In spite of this, Emerson began to implore Griffith to make a comedy with his good friend Douglas Fairbanks. Fairbanks, also a Broadway actor, was brought on by Griffith most likely due to his charm and good looks. However, during Fairbanks' first screen test, it was thought that he could not act. To appease Emerson and Fairbanks, Griffith allowed them to make a comedy. Emerson took to Daddy's files where he uncovered a plethora of comedies for Fairbanks written by Loos. While Griffith found scripts funny, he did not understand how the lines could be translated onto the screen. When Emerson suggested that they print the lines on the screen, Griffith scoffed claiming that people did not come to the movies to read. Tired of Emerson's pleas and knowing he and Fairbanks had contracts to fulfill, Griffith gave the green light for *His Picture in the Papers* to be made, the tale of Pete Prindle, the last son of a vegetarian health food manufacturer, who falls in love with Christine, who will only marry him if he gets his picture in the papers. Of course, he eventually gets his picture on the front page. *His Picture in the Papers* is a remarkably hilarious satire, earning praise from the *New York Times*. Loos' use of alliteration on several title cards is brilliant; the hilarity of the name Pete Prindle stands on its own. Loos is able to manipulate words in such a way that you anxiously wait for the next sharp title card to appear. After Pete shares a steak with the lovely Christine, the card reads: "Wherein it is shown that beefsteak produces a different style of love-making from prunes" (*His Picture in the Papers*) appears across this screen. This is one small example of Loos' outstanding wit in the film.

Loos' intertitles paired with the action of *The Mystery of the Leaping Fish* make it a gem of the era. The story surrounds a cokehead Sherlock Holmes type, named Cocaine Ennyday. Utilizing a small, simple gag such as the "Gentleman rolling in wealth" and then cutting to Ennyday sleeping in money is still entertaining to the modern viewer. Loos could have picked the word "money" or "dough," but she chose "wealth," which is the reason the joke lands so well—you don't expect it. The ending, in which Fairbanks is seen at the scenario office trying to get a job and is told "No, Douglas, you had better give up scenario writing and stick to acting" (Emerson, *The Mystery of the Leaping Fish*) is wonderfully unique, modern and meta. While Tod Browning is credited for story, it is not hard to believe Loos crafted this surprising and smart ending. It is no wonder that Griffith then entrusted Loos with writing the intertitles to one of his most famous films, *Intolerance*.

Most likely one of the first to view *Intolerance*, Loos thought Griffith was mental in trying to tell a story that jumped between four different periods of time. Fearless and determined, Loos took on the task of writing inter-titles for this three hour beast of a film. Until *Intolerance*, Griffith had mostly used subtitles to explain time, place, etc., but "...with *Intolerance* he allowed Loos a new freedom that resulted in wry titles such as: 'When women who cease to attract men often turn to reform as a second choice'" (Beauchamp and Loos 40–41). In 1917, *Photoplay* magazine dubbed Loos "The Soubrette of Satire." As the article so beautifully states, "The most important service that Anita Loos has so far rendered the screen is the elevation of the sub-caption, first to sanity, then to dignity and brilliance combined" (Johnson 148). More than one reviewer or historian has said that Loos' greatest contribution to silent film were intertitles. "One of her innovations was to prepare screen captions—these first appeared in 'Macbeth' in 1916–that then became standard practice. Her subtitles for 'Intolerance' in 1916 are considered classics of the genre" (Alden "Anita Loos…").

Loos, Emerson, and Fairbanks went on to team-up on several films: Fairbanks starring, Emerson directing, and Loos writing. In some cases, such as with *His Picture in the Paper* and *The Americano*, Emerson not only has a writing credit, but is listed above Loos. He asked her to share authorship and have his name listed first because it felt "undignified" for a man to take the back seat to a woman. Loos agreed, and most likely gained the same thrill she felt when lending her father that $5. She often spoke as though her writing was not of major importance. In an interview in *Interview* magazine in 1972, Loos was asked if her job became harder in the sound era. She replied, "It was never hard at all. I never took it that seriously" (O'Brien "Anita Loos: Gentleman…"). Perhaps in an effort to conceal her powerlessness over Emerson, Loos later wrote, "I had no pride in authorship because I never thought that anything produced by females was or even should be important" (*A Girl Like I* 181). In reality, Loos cared a great deal about her work and was perhaps a perfectionist. In *Without Lying Down: Frances Marion and the Powerful Women of Early Hollywood*, Cari Beauchamp writes, "Like Frances, Loos made light of her scriptwriting, saying once that the plot was developed, 'it was a breeze' and she had so much fun, it was almost a crime to be paid for it. But also like Frances, Loos got up before dawn to write and agonized over the words she chose" (Beauchamp 79).

When Fairbanks grew tired of sharing his spotlight with Loos and Emerson, the famous threesome went their separate ways. Emerson cited medical problems as the reason for the split and moved to New York, as he required the attention of specialists there. Loos followed. Emerson, or Mr. E as she often referred to him, was twenty years her senior. Loos claimed that she was unimpressed with Emerson upon first meeting him, yet in her memoir she wrote: "True, he was quite handsome; he was tall, his dark hair was turning attractively gray, and he had the somewhat romantic air of a semi-invalid" (Loos, *A Girl Like I* 99). In fact, Emerson was an intense hypochondriac. When Loos gained attention, Emerson fell ill. At one point, he became convinced he needed a donut cushion to sit on and took it everywhere he went. He also insisted that he had a serious throat problem, and so Emerson and Loos made pilgrimages to many specialists in both the States and Europe. Finally, a European doctor addressed Emerson's hypochondria with Loos. The doctor put Emerson under anesthesia, scratched his throat, and handed him a jar full of nodes, claiming they had been removed from his throat. Emerson was cured. Strangely enough, it was Emerson's neediness that drew Loos to him, she "was attracted to him out of the same maternal leanings she felt for her father, not out of a sense of needing to be protected" (Dolan 78). Loos' affinity for men like Beers and Emerson would ultimately be at the root of her most celebrated works. She wrote women who had all of the power over their men.

It is hard to believe that Loos pursued Emerson as he proclaimed that he never had been nor would he ever be faithful to just one woman. But like so many other women, Loos believed that she was different from his others. According to Loos, the finest moment of her life with Emerson came after he had his spleen removed. He took her hand, looked at his nurse and said, "Aren't I lucky at my age to have such a darling little sweetheart?" (Loos, *A Girl Like I* 181). Though a world-renowned writer, Loos desperately sought the approval of her Mr. E, and when that approval came, it was boiled down to one condescending line. That being said, during their early courtship, Loos grew tired of waiting for Emerson to settle down, so she took a play out of her seven-year-old, inner child playbook, left Emerson at the Algonquin Hotel in New York and moved to Long Island where she shared a house with fellow screenwriter, Frances Marion. Other suitors took notice of Loos, which caused Emerson to finally propose. While many friends felt the same way, Frances was the only one who spoke up citing that Emerson had a "constipated brain" and was manipulating Loos. Despite this warning, Loos married Emerson on June 15, 1919. Though she did not understand her friend's attraction to Emerson, Frances stood next to Loos as her maid of honor.

Loos and Emerson saw great success in New York professionally, making films with

Marion Davies and Constance Talmadge, and writing successful plays in between. The writing credit for one of Loos' greatest silent films, *The Love Expert* with Constance Talmadge, is shared with Emerson, though most film historians agree it is undeserved as this film is the perfect example of Loos' voice and her stellar wit and demonstrates her talent as humorist. Loos never simply states what is going on, which makes her intertitles genius. For example, one of her best titles sets up a scene in which the lead character, Babs, finds out that before Winthrop, the man she loves, can marry he must marry off his plain sisters and elderly Aunt Cornelia. Loos writes the following: "The next day Babs faced a domestic problem that would have made Ibsen green with envy" (Kirkland, *The Love Expert*). *The Love Expert* is also Anita's ability to satire sex at its best. The film makes light of the double standards for men and women. Babs' father finds her talking to a gentleman and scolds her saying, "A man like that will get you in compromising position, and then you'll have to marry him!" (Kirkland, *The Love Expert*). This is when Babs develops a scheme to trap Aunt Cornelia in her father's bedroom. It works beautifully and it forces him to marry her. Naturally, the father tries to get out of the situation first. However, Babs proclaims, "It's always the woman who pays!" (Kirkland, *The Love Expert*). Daddy vows to marry Aunt Cornelia, paving the way for Babs to marry Winthrop. As with most of Loos' works, her female characters go after what they want fearlessly, and Babs is no exception.

New York was good to the Emerson-Loos team as they thrived on both stage and screen. Furthermore, New York brought Loos and H.L. Mencken together and meeting Mencken would inspire her most famous work. When Loos finally met Menck—as she called him—she felt like she already knew him. She had been an admirer of Mencken for quite some time as he edited and wrote for the monthly *Smart Set*, a literary magazine that featured many up-and-coming authors. "My first impression of Mencken was of his arresting masculinity; he was smoking a big cigar which he held, like Pop, at a jaunty angle; aside from that sign of maturity, Henry Mencken looked like a young farmhand who was dressed in his best, with too much starch in his shirt and too high a collar. His boyish appearance made him all the more fascinating, for it arouses a girl's motherly instincts" (Loos, *A Girl Like I* 146). This is an extremely informative phrase. As if it was not apparent enough in her relationship with Emerson, Loos was inherently drawn to men that reminded her of her father; men who could not settle down and men who could never fully be hers. Loos writes about Mencken as if they carried on a love affair, using words such as "dates" and "romance" when referencing their relationship. However, it seems it was more of an intellectual affair, "He [Mencken] was to become yet another in what would be a string of love affairs of the mind, jousting with one-liners and all-night philosophical discussions, but they were rarely intimate liaisons that Loos might have hoped for" (Beauchamp, *Without Lying...* 110). While Mencken may not have exactly shared her sentiments, he did, at the very least, provide Loos with wit, banter, and the intellectual stimulation she missed with Emerson.

On a fateful trip from New York to Los Angeles, a Miss Mae Davis happened to be on the same train as Emerson and Loos. Davis was a blonde bombshell who had peaked Mencken's interest. As the train chugged across the country, Loos could not help but notice how the men were tripping over themselves in Davis' presence. "In the club car, if she happened to drop the magazine she was reading, several men jumped to retrieve it, whereas I was allowed to lug heavy suitcases from their racks while men, most particularly my husband, failed to notice" (Loos, *A Girl Like I* 265). While the witless blonde had captured Emerson's attention, it was Menck's affection for Miss Davis that drove Loos crazy. So Loos took to her notepad and sketched out what would become *Gentlemen Prefer Blondes*. Her audience at the time, was an audience of one, Mencken. "Had I been unsexual I might have written viciously, but I was in love with Mencken and had taken up my pencil in order to laugh into nothingness a blonde he cared more for" (Loos, *A Girl Like I* 266).

Gentlemen Prefer Blondes: The Illuminating Diary of a Professional Lady began as a series of stories in *Harper's Bazaar* (per Mencken's suggestion that Loos submit it to the publication). Due to immense popularity the published book appeared in November 1925 with the first printing selling out overnight. "The novel is a classic of American fiction and has been reprinted in dozens of languages, and the deliciously guileless gold digger Lorelei Lee has been personified on the stage and screen several times over" (Beauchamp and Loos 45). The first film adaptation graced the screen in 1928, but sadly the film has since been lost. It was adapted into a stage musical in 1949 starring Carol Channing, and that version was made into the 1953 musical film starring Marilyn Monroe and Jane Russell. While Loos had poked fun at sex before, Mencken declared that with *Blondes*, Loos was the first writer to make fun of sex.

Blondes is written as the diary of Lorelei Lee, a blond bombshell with a male friend, "A gentleman friend and I were dining at the Ritz last evening and he said that if I took a pencil and a paper and put down all of my thoughts it would make a book" (Loos, *Gentlemen Prefer...* 40). The book chronicles Lorelei and her best friend Dorothy's trip through Europe. A small wonderful detail in *Blondes* is how Loos misspells words and uses improper grammar throughout the novel, such as spelling "Freud" (as in Sigmund Freud) as "Froyd" or "opertunity" rather than "opportunity." Professor Laurie J.C. Cella observes, "...a closer examination of the grammatical errors suggest that Loos may have another aim: to put her readers in a position of false superiority comparable to Lorelei's hapless suitors" (Cella 48). At first glance, Lorelei is a just another dumb blonde, but the truth of the matter is, Loos has built Lorelei with many layers. As with Babs in *The Love Expert*, Lorelei is a woman who knows what she wants and exactly how to get it. While the audience believes it is her looks that land the gentlemen in her life, it is truly Lorelei's smarts. "Lorelei's seduction is shaped by her awareness of the very game she plays" (Cella 49). Lorelei is the perfect example of how Loos' views on relationships from an early age shaped her characters: Men go after Lorelei because she is the epitome of unattainable; Lorelei understands the thrill that gentlemen feel when they shower her with gifts; and Lorelei seems unintelligent on the surface, which means she'll remain inferior (or at least she will allow the men in her life think she is).

When examining Lorelei, this may be the alter ego that Loos so wanted to be; the woman who had the control over men. When in reality, Loos had very little control of the major male figures in her life. Her father never changed. While Loos adored him and all of his flaws, she spent her youth trying to control him. It started with that $5 she lent him. Despite what she writes, the thrill that she felt was hope; hope that maybe Beers would stick around with every dollar she gave and every secret she kept. Loos did whatever she possibly could to keep Emerson happy, including dedicating *Blondes* to him at his request; this was after he tried to stop the publication. Then there was Menck, who never seemed to love Loos the way she wanted him to, despite putting him on a pedestal. While Loos wanted to appear breezy like Lorelei, she put much effort into making it look like she was carefree. In a phone interview, Beauchamp talked about reviewing Loos' appointment books. She revealed, "Sometimes there would be a number like 102 or 103 written down and circled several times. This indicated her weight and that she had to lose a few pounds to get down to the 97 she usually weighed" (Beauchamp). Despite their differences, there is a piece of Loos in Lorelei: "Like Lorelei, Loos is singing her siren song and attempting to lure Mencken through an appeal to his intellect in making fun of the masses" (Dolan 78).

Playing opposite of Lorelei is Dorothy, the brunette. If Lorelei is Loos' alter-ego, then Dorothy her direct representative. Loos calls this out herself, "But as much as I owe Lorelei, I mustn't forget to add my thanks to the brunette Dorothy.... For in affairs of the heart I was Dorothy's most accurate prototype" (Loos, *A Girl Like I* 275). Like Loos, Dorothy is always standing by with a strong one-liner, "So Sir Francis Beekman wanted us to get out and look at the tower because he said that quite a famous Queen had her head cut off there one morning and Dorothy said 'What a fool she was to get up that morning...'" (Loos, *Gentlemen Prefer...* 40). Dorothy is the smart broad who is looking out for her friend at every turn, even though she knows that Lorelei has it handled. "As surely as that archetypal blonde is meant to represent the beginnings of Lorelei, so Loos's own position would be that of Lorelei's flapper sidekick, Dorothy Shaw ... a critic, a truth teller, and the voice of liberated, unhypocritical moral authority" (Dolan 75). William Faulkner had a particular affection for Dorothy. He wrote to Loos, "Please accept my envious congratulations on Dorothy.... But I wish I had thought of Dorothy first" (Anita Loos Papers).

Blondes is Loos' pivotal work. It earned her enough money that she no longer had to work, until Emerson squandered it all away. Around 1931, Mr. E declared that one of them had to go back to work, and that meant Loos so she left Emerson in New York and headed back to Hollywood.

The talkies were now in full swing. F. Scott Fitzgerald had been tasked by MGM to adapt Katherine Bush's play *Red Headed Woman*, which was a straight melodrama. However, according to Irving Thalberg: "Scott tried to turn the silly book into a tone poem" (Beauchamp 283). Thalberg called in Loos since Mencken had dubbed her the writer to poke fun at sex, Thalberg wanted to make *Red Headed Woman* something comical and fun. Loos accepted the challenge.

"For *Red Headed Woman*, Loos massaged what could have been a banal soap opera into a script riddled with double entendres and clever one-liners..." (Beauchamp and Loos 125). The film's main character is Lil Andrews, a stenographer who stops at nothing to get what she wants, which means seducing rich men. She has an affair with her married boss, Bill who leaves his wife for Lil. When Bill's family and friends refuse to accept her, she sleeps up with a richer man, only to have an affair with his chauffeur. When caught in the affair, Lil goes back to Bill, who is now back with his first wife. She then attempts to kill Bill, but she gets away scott free. Lil is seen at the end of the movie with a new older, richer gentleman getting into a car, with her actual lover, the chauffeur, driving them away. In short, Lil is a manipulative seductress who never sees her comeuppance. This is fantastic to see on screen because men were—and still are—often portrayed as acting without consequence, bur women rarely are. Loos writes a strong, multi-layered female character. When the audience first meets Lil, she is seen as this innocent secretary-type who has fallen for her boss. However, within minutes, we quickly watch her seduce him. Early on she says to Bill, "I'll be what you want me to be..." (Conway, *Red Headed Woman*) which is so telling of Lil and how she is able to trade up the men in her life. By all means, Lil is the epitome of an evil woman: She gets drunk, treats her best friend like a servant, and sleeps her way to the top. Nonetheless, there is something about Lil that is likeable—due in part to the incomparable Jean Harlow—but also to Loos' writing. Lil is quick, smart, and charming. In one scene, Lil asks the store clerk, "Can you see through this?" and the clerk replies, "I'm afraid you can, Miss." Without hesitation, Lil says, "I'll wear it" (Conway, *Red Headed Woman*). Above all, Lil is scandalous. It is said that *Red Headed Woman* was one of the movies that led directly to the Hays Code being enforced. Nonetheless, *Red Headed Woman* was a success. Enough people saw the movie as a farce, accepted it as such, and filled theatres. Loos had transitioned to talkies without any hiccups in her career.

Emerson decided to join Loos in Los Angeles, but Loos wanted him to fill his time so he wouldn't spend their money once again or make poor investments. She asked Thalberg to split her salary between her and Emerson, and he agreed, saying, "You are even more of a masochist than I am" (Beauchamp and Loos 128). By October of 1937, Loos and her brother Clifford checked Emerson into a sanatorium in Pasadena, where he was diagnosed with severe bipolar disorder. Loos would eventually find her Goldwyn contract locked in Mr. E's lockbox. She discovered she was being paid only half of what she was usually paid and that Emerson took the over a $100,000 signing bonus. Despite this, and despite the rest, Loos never divorced Emerson. He died in the sanitarium in 1956.

In 1939, Loos wrote the film adaptation of a Clare Booth Luce play entitled *The Women*. The play follows several female Manhattanites, particularly Mary Haines. Mary quickly finds out her husband is cheating on her from her cousin, Sylvia. Sylvia takes great joy in telling Mary this bit of gossip. Following along in the play script one can watch the movie to note what changes Loos made. First, Loos opens the film with two female dogs, or bitches, barking at one another, while the play opens with a bridge game. This is amazing and automatically sets the tone for the movie. The opening scene moves into a doggie spa, and then a ladies' spa. We immediately understand this over privileged, elite world. We see an overweight woman taking a mud bath complaining about worms. Another woman gets her wrinkles examined, "I hate to tell you this dear, but your wrinkles make the Rocky Mountains look like chiffon velvet" (Loos/Murfin, *The Women*). Loos skillfully manipulates and cut scenes from the Luce play. For instance, she cut the scene where Little Mary, Mary's daughter, is teased about her breasts and she calls girls tattletales and claims she hates them. This scene feels out of place in the play. Rather, Loos places Little Mary after a riding lesson, having fun with her mother. This focuses on a positive female relationship, such as a maternal bond, which ultimately inspires Mary to stand up for herself at the end. Little Mary also has a one-liner or two, proving that Loos makes even her youngest of female characters complex.

In addition, Loos cuts many characters or shrinks their roles, and focuses on just a handful of characters. While the play is confusing and muddy, the film moves beautifully. At the top of Act II, Loo adds a train scene that wisely sets up the next scene on the ranch, which is pivotal. Mary immediately develops a strong bond with Miriam and the Countess on the ride over cocktails, and these positive female relationships balance the backstabbing that ensues. Most importantly, is how Loos chooses to end this film compared to the stage version, which impacts the film, and what we as an audience take away. Mary decides to finally fight back with some gossip she learned about her husband's mistress, Crystal and her catty cousin, who had been co-conspiring as friends. She calls on her mother to watch Little Mary, who is curled up next to her, and says, "I've had two years to grow claws, Mother. Jungle red!" (Loos/Murfin, *The Women*). However, in the play, this is the last line of dialogue, and is addressed to Sylvia. The play then ends with Sylvia physically fighting Crystal, which leaves the audience with the final impression that women are mean and simple. In Loos' adaptation, Little Mary gets to witness her mother make the choice to get out of bed and fight for her family. The final beat of the film is Mary heading out the door, successfully winning her husband back. It has to be noted that Loos gives Crystal the best line of dialogue in the movie, not found in the play, "And by the way, there's a name for you ladies, but it isn't used in high society—outside of a kennel" (Loos/Murfin, *The Women*). This is a fantastic callback to the opening scene. Loos' adaptation of *The Women* is funny, charming, and still makes a clear statement on the affluent, women of high society. As Loos' *New York Times* obituary states, "One of her most praised scripts—some thought it superior to the play—was *The Women*" (Alden "Anita Loos...").

Perhaps it was no accident that *The Women* was Loos' next project after committing Emerson. In her version, we see Mary grow from a powerless, unaware housewife to a clever, strong, independent woman. While they are all strong-willed women, Mary is extremely different from Lil and Lorelei. It's almost as if Loos finally was in a place of peace and acceptance, no longer needing alter-egos; no longer feeling the need to live vicariously through the Loreleis of the world.

Loos continued to write throughout the rest of her life for a variety of mediums. Naturally, she wrote screenplays, such as *Susan and God* and the acclaimed *San Francisco* (which actually preceded *The Women*). She wrote two autobiographies, *A Girl Like I* and *Kiss Hollywood Good-by*; three if you count the *Cast of Thousands*; and four if you count *The Talmadge Girls*. Although, according to Beauchamp, *Kiss Hollywood Good-by* is very fictionalized and should be read as a novel. Loos' play credits include *Happy Birthday*, which she wrote for her friend Helen Hayes. She also adapted Colette's *Gigi* for the stage. Not to mention, Loos wrote many essays, articles, play reviews, and more.

Her collection at the New York Public Library for the Performing Arts, the Anita Loos Papers, is a telling compilation of many works, most from later in her life. Loos' review of a play, *The Killing of Sister George* by Frank Marcus, revealed a side of Loos not often seen. The review is titled *Are Lesbians People?* To be clear, Loos had no problem with lesbianism, as in *A Girl Like I* she writes fondly of her friends Elsa Maxwell, gossip columnist and professional hostess, and her life partner Dorothy "Dickie" Gordon. What the review showed was Loos' romantic side, rather than her witty, sassy side where she felt so comfortable. The last few lines read "For so the human heart behaves through all its ups, downs, tears, laughter and harrowing surprises. Well, my friend, that is Life and it is Art as they both have got to be, either in or out of the show shops." As with so many humorists, comedians, satirists, Loos was a woman who felt deeply, but would never let anyone know the depression or torture she sometimes felt. Once Beauchamp got to know Loos' niece, Mary Anita, well she asked to clarify rumors that Loos was a lesbian. The answer was no, yet Mary Loos also felt, "Not that Anita might not have been a lot happier if she had been. I can just see that tiny figure, almost fetal in an overstuffed chair, crying over some man. She so longed to be loved" (Beauchamp and Loos 204).

While Loos only stood at 4'11", she was larger than life. In reviewing her body of work a true American humorist who measures up to Lucille Ball, Carol Burnett, and Tina Fey was discovered. Her writing has made a cultural impact from the silent era that will continue until the end of time; Lorelei Lee is an archetype that is here to stay. Loos changed the way the film industry perceived and used intertitles, elevating humor in the silent era from Fatty Arbuckle making people laugh because of his girth to demonstrating true wit. Beyond that, she was able to brilliantly tackle gender role-reversal, giving women power and paving the way for films like *Bridesmaids* and *Trainwreck*. Anita Loos pioneered the way for females in comedy and showed the boys' club how it was done.

Works Cited

Anita Loos Papers 1917–1981. N.d. Essays and addresses undated, Box 1, Folder 4. Billy Rose Theatre Division, New York Public Library.
Anita Loos Papers 1917–1981. N.d. Short Essays 1968–1970, Box 1, Folder 3. Billy Rose Theatre Division, New York Public Library.
Beauchamp, Cari. *Without Lying Down: Frances Marion and the Powerful Women of Early Hollywood*. Berkeley: University of California Press, 1997.
Beauchamp, Cari, and Mary Loos, eds. *Anita Loos Rediscovered: Film Treatments and Fiction*. Oakland: University of California Press, 2003.
Cella, Laurie J.C. "Narrative 'Confidence Games': Framing the Blonde Spectacle in Gentlemen Prefer Blondes (1925) and Nights at the Circus (1984)." *Frontiers: A Journal of Women's Studies* 24.3 (2004): 47–62.
Dolan, Noël Falco. "Loos Lips: How a Girl Like I Talks to Gentlemen." *Women's Studies* 37.2 (2008): 73–88.
Essays and Addresses undated, Box 1, Folder 4. Anita Loos papers 1917–1981. Billy Rose Theatre Division, The New York Public Library.
His Picture in the Papers (1916). Wrs: John Emerson and Anta Loos, Dir: John Emerson, USA 62 mins.
"Interview with Cari Beauchamp." Telephone interview. Nov. 2015.
Intolerance Love's Struggle Through the Ages: In a Prologue and Two Acts. Wrs: D.W. Griffith and Anita Loos, Dir: D.W. Griffith. Triangle Film Corporation, USA 197 mins.
Johnson, Julian. "The Soubrette of Satire." *Photoplay* 1 Feb. 1917: n. pg.
Loos, Anita. *"Gentlemen Prefer Blondes": The Illuminating Diary of a Professional Lady*. New York: Boni & Liveright, 1925.
Loos, Anita. *A Girl Like I*. New York: Viking, 1966.
The Love Expert (1920). Wrs: Anita Loos and John Emerson, Dir: David Kirkland. First National Exhibitors' Circuit Co., USA 60 mins.
The Mystery of the Leaping Fish (1916). Wrs: Anita Loos and Tod Browning, Dir: John Emerson. Triangle Film Corporation, USA 25 mins.
The New York Hat (1912). Wr: Anita Loos, Dir: D.W. Griffith. Biograph, USA 16 mins.
Red Headed Woman (1932). Wr: Anita Loos, Dir: Jack Conway. MGM, USA 69 mins.
The Women (1939). Wr: Anita Loos. Dir: George Cukor. MGM, USA 133 mins.
Whitman, Alden. "Anita Loos Dead at 93; Screenwriter, Novelist." *New York Times*. 19 Apr. 1982: n.p.

The Nature and Genius of Alice Guy Blaché

KHANISHA FOSTER

It appears that much of Alice Guy Blaché's genius may have been in the doing of things. In her career she wrote, acted in, produced, and directed more than 1,000 films. She was present at the inception of sound in moving pictures, was arguably the first head of production at a major film company and went on to run her own company. In her memoir when she was exploring why she received such attention from the press in America she found it was because, "It is true that I had passed as a phenomenon, as for seventeen years I had been the only woman film director in the entire world" (Blaché 71). There are questions to be raised as to if she was the only female director during that time, but it seems undoubted that she was the most successful. This paper will be an exploration about the span of her career and how the woman who she became, began.

In an interview with Pamela Green the director of the soon to be released documentary *Be Natural*, a film that takes the exploration of Alice Guy Blaché's life and career to new depths, Green shared, "Anytime you mention early cinema, she has to be mentioned. If you talk about Hollywood before Hollywood, she has to be mentioned. If you talk about an artist and an entrepreneur at the time, she has to be mentioned." When asked about Blaché's relationship to her work, Green points out, "When she's born, celluloid is registered. She grows up with photography and she meets the beginning of cinema face to face, you know, at 23. Her story goes hand and hand with film. It's like her destiny." It is clear in Blaché's memoir that she felt linked to film from its start: "I have no pretense to making a work of literature, but simply to amuse, to interest the reader by anecdotes and personal memories concerning their great friend the cinema, at whose birth I assisted" (Blaché 1).

It is a very exciting time to talk about Guy as she was known in France before she was married, Mrs. Blaché as she was known in America after her wedding to Herbert Blaché, and Ms. Guy Blaché as she remained until her death. While there is a great deal of research, for decades her story was relegated to a few paragraphs in film history books. An undeniable pioneer in her field, lost films, repetitions of incomplete histories, and the recording of film histories by the dominant cultural group at the time, white American men, skewing those historical recordings in their favor. A series of actions have begun to unfold to correct her place in history starting with Blaché recording her story herself in memoirs actively written from 1947 to 1952. This caused her to reach out to Louis

Gaumont, son of Léon Gaumont, in a search for her old films. In return he gave a speech on "Madam Alice Guy Blaché, the First Woman Filmmaker" in Paris where he said "she has been unjustly forgotten" in 1954 (Simon 130–131). A series of honors followed and then, after her death in 1968 and a lull of almost 8 years, her memoir was published in 1976 on the heels of an early documentary about her work.

This very slow snowball eventually led to the American translation of her memoirs by Anthony Slide, an uncovering of more of her films, a few major books about her life, *Alice Guy Blaché: Lost Visionary of the Cinema* by Alison McMahon and *Alice Guy Blaché: Cinema Pioneer* published by the Whitney Museum of American Art as partner to an exhibition on her work. An epic undertaking that prepared Green's team for their documentary, five years in the making, and which uncovered more information and films hidden for years. The interview with their team revealed a lot, but perhaps with the final unveiling of the film this paper will be quickly outdated. Green found the perfect words for the quest to unveil Blaché's place in cinematic history, "She's like a porcelain doll that's broken into pieces, all over the world, over a span of 100 years that we've had to collect together to try to get a face of who she was as a person and who she was as an artist." The following is an attempt to align some of those pieces and paint a clearer portrait of the artist.

A portrait of film pioneer and writer/director Alice Guy Blaché, circa 1910. Guy Blaché directed over 100 synchronized sound films before 1907 and shot close-ups well before D.W. Griffith (courtesy the Academy of Motion Picture Arts and Sciences' Margaret Herrick Library).

Blaché's parents, mother Marie Clotilde Francine Aubert and father Émile Guy, had an arranged marriage in Paris and days later moved, by ship, to Chile where he was a successful book seller and owned a chain of bookstores in Valparaiso and Santiago. This may lead one to wonder if Guy was a mixed race woman, though both her parents were of French descent. Yet when Marie was pregnant with Blaché, her fifth child she insisted on having this baby in France though all the previous siblings were born in Chile. The reason that she gave, and Blaché repeated in her memoir, was so that Marie wanted to have one child who was "born French." Alison McHahan heard that there may be another reason for having the baby abroad, "Roberta Blaché, Alice Guy's daughter-in-law, who knew Guy intimately at the end of her life, told me how Guy would recount with glee a kind of "family legend": Marie, Guy's mother, took the precaution of going to France to give birth to her fifth child because she had been having an affair with one of the Chilean vaqueros on the hacienda. If the child was not Émile Guy's this could have been obvious at birth, so it was prudent to give birth far away from prying eyes. When pressed to confirm this story, Alice Guy would simply shrug, with a twinkle in her eye" (McMahan, xxxvii).

There is no way to verify her parentage, but another unusual step followed. Émile was there for the birth but returned home to Chile shortly after. Blaché's mother followed as soon as she was able, but they did not bring their daughter home with them. Blaché lived instead with her grandmother and said of the ordeal, "This abandonment caused me no harm: my grandmother loved and spoiled me. She lived in Carouge, a Geneva suburb dear to artists" (Blaché 3). In fact, it seemed more of a shock three years later when her mother came to bring her home and Blaché had no idea who she was. These quick adjustments to new settings would become a trend in her childhood and her life.

Blaché lived a few more years in Chile before being whisked away to boarding school along with her three sisters at the Convent of the Sacred Heart, in Viry on the Swiss border. Shortly after, as she describes it, "a series of catastrophes put an end to our imprisonment [the Convent]. In Chile violent earthquakes, fire and theft ruined my parents" (Blaché 10). She was sent to a less expensive Convent in Ferney. Following her brother's death at 17 from a rheumatic heart and her father's death soon after, Blaché moved back to France with her mother. Her sisters moved on to their adult lives. Shortly after arriving her mother "…was named director of the Mutualite maternal, a society created by the textile unions to aid needy women workers entering on maternity" (Blaché 11). These quick life changes caused Blaché to see herself in different lights. When she was in Chile, "After two years of this happy life full of gaiety, of sunshine," she said of herself, "I had become a black little person, speaking only Spanish" (Blaché 8). As a teenager alone with her mother in France, "…my mother took me with her to aid in her work. My debut was difficult. I was to perfection the little white goose of the period. A bit of a snob, I felt the suburban people to be a different class of being. A few visits sufficed to waken my sympathy, my pity, often my admiration" (Blaché 11). As Alan Williams put it, "Guy could be a free-spirited, Spanish-speaking little girl in Chile one year and a submissive student in a gloomy Swiss convent the next—or, later in life, at the very top of her profession in Paris one year and then unemployed the next in Cleveland, married to a man of clearly lesser abilities than her own" (Simon 34). This ability to transfer the way she saw herself showed in her cinematic work as well.

There is a curiosity about how one becomes a female leader in a field dominated by men. Blaché did not set out to be a film director; the profession did not yet exist. It grew up around her. She began as a typist and stenographer. Her stenography teacher told her of an opening at Comptoir général de Photographie and wrote her a letter of recommendation. The man she came to see, the director M. Richard, was not in so she was referred to Léon Gaumont. She recounts their first meeting:

> Timidly, I offered him my letter of introduction. He read it, examined me in silence and finally said: "The recommendation is excellent, but this post is important. I fear, Mademoiselle, that you may be too young."
> As my hopes crumbled.
> "But sir," I pleaded "I'll get over that."
> He looked at me again, amused.
> "Alas, that's true," he said "you shall get over it. Well let's try" [Blaché 16].

She was hired. Well before the days of constant selfies there was a unique thrill to working in photography. "In those days photography reigned. All the aristocrats, all the scientific world, all the artists (writers, painters, sculptors), the diplomatic world and even the demi-monde made photographs" (Blaché 17). As a result of her new environment Blaché met top physicists, doctors, astronomers, and geographers, and her hunger for knowledge and comfort with new environments readied her to learn. "I knew nothing of this art. I had to familiarize myself with sizes of plates, the variety of papers, the chemical products, the different camera names, their qualities, focus-lengths, shutters, etc." She did so in preparation to work alongside the greatest minds of the day. "This meant that Guy, probably without realizing it, was in a front row seat to witness one of the greatest social transformations of recent memory: the drive to mechanization. Some of her earliest films were parodies the scientific films that she helped the scientists produce" (McMahan 18). Alice was well aware of the thrill and responsibility of creating work at such a high level. In the United States it may have been Edison driving the patents, but it was mostly artists utilizing the cameras. Blaché had a whole different entrance into film. The Gaumont Company and Blaché herself aided in the study of the respiration process of comparing humans and dogs, recorded the first x-ray experiments with reels, experiments with compressed air, studies of bees, oceanography. She said of the work, "Science was not absent from our activities" (Blaché 42).

Blaché's rise through the company happened quickly. Gaumont wanted to accompany a presidential voyage to Algeria, Blaché stepped up to take over duties while he was away and earned his respect, a raise, and an increase in responsibilities. Blaché was in the room when Georges Demeny demonstrated the *phonoscope* for the first time. In July of 1895 Gaumont took over the company and hired Alice as office manager. She asked if she "might write one or two little scenes and have a few friends perform in them" (Blaché 26–27). He agreed as long as she did such work on her off hours. Suddenly, in the midst of working long days, Blaché was making movies. Green described the early days of making movies at Gaumont this way, "I call them the first class of Silicon Valley 1905, 'cause their initial films are like Vines, Instagram, Youtube movies. It's very similar, and we're doing the same thing today when we use new technologies to experiment."

Sixty-three of the movies that Blaché made while working for Gaumont are collected on the DVD Gaumont Treasures. Disk 1 is dedicated entirely to Blaché. While just a drop in the bucket of the work she did when she was there, it is a fascinating exploration of how quickly her work and voice grew. The films start as actuality films, "films of notable events such as parades of the newly-invented automobiles or lifestyle scenes of people engaged leisurely activities" (McMahan 16). In Blaché's case she films boys swimming in a stream, dog tricks, moments captured abroad. The films taken in Spain are quite lovely. These moments of catching life in other countries become key when we look at the American silent films that evolved later. Often for those films, whether they were trying to portray China, France, of even Africa, there seemed always to be palm trees in the background and a beautiful beach. Blaché, however, was documenting other regions and using that knowledge in her fiction films. In terms of fiction, it should be addressed that many film historians infer that Blaché made the first fiction film. It is key to remember as technology evolved internationally at a very similar pace it is almost impossible to name the true winner of this race, but many historians have suggested that it was either Blaché or Mèliés. According to Blaché's timeline in her memoir, she beat Mèliés to the punch, but that isn't the end of it. "So, if we take Alice Guy's word for it, she made her first fiction film before Mèliés made his; but since L'Arroseur arrosés made and publicly screened before either of them made their films the debate over whether Guy or Mèliés was the first fiction film director is moot" (McMahan 13). She was one of the first though. Translated as *The Cabbage Fairy*, one of her earliest films, is considered one of the earliest works of fiction in film. All is not lost, "Alice Guy, though not the first person to make a fiction film, was among the first to make the transition from the cinema of attractions to narrative cinema, and that earlier than previously supposed" (McMahan 42).

Blaché's sense of humor developed very quickly. In *Madame's Cravings* (1906), we watch a pregnant woman steal a lollipop from a child, then some absinthe, a beggar's herring, and a pipe all to satisfy her needs. It's hilarious and also shows one of Blaché's early innovations, the close up reaction shot. Historians credit D.W. Griffith with the first close-up in 1908, but the shot he actually used, a long shot that gives a vignetted effect, Blaché had used several years earlier. "She appeared to abandon these approaches quickly in favor of simply moving the camera closer to the actors in order to get a closer shot" (McMahan 40–41). We also see her sense of humor in *The Drunken Mattress* (1906), where a drunken man passes out in a mattress-makers unfinished mattress and is therefore sown in. Many of Blaché's favorite storytelling choices are revealed in this film. She seemed to like physical as well as acrobatic comedy, chase scenes, and gender swapping. There is such adventure in this early work, one might think it is all impromptu, but Blaché is careful to clear that up:

> Many people who have never set foot in a studio before 1930 ... and perhaps even since then ... believe that we use to work without scenarios. Nothing could be more false. Except for the very earliest films of the twenty or twenty-five meters everything was prepared in advance: the story written with care, the cast, decor, the costumes prepared in detail and distributed at each shooting. Otherwise how could we have avoided going down in disorder" [Blaché 45].

One of her scenarios is printed in her memoir, but for many Blaché films it is difficult to decipher which she has written. Since she was looked on as a director, history has tracked her that way.

In 1897 Gaumont made Blaché head of film production, a position she held for 11 years. The work during that time grew in many ways, camera tricks which Blaché quickly mastered evolved at a rapid pace, but the industry was moving as quickly, "The other film producers who sprang up concurrently used our discoveries as soon as we made them" (Blaché 31). Her fast evolution would prove helpful later in her career when she went to America,

> the American studios being already ... better equipped than our own. However, their ignorance of certain procedures really astonished me. The first time I asked my cameraman to get a special effect (on that occasion, a man walking on water) he told me that this was impossible. I had to insist and to guide him, step by step, to obtain a result with filled him with adoration and earned me his respect [Blaché 69].

In fact, Guy's work at Gaumont was advancing so quickly that she had accomplished something that many film history books report to have happened more than 15 years later, sound.

The *Chronophone* was a staple technology at Gaumont Company as early as 1900–1901. Gaumont thought it was the future, trying to generate revenue from it for over 20 years, some more successful than others. Upon discovering the intense effect the chronophone had on Blaché's life in general and the industry specifically McMahan reflected that she found herself forced to "re-evaluate one of the "grand-narratives" of the early cinema: the idea that silent cinema came first, and synchronized sound cinema came belatedly after, and that sound has always been a modest handmaiden to the film image" (McMahan 43). Blaché's films from 1906 were filled with sound: a rooster crowed, famous Opera and French folk singers, dancers accompanied by music. Color also appeared onscreen for many of these films. McMahan reports, "…there is no question that she played a key role in early sound film production, as she directed over 100 synchronized sound films between 1902 and 1906" (McMahan xxxii). The effect of the *chronophone* on her life cannot be underestimated, either, as it led her to her husband, to America, and eventually to the end of her career.

When German clients found the *chronophone* complicated, they called Blaché to travel to Germany and explain the product. She didn't know the land or the language so Gaumont assigned Herbert Blaché (Herbert), their new sales representative, as her interpreter. According to Blaché they fell in love and were married by Christmas. Again she offers him no flowery language and her real romance seems to be with film and travel, but when Herbert is sent to live in Cleveland immediately after their marriage to market Gaumont products, Blaché gives up her impressive post at Gaumont to go with him. Herbert was to establish a *chronophone* franchise, a marketing partner to two American businessmen who had bought the rights. He made no income for the first nine months and they lived off of her money. She was also pregnant during the time, but in her memoirs she only mentions her children much later and very briefly. More important to her was the founding of her own production company, Solax Studios, in 1910.

Solax

The beginning of Solax, Blaché's film company in Chicago, seemed to be a happy endeavor. Herbert was still contracting with Gaumont in a large space Gaumont had set up there. Blaché had a reminiscent and active response to the studio, "The Gaumont studio was not being used every day. The temptation was too strong; I resolved to rent it and try making a few films" (Blaché 67). On September 7, 1910, Blaché founded Solax Studios. "Herbert Blaché was the "presiding spirit," George A. Magie was the business manager, and Alice Guy Blaché was in charge of film production" (McMahan 75).

A banner that read "Be Natural" hung in the studio, a basic truth of Blaché's style that had carried over from France. "Madame Blaché has very little patience for the film censors. She is French and believes in realism. She argues that the public should be the judge" ("Facts and Fancies" 293–294) As to the beginnings of Solax,

> When she married Herbert Blaché she came to America as the dutiful wife and counselor of Gaumont's representative in this country. She was quick to see the possibilities of an independent plant and with her own money, she organized The Solax Company; built the establishment on a plot of ground joining the Gaumont works at Flushing, L.I.; assumed the presidency, gathered about her the talent required and superintended and managed every detail ["Facts and Fancies" 293–294].

Blaché described each aspect with glowing pride,

> [a friend] gave our studio an installment unique at that time: an entirely removable ceiling, real keyboard for lights, spot-lights, etc. Our cameras, projectors, printing, perforation, were by Bell & Howell, whose reputation is well known. Finally, our film supplier was Kodak, which had arrived at an unequalled degree of perfection [Blaché 69].

During her time at Solax Blaché mostly focused on cowboy stories, military films, and melodramas. She owned and ran the studio from 1910 to 1914.

Some published texts describe Blaché as conservative, but her movies for the most part were not. She loved gender swapping, played with oral fixations, showed pregnancy onscreen 50 years before Lucille Ball could say the word pregnant on television. Blaché showed women as heroes, saving a man falling off a cliff, and used them in their own stunts. In *The Consequences of Feminism*, she has the whole society flip gender norms completely. The men are caring for the babies and homes and taking on feminine traits of the time, 1906, while the women are abandoning families and smoking cigars at the social club. In the end the men revolt against their treatment. It is hilarious and subversive. Pamela Green talks about the film, "Filmmakers go by personal experience and she used comedy to address certain aspects, maybe get away with it. *Consequences of Being a Feminist* [how she translated the title] is probably one of our favorites because she basically says what if, what if women were in charge?" Green also shared that Blache remade this film and imagined it taking place in 2000.

Blaché was also, as far as we know, the first film director to hire an all African American cast. *A Fool and His Money*, about a poor man who wants to get the girl, came out in 1912. According to Pamela Green, "It was supposed to be a mixed cast, and the Caucasian cast said no. So she said, fine. She did it all African American." Green believes the initial casting would have been, "a White man in love with Black Venus." We cannot be sure. The movie was filmed in Balché's home and utilizes her automobile. She also directed *A Man's Man* which had a Jewish central character shown in a positive light. With the anti–Semitic nature of the films surrounding its release she must have made an active choice to tell the story this way. Neither of these films are perfect. The text for advertisement is atrocious. For *A Fool and His Money* in particular, "The story is a satiric comedy dealing with the pretentions of colored folks. The way they ape and imitate their White brothers forms the basis of the story" (McMahan 149). To be fair, the synopsis does not show this careless language. This is a problem we still see in film marketing today, a fundamental misunderstanding of cultural groups and how to appropriately and honestly represent them. However, McMahan captures an important perspective, "At the same time, we can read some sense of identification between immigrant and disenfranchised blacks; at the very least, we can recognize a willingness to put Jewish characters (*A Man's a Man*) and blacks (*A Fool and His Money*) at the center of melodramas that incorporate stereotypical tropes but also undercut those tropes." We are still unclear of the cultural circumstances of her birth as well, but we do know that she had felt a part of communities of Color in her youth.

Even with her work speaking volumes about her point of view, whether it be through the lens of gender, immigrants, or simply as a brilliant artist, a male film critic in 1912 described Blaché this way, "This is a woman's era, and Madame Blaché is helping to prove it without any fuss at all. She only favors suffrage when satisfied that women are ready for it, and she is so modest about what she had done in the Gaunt and Solax companies that I had to depend upon others for any detail relating to her remarkable career in the production of moving pictures" (Harrison, 1007–1011). Are we to believe this demure telling of the woman who led over 1,000 films? This was her take on being a woman in the burgeoning industry:

> Perhaps I should not have been able to accomplish so much in any other country, particularly in France. I am a woman. Do you understand? Here [United States] in a general way, the fight and victory is to be strong, irrespective of sex. It is not so where I come from. In France we are women, just women, to be treated with all due deference by then of breeding and to be pampered and showered

with affection. Women are constantly in a state of dependence, and not likely to exercise their reason with freedom. Art in some forms is practically the only field open to them. There are exceptions, of course, but they are rare [Gates 28].

There is much debate among film historians about how much Herbert had to do with the end of Blaché's career. It is a legitimate question since she had been on a steady rise before she met him and then the challenges came. Anthony Slide explores this in his introduction to her memoir:

> It is perhaps not unfair to suggest that Herbert Blaché was in part responsible for the demise of his wife's directorial career. He promoted himself over and above his wife wherever possible, even having her work as his assistant. The writing was on the wall as early as 1913 when Blaché forced the closure of the Solax Company, so closely associated with Alice Guy Blaché, and in its place formed his own organization, Blaché Features [Blaché, vi].

As she described the end, "My husband, having finished his contract with Gaumont, had taken the presidency of Solax. I abandoned the reins to him with pleasure. I never attended any of the conferences where the Sales Co. composed the programs; I would have embarrassed the men, said Herbert, who wanted to smoke their cigars and to spit at their ease while discussing business" (Blaché 79). Herbert started his own company under the same roof, some say to mark his independence from both Gaumont and his wife's success. The details of the closing are murky. "The usual assumption is that Solax went bankrupt at that time. It was not actually the case. In 1914, the company merged with another concern; the physical plant was sold as a part of bankruptcy proceedings in 1920" (McMahan 43). In the end, Herbert's new venture, Blaché Features, absorbed Solax.

Did Herbert ruin her career? Blaché seems to find there were contributing factors that did not appear to help, for instance his ties to the *chronophone* and it ultimately not being the future of film. Solax's early success made his short comings on his ability to represent Gaumont in the U.S. more visible. Perhaps he gambled. Blaché refers to him losing badly in the stock market and after their marriage many of her American films dealt with gambling husbands. Blaché mentions how he mishandled deals for her film releases which she had to fix. Still, with all of this Blaché never blamed her career endings on Herbert.

About his leaving her she simply wrote, "My husband, in middle-age crisis, had gone to California with his principal actress" (Blaché 95). This is how she first introduced possible trouble in their marriage as she wrote her memoir, but then she went right back to discussing her work. When she ventured out on her own with her children, to try and make films independently she caught a strain of influenza so strong that several members of her crew died. For her recovery she and the children returned to live in the same state with Herbert, "My husband, passing through New York, came to see me. I believe my sad look moved him. He asked me to rejoin him as soon as I could. Six weeks later my children and I took the road for California" (Blaché 97). Even though she seems to have completed the memoir the year before his death, it was not published until much later, and she never concludes their story, or gives very many details.

What remains the most clear about Blaché after all of this research, is that she was driven by the work. Her mind was both creative and technically driven. She was as much scientist as she was artist. As to why she succeeded, several factors come to mind. She was at the right place at the right time. She was adaptable to different environments. She was a work horse. She was daring with new inventions and techniques, but mostly she did not seem afraid to fail. She seemed afraid to stay the same. She said of herself in the industry, "There is nothing connected with the staging of a motion picture that a woman cannot do as easily as a man, and there is no reason why she cannot completely master every technicality of the art" (Blaché 195).

WORKS CITED

"Facts and Fancies About a Woman You Know or Ought to Know." *Motography*, Vol. VIII, No. 8, October 12, 1912, 293–294.

Gates, Henry H. "Alice Blaché: A Dominant Figure in Pictures." *The New York Dramatic Mirror*, Vol. LXVIII No. 1768, November 6, 1912, p. 28.

Green, Pamela. Personal Interview. 16 November 2015.

Guy Blaché, Alice. *The Memoirs of Alice Guy Blaché*. Trans. Roberta and Simone Blaché. Edited with an introduction by Anthony Slide. Lanham, MD: Scarecrow Press, 1996.

Guy Blaché, Alice. Woman's Place in Photoplay Production. *The Moving Picture World*, Vol. XXI, No. 2, July 11, 1914, p. 195.

Harrison, Louis Reeves. "Studio Saunterings." *The Moving Picture World*, Vol. XII, No. 11, June 15, 1912, 1007–1011.

McBane, Barbara. "Imagining Sound in the Solax Films of Alice Guy Blaché: Canned Harmony (1912) and Burstop Holmes' Murder Case (1913)." *Film History: An International Journal* 18.2 (2006): 185–195. MLA International Bibliography. Web. 10 Dec. 2015.

McMahan, Alison. *Alice Guy Blaché: Lost Visionary of the Cinema*. New York: Continuum International Publishing Group, 2002.

Simon, Joan, ed. *Alice Guy Blaché: Film Pioneer*. New York: Whitney Museum of Art, 2010.

"You'd better learn to hold your liquor"
Bess Meredyth and a Career in Early Hollywood

SYDNEY HAVEN

Bess Meredyth was arguably one of the most successful screenwriters (male or female) of the silent era, and yet very few details of her life and work have ever made it into print. Even her son, John Meredyth Lucas (who later became a screenwriter himself), was unable to offer much information when writing his own memoir: "It, unfortunately, never seemed important that I learn Mother's early history. She never wrote it, only mentioned a few disconnected anecdotes. I never asked. By the time the questions were formed, the answers had died" (Lucas 19). He was, however, able to paint an entertaining portrait of a brilliant woman with an outrageous sense of humor who spent time both at work and away fending off advances from Hollywood heartthrobs and teaching her pet Mynah bird how to swear (36, 61).

Bess Meredyth was born Helen Elizabeth MacGlashan in Buffalo, New York (Beauchamp 42). When she was a teenager, her father arranged for her to be sent to Detroit to live with three of her aunts so that she could receive proper music instruction. Aunt Agnes Woodward taught whistling, and she organized a touring group called The Agnes Woodward Whistling Chorus, which later performed at an Embassy Club luncheon after Meredyth had established herself in Hollywood, much to Meredyth's mortification (Lucas 18). She learned piano from these eccentric aunts, and returned home to where her father managed a local theater (Sturtevant).

At her father's theater, she obtained her first stage work: "She did Pianologues, playing while singing or reciting, an acceptable act in the innocent vaudeville of those days" (Lucas 19). Meredyth's work in the theater allowed her to move to New York City, where, after some stage work and vaudeville touring, she found herself involved in the brand-new, not yet respected medium of motion pictures (Lucas 19). She acted in early silent films in New York, then was diagnosed with "a possible case of tuberculosis" and moved to the warm, dry climate of southern California (19).

In 1911, Meredyth began working as an extra at the Biograph Company, and eventually wound up as a stock player for D.W. Griffith. In addition to acting at Biograph, she also began to write and direct one- and two-reeler films. It had occurred to Meredyth that she could make more money if she both wrote and acted, so she began doing so for several different studios (Beauchamp 42). Here, the timeline becomes a bit convoluted, as no source can agree on the exact dates in which events occurred. John Meredyth Lucas stresses the importance of a 1914 film entitled *The Desert's Sting*, in which Meredyth starred alongside future screenwriter Jeanie Macpherson and a successful actor named Wilfred Lucas, whom Meredyth later married in 1917, and who became John Meredyth Lucas's father (Lucas 21).

Victoria Sturtevant, in an article for the Women Film Pioneers Project, says that the couple left Biograph in 1914 to run their own unit at Universal. In 1918, Meredyth wrote the script for *Tarzan's Romance*, starring Elmo Lincoln and co-directed by Meredyth and Wilfred. Lucas recounts a scene in which the star, Lincoln, refused to run barefoot across a patch of rocky ground, so Meredyth removed her own shoes and assured Lincoln that it would not be a problem. She said, "Watch!" and took off running across the rocks. "Just don't press down hard," she said. Then she urged Wilfred to roll the cameras, and the scene was shot before Lincoln was able to notice Meredyth's bleeding feet (Lucas 21).

Writer Bess Meredyth, circa 1920. Truly committed to her craft, Meredyth once smuggled a film out of Rome by hiding the film cans in her hatbox after the Italian government ordered the film be confiscated (courtesy Cari Beauchamp).

Sturtevant refers in her essay to the period from 1914 to 1920 as "Meredyth's most prolific, a period during which she wrote, acted, and directed motion pictures with her husband." Their son John was born in 1919. In 1920, Meredyth and Wilfred moved to Australia with their son to make films. In Australia, Meredyth was able to become more involved in the production of her films, including cutting and titling (Sturtevant). Meredyth and Wilfred stayed in Australia for only a year, and when they returned to Hollywood, Meredyth "literally hung out a shingle and hers was the only individual name listed in the Los Angeles phone book under Scenario Writers" (Beauchamp 155).

When she returned to Hollywood, Meredyth retired from acting to focus on writing full time. She formed many vital, lasting friendships, including a very close friendship with Frances Marion, with whom she shared "a strong sense of humor and fierce ambition" (Beauchamp 43). She was also incredibly loyal to studio executive Irving Thalberg, whom she said was the reason she survived the transition from silent films to sound (306). In 1924, MGM sent Meredyth to Italy to "rescue" the production of *Ben-Hur*, which was running behind schedule and over budget. She replaced fellow screenwriting pioneer June Mathis and was given the "coveted job" of rewriting the script (195). Though she is only given credit for "continuity," she essentially supervised the entire production, according to Sturtevant.

While on the set of *Ben-Hur*, Meredyth christened the enormous, extravagant set "The Hur House," and the Italian crew "were greatly puzzled by the amusement this aroused among the American crew" (Lucas 30). Meredyth orchestrated an elaborate scene that involved gigantic war ships locked in a naval battle. The ships made a planned collision with each other during shooting, necessary for the scene, and some of the extras, who were real Italian soldiers, fell into the water. Unfortunately, no one was sure whether anyone had drowned, so the police ordered a head count. The government ordered the film to be confiscated. Meredyth hid the film cans in her hatbox and smuggled them aboard the Rome-Paris express, getting the scenes out of the hands of the police. The film survived, none of the extras had drowned, and Meredyth proved once again what she was willing to do for her career (30–31).

When filming was complete and Meredyth returned from Italy, she and Wilfred divorced (Beauchamp 195). She spent the next few years adding film after film to her résumé and nurturing the friendships that would carry her into her old age. In 1929, while writing *Noah's Ark* at Warner Brothers, Meredyth met and married the film's director, a Hungarian who changed his name from Mahala Kurtez to Michael Curtiz (306). Curtiz would be the third and last man whom Meredyth married; the first was done on a dare in high school, when she married a member of the football team after one of the games. Since that marriage did not have the approval of either of their parents, it was quickly annulled, and rarely spoken of again (Lucas 19).

For the next few years, Meredyth continued to cultivate an enormously successful screenwriting career. Meredyth was one of the thirty-six artists—including fellow screenwriter Jeanie Macpherson—who founded the Academy of Motion Picture Arts and Sciences in 1928 (Sturtevant). Her name can be found in more than a dozen Academy bulletins as a member of the Awards of Merit committee, which was one of the first committees established. In all of the bulletins that list Meredyth as a committee member, she is often the only woman in the group ("Bulletin"). The first Academy Awards were held in 1929, and Meredyth was nominated for two screenplays: *Wonder of Women* and *A Woman of Affairs*, which was adapted in 1928 from the novel *The Green Hat* and starred Greta Garbo (Sturtevant).

Most unfortunately, in 1936, Irving Thalberg died, and with him died the careers of many wonderful artists, including that of Meredyth, who had always been loyal to Thalberg, referring to herself as "a Thalberg man" (Beauchamp 248). When he died, and the regime changed at MGM, Meredyth's contract was dropped and she was given two options: leave the studio, or come in with a new contract as a "junior writer" (340). However, in the early 1930s, Meredyth had begun suffering from what her son speculated were "anxiety attacks" (Lucas 62). These continuing attacks, combined with the stress of Thalberg's death and losing her contract, led Meredyth to announce her retirement in 1938. She spent most of the rest of her life voluntarily bedridden (Lucas 222).

Though her last writing credit was in 1941 with *That Night in Rio*, Meredyth continued to assist her son in his work by acting as his story editor, reading and editing his scripts (Beauchamp 375). She served as an unofficial and uncredited contributor on Michael Curtiz's 1942 film *Casablanca*. Julius Epstein, one of *Casablanca*'s screenwriters, remembers, "When we had a story conference and Mike came in the next day and made criticisms or suggestions, we knew they were Bess Meredyth's ideas, not his, so it was easy to trip him up. We'd make a change and say, 'What do you think, Mike?' and he'd have to go back and ask Bess" (Beauchamp 357). This indicates that Curtiz was secretive about Meredyth's input and attempted to take all the credit himself, but Lucas adds that when Curtiz would express displeasure, and the writers would ask him to elaborate, he would say, "I don't remember what the hell Bess tell me [*sic*]" (Lucas 142). From Lucas's perspective, Curtiz seemed to respect Meredyth very much—if one is willing to overlook, as Meredyth was, the numerous affairs that Curtiz had during their marriage.

When Curtiz traveled to Italy in 1960 to make the film *Francis of Assisi*, he informed Meredyth's nurse that he would not be coming back. He then informed Meredyth of the news in a letter; he did not want to divorce her, but he was not coming home (Lucas 222). Still, Meredyth kept a room for him in her home, where he would come and stay from time to time until his death in 1962 (Beauchamp 375). After living much of her late life surrounded by in-home nurses and maids, Meredyth spent her last years at the Motion Picture Country House and Hospital. There, one day in mid–July 1969, Lucas received the call telling him that his mother was dying. Meredyth was aware that something was wrong, so she asked the date. When her son told her it was July 13, Meredyth worried that she was going to die on the thirteenth (Lucas 247). Today most sources, including Beauchamp, say that Meredyth died on July 13, 1969; however, her son says she died on July 14, 1969, at two o'clock in the morning (Lucas 247). Despite her multiple marriages, and the fact that she was legally Mrs. Michael Curtiz upon her death, Lucas chose to bury her under the name Bess Meredyth, "the name she had made for herself" (248).

Meredyth's story is unfortunately one that is commonly found among female writers of the era; an insanely talented, fiercely intelligent woman who thrived for a time in a male-dominated industry, who helped shape the industry into what it is today before being pushed aside. Some of the women fought to keep their careers; some of them, like Frances Marion, turned to other artistic pleasures, such as music and painting. Meredyth, tragically, crawled into bed and succumbed to her anxiety and depression.

The most admirable thing, however, is that she kept her sense of humor. Lucas recounts stories of the pranks Meredyth pulled on her nurses. On one occasion, Meredyth went to the bathroom, and a short time later, the nurse went in to check on her. She found Meredyth lying on the floor with a bottle of sleeping pills scattered around her. The nurse panicked and was frantically calling the doctor when Meredyth said, "Got you!" (Lucas 245). Another nurse wore a hearing aid, and Meredyth very slowly turned the volume down on the television, bit by bit, until the nurse turned up her hearing aid as far as it would go. Then Meredyth would blast the television at full volume. The nurse thought something was wrong with the batteries in her hearing aid for a long time before she finally figured it out (245). Meredyth also sent her son a telegram on the first day of shooting of a film he had written:

> Have you a small part for me? I was a star of the silent films. I also did some writing before the pictures talked and the trains ran on schedule. If interested please contact me and perhaps you also have something for my husband who directed pictures in Hungary [Lucas 163].

She signed the telegram, "Mrs. Genius Martyr."

Another one of her major (and potentially most challenging) endeavors was being a working mother in Hollywood. As Lucas states in his book, "Her career came at a time when working in a male world required a lot of guts and full-time attention to the job" (Lucas 124). From studying Lucas's memories of Meredyth, she seems to have taken a more hands-off approach to raising her child, leaving him to the care of the household help. That is not saying that she did not feel love for her child. But she simply could not be both a successful working woman and a full-time, hands-on mother. Lucas recalls Meredyth saying to him that when she found out she was pregnant, "it was too late. Otherwise you'd have joined your little brothers and sisters down the toilet" (123). It seems callous to say such a thing to a child, but Meredyth always treated her son like an adult. After one of her and Curtiz's famous parties, during which her twelve-year-old son became incredibly drunk off of stealthily obtained glasses of punch and had inappropriate relations with a middle-aged Hollywood housewife in the Curtiz's garden, Meredyth told her son, "If you're going to drink, old man, you'd better learn to hold your liquor" (15).

Meredyth was known during her career for her "ability to handle sticky situations in a way that helped the studio run smoothly" (Sturtevant). A prime example of this was MGM sending her to Rome to clean up the production of *Ben-Hur*. As Sturtevant wrote, "Meredyth was very much at home with the masculine ethos of action filmmaking." Meredyth had a wonderful sense of humor, and today she would probably be described as "one of the guys." Gene Fowler, with whom Meredyth wrote *The Mighty Barnum* in 1934, wrote a dedication to her in *Timberline*, one of his first best-selling books: "For Bess Meredyth—my pal. A man's man. With deep appreciation for one of the finest associations I have had in this or any other professions (including my pimp days at Bryn Mawr)" (Lucas 106).

Meredyth also possessed an admirable ability to fend off advances from multiple Hollywood heartthrobs with "a wry retort," which would have been incredibly helpful considering she worked closely with many male actors in a predominately male genre (Sturtevant). During her work on *Ben-Hur*, Meredyth was propositioned by the star Ramon Novarro, whom Lucas describes as "second only to [Rudolph] Valentino as a heartthrob during the '20s" (Lucas 29). Meredyth and Novarro were riding in a horse-drawn carriage when Novarro made his advances. Meredyth rebuked him, and he admitted that he had confessed to a priest that he had sinned with her. Meredyth asked him how he could have committed such a sin without her knowledge, and Novarro said that as a Catholic, the desire was as bad as the actual act. He then ran off into the rain, leaving Meredyth to ponder his actions (Lucas 29).

On another occasion, while working on *The Sea Beast* with John Barrymore, who had been nicknamed "the world's greatest lover," Barrymore took Meredyth on a boat ride around the island where they were shooting the film (Lucas 35, 36). While they were in the boat, Barrymore suddenly shut off the motor and kissed Meredyth. Meredyth drew away, questioning his actions, the reasons of which, he told her, should be obvious. She said to him, "Look, Jack. I know you're the Great Lover. The whole world knows you're the Great Lover. You don't have to prove it—certainly not to me." Barrymore pondered this, and then laughed and said, "Damn right. We're friends, which is a hell of a lot better. Bess, I love you." After he kissed her forehead and was content, Meredyth responded, "You don't have to be *that* relieved" (Lucas 36).

The purpose of these anecdotes is to explain Meredyth as a feminist role model. Meredyth understood, in the era in which she lived and worked, that to be seen as an equal among the men, a woman must behave like a man. She earned the respect of countless male actors, directors, and fellow writers during her career by using her wit and her outrageous sense of humor, and her relationships with these men are what led her to the roles that allowed her to prove her worth. However, in the course of behaving like a man, Meredyth did not lose her femininity. Some may argue that her more masculine behavior is anti-feminist, and that in the fashion of true equality, she should be respected for being and acting like a woman. However, in the era of Hollywood in which she worked, which was and continues to be prominently masculine, added to the fact that she worked in a very male profession, Meredyth played to her strengths. For a while, until Thalberg died, it paid off. She was fearless and confident, a true leader in the industry.

However, Meredyth was equally adept at writing women's films. She adapted the novel *The Green Hat* into the film *A Woman of Affairs*, which was not an easy task. The novel was filled with subjects classified as indecent including "venereal disease, alcoholism, infidelity, unwed pregnancy, and suicide" (Sturtevant). Meredyth was given the task of writing a cohesive, appealing story while working around the Production Code stipulations. If her Academy Award nomination for best adapted screenplay is any indication, she succeeded. *A Woman of Affairs* contains a coherent plot with clever metaphors that carry throughout the entire film. The characters are as fully developed as characters could be in the 1920s. Even Greta Garbo's character, Diana, who is viewed in a negative light by most of the other characters throughout a majority of the film, has the proper motivations for her actions which help garner the audience's sympathy and cause viewers to root for her. The film ends with Diana sacrificing her own happiness for her one true love, John Gilbert's Neville Holderness, by crashing her car into the tree under which he first declared his love for her. Her death allows him to marry the "good" woman, Constance.

One of Meredyth's most well received films was *Don Juan* (1926), the story of the infamous Great Lover, played by John Barrymore, Hollywood's Great Lover. In fact, it was widely known that during filming, Barrymore was having a passionate and dramatic relationship with his leading lady, Mary Astor (Lucas 35). This film is much different in tone than *A Woman of Affairs*, and it is obvious that the story was written more for a male audience, while using the handsome Barrymore to appeal to the female demographic. It seems surprising that so much was allowed to pass by the Production Code; some of the costumes were quite revealing and risqué, and there was an awful lot of passionate kissing. Meredyth's vaudeville background seems to have come into play with this script. It was funny and satirical, mocking both the ruling class of Rome, the Borgia, as well as very firmly declaring that Don Juan's amorous endeavors were not as glamorous as often portrayed. Indeed, at the end of the film, Don Juan heroically rescues his true love from her lecherous admirer and they ride off into the sunset together, the maiden having successfully tamed the Great Lover.

Possibly, Meredyth's most well known film was *Ben-Hur*, though she did not write the original adaptation. She is credited with getting the production back on track and on budget, and she's listed under "continuity" in the film's credits. *Ben-Hur* was not as tightly written as *A Woman of Affairs* or *Don Juan*. Some of the plot points are attributed to miracles performed by Jesus, which comes across as a bit of a letdown. Meredyth choreographed the famous naval battle sequence—the one that caused all of the trouble with the Italian authorities—and was spectacular to watch. There was so much action and drama, and it was much more violent than expected. The Production Code seemed to have been more concerned with avoiding the representation of sexuality than that of violence. As was the custom, the hero of the film, Ben-Hur, emerges victorious from a climactic chariot race with his enemy, Messala, and is reunited with his family, who Jesus miraculously cures of leprosy.

In 1926, Meredyth wrote a film adaptation of Herman Melville's *Moby Dick* entitled *The Sea Beast*. In a review of the script, Marsha McCreadie marvels that Meredyth kept her scenario so similar in tone to the original novel. She points at a specific section as an example, taking an excerpt directly from the script: "Showing the surging, restless water—nothing else. This is the first and last scene in the picture and is symbolical [sic] of the fact that while great loves and tragedies occur—lives are lost—hearts are broken—the sea remains unchanged, leaving no record of what has gone before." This is a beautiful example of the level of talent that Meredyth brought to Hollywood. McCreadie also mentions Meredyth's characterization of Captain Ahab. Meredyth turned Ahab into a more appealing figure to audiences, giving him motivations for his actions. He is rebuked by the woman he loves because of his peg leg, and his broken heart justifies his repulsive behavior later in the film. The film is also an unusual role for John Barrymore, who plays Ahab; it is not his typical romantic role. With this script Meredyth gave him the chance to test his talents as an actor. The film also depicts a happy ending, in which Ahab returns safely from his voyage, which differs from the tragic ending of the original novel.

These few examples pulled from Meredyth's impressive body of work accurately encapsulate her ability to write for many a genre. They also show how successful she was with adaptations; she was a master of staying true to the tone of the original source material, while creating a unique story entirely her own. Meredyth may not have written down her memoirs, and many of her accomplishments and personal stories may be lost forever. But her impact on history remains firm. She was and continues to be a source of inspiration for women who aspire to a career in Hollywood. Bess Meredyth was fierce, intelligent, hilarious, and fearless, and she never allowed her weaknesses to define her.

Works Cited

"Academy Story." Oscars.org. n.d. Web. 6 Dec. 2015.
Beauchamp, Cari. *Without Lying Down: Frances Marion and the Powerful Women of Early Hollywood.* Berkeley: University of California Press, 1998.
"Bulletin #7." AMPAS Reference Collection. Academy of Motion Picture Arts and Sciences. 1 Feb. 1928. PDF file.
Don Juan (1926). Wr: Bess Meredyth, Dir. Alan Crosland, Warner Bros., USA 110 mins.
Lucas, John Meredyth. *Eighty Odd Years in Hollywood: Memoir of a Career in Film and Television.* Jefferson, NC: McFarland, 2002.
McCreadie, Marsha. "Pioneers." Films in Review 46. ½ (1995): 22. Academic Search Complete. Web. 13 Nov. 2015.
The Sea Beast (1926). Wr: Bess Meredyth, Dir: Millard Webb. Warner Bros., USA 76 mins.
Sturtevant, Victoria. "Bess Meredyth." In Jane Gaines, Radha Vastal, and Monica Dall'Asta, eds. Women Film Pioneers Project. Center for Digital Research and Scholarship. New York: Columbia University Libraries, 2013. Web. September 27, 2013.
A Woman of Affairs. Dir. Clarence Brown. Perf. Greta Garbo, John Gilbert, Douglas Fairbanks, Jr., Lewis Stone. MGM, 1928. Film.

The Best Revenge Is Outliving Them All
The Life and Heartbreak of Frederica Sagor Maas

MIKAYLA DANIELS

Frederica Sagor Maas was a screenwriter whose career spanned decades and was full of imagination, hard work and disillusionment. Taking a decade to write her memoir, which she finally published at the ripe age of 99, Maas expressed her feelings for the Hollywood industry and how her husband Ernest and she saw their ideas stolen and turned to trash before eventually being accused of communism and being blacklisted. This is a woman who did not rise to high fame in the industry but whose story should be told for it is one that many others faced.

Frederica was born in 1900, the youngest of four daughters in a Russian Jewish immigrant family. Her introduction to cinema started early when her father took her into the city for excursions. On these trips her Papa, as she loving refers to him in her memoir, would give her money to get a candy from a machine with the promise not to tell her mother. He also was the one who took her to see her first film, "Another secret we shared was my first visit to a nickelodeon ... we had to stand in the back because the place was packed. Papa posed me on his shoulders so I could see" (Maas 4).

Her first picture was *Sampson and Delilah*. She recalls how she didn't understand the final images of Sampson tearing down the temple at the time but that it later became more significant to her. Though she had no dreams of becoming a film writer at that time, the love for the medium was set in motion early enough that when she needed a life change she came back to it.

Growing up in New York she attended an all-girls school that she felt "spoiled me for high school and even college" (Maas 10). She was inspired by her literature teacher, Miss Brooks, who recited Longfellow's "Evangeline," "dramatizing those beautiful lines and making the poem real for us" (Maas 10). In an era where women were more often expected to want to be wives than independent individuals, positive female influences gave her hope and strength. Perhaps because of these encounters with inspirational, strong women, Maas was better able to weather what would come into her life during her career in Hollywood. The strong family life that she grew up with included friends and neighbors whom she spends a good amount of time fondly speaking of in her memoir. The way she writes of her experiences she gives away the internal strength she achieved as a woman who knew herself: "I remember when I was 17 or 18, marching in a New York parade, right before women got the vote. I marched in the schoolteacher segment, because my sister was a schoolteacher. I remember we held hands, and I remember how I felt. My God, I thought I was revolutionizing the world." (Salon).

While she had originally wanted to be a doctor, her family felt that she was too beautiful to spend the cost of a six-year college degree when she could easily marry well. Not the type of woman to simply give up and wait for marriage Maas had to come up with another reason to go to college at all. As was typical of a large family living in 1920s New York money was tight. She used that fact to convince them to send her to a journalism program. Working at a newspaper would bring in a much-needed income, so at the age of 17, Maas entered Columbia College in New York.

When Frederica arrived at college it was not what she had envisioned. She felt that her instructors were "average" much like her high school instructors had been. Maas also wrote that part of her bad experience may have been due to the fact that she was an off campus student. Instead of participating in the college campus life that gives one a sense of belonging and socialization, she worked and went to classes. Maas says she did not enjoy college at all and at one point came close to having a first-class nervous breakdown and that she felt ill before every class (Maas, 13). Her mother noticed the stress her youngest daughter seemed to be having and in a moment of release Maas told her how much she hated it there but didn't want to disappoint them since they had been paying her tuition. Her mother calmed her fears and told her not to worry about and that "Your Papa and I would not be sending you to college if we did not have the money" [Maas 14].

Still, Maas never finished her degree, but the writing bug hit her. After a summer working as a copy girl at a newspaper, she entered the film industry when she answered a want ad for an assistant to the story editor at the Universal Pictures branch in New York City. Her family at first was not pleased but "the fact my salary was a whopping 100 dollars a week may have influenced my sisters and father a bit" (Maas 16).

She had an office next door to her boss, and while her title was "secretary," she also functioned as a reader, taking scripts home to analyze. So inspired in her job Maas recalled endless nights pouring over manuscripts and scenarios. Feeling the fever to become a film writer herself, she sent away for the book *How to Become a Screenwriter*

An undated publicity photograph of writer Frederica Sagor Maas. A woman of many talents, Sagor Maas credits herself as the stylist to Hollywood newcomer Lucille LeSuer—whom the world would come to know as Joan Crawford (Academy of Motion Picture Arts and Sciences' Margaret Herrick Library).

I, published by the Palmer school of Hollywood. Famed film titles writer and author of *Gentlemen Prefer Blondes*, Anita Loos once wrote about the many of these types of scams created for unknowing young writers. After shelling out fifty dollars she learned that it was all a moneymaking scam. Her boss at the time, John Brownwell, told her that if she wanted to learn how to write for film her best way was to watch them.

History is full of great filmmakers who never received a formal education but learned by watching films. With Brownell accompanying her to films to explain things to her as they watched, she gained a better sense of how to write than any school at the time could have given her. Maas would view the same film at least five times so that she fully understood every part of it, from shots to story to the way the actors worked. She writes that her favorite films were by William de Mille. While his brother Cecil was more successful and well known, she felt that William was the true artist and his brother was a "showman pretender" (Maas 18). In 1923 she was promoted to Story Editor but only stayed for a year before leaving for Los Angeles.

According to her obituary in the *LA Times*, "When the bosses she later called "chauvinistic honchos" refused to help her become a screenwriter, she left for Hollywood. She was 23." She moved to Hollywood in 1924 and as was true for many young women, those who were considered good looking were pushed towards being seen on screen. Being the strong willed woman that she was, Maas decided she still wanted to be a writer. While in Hollywood Maas wrote the screenplay for the adaptation of *The Plastic Age* (1925) based on a novel that she had acquired while at Universal, only to have it rejected by Carl Laemmle for being too "dirty" (Vatsal 46). She eventually arranged its purchase by her friend B.P. Schulberg, who produced the film as well. It was fortuitous for Maas that the producers cast emerging star Clara Bow. The film was a huge success and even secured Maas a contract with MGM for 3 years for $350 a week. This should have been the huge breakout for Maas that shot her name into history, yet film history seems to have largely forgotten about her after her tragic life to come.

Her first script was a huge success and she was only 24 at the time it was made. How is it that a woman with a large box office hit and a new contract with a large studio would one day contemplate suicide? Well, Maas learned quickly the cruel hand of Hollywood, which sometimes still takes as fast as it gives. With her 1926 film *Dance Madness* she quickly saw that credit in the business was not so simple to receive, and every writer wants credit for what they create. This was the first and only time that it happened to be in her favor, much to her own surprise. The original script had been adapted by Alice D.G. Miller, also at MGM, and Maas herself merely made a few strategic changes. Needless to say Miller wasn't happy and Maas was learning how MGM worked.

One day she was told to write a scenario based off of nothing more than a title, *His Secretary* (Maas 73). Maas took that title and ran with it, from there, she came up with everything, plot, and characters. She wrote a twenty-page outline and passed it off to another writer, Carey Wilson who read it, made a few changes and handed it off to the boss. When it came back across her desk, Carey Wilson had been given the written by credit. Maas was furious: "There it was in black and white.... I could not believe it but there it was: adaptation and scenario by Carey Wilson" (Maas 74). At the time, whichever writer was the last person on the project, received the full credit. Maas experienced the frustration of many writers at the time: no one to support them. This issue would help motivate the creation of the Writers Guild of America (WGA), but came too late for Maas' career. She recalls those days as ones where the WGA was weak: "If you had a valid grievance the guild would mildly protest for you—write a polite letter" (Maas 69). She further explains that a writer had to be very careful about filing those grievances, which could mark you as a troublemaker to producers and studios alike.

Maas recounts "I wrote every one [of the early Norma Shearer pictures] and received credit for none.... The worst part was that there wasn't a blasted thing I could do about it" (Vatsal 24). The credit she would have received on the films would have furthered her career, but without the credit, it is as if she never produced quality work. This again is part of a larger issue for future film historians, trying to construct early screenwriter's proper credits. As a result of this her last film credited with MGM was the 1926 film *The Waning Sex*, though originally F. Hugh Herbert received that credit. Maas was devastated. She wrote the bulk of that screenplay and yet another writer was credited for it. She was not one to stand quiet, so she complained to the producer. While she did end up with shared credit on that film, subsequently she was fired from MGM.

Maas then wrote two films for Tiffany Pictures, founded by female film star Mae Murray and her husband, director Robert Z. Leonard. Maas says that the way it was run was small and everyone had one job. She seemed to enjoy the two films she made for them. Maas worked well with director Louis Gasnier on *That Model from Paris* (1925). "I held a high regard for his ability, his love of work" (Maas 113). The film definitely showcases her writing and has an artistic sense, perhaps due to the close relationship with the director. *That Model from Paris* feels more of a collaboration between artists, rather than a bunch of separate people working on a film, as at the big studios. Sadly, when Murray and Leonard divorced, Tiffany Pictures closed shop and Maas moved to Paramount for one year.

Her time at Paramount was short and Maas herself says that "I worked on four stories... *It* (1927), *Red Hair* (1928), *Hula* (1927), starring Clara Bow, and *Rolled Stockings* (1927), starring Louise Brooks" (Vatsal 147). When researching her credits at Paramount, the only credit she is given in The American Film Institute is *Rolled Stockings*. The U.S. Library of Congress list her credit for *The Plastic Age* while the Library and Archive for Canada lists her as having writing credit for *That Model from Paris* (1927). With so few records left it is frustrating to see how Maas may fade from history entirely. How many writers have to disappear from the history books before the world takes notice? Credits are the only way to prove what you have accomplished in film.

After leaving the studio system, Maas married fellow writer Ernest Maas. He had a few writing credits himself at the time of their marriage "Ernest Maas had nearly 20 credits, including *His Secretary* in 1925 and *The Waning Sex* the next year. Both films starred Norma Shearer, who was a good friend until Maas unsuccessfully warned her against marrying Thalberg" (*LA Times*). They worked on several projects together, most of them unrealized. Then they lost $10,000 in the 1929 stock market crash and were left in financial ruin. "They survived by writing movie reviews and turning out screenplays but all but one, *The Shocking Miss Pilgrim*, a 1947 release from which Mrs. Maas took as the title of her memoir, was rejected" (*N.Y. Times*).

With most of their writings between 1938 and 1950 never seeing the light of day, the couple went into a deep depression. In a 1999 Interview with *The San Francisco Tribune* she says that they were "hopeless, humiliated and having little money, the couple drove to a hilltop overlooking Hollywood with the intention of committing suicide in their Plymouth. Clutching each other, they started sobbing and realized that "none of these things mattered. We had each other" (*San Francisco Tribune*). Fed up with the industry,

Maas took a job at an insurance agency, but they continued to freelance when they could. After their one huge success, adapting the novel *Miss Pilgrim's Progress,* they gave up all together. Though they finally retained a written by credit and had a project produced and distributed, the couple described the film as "brutal disfigurement" of their original idea when it debuted in 1947 as a Betty Grable musical renamed *The Shocking Miss Pilgrim* (Vatsal 239).

Making waves doesn't tend to make a person popular and that seems to definitely have hurt her in her career. The communist scare and the Hollywood blacklist didn't help, "When the Communist witch hunt hit Hollywood, Maas and her husband, also a screenwriter, were suspected of harboring Bolshevik views and were forced to embrace other professions" (Shreve). The couple were interrogated by the FBI, and the investigation ceased once they left the Hollywood system. Her Hollywood story would end there if not for the release of the memoir she wrote in 1999, ironically titled after her biggest hit, *The Shocking Miss Pilgrim.* Much like the memoirs of fellow female screenwriters Adela Rogers St. Johns and Anita Loos, by the time of publishing, Maas had outlived her peers. Her book gave Maas a revenge of sorts as she wrote, "I can get my paycheck now. I'm alive and thriving and well, you S.O.B.'s are all below." When he reviewed the book, noted film historian Kevin Brownlow raved about her industry secrets and her "Trashing Hollywood legends ... but the results are captivating" (*Publishers Weekly*). Jayne Plymale wrote: "She quickly learned to forego integrity in the name of profits and was not above denigrating what serious reputation she might have cultivated by adapting vacuous star vehicles for the likes of Norma Shearer and Clara Bow. Her reward? The occasional credit, when the powers-that-be deigned to dole out accolades."

Even after her death her memoir was still being reviewed, but not always praised: "Sagor's various tales of mistreatment, misogyny, and discrimination have been taken as the absolute truth by the politically correct crowd," writes Andre Soares at the Alt Film Guide. "The way Hollywood men treated Sagor and/or other women—plagiarism, prostitution, power trips, etc.—is supposed to serve as proof of how intelligent, driven females suffered in the hands of ruthless, sex-crazed male animals in the American motion picture industry" (Hudson, *The Daily*).

During the book's original release, Maas gave a series of interviews. While most recalled the issues in old Hollywood, she also gave her thoughts about the films of the current era. Maas, as a strong female writer, was not impressed with the state of the industry at the time of her interview,

> There's no lack of material, there's just lack of incentive to make anything else but what they consider box office. And, hell, who can dispute them? Pictures are making money. And people are getting stupider and stupider. They'll pay seven and a half dollars to see a motion picture and it's all in the same vein: sex, sex, sex, sex, sex and violence, violence, violence, violence. You know what they've done? They've taken the vulgar, low part of old-fashioned vaudeville—all those terrible little acts—and they've put it on TV [Salon].

Even at 99, she was looking for story in films.

Also in 1999 she attended the fundraiser for The Booksmith, which sold books and organized author signings for the San Francisco Silent Film Festival. The organizer Tom Gladysz said

> The Booksmith also held an event at the store with Maas the night before, and sold 60 copies of her autobiography. Gladysz chose to interview Maas—whose vision is impaired but is otherwise spunky and upbeat—instead of doing a traditional reading. It was Maas's first and only bookstore event.

Maas told Gladysz that "Outliving everybody brings a triumphant feeling" [John High, *Publishers Weekly*].

Maas lived another 12 years after publishing her memoir. Even in her late '80s and '90s she was working to try to let people know about a history that wasn't being told. Maas first contacted the Women Film Pioneers Project at that time and worked to help give them more firsthand history of early women in film. She seemed to be a strong, intelligent and thoughtful woman from her childhood to her death. While history may have yet to give her the place in it she deserves, at least she still wanted to give history a hand.

Works Cited

"Forecasts: Nonfiction." *Publishers Weekly* 246.21 (1999): 56. *Academic Search Complete*. Web. 11 Dec. 2015.

"Frederica Sagor Maas, "Hollywood's 'Shocking Miss Pilgrim,'" *The Forward*. Web. 3 Dec. 2015.

High, John. "Lights, Camera, Bookselling Action." *Publishers Weekly* 246.33 (1999): 29. *Business Source Premier*. Web. 11 Dec. 2015.

Hudson, David. "Frederica Sagor Maas, 1900–2012 on Notebook." *MUBI*. 7 Jan. 2012. Web. 12 Nov. 2015.

Maas, Frederica Sagor. *The Shocking Miss Pilgrim: A Writer in Early Hollywood*. Lexington: University Press of Kentucky, 2010.

Plymale, Jayne, et al. "Book Reviews: Arts & Humanities." *Library Journal* 124.10 (1999): 116. *Academic Search Complete*. Web. 11 Dec. 2015.

Shreve, Jenn. "The Shocking Frederica Sagor Maas." *Saloncom RSS*. 1 Aug. 1999. Web. 4 Dec. 2015.

Vatsal, Radha. "Frederica Sagor Maas." In Jane Gaines, Radha Vatsal, and Monica Dall'Asta, eds. *Women Film Pioneers Project*. Center for Digital Research and Scholarship. New York: Columbia University Libraries, 2013. Web. September 27, 2013. https://wfpp.cdrs.columbia.edu/pioneer/ccp-frederica-sagor-maas/.

Silent Screenwriter, Producer and Director
Marion Fairfax

SARAH PHILLIPS

Marion Fairfax, while almost entirely unknown today, is an everywoman example of the plight of female screenwriters of the silent era. From the origins of her career through her mysterious disappearance from the Hollywood scene after the advent of talkies, there is little information available on her work as an actress, playwright and screenwriter and the information that is available is not consistently correct.

Marion Fairfax was born Marion Josephine Neiswanger on October 24, 1875, in Richmond, Virginia. On June 7, 1899, she married Tully Marshall at high noon in New York City (Neiswanger). Marshall began his career as an actor on the Broadway stage, having been in four Broadway plays at that point. Fairfax soon joined the acting profession with *The Triumph of Love* at the Criterion Theatre in 1904, and *Bedford's Hope* at both Haverly's 14th Street Theatre and the America Theatre in 1906. Marshall, now a popular comedic actor, was in six plays during this time, and quite quickly, Fairfax turned to writing a play that both she and her new husband could appear in together. This play, the first and only one produced by The Tully Marshall Company, was *The Builders*, which played at the Astor Theatre in 1907 for 16 performances.

Fairfax followed this run by writing *The Chaperon* [sic], which neither she nor Marshall starred in, and which played at Maxine Elliott's Theatre from December 1908 to February 1909, for a total of 62 performances. At the same time, in December 1908, she had a play running in New Haven, Connecticut at the Hyperion Theatre called *The Ways and The Means*, which was an adaptation of a book called *Mr. Crewe's Career* written by Winston Churchill in the same year. For her adaptation, she worked for Comstock & Gest Inc. out of New York, and the contract she signed offered $500 upon signing, 2.5 percent of the first $5000 gross weekly receipts, then 5 percent after the first $5000 gross weekly receipts (Comstock).

Her next play, which she both wrote and directed, would become her most successful stage production. *The Talker* starred her husband in the type of comedic role that had become his forte. Produced by Henry B. Harris, whose previous smash hits had mostly been by writer James Forbes, *Talker* opened at the Harris Theatre in January 1912, and ran 144 performances until May 1912. Personal letters abound in the Motion Picture

Academy library congratulating Fairfax on her writing, and Marshall on his performance. A review from *The New York Dramatic Mirror* on January 10, 1912, praised it as "a mighty human little play, with a real idea behind, and real people to work out the idea in human, logical shape," and then states, "If the public doesn't keep the play here a long time it will be because New York doesn't know good American drama" (Harris).

Later, there appear a couple of contracts in her personal records wherein she agrees to allow other companies to translate her plays, including *The Talker, Work*, and *Eager Heart*, in French and Italian, while another agreement only wanted *The Talker* translated into something for Denmark, Sweden, Norway, and Finland. Another agreement with leasing agent Sanger & Jordan allowed them to lease the production and publication of the play *The Eager Heart* exclusively. Interestingly enough, the beginnings of Fairfax's success begin to show through in this document from 1914 where she crossed out the part allotting "50% of all royalties and license fees" to the producers and wrote in "10%" (Sanger). The contract was agreed to, though not much is found on *The Eager Heart* after this besides a promise of production in Vancouver.

Following *The Talker* in 1912, there was a two-year break in produced stage content, which is a bit unusual following such a financial and critical hit. It can be assumed that Fairfax was writing plays, since not all of her plays written appeared on Broadway, but also one letter from Anne Banning in July of 1914 was particularly illuminating. In it she states, "I am so distressed to hear of your continued illness, and am sending these flowers just to express to you how much I miss you…" (Banning). Unfortunately, an undisclosed illness would trouble Fairfax for the rest of her career, and it can be assumed that this illness was also the cause for the brief absence of her work on the Broadway scene during this time.

In September of 1914, Fairfax wrote *A Modern Girl*, which was produced by The Shubert Organization at the Comedy Theatre, but only ran 17 performances. The following year, October of 1915, she had *Mrs. Boltay's Daughters* produced by Harrison Grey Fiske and George Mooser, also at the Comedy Theatre, and also running for only 17 performances (Marion, IBDB). Marshall, meanwhile, had found success as a director in early 1915 in a play called *The Trap*, which ran at the Punch and Judy Theatre for 100 performances until it closed in April 1915 (Tully, IBDB).

Writer Marion Fairfax, circa 1920. A famous playwright and a very successful screenwriter, Fairfax developed her own production company in 1921 (Academy of Motion Picture Arts and Sciences' Margaret Herrick Library).

With none of Marion's recent plays taking hold on the Great White Way, it must have been with relief that the announcement in *Motion Picture News* came in April 1915 that, "The Lasky Feature Play company has entered into a contract with Marion Fairfax, the New York dramatist, who will leave for the studios in Hollywood this week. The scenario department of the Lasky Feature Play company is completely in the charge of William C. de Mille..." (Marion, MPN) Shortly thereafter, Marshall and Fairfax began showing up in the captions of photos in various film industry publicity magazines, and listed as names in the litany of attendees at various Hollywood functions.

Fairfax's first scenario at Lasky was an adaptation of the James Forbes hit play *The Chorus Lady*, which had been first produced for the stage by Henry B. Harris in New York. Harris had also been the producer for her smash hit *The Talker*, so it can be assumed that her relationship with both must have smoothed the way for adaptation rights talks. From here, Fairfax wrote in several different genres, including comedy, drama, and westerns, for a couple different directors, all under the Lasky banner, until she co-wrote *The Blacklist* with William C. de Mille. Based on a 1915 Colorado mine strike, this film began a five-drama-film streak in 1916 where Fairfax wrote the scenario and de Mille directed. Following this, she adapted her stage script *The Chaperon* in 1916, for Essanay Film Manufacturing Company, best known for the early Charlie Chaplin comedies, with Arthur Berthelet directing. Then, back again she went to Lasky, and as she was under contract there, it can be assumed that Lasky didn't want *Chaperon*, but she was determined to have it made, so she sold it elsewhere.

Fairfax churned out an average of six scenarios per year from 1917 through 1919, gaining prominence each year for her work. In 1917, she was paid $669.34 for *Secret Game*, out of a total production budget of $19,108.50 (Paramount, *Secret Game*). In 2015, that would be the equivalent of $12,437.07 out of a total budget of around $350,000. To give some context, that would fall in the 2015 Writer's Guild Low Budget agreement, and would require a fee of $23,348. However, in Fairfax's day, films were shorter, and *Secret Game* was a five-reeler, which means it ran nearly 60 minutes. Also, in 1917, the union formation of the Screen Writers' Guild was still sixteen years away, so those fee standards had not yet been set.

Two years later, Fairfax was paid $1136.36 for *The Roaring Road* script, out of a budget of $28,833.21 (Paramount, *Roaring Road*). In 2015, that would amount to $15,622.52, out of a total budget of around $395,000. Still not the highest paid scenario writer, but she was averaging six films per year, and *The Roaring Road* was again a five-reel scenario. *The Roaring Road* is one of the few extant films available from Fairfax's history. Directed by James Cruze, and produced by Paramount Pictures (which may be why it has survived), it is a fun racing film that focuses on the passion a young man has for racing. The only thing that holds more weight for him is his passion for a young woman. Fairfax often wrote genres that went against the expectation of female writers, both then and now, including sport films such as *The Roaring Road*, westerns, science fiction. Between 1917 and 1918 Fairfax also wrote a series of films featuring Japanese actor Sessue Hayakawa in Eastern-themed stories that made him the hero, not the villain, as was the trend in the post–World War I years (Slater).

Around this time, Marion's contributions to the screenwriting profession were beginning to be recognized. In early 1919, she received a letter from the California State Library requesting author's versions of her past works and future manuscripts to file away (Suggett). But by the end of 1919, Marion's contract was up for renewal with Lasky, which would soon merge with Famous Players. Instead, Marshall Neilan, who had first worked with Fairfax in the film *Freckles* in 1917 for Lasky's production department, but with whom Fairfax had been friends from her early days on Broadway, formed Marshall Neilan Productions. He signed Fairfax for his next four productions, which were to be distributed by First National. Also, an agreement was reported that following those four productions, Marion Fairfax Productions was to be set up in "a working arrangement with Mr. Neilan.]" (Marshall, *Exhibitor's Herald*).

Fairfax indeed wrote four scripts in 1920 for Neilan, and one, *Dinty*, was often referred to in the following year's advertisements with the now familiar brought-to-you-by-the-same-team-that-brought-you-*Dinty* pitch. This is where it gets interesting, and quite insightful into, perhaps, the way that female-led production companies often fell apart after one production. The first thing to consider is the marketplace they were entering. Marion Fairfax Productions began in early 1921, just when the smaller film houses were beginning to merge together to gain strength. It was also when higher production values were expected. Production houses that began even as late as 1915 still had a little wiggle room for failure, as the cost of production was lower, and the expectation of audiences hadn't yet become as analytical. By 1921, production costs were ballooning, along with a national recession between 1920 and 1921. While the recession didn't seem to affect Fairfax directly in regards to work (she wrote four films each year), it could have affected the taste of an audience. If they could no longer afford to see multiple films per month, but only one or two, they would have to make choices.

Marion Fairfax Productions was organized in 1921. In April, there is a telegram from her first Hollywood employer, William C. de Mille, welcoming her to the fray, and stating "I am glad and afraid to welcome you as a competitor. At least I will learn from your work and I wish you every success in the world. You don't need good luck only opportunity." Also in April, she was interviewed for the *Exhibitor's Herald*, a trade paper for film exhibitors, where she stated:

> The formation of Marion Fairfax Productions is not the result of a sudden decision of an overnight idea. It is the realization of a plan that I have studied and worked out for over a year. I believe there is a place for the combination of literary effort and motion picture presentation, just as there is a place for the combination of literary achievement and stage presentation [Marion, April 1921].

By May, an article announced that she will direct her own pictures, and then qualified that decision by explaining that she "has staged a half dozen of her own plays on Broadway with marked success," and that "well-known men will assist" her. Among them Hugh McClung was mentioned as helping "further facilitate her physical direction of the scenes and preparation thereof" (Marion, May 1921). Another advertisement stated they were only looking for a first-rate, well-known cast. The first movie, *The Lying Truth*, was filmed sometime between early May and the end of July 1921, as a letter praising the first cut was dated July 26, 1921. While the film itself has been lost, the script is quite insightful into Marion's style and voice. The shooting script is set in "Southeastern Missouri in 1900" though other sources have stated that it is set in Ireland (Slater).

The story follows a young boy, Bill O'Hara, whose mother dies in childbirth. His father, a poor man, asks the owner of the local newspaper to adopt him so he won't be raised motherless. The family agrees, and he is raised next to the couple's son, Sam Powers. Bill grows up to be an upstanding man who is less loved by his adopted parents than his troubled brother, Sam. One day, Sam comes home from college, having been expelled for drinking, debt, and cocaine (an interesting note is the accepted use of cocaine as a regular vice in the '20s, versus modern days). Sam's father, who is on his deathbed, makes

Sam promise to never touch cocaine again. When he finds out he has used it again, the elder Powers leaves the newspaper to Bill, not Sam, as his birthright, and the whole town, which has no knowledge of Sam's vices, is immediately against Bill, thinking him a swindler.

Throughout the entire film, the tension builds, and we clearly understand the motives of all the characters, and have empathy for all. Both main characters have difficult struggles and clear wants: Bill wants to save the drowning newspaper, and Sam can't beat his addiction to cocaine. Fairfax's masterful weaving of the two stories has them intersect with both journeys ending at the same time—Bill has set up a fake murder at a local cove, complete with a broken boat and staged fight footprints, to attract national attention and sell more papers. Meanwhile, Sam's struggle has ended in suicide just around the corner from the cove, and all fingers point to Bill's jealousy. The climax comes when the entire town, resorting to mob justice, chases Bill to the newspaper and begins ransacking the place, trying to hang Bill. Only when Bill's adopted mother, who always protected Sam over Bill, brings Sam's suicide note to the sheriff, does the whole town realize they were about to hang an innocent man.

A commentary on small-town politics, and also the hotheaded ability to jump to conclusions about anyone, seems to be a running theme in Fairfax's scenarios. While a few sources have looked at her ability to make a socially unlikeable character likeable, one of the more striking things is how well she wrote her male characters, but how very often, her women were flat or clichéd. In *The Roaring Road*, she created a pretty but boring daughter there only to motivate the man to chase her, while in *Sherlock Holmes* (1922) his love interest does nothing to illicit interest from this extraordinary man except meet him and be pretty. Likewise, in *The Lost World*, an early dinosaur film, the daughter of the lost explorer does very little except to feel faint, and be fought over by two different men. One exception to this observation is *Through the Back Door* (1921), written for Mary Pickford, where Pickford's character had clear motivation. Incidentally, this is also the film that is often referred to when talking of clever inter-titles, as it contains the line, "If it were not for New York hotels, where would elopers, divorcees and red plush furniture go?." Fairfax left physical evidence of her organization as a director on the physical copy of the shooting script, now residing in the archives. There are light pencil markings which look like little x's through various scenes, perhaps made after they were shot. Other markings are arrows connecting scenes. On page ten, a pencil-scrawled "fade out" appears between the x's and arrows.

The Lying Truth didn't do very well, from what studying its history can tell. However, it may not be because it lacked merit. In an edited review document from an unnamed executive at First National Pictures, who had distributed many films Fairfax had written, *Lying Truth* is praised as "unusually strong" and "extraordinarily fine." Later in the document the same executive noted, "I should vote for this as a First National attraction" (L.M. Production document). Ads for *The Lying Truth* began appearing in trade magazines, stating that they were arranging for distribution. Shortly thereafter, in September, Fairfax was signed onto another Marshall Neilan–directed film, *Sherlock Holmes*, starring and produced by John Barrymore. For this effort, she was paid $4000 to complete the continuity in five weeks, which in 2015 would amount to around $53,000—a raise for someone who had risen to prominence through headlining her own production company.

In 1921, while her production team was trying to sort out distribution, with constant promises of such in the press, Fairfax was keeping busy. She spoke publicly more often, especially to the Press Club and women's groups (Breeze). She became more involved in the Los Angeles Tuberculosis Association (which may or may not indicate her recurring illnesses). She became more active in the Writer's Club, even inviting Charlie Chaplin to the December dinner-dance (Fairfax, to Chaplin). Scrawled below the invitation, she wrote, "He came although I was warned he 'never accepts invitations.'" Such commentary is littered throughout her personal papers, and gives incredible insight into her true feelings about the goings-on around her.

Then in February 1922, in *Exhibitor's Herald*, an article appears that states *The Lying Truth* will be part of the first offering of five films by a new distributor, American Film Company, though *Kendall's Cardigan* was the film mentioned in all the headlines, with *The Lying Truth* lost among the fine print (Kendall). John Jasper begins to appear in Fairfax notes as someone to blame as her films began to receive less attention. Jasper had left Charlie Chaplin studios in 1919 to start his own production company. He bought some land and built three production stages in Hollywood, named "Hollywood Studios, Inc." By 1920, Marshall Neilan and Marion Fairfax had set up shop at Jasper's studio, along with a few others. (Robinson Hope) In early 1921, in Variety, an article states that Jasper and Fairfax were working together, with Jasper as production manager, "and it is generally understood building the principal financial interest in the productions." Filming of *The Lying Truth* began, after which came the subsequent distribution delay, and another interesting venture, shown in a contract from March 1922, between Jasper, Fairfax, and Edward Tanaka. The new contract appears to set forth an agreement where Fairfax and Jasper would send scripts to Japan to be made by Tanaka, and those films would then be distributed by Jasper and Fairfax in the States. Written on the contract, in Marion's scrawl, is a sentence blaming Jasper, whom she calls Jack. "He ruined by over cranking" (Tanaka, et al.). She then reiterates this in her scrawl at the bottom of a personal letter from Tanaka. He wrote that set design was going well, but Fairfax scrawled "Jack Jasper, by privately instructing Tanaka to grind at speed used in screen farces—caused Tanaka to ruin a beautiful picture—and leave me holding the bag! Jack is impossible" (Tanaka letter).

Following this, *The Lying Truth* came to the market, but box office suffered from the reviews of exhibitors and a marked lack of advertising. In late 1922, one review stated, "A very good one-day program picture, but not a special. Played two days with heavy loss. Paid three times its worth. Sold to me as a special" ("What the Picture Did for Me"). After that not much was heard about *The Lying Truth* for a while, but Fairfax kept busy making speeches, editing and titling *Youth to Youth* (1920), (Engel) helping Reginald Barker with editing suggestions on *Hearts Aflame* (1923), (Barker) and entertaining another foreign venture with George Mooser in India (Mooser).

Then, in October 1923, the truth surfaced. A letter from United Producers & Distributors appears in Fairfax's personal papers. While the contents of the letter seem of little importance, her scrawl says it all. At the top of the letter, she wrote, "*Lying Truth* release—Great mistake to go with absolutely new release which was soon crowded to wall—instead of giving it to First National. John Jasper's doing" (Leonard). So we can see that Fairfax's working relationship with John Jasper was much of the undoing of her production company, at least for a while.

That was not the end of Marion Fairfax Productions, however, as other researchers have claimed. Though she did take a short break from producing her own pictures, she continued writing for other production companies in what appears to be a freelance capacity. She also stepped into the world of editing for First National. On *Sundown* (1924) for First National, Earl Hudson sent her a telegram requesting a daily report on the rushes, essentially asking for the equivalent of a director's opinion on the progress of the filming. (Hudson, 1924) She would later write and edit *The Lost World* (1925) for Hudson.

Throughout the early and mid–'20s, Marion's services were clamored for, indicated by one telegram from Hudson announcing that Sam Katz, the head of the legal department for First National in New York, saw *Her Temporary Husband* (1923). In Spring's words, "I really have not laughed so hard since *The Hottentot*. I think the picture is a whow [*sic*]!" Below, scrawled in blue ink, all-caps, "Fairfax's always a winner—Don't ever let he(r) get away—Tons knows she is both restless and damn i(n)dependent—Sam" (Hudson, 1923). In another telegram from Hudson in 1924, regarding *Lilies of the Field* (1924), he writes "*Lilies* going tremendously public greatly enthused stop positive we have sensation hit to our credit kindest regards, Sam Katz." Below, again in all-caps blue ink, "Fair wins again—Sam" (Hudson, 1924). Hudson continued sending communications, from telegrams to radio messages, asking Fairfax to work on a number of upcoming films. After a litany of requests, he states, "It is very important to me that you do not work too hard. Under no circumstances forget the absolute necessity to me you are and incidentally and other wise I won't let you finish Lost World script" (Hudson, Radio Message from Texas No. 3).

By the end of 1924, Fairfax was ill again. The production manager of First National wrote her an acknowledgment that she would no longer be coming east, on account of her illness. He expressed his disappointment, as he "cannot help but appreciate your valuable services in connection with the First National Productions, and am just wondering when you have recovered your health—if there is anyway we could fit you in with whatever units may be working on the coast—whether you will discuss this matter with us before making other arrangements" (Rowland). By early October, Fairfax had changed her mind and was indeed planning on heading east to handle the editing, titling, and general editorial direction of *The Lost World*, possibly her best-known film to date (McCormick *and* Rowland).

The Lost World was an adaptation of Arthur Conan Doyle's famous dinosaur novel, and the film itself did the story justice. Fairfax both wrote the adaptation and directed the editing. After the massive success of *The Lost World*, which broke records, Fairfax was more in demand than ever. In another telegram sent by Hudson in February of 1925, he expresses a desire for her to return to New York because they have four films in production, as well as four in pre-production. He had proposed to his boss that she come back to New York to take charge of the editing and titling of the four films in production, then beginning "at earliest practical moment" for her to have a "unit of your own." He followed this up with continued compliments on *The Lost World*'s advance sales (Hudson 1925).

By late 1925, ever resourceful, Fairfax began a new partnership, this time with Sam E. Rork. Motion Picture News reported that Rork and Fairfax, both independent producers, had joined forces to share technical staff while producing their own films. "This arrangement was used in connection with Rork's latest comedy *Clothes Make the Pirate*. This picture was produced in New York but the same production staff will accompany the producers to Hollywood where Miss Fairfax's first production *The Desert Healer* will be filmed" ("Rork-Fairfax Have New Plan"). Interestingly enough, Fairfax wrote *Clothes*

Make the Pirate (1925) and was credited as supervisor and writer, which, according to this article, would be correct. However *The Desert Healer* is credited solely as a Sam E. Rork production by all modern digital accounts, except the historical documents don't seem to reflect that.

In *Motion Picture News* in March 1926, *The Desert Healer* is again referred to as a Marion Fairfax Productions project, "in collaboration with Sam E. Rork" ("Algerian Village Erected for *Desert Healer*"). It was later re-named *Old Loves and New* and released by First National. In April, a letter from the National Board of Review of Motion Pictures notified Mr. C.F. Chandler of First National that the film had been selected for the Photoplay Guide because of its "technical handling and sustained interest" (Barret). Written by hand across the letter, in a different scrawl than Fairfax's, was an arrow pointing at the title and "Marion Fairfax Productions," with another "ATT M.F." So, *Old Loves and New* was technically the second Marion Fairfax Productions picture.

In 1926 Fairfax wrote *The Blonde Saint*, which was to be her final picture. There are two things that point to this being Fairfax's film. In a letter from Fairfax to S.P. Trood of the Public Relations Counsel, she wrote, "About the boats;—I have decided to do the trick shots after I have completed my picture, and I will then be rid of my big salary sheet and can take my director and staff off by ourselves and fuss around until we get what we want. This will probably be about the middle of September…" (Fairfax, 1926). She wasn't in production on any other film, and this letter indicates she was carrying the balance sheet for the crew, thus it was a Marion Fairfax Productions film. Secondly, and probably most telling, was a Western Union telegram to Sam Rork in November of 1926 from First National, expressing pleasure in *The Blonde Saint*, to "you and Marion Fairfax." Scrawled across the telegram is "2nd Marion Fairfax Production for First Nat'l."

By September, Fairfax was ill again, possibly the worst she had experienced. In a personal letter to Fairfax from Alfred Hustwick of Famous Players–Lasky, he says he had met her husband, Marshall, at First National, and

> … was surprised to learn from him that you had been having such a wretched time, but was very glad to hear that you are on the road to recovery. Although it is a long time since we saw each other, I want you to know that I'm still interested in all the old friends of the early Writer's Club days. Here's hoping that Marion Fairfax will soon be well and strong again and occupying her old place in the activities of the picture world—a place that no one else could ever fill with quite the same charm and dignity [Hustwick].

Whether Fairfax had come to an agreement with Sam Rork about production ownership based on her impending illness, or whether he had taken advantage of her weakened state while negotiating titling on the First National distributions, will never be known. What is known is that Fairfax all but disappeared from screenwriting and the filmmaking business after the end of 1926, as did many female-led production companies.

Fairfax, ill in 1926, ceased writing screenplays. She did not, however, cease writing. She wrote a column called "Marionettes" for *Rob Wagner's Script* magazine, which was upbeat and playful, though she did admit, "I haven't been inside of a studio for a couple of years," and then, "I believe it's worse to be a semi-invalid than a whole one." In another column, she states, "The Doctors stabbed me with some of their new-fangled serums, determined to make me well at all costs (to me) and I took the count in the first round. After this last experience I've made up my mind to continue to enjoy ill health in my own little way instead of 'getting well' in theirs" (Fairfax, "Marionettes").

Ever-positive Fairfax appears to have left the business from ill health. Much later, sometime around 1940, she received a letter from the Poet Laureate of Texas, Lexie Dean Robertson, praising an enclosed poem by Fairfax. (Robertson) Another letter from a magazine editor praised her "stories" (Alvord). Finally, she sent in at least one story in 1946, three years after her husband's death, to the Junior Order of the Torch Bearers for a weekly "monograph" called "The Torch" (Freeman).

Many of the female-led production companies from the silent era were lost in the short-lived but powerful recession between 1920 and 1921, including The Eve Unsell Photoplay Staff, Ida May Park Productions, Margery Wilson Productions, Vera McCord, Lillian and George Randolph Chester, and Cathrine Curtis Corporation (Mahar, 185). But later on, in the late '20s, a more likely culprit was the industrialization of the film industry as more Wall Street investors were lured from the East. Once talkies insisted upon their adoption, and expensive sound stages were inevitable, a few theories exist about the great migration of women away from behind the scenes. Historian Giuliana Muscio muses that "with the introduction of sound probably some of these writers did not want to learn the new tricks of the business, because they were not that young anymore." She also considers that, as the studios became larger machines and producers were given more power,

> This changed the nature of the collaborative relation of writer/producer into a power struggle. The construction of Writers' Buildings in the studio lots and the new schedules of work from eight to five probably were not too appealing to these writers, who were used to working at home. Most of all, their feminine quality was represented in their ability to cooperate in a team, to do a little bit of everything, and thus, they did not fit too well in a rigidly specialized schema of work [Muscio, 306].

Karen Ward Mahar has another theory that seems plausible. She argues that when Wall Street investors arrived in Hollywood,

> the presence of women in its ranks came under greater scrutiny. Women in the American film industry had thus far enjoyed more latitude and leverage than women in any other industry, including the stage. But women in powerful and visible positions were not the norm for most industries, particularly the financial industry [Mahar, 186].

In truth, perhaps it was a combination of both. If a group of people, regardless of gender, become used to a certain way of working, and come to expect that from a workplace, and that environment suddenly changes, then naturally the population should dwindle. Likewise, a lack of drive to adapt to the new surroundings, or the fact that the people in power consciously or subconsciously hire fewer numbers of that group of people effects such a population. Whatever the reason, Marion Fairfax essentially retired in 1927, though she lived until 1970.

WORKS CITED

"Algerian Village Erected for *Desert Healer.*" *Motion Picture News*. Motion Picture News, 15 March 1926: 1193. Print.

Alvord, Adeline. Letter to Marion Fairfax. 14 March 1940. The Marion Fairfax papers, Margaret Herrick Library, Academy of Motion Picture Arts and Sciences. TS.

Banning, Anne. Letter to Marion Fairfax. 3 July 1914. The Marion Fairfax papers, Margaret Herrick Library, Academy of Motion Picture Arts and Sciences. MS.

Barker, Reginald. Telegram. 16 November 1922. The Marion Fairfax papers, Margaret Herrick Library, Academy of Motion Picture Arts and Sciences. TS.

Barret, F.C. Letter to Mr. C.F. Chandler. 16 April 1926. The Marion Fairfax papers, Margaret Herrick Library, Academy of Motion Picture Arts and Sciences. TS.

Barrymore Productions, John. Letter of agreement to Marion Fairfax. 28 September 1921. The Marion Fairfax papers, Margaret Herrick Library, Academy of Motion Picture Arts and Sciences. TS.

Breeze, Rita Green. Letter to Marion Fairfax. 28 October Year Unknown. The Marion Fairfax papers, Margaret Herrick Library, Academy of Motion Picture Arts and Sciences. MS.

Comstock & Gest. Inc., and Marion Fairfax. Contract to produce *Mr. Crewe's Career*. 10 October 1908. The Marion Fairfax papers, Margaret Herrick Library, Academy of Motion Picture Arts and Sciences. Print.

de Mille, William C. Telegram. 16 April 1921. The Marion Fairfax papers, Margaret Herrick Library, Academy of Motion Picture Arts and Sciences. TS.

"Digest Pictures of the Week." *Exhibitor's Herald*. Exhibitors Herald, 15 April 1922. Archive.org. PDF file image scan of Print.

Engel, Jos. W. Letter to Marion Fairfax. 15 September 1922. The Marion Fairfax papers, Margaret Herrick Library, Academy of Motion Picture Arts and Sciences. TS.

Fairfax, Marion. Letter to Charlie Chaplin. The Marion Fairfax papers, Margaret Herrick Library, Academy of Motion Picture Arts and Sciences. TS.

_____. Letter to S.P. Trood. 7 July 1926. The Marion Fairfax papers, Margaret Herrick Library, Academy of Motion Picture Arts and Sciences. TS.

_____. "The Lying Truth." Shooting film script. 1921. The Marion Fairfax papers, Margaret Herrick Library, Academy of Motion Picture Arts and Sciences. TS.

_____. "Marionettes" recurring column. Rob Wagner's Beverly Hills Script Magazine. No Date. The Marion Fairfax papers, Margaret Herrick Library, Academy of Motion Picture Arts and Sciences. Print.

Freeman, J. Duane. Letter to Marion Fairfax. 25 July 1946. The Marion Fairfax papers, Margaret Herrick Library, Academy of Motion Picture Arts and Sciences. TS.

"Harris—The Talker." *The New York Dramatic Mirror*. The New York Dramatic Mirror, 10 Jan. 1912. Print.

Hudson, Earl. Letter to Marion Fairfax. No date. The Marion Fairfax papers, Margaret Herrick Library, Academy of Motion Picture Arts and Sciences. MS.

_____. "Radio Message from Texas No. 1." No date. The Marion Fairfax papers, Margaret Herrick Library, Academy of Motion Picture Arts and Sciences. TS.

_____. "Radio Message from Texas No. 3." No date. The Marion Fairfax papers, Margaret Herrick Library, Academy of Motion Picture Arts and Sciences. TS.

_____. Telegram. 6 December 1923. The Marion Fairfax papers, Margaret Herrick Library, Academy of Motion Picture Arts and Sciences. TS.

_____. Telegram. 6 March 1924. The Marion Fairfax papers, Margaret Herrick Library, Academy of Motion Picture Arts and Sciences. TS.

_____. Telegram. 2 January 1925. The Marion Fairfax papers, Margaret Herrick Library, Academy of Motion Picture Arts and Sciences. TS.

_____. Telegram. 12 February 1925. The Marion Fairfax papers, Margaret Herrick Library, Academy of Motion Picture Arts and Sciences. TS.

Hustwick, Alfred. Letter. 7 September 1926. The Marion Fairfax papers, Margaret Herrick Library, Academy of Motion Picture Arts and Sciences. TS.

Keegan, Rebecca. "The Hollywood Gender Discrimination Investigation Is on: EEOC Contacts Women Directors." *The LA Times*. The LA Times, 2 October 2015. Web. 10 Dec. 2015.

"Kendall's 'Cardigan' First Offering of American Releasing Corporation." *Exhibitor's Herald*. Exhibitors Herald, Feb. 25 1922. Archive.org. PDF file image scan of Print.

Lasky, Jesse L. Feature Play Company. Letter of agreement to Marion Fairfax. 18 January 1918. The Marion Fairfax papers, Margaret Herrick Library, Academy of Motion Picture Arts and Sciences. TS.

Leonard, F. Letter to Marion Fairfax. 10 October 1923. The Marion Fairfax papers, Margaret Herrick Library, Academy of Motion Picture Arts and Sciences. TS.

L.M. Production document, editorial summary. 26 July 1921. The Marion Fairfax papers, Margaret Herrick Library, Academy of Motion Picture Arts and Sciences. TS.

The Lost World (1925). Wr: Marion Fairfax and Arthur Conan Doyle, Dir. Harry O Hoyt. First National Pictures, USA 106 mins.

Mahar, Karen Ward. Women Filmmakers in Early Hollywood. Baltimore: John Hopkins University Press, 2006. Print.

"Marion Fairfax." *IBDB: The Internet Broadway Database*, 10 Dec. 2015. Web.

"Marion Fairfax Completes Plans for Initial Independent Features." *Exhibitor's Herald*. Exhibitors Herald, 23 Apr. 1921: 58. Print.

"Marion Fairfax, Dramatist, Is with Lasky." *Motion Picture News*. Motion Picture News, Apr. 1915: 64. Print. The Marion Fairfax papers, Margaret Herrick Library, Academy of Motion Picture Arts and Sciences. TS.

"Marion Fairfax Will Direct Own Pictures." *Exhibitor's Herald*. Exhibitors Herald, 7 May 1921. Archive.org. PDF file image scan of Print.

"Marshall Neilan Again Signs Marion Fairfax." *Exhibitor's Herald*. Exhibitor's Herald, 16 Oct. 1920: 41. Archive.org. PDF file image scan of Print.

"Marshall Neilan Leaves for East—Wife Starts Divorce." *Variety*. Variety, Hollywood, 18 February 1921. PDF file image scan of Print.

McCormick, John. Telegram. 9 October 1924. The Marion Fairfax papers, Margaret Herrick Library, Academy of Motion Picture Arts and Sciences. TS.
McGann, Anabel Parker. Letter. No date. The Marion Fairfax papers, Margaret Herrick Library, Academy of Motion Picture Arts and Sciences. MS.
"Mr. Crewe's Career Staged." *New York Times*. New York Times, December 29, 1908. New York Times Archive Site. PDF file image scan of Print.
Mooser, George. Letter to Marion Fairfax. 4 April 1923. The Marion Fairfax papers, Margaret Herrick Library, Academy of Motion Picture Arts and Sciences. MS.
Muscio, Giuliana. Women Screenwriters in American Silent Cinema, Chapter 13 in "Reclaiming the Archive: Feminism and Film History." Wayne State University Press. Detroit. 2010. Print.
Neiswanger, Joseph. Marion Fairfax and Tully Marshall wedding announcement. 1899. The Marion Fairfax papers, Margaret Herrick Library, Academy of Motion Picture Arts and Sciences. TS.
"Opposition in Maryland." *Sacramento Union*. Sacramento Union, Number 25949, 2 April 1922. PDF file image scan of Print.
Paramount Pictures. Production Summary for *Secret Game*. 1917. The Marion Fairfax papers, Margaret Herrick Library, Academy of Motion Picture Arts and Sciences. TS.
_____. Production Summary for *The Roaring Road*. 1919. The Marion Fairfax papers, Margaret Herrick Library, Academy of Motion Picture Arts and Sciences. TS.
The Roaring Road (1919). Wr: Marion Fairfax, Dir: James Cruze. Paramount Pictures, USA 58 mins.
Robertson, Lexie Dean. Letter to Mrs. Marshall. No date. The Marion Fairfax papers, Margaret Herrick Library, Academy of Motion Picture Arts and Sciences. TS.
Robinsonhope.com. Hollywood Center History Timeline, 8 Dec. 2015. Web.
"Rork-Fairfax Have New Plan." *Motion Picture News*. Motion Picture News, 7 November 1925: 1247. Print.
Rowland, R.A. Letter to Marion Fairfax. 26 September 1924. The Marion Fairfax papers, Margaret Herrick Library, Academy of Motion Picture Arts and Sciences. TS.
_____. Telegram. 9 October 1924. The Marion Fairfax papers, Margaret Herrick Library, Academy of Motion Picture Arts and Sciences. TS.
Sanger & Jordan, and Marion Fairfax. Contract to lease out *The Eager Heart*. Print.
Sherlock Holmes (1922). Wr: Marion Fairfax, Dir: Albert Parker. Goldwyn Pictures Corporation, USA 85 mins.
Slater, Tom. "Marion Fairfax." In Jane Gaines, Radha Vatsal, and Monica Dall'Asta, eds. Women Film Pioneers Project. Center for Digital Research and Scholarship. New York, NY: Columbia University Libraries, 2013. Web. 27 September 2013.
Spring, Sam. Telegram to Sam Rork. 4 November 1926. The Marion Fairfax papers, Margaret Herrick Library, Academy of Motion Picture Arts and Sciences. TS.
Suggett, Laura. Letter to Mrs. Tully M. Phillips. 10 February 1919. The Marion Fairfax papers, Margaret Herrick Library, Academy of Motion Picture Arts and Sciences. TS.
Tanaka, Edward. Letter to Mr John Jasper. 1922. The Marion Fairfax papers, Margaret Herrick Library, Academy of Motion Picture Arts and Sciences. TS.
Tanaka, Edward, Marion Fairfax and John Jasper. Production and distribution agreement. March 1922. The Marion Fairfax papers, Margaret Herrick Library, Academy of Motion Picture Arts and Sciences. TS.
Through the Back Door (1921). Wr: Marion Fairfax, Dir. Alfred E. Green and Jack Pickford. and Gerald C. Duffy. Mary Pickford Company, USA 89 mins.
"Tully Marshall." *IBDB: The Internet Broadway Database*. Web. 10 Dec. 2015
"What the Picture Did for Me." *Exhibitor's Herald*. Exhibitor's Herald, 21 October 1922. Archive.org. PDF file image scan of Print.

Smart Girl in Charge
Eve Unsell

LAURA KIRK

Eve Unsell was one of many early female pioneers in the new art form of cinema whose work weaved many famous players of the era together. During her career, she accumulated nearly 100 credits as a screenwriter. Mentored by some of the most prominent producers in the history of American theater and then film she flourished, it is important to consider the climate in which she worked and conquered. Though she wrote for notable stars including Mary Pickford, Lon Chaney, Clara Bow, Baby Peggy and Jack Benny the repetition in her career was not with directors or actors or genre but with producers. Many credits are with Paramount Pictures, or Famous Players–Lasky and with B.P. Schulberg. Genre and themes across her body of work were typical of the time period consisting of melodramas, romances, crime dramas, mysteries, and society dramas. She found her forte in the adaptation of short stories, novels, and plays, a hallmark of the era. The tricky chore of adapting others' work was one her well-educated, literary background sustained. During these formative years, women dominated the film industry. By studying her career, one can gain perspective of how women navigated a rapidly changing field due to evolving formats and distribution comparable to today's demand for content due to multiple platform engagement by audiences. Only by direct confrontation and examination of the business of film armed with the knowledge of history can women take charge again. Eve Unsell's success was due to her education, reputation, skill, work ethic, and independence fired directly in the face of gender inequity.

Though she was born in Chicago, Unsell grew up the daughter of a successful merchant in Caldwell, Kansas making her trajectory from college to theater actress to trusted writer to executive all the more dramatic. She was placed in charge of scenarios at a new British Lasky company and relocated to Europe according to the article "Fame for a Kansas Girl" in the *Kansas City Kansan*, written by columnist Alma Whitaker (Fame 1919). This was the age when women were listed in headlines as girls no matter their age or accomplishments. Whitaker describes Unsell as bright, dear and with all sorts of college degrees! Her degrees were from Hardin College, followed by a B.A. from Christian College in Columbia, then additional education at Emerson College in Boston where she studied drama and literature (Whitaker A. 1931). Kicked out of Hardin for lighting a firecracker in the chapel demonstrates independent behavior in settings with firm expectations of behavior for women. This kind of social emancipation laid the groundwork for her move from the Midwest to New York City. It also served her ability to think outside the box and create work for herself in later years. This quality would be necessary when encountering larger than life men in power. During this time period, women who didn't marry young were more likely to move away from home.

Starting in New York she worked for American theater legend, David Belasco. In Belasco's book, *Through the Stage Door*, he advised women to put off marriage so as not to encumber careers. He lamented his search for plays taking more energy than actual productions. If the written form was solid everything else would fall into place. He looked down upon motion pictures for many reasons. The constant interruptions to remind the viewer what the story was about made inter-titles a curse. He defended perceived competition pointing out theater quality would always persevere over film because it didn't have to dumb down to the masses to stay viable (43, 209). In an article penned for the *New York Times*, Belasco declared every woman believed she could be an actress due to her inherent "nature." He knew because he faced this onslaught of women with this embedded dream every day of every year. Additionally, he describes "mature women … long past their first blush of youth … the most pathetic" (Stage-Struck Women). A strong sense of identity would be necessary to propel women from these attitudes. Later Unsell "was a play reader and constructionist with Mrs. H.C. de Mille" or Beatrice as she was also known, mother of Cecil and William (Belasco 43, 209). During her time as a reader, Unsell learned "plot detection." So the networking continues. Later Belasco would moderate his low opinions of the art form and collaborate with J.L. Lasky. Between the years 1913 and 1916 many plays were adapted into films and distributed with limited release. Unsell's credits and affiliations correspond with this practice (Tibbets 77).

An undated publicity photograph of writer Eve Unsell. Writing on nearly 100 films during her lifetime, Unsell was also known to use the pseudonyms Oliver W. Geoffreys and E.M. Unsell (Academy of Motion Picture Arts and Sciences' Margaret Herrick Library).

To supply demand early Hollywood turned to popular novels for story ideas. Films of the era were cross-promoted as photoplay editions of the novels released with added production stills as a tie-in. Emil Petaja was a fan and early scholar of this form as well as an avid memorabilia collector. His book *Photoplay Edition* has the closest version of a complete list of this form including more than 400 titles. In his preface, he advises that the films were "loosely adapted" then sold with the adage "Read the book, then see the picture!" This appealed because audience goers could "relive" moments from the film back at home (Petaja 1975). An example of this from *The Plastic Age* is a still of Clara Bow tugging her man and encouraging him with the line: "COME ON—I KNOW WHERE THERE'S LIQUID REFRESHMENT!" (Marks 204).

The Eagle's Mate (1914) starring Mary Pickford and produced by Famous Players Film Company is one of Unsell's first credits for scenario writing. Based on the novel by Anna Alice Chapman the front cover advertises a beautiful and girlish heroine perfectly suited for Mary Pickford. The copy also describes her as "tantalizingly virginal." However that appealed one does not want to imagine. No wonder groups formed to censor Hollywood. The dialogue in the novel is rich with the vernacular of the characters. The feisty Anenome and the love of her life, Lancer pay homage to classic story telling such as Shakespeare's *Taming of the Shrew* or Chekhov's *The Brute*. In a still from the film Lancer and Anenome face off and the caption reads: "YOU WANT TO STEAL ME FOR YOURSELF!" "NO, I WANT TO WIN YOU!"

Anenome agrees to marry Lancer under the condition they will divorce in six months if she doesn't love him by then. Anenome discovers she loves him after learning of his death. Melodramatic indeed is his sudden appearance during violent chaos to return to her side building to a kiss worthy of the big screen (Chapin 105, 236, 295–6). The adaptation of this novel, filled with pages of torrid dense dialogue, and boiling titles down to two sentences proved a gargantuan task, but Unsell was up for just such a task.

Famous Players–Lasky was formed when Adolph Zukor and Jesse L. Lasky merged their resources with Paramount acting as a distributor with block booking that guaranteed entire slates of films to be shown in theaters. Their biggest star was Mary Pickford so Unsell was off to a great start after her time in the theater with Belasco (Stanley 1978). Unsell would go on to create numerous projects for them and eventually take charge of scenarios for a newly formed British Lasky company in 1919. Unsell communicated with Motion Picture News through her husband Lester Blankfield after a "flying visit" (travel by air was new) to see his wife. Unsell described her findings about the British and how they responded to American Cinema. She reported they were critical but that American Films are well received and numerous. Her review sounds as if America did it better for less money. On a personal note, she reports no disrespect and admires the culture of the women she encounters, though finds it hard to see screens through dense smoke since women smoke in her new work country (American Pictures, 1919). In London one of her first employees was a young Alfred Hitchcock who designed title cards (Dick 17) presumably under Unsell's tutelage on such films as *The Call of Youth* (1921). Unsell is credited with teaching Hitchcock "the ins and outs of story and screenplay mechanics as well as adapting novels for film" (Elliot, 2010).

Years later, Unsell would return to New York to act as president over her namesake company: "Eve Unsell Photoplay Staff, Inc." which would prepare continuities for Famous Players–Lasky (Miss Unsell Heads, 1921). A New Year Greeting ad in Variety dedicates her company's intent to meet a "higher scenario standard." The ad lists Katherine MacDonald as the star of upcoming efforts. It also lists the many stars and directors Unsell wrote for as well as "Celebrated Authors" whose works she adapted. In the small print at the bottom left-hand corner she is listed as president, at the right, her husband Lester Blankfield is listed as the secretary and general manager of the entity (Eve Unsell Photoplay Staff, Inc., 1921). Their collaboration kept her name front and center. By this time her talent was well established and respected. This wave of independent companies emerged between the years of 1916 and 1923 so much so that it was described as an epidemic as noted by author Karen Ward Mahar in her book *Women Filmmakers in Hollywood* in the sixth chapter about the "'her own company' epidemic." (154) Mahar further clarifies and distinguishes Unsell's company as a "freelance writing service provider" along with Unsell's described desire to "bring filmmakers and authors to a new level of mutual understanding" (185). This was likely a mission she was dedicated to at this point in her career.

Also under the umbrella of Famous Players was producer B.P. Schulberg. Schulberg started work for Famous Players in 1912, left for a while, then returned in 1925 as a replacement for Cecil B. DeMille as general manager (Dick 16). In the mix, Unsell would work on numerous pictures under Schulberg. Both educated and traveled people, they seem to have enjoyed a mutual respect for each other. This collaboration was promoted in the *Los Angeles Times* with the dramatic declaration that "they promise, they are going to wrinkle day and night over the problem of better stories" (Kingsley 1922). It is interesting to also note in the article that Schulberg is credited with "persuading her to stop the drudgery of adapting scenarios from other people's stories and devote herself to writing her own." According to a letter written by R.J. Huntington about Unsell's own view on "The Apathy of Authors" he respects but disbelieves some of her claims about the "swamping of the scenario department with worthless material." He criticized her opinion and stated: "the screen cannot be made an outlet for "loose" ideas and banal plots." Huntington blames the excess of poor product flooding the theaters for inspiring the poor imitations submitted to studios. Critical of the numbers of adaptations and their spawn he calls for independent thinking from producers, better readers making those choices and original stories as the antidote (Huntington, 1923).

Yellow Fingers (1926), based on the novel by Gene Wright, was a yellow peril exploitation film story of a "white girl saved from clutches of an Oriental" (Vogel 2010). Unsell earned sole writing credit for this film featuring Olive Borden. "Yellow Peril" is a term defining an ideology that was most prolific between 1890 and 1924, expressing fear of a danger posed to the West by intermarriage, population domination, and ultimately the fear that the United States could potentially become completely Oriental. "Inbreeding" among races and the danger white women faced was wide spread with many feared races othered; the more foreign or different the stronger call to defend and examine this perceived threat within the frames of films of the period. (Thompson 18). In *The Cheat* (1915), Cecil B. DeMille spectacularly exploits the aforementioned fears in the tale of a gambling married woman's loan to be paid with her virtue to the wealthy Japanese character who threatened said virtue. According to Turner Classic Movies when the film's re-release offended Japanese allies during World War I, the nationality and name were changed from Japanese to Burmese. (Fristoe n.d.)

In the film *Shadows* (1922) starring Lon Chaney and produced by B.P. Schulberg, Unsell shares adaptation credit with Hope Loring based on the story *Ching-Ching Chinaman* (1917) by Wilbur Daniel Steele. Louis F. Gottschalk wrote the music for both D.W. Griffith's *Broken Blossoms* (1919) and *Shadows*. Unsell later collaborated with Gottschalk on the musical *Ching Ching Chinaman* (1923). Unsell's lyrics include the phrase "Winky, Chinky, Blinky Chinaman" (Garrett). Race and stereotyping are also apparent as exemplified with the work ethic of the title character and the mysterious ways he moves about. (Maurice, 2008). The opening titles are exemplary of Schulberg and Unsell's literary and educated approach to telling a story:

> To every people, in every age, there comes a measure of God to man—through man.... Even today, Wisdom may dwell among us, in humble guise, unknown, despised, until its mission fulfilled, it slips back into the mystery from whence it came.

A philosophical and literary opening to the film not leveled at the masses might be chastised by moguls insisting viewers don't go to the movies to read. Lon Chaney received rave reviews as the Chinese launderer, Yen Sin—"The Heathen" who washes up onto a fishing village of Urkey where Sympathy Gibbs and her abusive husband live. After the storm takes Dan Gibbs and Yen Sin washes up only to be outcast for not observing the Christian rites of lives lost, the character of Minister John Malden calls out the hypocrisy of Christian faith with such titles as: "For shame! Our Brother! Christ died for such as he." The conversion story continues as he professes: "I would give my life if I could make you believe." By this, the solution to the peril is to convert Yen Sin to Western culture completely rather than allow his culture to threaten ours. For all to be assimilated to White Christian culture was what was best for them with preserving American culture the ultimate goal. Unsell's titles depicting the vernacular and dialect of the Chinese man were filled with the requisite replacement the notoriously difficult consonant "r" with "l" along with simple mistaken grammar such as his lines from his death bed: "Yen Sin go back China way pletty quick now—get Mista Minista—please." Or, in his sudden willingness to: "confessee" for the "minista flen of mine."

Yet in the same scene, he appears to understand normally spoken complex English when he responds and nails Nate Snow to protect his loyal friend and expose the blackmail that has persecuted the Godly minister. When the minister forgives Nate for horrible cruelty Yen Sin is so moved by his example he does finally believe in this great faith that would inspire such a generous move. Thus the heathen is claimed for the Kingdom and for America and the film ends along with a cinematic kiss from the love interests.

Another Schulberg collaboration is *The Plastic Age* (1925) based on the novel by Percy Marks, starring Clara Bow. Fredrica Sagor Maas obtained the galleys and took the novel out herself gaining a contract to write the screenplay. Sagor describes Schulberg as someone who liked women but was polite when rejected (Maas 2010). Unsell is never mentioned in Sagor's autobiography. A first-time writer would likely not have the craft needed no matter the raw talent. According to archivist Hilary Swett at the Writers Guild Foundation, "Writing credits in the teens and 20's were not codified as they are now. This was one of the reasons screenwriters organized in the first place. Loosely organized in 1920, the Screen Writers Guild formally organized as a union in 1933 and that is when the official records begin. Unsell joined the Guild and is mentioned on the rosters from 1933–35." Since contracts with writers were governed by studios, there was never any bargaining power so credits up to the time of the union were loose and hard to analyze. Sagor offered, "…credit on a script usually went to the last writer brought on to do a rewrite…. Once in a while, there might be a sharing of credit with one of the previous writers, providing he or she had sufficient clout to demand it. Otherwise, the last writer hired snatched the merry-go-round gold ring" (Banks 2015). Unsell surely had sufficient clout to take this credit from Maas.

The film *Captain January* (1924) is based on the children's book by Laura E. Richards. It features the irrepressible child star Baby Peggy. The titles are simple and straightforward. In the book, the girl is ten years old and has extensive dialogue and scenes not included in the film. The child actress was five years old when the film was made so the dialogue had to be adapted both to fit the constraints of titles and its star. The handling of adoption themes is nuanced and ahead of its time. In the sequence leading up to the possible move from her beloved Captain Daddy who discovered her washed up in a storm and the only parent she has ever known the titles and action are as follows: Baby Peggy discovers Captain Daddy showing the locket with her mother's photo to her aunt so she exclaims: "He's telling her my story…." Both in the book and the film the girl loves to hear her adoption story, which in today's adoption culture is also encouraged. Then we learn that her "real family" has been found. Today the word "real" is discouraged when referring to adoptive parents.

Then, when asked if she will go and live with her aunt and uncle to be their little girl she replies, "But I can't belong to different people, 'cause I'm just one—I'm Captain Daddy's little girl." Not looking at her, Captain Daddy tells her he wants her to go. Figuring this out she takes his face slowly looks at it and cries, "Daddy Judkins, that's a—great—big—Fib!" Deeply hurt and confused she cries and clings to the only parent she has ever known. In the book due to her age, the freedom of narrative and pages of dialogue, a more complicated scenario is depicted with the aunt and uncle. It culminates in a threat of suicide if she is taken from her father figure. She tells him that he "lies" rather than "fibs" and jumps out a window. So goes the adaption of the book. As Belasco chastised film—the mass audience calls the shots and in this case the star when it comes to story. Still, Unsell captures the heart of the importance of the scene however truncated.

In one of her final films, *The Medicine Man* (1930) Unsell is listed on IMDb as the writer with adaptation credit for this play by Elliot Lester. Ladye Horton is credited with the screenplay and this is the sole credit found for Horton. Again, Unsell was likely brought in to bridge the gap between a new screenwriter and the original playwright. The film introduces a young Jack Benny in the charming but not necessarily comedic title role. In the transition from silent films to "talkies" it is striking to think of the sheer amount of dialogue suddenly required to tell the story. The writing supports Benny's charm and wit. Lines like "and up jumped the devil" affirming Hulda's arrival typifies the style of the film. The indignity of the older women catching Betty and John kissing shifting to their curiosity and desire to drive closer for a better look demonstrates character behavior. A particularly effective moment is an intense whipping scene that is heard but not seen leaving the horror to our imagination. The "all is lost" moment of the train pulling out to the conclusion of the hero and heroine getting married is classic structure that a seasoned veteran such as Unsell would capitalize on in adapting a story. The reliable melodrama format of a woman endangered (by a brutal father) and getting saved by the hero she falls in love with is effectively in place in the screenplay Unsell adapted.

Very little is known about her personal life save her beginnings in Kansas, well claimed by local newspapers to entertain the small town inhabitants while celebrating their local merchant, her father. There are elements of joy, respect, and most certainly astonishment to see a female rise and lay claim to so many credits. Her marriage to Lester Blankfield from 1911 until her death did not seem to encumber her and in fact seemed to support her. He worked with her company and they co-wrote plays together as evidenced by copyrights in 1919 with the Library of Congress. Various columns in periodicals throughout their union documented their travel and participation in social events. A year before her death, *The Film Daily* reported a vacation from the editorial department of a company in Detroit to travel to New York with her husband who was selected as a speaker for the Democratic national committee. (Alicoate 1936). There is no mention of children, which seems to have allowed her to travel and work freely.

Toward the end of life, she enjoyed a Malibu Beach cottage she named "Me-Likee" probably due to a true enjoyment of being an early settler in stunning Malibu, but perhaps also influenced by dialogue written in exploitative dialect (Nye 1928). Malibu in the twenties was a far cry from modern-day Malibu, accessible by the Pacific Coast Highway and freeways as a commute to the studios. Then the area not being fully developed was dominated by the nature that edged up to it. At the time of Unsell's death, her neighbors were "90% movie people who loved the sea and the isolation" (Ripton 1964). For a career such as Unsell's, an obituary consisting of two sentences is not acceptable (Obituary 5, 1937). She receives a more detailed description of her interactions with a baby seal she nurtured in the same year in the same publication (Whitaker A. 1937). Her film credits become sparse after 1926. Her death occurred four years after her last credit. At age 50, a filmmaker's life ended after a brief undisclosed illness at the outreaches of the town she helped build both as a writer and woman in power.

For nearly all women the changing industry took a different kind of control as procedure and production shifted again to satisfy gender portrayal acceptable to censors and mass audiences. Losing autonomy many women turned away from the field at once as the glass ceiling hardened. Jane M. Gaines asks what happened to these women and names her chapter in the Wiley-Blackwell History of American Film, "pink-slipped" with "intended irony" because there is no paper trail to confirm a widespread systematic conspiracy to bar women from writing, directing, or producing film just as there is no similar proof today (Gaines 2011). Analyzing how women dominated the field during shifting distribution platforms is a crucial application for today's questions. In May of 2015, the ACLU requested an investigation of the hiring practices of studios, networks and talent agencies (Buckley 2015). In August 2015 in Los Angeles, a panel discussion hosted by the Stephens College MFA in Screenwriting followed up on this inquiry with the question: "Is there a legal remedy for gender discrimination in Hollywood?" In the discussion, there was a call for awareness and education. The industry must look squarely at its own numbers to understand the unconscious bias dominating the field. Hires were and are consistently of individuals already known and trusted by those in power.

Unsell's repeated work with studios and producers represents her work ethic. Lasky, Schulberg and others kept hiring her because they knew she could get the job done and done well. As we examine the women working in early Hollywood we reclaim history and regain the foundation set by these pioneer women filmmakers. As Albert Camus said, "Those who don't know the past are doomed to repeat it." Evolve or become extinct. While her name is missing from the index of a broad survey of film history books of the era it is clear, though not famous, Eve Unsell was a player who surely merits our regard.

Works Cited

Alicoate. "Eve Unsell in New York." *Film Daily* 6 August 1936. Web. Lantern 8 Dec. 2015.
"American Pictures Dominate Abroad Says Eve Unsell." New York, December 1919.
Banks, Miranda J. *A History of American Screenwriters and Their Guild*. New Brunswick: Rutgers University Press, 2015. ProQuest. Web. 8 Dec. 2015.
Belasco, David. "Seeing Four Thousand Stage Struck Women Every Year." 5 September 1909. Timesmachine.nytimes.com. 31 August 2016.
_____. *The Theatre Through Its Stage Door*. New York: B. Blom, 1969.
Buckley, Cara. "A.C.L.U., Citing Bias Against Women, Wants Inquiry into Hollywood's Hiring Practices." *New York Times*. 12 May 2015. NY Times. Web. 8 Dec. 2015.
Chapin, Anna Alice. *The Eagle's Mate*. New York: Grosset & Dunlap, 1914.
Charlie Achuff, Madeline F. Matz. Eve Unsell. Women's Pioneer Film Project. Web. 31 August 2016.
Dick, Bernard F. *Engulfed: The Death of Paramount Pictures and the Birth of Corporate Hollywood*. Lexington: University Press of Kentucky, 2001.
Elliot, A.R. "The Scary Discipline of Alfred Hitchcock Wow 'Em." *Investor's Business Daily* 12 May 2010. ProQuest.Web. 8 Dec. 2015.
"Eve Unsell Photoplay Staff, Inc." *Variety* 7 January 1921. ProQuest. Web. 8 Dec. 2015.

"Fame for Kansas Girl." *Kansas City Kansan* 22 July 1919: 1. Copyright 2015. Newspapers.com. Web. 12 Sept. 2015.
Fristoe, Roger. "The Cheat." n.d. TCM. Web. 7 Dec. 2015.
Gaines, Jane M. "Pink-Slipped: What Happened to the Women in the Silent Film Industry?" Corporate. Wiley-Blackwell History of American Film Volume 137 Issue 3. West Sussex: John Wiley and Sons, Inc, 2011. 162.
Garrett, C.H. "Chinatown, Whose Chinatown? Defining America's Borders with Musical Orientalism." *Journal of the American Musicological Society* (n.d.): 119–173. ProQuest.Web. 7 Dec. 2015. http://www.imdb.com/name/nm0881333/. n.d.
Huntington, R.J. "Scenarios and Producers." *New York Times* 25 November 1923. Timesmachine. Web. 8 December 2015.
Kingsley, G. "Flashes." *Los Angeles Times*. 21 July 1922. ProQuest. Web. 8 Dec. 2015.
Maas, Frederica Sagor. *The Shocking Miss Pilgrim*. Lexington: University Press of Kentucky, 2010.
Mahar, Karen Ward. *Women Filmmakers in Early Hollywood*. Baltimore: Johns Hopkins University Press, 2006. Print.
Marks, Percy. *The Plastic Age*. New York: Grosset and Dunlap, 1925.
Maurice, A. "What the Shadow Knows." *Cinema Journal* (2008): 68–89. ProQuest.Web 7 Dec. 2015.
"Miss Unsell Heads Movie Corporation." *The Wellington Daily News* 21 January 1921. Newspapers.com Web. 15 Nov. 2015.
Nye, M. "Society of Cinemaland." *Los Angeles Times*. 12 August 1928. Web. ProQuest 8 Dec. 2015.
"Obituary 5." *Los Angeles Times*. 8 July 1937. ProQuest. Web. 8 Dec. 2015.
Petaja, Emil. *Photoplay Edition*. San Francisco: Sisu, 1975.
Ripton, R. "Stars Partied While Malibu Burned, Recalls Pioneer Colony Resident." *Los Angeles Times*. 27 September 1964. Web. ProQuest 8 Dec. 2015.
Stanley, Robert Henry. *The Celluloid Empire: A History of the American Movie Industry*. New York: Hastings House, 1978.
Thompson, Richard Austin. *The Yellow Peril*. New York: Arno Press, 1978.
Tibbets, John C. *The American Theatrical Film: Stages in Development*. n.d.
Vogel, Michelle. *Olive Borden: The Life and Films of Hollywood's "Joy Girl."* Jefferson, NC: McFarland, 2010.
Whitaker, A. "Sugar and Spice." *Los Angeles Times*. 13 June 1937. ProQuest. Web 8 Dec. 2015.
Whitaker, Alma. "They Get $1,000 to $5,000 for a Story!" May 1931. *Screenland*. Web. 16 November 2015.

The Glorious Ms. Glyn

Amy L. Banks

To study the writer Elinor Glyn is to study the history of sex appeal. Her graceful, stately, English elegance touched everything she wrote and her protagonists all make lasting impressions upon viewers and readers with their stunning sexuality and physical prowess. Agonizing love stories and wild, imagined sex are Glyn's lasting gift to us, along with the most important concept of all, Glyn's proffered "It," a term she coined to explain the mysterious sex appeal some lucky people possess.

Glyn's experiences as an English barrister and landowner's (Mrs. Clayton Louis Glyn) wife, I believe, form the basis of much of her work. The nuances of high society and high language associated with a life of pleasure and wealth are a recurrent theme through her available works. Glyn's unhappy marriage and subsequent love affairs also appear to provide much fodder for her written body of work; *Three Weeks* was reportedly based on her affair with the 16-years-younger Lord Alistair Innes Ker and she had a long-running relationship with George Nathaniel Curzon, 1st Marquess Curzon of Kedleston. Her daughters, Margot and Juliet, both married into aristocracy and Glyn's sister, Lady Duff Gordon (a survivor of the *Titanic*) also provided inspiration for her writing. Even Glyn's own physical features—blazing red hair, for example—are borrowed to embolden a ferocious lady protagonist. Her well-documented love of cats is also evident in her work, from the descriptions of the lady character in *The Reason Why* being continually described as having panther-like qualities to the female protagonist in *Three Weeks* writhing upon a tiger skin in front of a fireplace.

Though Glyn lived and died long ago (1864–1943) her study in sensuality lives on in any number of female stars considered sexual icons today, those who may not possess perfect physical qualities, but certainly possess "It." For example, Julia Roberts with her oft commented upon non-normal nose comes to mind, Sarah Jessica Parker and her foot-shaped face, Angelina Jolie has puffer-fish lips or Scarlett Johansson with her overall presentation are great examples of modern actresses who have "It." Though not immaculately physically perfect, these women are all perfectly beautiful and possess a magnetism that makes it impossible not to stare at them. Glyn provided us with the name for what they possess.

Glyn was a prolific writer, at one point publishing a book a year to keep her family's dwindling finances afloat. Though she only came to Hollywood after the death of her husband in 1920 (her novel *The Great Moment* was in production), she wrote several screenplays, directed films, and was instrumental in assisting Rudolph Valentino and

Clara Bow in their ascension to stardom. Even though Glyn reigned in Hollywood for only about a decade, 27 films were produced from her stories, novels and screenplays. (Barnett and Weedon 1). For the remainder of her life, Glyn traveled between L.A. and Brighton, U.K. and was a major member of the Hollywood in-crowd. Her immense popularity sparked Anita Loos to joke, "If Hollywood hadn't existed, Elinor Glyn would have had to invent it" (Merriman).

Madame Glyn, as she branded herself, came to Hollywood at the behest of June Mayo of Famous Players–Lasky Corporation. At the time she was 56 years old, and had only been to America once before (when she was 42). Her initial contract with Jesse Lasky was for $36,364 annually and enough time off for a yearly trip to Europe. The success of *The Great Moment* in 1921 cemented Glyn's position as a writer

A publicity photograph of screenwriter Elinor Glyn on set in October 1923. Tame by today's standards, Glyn's scandalous romantic fiction had a huge influence on pop culture in the early 20th century. She popularized the concept of "It"—a certain type of sex appeal—and made Rudolph Valentino, Gloria Swanson and Clara Bow stars (Academy of Motion Picture Arts and Sciences' Margaret Herrick Library).

in Hollywood. In 1922 her contract with Lasky concluded and Glyn moved on to work for Metro-Goldwyn-Mayer, writing the screenplay adaptation of her novel *Three Weeks*. She was to direct the film as well but demurred to King Vidor (it's unclear whether that was by choice or not). The film was released in 1924 and was a huge success. Glyn's *Man and Maid* was released next in 1925 and other hits were to follow. (Cummings).

The film that made Clara Bow a star (and justifiably so!), *It* (1927), is a twisty tale of love and misunderstanding, which first appeared as a serialized story for *Cosmopolitan* magazine. The highlight of the film was the meticulously orchestrated meet-cute of Bow's character and the object of her affections, Mr. Waltham. The clever shop girl fails at several attempts to catch the eye of her would-be suitor, finally positioning herself in the right place at the right time. The pay-off is sublime, and the scene gives audiences a calculated happy-down-to-the-toes, curly feeling.

Film historian Rosanne Welch commented, "In a way, Glyn and Bow are the warped side of Frances Marion and Mary Pickford." Bow starred in *It*, based on Glyn's story; she also starred in the 1928 film *Red Hair*, which was based on Glyn's 1905 novel of the same name. Indeed, Glyn wrote the role that brought Bow to the height of stardom, much as Marion did for Pickford; the warped side is that stardom destroyed poor Clara Bow, where Pickford flourished. Sadly, *Red Hair* is presumably lost to history save for a few tiny clips housed in the UCLA Film and Television Archive. *It*, however, is fortunately extant and proves to be one of those silent films that is so good one loses oneself to the story and doesn't suffer for the lack of audible dialogue. Bow's expressive, beautiful eyes tell the emotional tale while Glyn's title cards sufficiently fill in the rest. And Glyn's cameo of herself in the restaurant scene was also marvelous (seeing the object of my research alive and perambulating was delightful).

Unfortunately, time has not been kind to the remaining copies of the classic love story *Such Men Are Dangerous* (1930), based on a Glyn story, yet the film does not fail to delight. *Dangerous* begins with a man and a woman marrying. The woman is young and lovely, her groom older, bent and apparently unattractive, according to the dialogue. On their wedding night Eleanor, the bride, slips away into the night and heads back to her society-climbing, gold-digger sister's house. Oddly, the sister appears to be married to a very effeminate dandy, who fancies himself a ladies' man. It is implied that Eleanor has run off because her new husband is ugly. However, we know that she actually left because her husband lavished her with cash and gifts, bestowed by his secretary, and she found that cold and distasteful. It seems that Eleanor is a lusty young gal with heart aflame; her sister encouraged the marriage on account of the financial stability it would provide, but Eleanor requires love and realizes her mistake.

Never mind, because the new husband goes missing. That's right, he up and disappears, is presumed dead, and Eleanor apparently becomes a rich, young widow. Except in a common cliché of such films, he isn't dead at all! He's hiding out at a sanitarium, becoming fabulous with the help of a kindly plastic surgeon who, as it turns out, had a hospital saved during the war on account of sweet husband's cash donations. When the bandages come off, the nurse comes in and can't avert her eyes from the husband's awesome sexiness. The husband's secretary (Paul) has shown up, the husband has sent for him. Paul doesn't recognize his boss till prompted and a happy reunion ensues! Now the newly dapper gentleman is on a quest to win back his bride! He learns she's living in Paris and sets out to seduce her, which he accomplishes through a series of not-very-complicated actions. Truly, she is ripe for the picking, and low-hanging fruit to boot. As the moment of ravaging is upon them, the husband has a change of heart. He has fallen in love with this easiest of pickings and huzzah, she loves him as well. Then he pontificates his predicament; comes clean, as it were. She is shocked. He is heartbroken. But then she relays that she hasn't spent any of the money he left her, he has changed for the better, and they kiss and ostensibly consummate their relationship. The end. The plot may seem formulaic by today's standards, but, it was original enough to be completely novel in its era and charming and entertaining to historians and film aficionados today.

Glyn appears in modern popular culture via the 2001 drama *The Cat's Meow*, which tells the tale of Thomas Ince's 1924 birthday cruise on W.R. Hearst's yacht, and his subsequent death under mysterious circumstances. As written by Steven Peros (adapted from his play) the character of Elinor Glyn (portrayed by Joanna Lumley of *Absolutely Fabulous* fame) narrates the story. Ince's birthday cruise is attended by many Hollywood-connected guests, Glyn being one of them. Over the course of the journey we see that Marion Davies (played by Kirsten Dunst), who is Hearst's (Edward Herrmann) mistress, is also having a questionable relationship with Charlie Chaplin (played by Eddie Izzard). This causes Hearst to fly into a rage and shoot Chaplin in the head—but alas, it's a case of mistaken identity, and it is Ince who suffers the head wound.

The boat is docked, the barely alive Ince is delivered home by private ambulance and the rest of the guests either have no clue what actually happened, or are bribed by Hearst into silence. In real life, there has been no revelation of what happened to Ince; his death remains a mystery. In fact, it remains a mystery to all in attendance on the cruise.

In the film Glyn is written as a gorgeous society bell of a tad past prime age, elegant and coy and a good friend to Chaplin, Hearst and Davies alike. Glyn seems to take a motherly role in guiding Davies back to Hearst's arms and out of Chaplin's, telling the younger Davies that a life with Chaplin would never lead anywhere (though Chaplin is single and Hearst has a wife and children). Davies takes her advice and stays (in the film and in real life) with Hearst till his death at 88 years old. In researching Glyn's presence in Hollywood history, it would seem that she indeed did move in the top echelon of society's circles. At the time frame of this movie in her real life, Glyn's husband had died, she had relocated to Hollywood, published many books and was a regular contributor to Hearst's *Cosmopolitan Magazine*. It also did appear that she coached many actors/actresses in mannerism and the proper way to behave in society. The film indicates this type of relationship not only with Davies, but also with Chaplin and others. Fifty-eight years after her death, Glyn is still influencing pop culture—so much so that she is selected to narrate the film, illustrating her enduring impression and her timeless fame.

The Glyn book, *Three Weeks* (1907), was originally serialized in the Hearst publication *Cosmopolitan* and later adapted by Frances Marion into the 1924 film starring Aileen Pringle as the mesmerizing Queen, and Conrad Nagle as innocent Paul Verdayne. Though tame by modern standards, the book caused an uproar upon publication due to its immoral themes of love and lust. For modern readers the book seems dramatic to the extreme, overly sentimental, and overwrought with the imagined scent of flowers (mainly roses) described thoroughly on most every page. The gist of the story is that Paul, a young English aristocratic rube, falls in love with an ugly farm girl and his parents send him on a long vacation to forget about her. Whilst dispatched to Switzerland the gullible Paul meets an enchanting older woman who seduces him, deflowers him, enchants him, then dumps him over the course of three weeks. She later bears his child and is murdered by her husband. Paul pines and whines miserably for several years, then discovers his son will be the king of a throne in Russia. The immorality of a married woman performing such shenanigans seems to have caused mass panic—and of course, book sales—when it was first published.

The fact is, by modern standards, the book itself isn't pornographic in any way. No actual sex scenes are described (though alluded to) and the relationship itself is described in minute, sappy detail. Of note, the Queen was referred to over 20 times as having snake-like qualities, therefore leading the reader to assume her evilness. For instance, Paul watches the lady recline and muses, "Her figure so supple in lines, it made him think of a snake" (Glyn 23). On page 38 the lady, "quivered again with the movements of a snake," and wears a garment "like a serpent's tail." On page 55 the lady's passion is described as, "A madness of tender caressing seized her. She purred as a tiger might have done, while she undulated like a snake." Added to that, there is an entire scene in which the Queen writhes on the tiger's skin that culminates in Paul's bold profession of desire to become the lady's lover. The scene also inspired the unattributed yet memorable light verse: Would you like to sin / With Elinor Glyn / On a tiger skin? / Or would you prefer / To err with her / On some other fur?

The book was significantly scandalous for its time, and also introduced the theme of having "It" before Glyn had fully fleshed this out as a concept. It would not be until the 1927 publication of Glyn's book *It* that she would define the theory, but Mme. Zalenska clearly had "It." Described simultaneously as a snake, tiger, Queen, princess, etc., but also described as not being overly attractive, she still manages to land the strapping blonde

God Paul (as he is sometimes described) and inspire the loyalty of all her servants, though she is shown many times being irate, mean and even abusive to them. Clearly Glyn had a vision of what constitutes sex appeal, and carried that theme through her work.

This theme of "It was also evident in the 1912 Glyn book *The Reason Why*. Every bit as dramatic as *Three Weeks* but without the heavy sexual innuendo, the lady protagonist was also in possession of mass amounts of 'It'" before Glyn had a word to adequately describe the phenomenon. Zara Shulksi, niece of financier Francis Markrute and awkward bride of the strapping Lord Tancred, is described as: "Firstly, she had that arresting, compelling personality which does not depend on features, or coloring, or form, or beauty. A subtle force of character—a radiating magnetism—breathed from her whole being" which is the very definition of "It." She is further described as, "Rather tall and very slender; and yet every voluptuous curve of her lithe body refuted the idea of thinness. Her head was small and her face small, and short, and oval, with no wonderfully chiseled features, only the skin in its white purity—not the purity of milk, but the purity of rich, white velvet, or a gardenia petal." (Glyn 9). Clearly, the lady is described in glowing terms, yet not as overly attractive facially. Her personality, also explained thoroughly throughout the text, is not all together pleasant. Yet every male character in the book and the readers of the tome are expected to be mesmerized by her character as if by magic. She is described over 17 times as being panther-like in her hunted, defensive anger and truthfully acts extremely unkind to just about everyone she encounters. Yet somehow all grovel to be in her presence and gain her favor.

The Reason Why echoes many of the same themes as did *Three Weeks*. For instance, the lady in both books is of mysterious, royal heritage that is alluded to but not disclosed until much, much later. Relationships in each book take on tragic, twisted, farcical longing for much of the text. Both male protagonists are English and from very rich families. Both women have awful, brutish first husbands who end up murdered. Both stories have sympathetic old male characters who listen sadly to the problems of the young and wish to help but don't really know how. Both male protagonists are very attached to their dogs. It goes on and on. The main differences within the texts are that *The Reason Why* has a happy ending and *Three Weeks* does not. Also, *Three Weeks* is ostensibly riddled with maniacal sex (though only alluded to) and nobody is having sex at all in *The Reason Why*.

A prolific author of novels, Glyn also published abundantly in the short story genre. She was often published in Hearst publications and it appears her work was quite popular. Nothing in the body of Glyn's other work seemed to match her article, "Marriage," published in 1913 in *Good Housekeeping* magazine. Perhaps this article was a nod to her formal English background or maybe a sarcastic comic acknowledgment of her own unhappy union or, sadly, her actual opinion of the institution. Equally comic and depressing, this article details Glyn's views that are firm, antiquated and can be interpreted as insulting to both sexes. For example, Glyn says that women have imagination and men have polyamorous instincts. Men are to use words to please a woman instead of actions, and women are expected to understand and realize that rallying against this idea of polyamory is to question God's intentions. She asserts, "Whatever we choose to say in contradiction to this resolves itself into empty words, the fact of nature remaining" (Glyn 348). Glyn writes, "Monogamous marriage is an ideal state, not a natural state, and it must be admitted to be such, and lived up to as an ideal, not undertaken with the notion that fidelity in a man is a natural and infidelity an unnatural thing" (348). The thing is, this ideal is not held towards women. Glyn states woman "becomes promiscuous only under certain conditions," and "She has only to resist perverted desire, which is an exotic growth, the outcome of civilization" (Glyn 348).

The article lists all the reasons for woman to be faithful and man to not be, such as the propagation of the species (man) and purity of offspring (woman). Glyn asserts that as the loss of woman's instinct to propagate a pure species dwindled, she became a "vicious creature" (Glyn 348). She also indicates that the only reason man has to be faithful is the church, and if he is not church-minded, then the fear of being found out is his only impetus. She warns, however, that, "There are numbers of good and honest characters who do not feel convinced that entire fidelity in man to one woman was intended by the Creator, and who therefore feel no degradation in the latitude they allow themselves" (Glyn 349). So fidelity in man is, for all intents and purposes, a lose-lose proposition? Glyn's admonishments for women in unhappy marriages are harsh and of the accept-your-lot-in-life variety. She writes, "A woman disgusts or bores a man, and then bewails her sad lot, and calls the man a brute for being indifferent and a shameful creature for looking elsewhere for consolation" (349). She tells each woman to take stock of her situation and, "ask herself whether she herself threw dust in her own eyes as regards the character of her husband, whether he deceived her in this—or whether they just drifted together, each to blame as much as the other, through the attraction of sex and the cruelty of ignorance." Finally, she tells women, "if she is sensible, she will use the whole of her intelligence to make the best of it" (Glyn 350). So it seems we are to assume then that men are unfaithful, women should accept that, marriage is impossible and women ought to avoid any further discussion of the subject.

Other largely outdated views include the statement that, "Woman is as willing to be ruled as ever she was—she always adores a master" (Glyn 350) and "A really noble and unselfish woman would never consider her personal emotions before her duty to God and to her neighbor" (Glyn 350). She also blames the woman for her own unhappiness stating, "It is because the outlook of woman is, as a rule, so pitiably narrow and self-centered that she often makes a useless and unhappy wife, and shipwrecks her own and her family's future" (Glyn 350). Glyn does offer some sound thoughts on the subject of marriage, however. She speaks of man and woman joining, saying, "They solemnly stand there and make vows about an emotion over which they have no more control than they have over the keeping of the wind in the south" (Glyn 351). She admonishes woman to think long and hard before entering into marriage, and to do so as an enlightened person, not as someone playing the lottery. She concludes by saying, "Before undertaking to play that most difficult part of wife, every girl ought to ask herself–Does she care for the man enough to make her use her intelligence to understand him, and try to keep him loving her?" (Glyn 351). The one particular sentiment that seems to have stood the test of time is, "Truth alone remains at the end of the year" (Glyn 352).

"Why I?" is a short story by Glyn of the supernatural variety, published in *Hearst's Magazine* in December of 1913. Billed as, "a ghost story befitting the Yule Tide tradition in fiction, but all perfumed with the mingled odors of dead rose leaves and old lavender" (895), it is all Glyn. Though not with a Christmas theme, the story itself seemed to be a gift to readers. Of course the protagonist is an Englishwoman, as is the case in so many Glyn stories. She happens to be 37 "but fresh of face" (Glyn 897), a widow, and living with her uncle in the English countryside. The two visit Paris together, and then Versailles, and she has a supernatural encounter with a ghost bent on sending a letter. The older woman appearing younger is a theme discovered in many of Glyn's stories, and the theme of being a widow is also a common device in her work. In *The Reason Why*, an older-but-appearing-much-younger character lives with her elderly uncle in the English countryside and the main protagonist is a widow who lives with her English uncle. She is also quite fond of having characters send letters, as this motif is present in most all of her fiction writing. So, Glyn was not afraid to recycle a detail or two. The story is full of romantic prose and elegance, especially as the protagonist meets the recipient of the ghost's letter, an elderly Parisian woman of noble ancestry with a tragic romantic past. There are rosy cheeks and grand sighs and the drinking of hot beverages in a salon. Very short, but very ostentatious, and very Glyn.

"Her Hour of Love" is another Glyn short story printed in 1911 in *Cosmopolitan*. In it the young bride Winifred is fretfully wed to the wheelchair-bound Ernest, who was shot in the war (they had been engaged before he was injured). Her family has disowned her for marrying a man they refer to as "a cripple" and the two live in seclusion in the English countryside with their elderly servant James and Ernest's loving dog, Tom. Ernest's old Eton friend Sir John Harrington lives nearby and becomes a frequent visitor. Unfortunately, he also falls longingly, painfully, dreadfully and unproductively in love with Winifred, who comes to love him back in an equally powerless, enfeebled, and fruitless manner. True to Glyn's style, Sir John is a gorgeous, eligible bachelor who hasn't yet found the right woman till he does, and she is completely inappropriate. What are they to do? John goes on a trip to forget her, and she throws herself into the task of being the best wife she can. She dotes on her frail husband while Sir John travels abroad unhappily with his mother. Eventually John comes back to see Winifred one last time to tell her he is leaving for good. Of course he does this in a highly dramatic way, with tremulous voice and sad eyes, saying, "I have come to say good-bye to you, my darling white dove. For I cannot crush that which is in my heart any longer. If I stayed it would burst out." (Glyn 842). She's too emotional to answer him, so they share a meaningful look and he leaves. She rushes home to find her husband has died.

With a moral compass the size of Canada, Glyn ruled the English countryside with an iron fist of romantic prose. One wonders if *Cosmopolitan* readers of the last century truly enjoyed this style, but yet finds it compelling to read at the same time. I look forward to collecting all of Glyn's dusty tomes and binge-reading them when the weather is bad and there's nothing better to do than hide in bed with hot tea and the tales of lusty, depressing English men and women.

Works Cited

Barnett, Vincent L., Weedon, Alexis. *Elinor Glyn as Novelist, Moviemaker, Glamour Icon and Businesswoman.* Burlington, VT: Ashgate, 2014.
The Cat's Meow (2001). Wr: Steven Peros, Dir: Peter Bogdanovich. Lions Gate Films, USA 114 mins.
C.D. Merriman for Jalic Inc. *Biography of Elinor Glyn*. The Literature Network. 2005. Web 27 November 2015. http://www.online-literature.com/elinor-glyn/.
Cummings, Denise. "Elinor Glyn." Women Film Pioneers Project. Columbia University Libraries Information Services, 2013. Web. 8 Dec. 2015.
Glyn, Elinor. "Her Hour of Love." *Cosmopolitan* November 1911: Pages 836–842.
_____. "Marriage Question." *Good Housekeeping* September 1913: Pages 347–352.
_____. *The Reason Why*. New York: D. Appleton and Company, 1912.
_____. *Three Weeks*. AEgypan Press, 1907.
_____. "Why I?" *Hearst's Magazine* December 1913: Pages 895–901.
It (1927). Wr: Elinor Glyn, Dir: Clarence G. Badger. Famous Players–Lasky Corporation, USA 72 mins.
Roach, Joseph. *It*. Ann Arbor: University of Michigan Press, 2011.
Such Men Are Dangerous (1930). Wr: Elinor Glyn, Dir: Kenneth Hawkes. Fox Film Corporation, USA 83 mins.

Fearless and Fierce
June Mathis

Lauren Elizabeth Smith

June Mathis, one of the most prolific screenwriters of the Silent Era, not only wrote cinema, she lived it. Mathis traumatically passed away at the young age of 40 in the same place she began her career as an entertainer, the stage. The *New York Times* reported her dramatic demise in a front-page headline: "June Mathis Heart Victim" after Mathis died suddenly of a heart attack while attending a play at a New York theatre. Mathis lived out what cinephile critics would later coin "cinema 360," or when a character starts and ends in the same place, physically, but is forever changed, emotionally, by their journey. Within her 360-degree adventure, Mathis acted, she wrote, she produced and, most notably, she had an eye for discovering silent movie magic. Her emphasis on the eyes would trickle into her work, for she once admitted in an interview, "I first notice the eyes. There I find what I call soul, and by this alone, I judge" (Tildesley 94). Analyzing Mathis' unique and influential eye creates a tribute to her life and acknowledges the career path she pioneered for women in the cutthroat world of filmmaking.

Mathis was a woman of many talents who wore many hats. The first hat she ever tried on was that of a vaudeville performer and from the start, it was a successful fit. The age of her actual premiere on stage varies in separate accounts; however, it is confirmed that she was young and her first performance was reciting at the Ladies Auxiliary of the Democratic County Committee in October 1898. Following her performance, the local paper remarked, *"Little June Mathis recited in charming style."* Mathis continued to swoon her audiences with her captivating recitals. Her proud hometown of Salt Lake City would later deem her, *"The Cleverest Child Elocutionist in this part of the country"* (Pickford 277). This cleverest child, June Beulah Hughes, was born in 1887 in Leadville, Colorado to Virginia "Jenny" Hughes. There is much controversy over Mathis' birth father. "Mathis claimed that her father was Dr. Phillip Hughes from Wales and died when she was a baby. No Phillip Hughes appears in the census. Silent film stars would often usually cite a parent's absence as a death to save from embarrassment" (Pickford 276). The truth lies somewhere between Mathis' version and her mother moving the family to Salt Lake City where she married the city's renowned pharmacist, William Mathis. Mathis was very fond of her stepfather and immediately took his last name as her own. Shortly after settling in Salt Lake City, Mathis began touring the vaudeville circuit with her grandparents, filling theatres from Chicago to New York City. Back at home, a beyond

A publicity shot of screenwriter June Mathis at her desk working on a script in 1925. Mathis always wore an opal ring when she wrote. She was convinced it brought her ideas (Academy of Motion Picture Arts and Sciences' Margaret Herrick Library).

proud papa, William, would post June's rave reviews in the window of the Mathis Drug Store.

From a young age Mathis proved she could earn her own keep. However, her stage success didn't come without stage scares. Her ongoing heart problem had her hopping from hospital beds to rehearsals. With her health manageably intact, Mathis was signed to play in *The Fascinating Widow*, a role that would give her great acclaim. She toured with the production, which sold out 20 weeks in Chicago. "Mathis noted that while touring *Widow*, a local newspaper had asked her to write an article for them. After she had done so, the editor commented that she was a good writer; why not try that for a profession? Mathis was flattered but still unsure of leaving the stage" (Pickford 279). She gained certainty and confidence through education. After two years of schooling, Mathis traded her weathered vaudeville hat for a shiny writer's cap.

One of the characteristics that set Mathis a part from other writers and filmmakers of her time was her determination to study the art of filmmaking, not only for the art's sake but the artist's sake. Gus Hardy of *Scenario-Bulletin Digest* points out, "Her debut as a motion picture writer was vastly different from the average person who gets a story idea, spends a half an hour writing it—ships it off to a motion picture company and in two weeks receives the story back plus a nicely worded rejection slip" (5). Even today, the question of whether or not a filmmaker should invest in education often leads to a heated debate. The opinions on the subject are spilt smack in the middle. One side feels education is invaluable and necessary; the other sees it as a waste of time, that the time spent studying the craft should be spent out in the industry working. It is clear that Mathis valued education, even if it was self-education. Hardy further comments, "She didn't make the mistake of submitting a 'half-baked scenario.'" She never tried to sell herself before her two years were up, that she knew the fundamentals, the basic principles of the art she was entering" (5). In order to avoid being considered a half-baked writer, Mathis buried herself in literature. She read everything from Shakespeare to De Maupassant. Mathis pays homage to Shakespeare in the writing and staging of the Romeo and Juliet–esque balcony scene between Juan and Carmen in *Blood and Sand*. Ultimately, her tenacity to self-educate paid off. The cleverness and dramatic moments in her scenarios and screenplays turned studio heads and attracted audiences, earning her a respectable salary and a profound reputation. How refreshing it is to learn that Mathis' success wasn't on account of "luck" or running into the right person at the right time; but rather, it was on account of her sleepless nights studying and her eagerness to feed her mind with the greats that wrote before her.

After two years of studying the nuts and bolts of filmmaking, Mathis tried on her writer's cap and entered a film story–writing contest. Although her entry didn't win, her scripts gained the attention of several studio heads. In 1915, she was offered a position at Metro Pictures who would go on to make and distribute her first film, *House of Tears*. Mathis climbed the ranks quickly, and after just two years was made head of the Scenario department, making her the first female film executive in history. In 1918, Mathis could wear any hat she wanted. From producing, casting, writing and editing, Mathis became one of the most powerful women in Hollywood. "Unlike other women who were paid with a high salary, Mathis was strictly behind the scenes, and no such expectations were made of her to preserve some sort of image. Though Mathis never achieved the wealth and independence that Mary Pickford did, she was the highest achieving, ranking and paid female who did not appear on camera" (Pickford 283). During her twelve-year reign in Hollywood Mathis would write and oversee over 100 films.

Just because Mathis worked behind the camera, doesn't mean she was free from scrutiny. Women in Hollywood are marked with one of two labels: Sex Kitten or Frumpy Mother. Mathis' short, stout frame clothed in modest attire and topped with frizzy locks put her into the frumpy mother category. This was especially written and said of her when she stood alongside her most valuable discovery, suave silent film star, Rudolph Valentino. However, her gutsy and adamant personality backed up by her writing talent made her looks a minor concern. Film historian Hala Pickford argues,

> After a string of successes with Valentino, Mathis continued her executive career, becoming more renowned and well paid then the year before. Not only was she not a old frumpy woman, but she was a bit of a man-eater, dating many of her protégés. At a time when so few women had power, Mathis ruled the film world despite being completely behind the scenes [276].

Mathis wasn't fighting the fight to be taken seriously alone. She had other female screenwriters such as Francis Marion, Anita Loos and Jeanie Macpherson by her side. Still, Mathis rolled with the punches when they came for her, from all directions. Pickford elaborates,

> Though not as stylish or slim as Anita Loos or Frances Marion, Mathis made up for her looks with a wit and noted bubbly personality. One interviewer said of her, "*She has wide cheeks, full grey eyes and what she frankly calls 'fat, to nourish the nerves.' Her poise is perfect. She gives the impression of tremendous reserves of energy.... Miss Mathis is thoroughly feminine*" [288].

Her tremendous energy and full grey eyes would give way to one of the greatest silent film affairs of all time.

Mathis was married to hotheaded Italian, Sylvano Balboni whom she met on set of her film *Ben Hur*, for the last three years of her life. However, it would be her relationship with a different Italian, actor Rudolph Valentino, that would define and haunt her career and reputation for all of eternity. Although Mathis can be credited with achieving a multitude of movie milestones, she will be forever shadowed by her discovery of Valentino. Was it a mentorship? Was it a love affair? Was it professional, or was it strictly a mother-son situation? The friendship between Mathis and Valentino still remains unknown territory. However, what is public knowledge is that Valentino was forever indebted to Mathis for launching him into stardom, and he sincerely treasured her for that:

> However he was found, Valentino would always speak fondly of Mathis saying, "*For seven long years, working hard, playing small parts in sometime atrocious pictures I labored to be 'found.' But it was June Mathis who opened the door of opportunity for me. She discovered me, anything I have accomplished I owe to her, to her judgment, to her advice and to her unfailing patience and confidence in me*" [Pickford 291].

After Mathis cast Valentino in her anti-war sensation, *The Four Horseman of the Apocalypse* the silent film big screen was never the same. Mathis wrote five more leading roles for Valentino that made him not only a film icon, but also a "Latin Lover" and perhaps Hollywood's first heartthrob.

If there was any man to have threatened the dynamic duo, it was director Rex Ingram, whom Mathis is also credited with discovering. "Ingram had been directing B films since 1914, and after their collaboration on *Four Horseman* the two were said to be inseparable, spending extremely long days at the studios on her masterpieces" (Pickford 286). The three collaborated on *Four Horseman* together, a box-office success that would prove to be the beginning and the end of the mighty trio. Ingram reportedly stole the beautiful extra gal, Alice Terry, from Valentino's fingertips, took her to dinner and married her. The marriage rocked Hollywood. After the scandal hit, Adela Rogers St. Johns applauded Mathis' maturity, "In public June showed the magnificent condescension of a duchess. If her heart broke in private, nobody except her friend Rudy knew it. Nothing could shake the friendship between June and Rudy" (Pickford 291). St. Johns was correct. Nothing separated these two artists, even after Valentino died from an abdominal infection at just 31 years old. Following his death, Mathis bid on the empty plot next to him. A lawsuit ensued between the two Italian families; Balbonis versus Valentinos. "Mathis said of the borrowed crypt, 'He is my guest in my future home, and I don't intend to ask him to leave'" (Pickford 307). Before the case was decided, Mathis' heart gave out. Valentino and Mathis, both gone too soon, died within a year of each other. Whether they were film fellows, friends, aficionados or like family, these two were often in sync on multiple levels. Today, Mathis and Valentino rest in peace, side by side, at Hollywood Forever Cemetery in Los Angeles.

To pigeon hole Mathis into a particular genre, style, or theme is almost impossible. From war epics (anti and pro) to melodramatic romances to comedy, Mathis immersed her written word in multiple genres and explored a number of themes and styles within these reels. Perhaps it was her executive power that allowed her to exercise such genre freedom and granted her the ability to make such bold statements on the big screen. However, sifting through her voluminous film portfolio (107 writing credits) there are patterns and tendencies that a critic is likely to detect when watching a Mathis movie. Although Mathis was known for her butchering talents, she once cut Erich von Stroheim's ten-hour epic masterpiece *Greed* (1924) down to a manageable, equally as epic, *Thriller*—many of her films exceed two hours. Her films often cover an emotional and dramatic moment in history that requires extensive attention and coverage. A Mathis movie is built on elaborate sets, full of extras and lead characters that are dressed in grandiose costumes, all qualities that prove her films were at the forefront of big-budget blockbusters. Digging underneath the technicalities, Mathis rooted her flicks in spiritual sentiment and mysticism, challenged gender codes, toyed with sexuality, and often left the audience with a harrowing life truth to savor and continue to chew on after they left the theatre.

More often than not, audiences read a Mathis movie before they were invited to watch it on screen. She had an eye for adapting films from critically acclaimed and celebrated novels and plays. Early in the silent days of cinema, completely original concepts were sometimes hard to come by and could be even harder to sell. Buying a new story meant taking a risk, and this was a bet studios were not necessarily willing to gamble. As a result, adaptations were very popular and they were especially popular with Mathis. Her successful adaptation process is demonstrated in her most beloved and revolutionary films: *The Four Horseman of the Apocalypse* (1921), *Blood and Sand* (1922), *The Saphead* (1920) and *Camille* (1921); all of which will be discussed and dissected further. Film historian Hala Pickford defines the Mathis masterpiece best, "Most of her films were somewhere between the two genres, using drama and humor, with a heavy dose of spiritualist themes about redemption and the power of belief. Mathis' masterpieces seem to be quite long, considering they stay consistently entertaining speaks well of her skill" (Pickford 280).

Mathis had been certain from a young age that she could make a spectacle bigger and better than anything seen or heard before, and the shot heard around the world was exactly what she did with *The Four Horseman of the Apocalypse*. *Four Horseman* is Mathis' most significant screenwriting contribution for it not only satisfies all requirements of the Mathis masterpiece, but, equally as important, it situated her as one of the most powerful woman in Hollywood to date. It was her casting of Valentino and her selecting director Ingram that ultimately determined the huge success of the film. Under Mathis' rule, "*Four Horsemen* would be the highest grossing film of 1921 beating out Charlie Chaplin's *The Kid*. It would gross $9 million (in 1933 dollars) and be the 6th best-selling silent film ever" (Pickford 287). Its monetary gains matched its cultural revenue, which is fascinating considering at the time, the United States was rampant in xenophobia. The film popularized the Argentinian dance, the tango, and proved that a dark-skinned actor, given the chance, was more than capable of carrying the weight of an American film.

When the film was released, playwright Robert E. Sherwood wrote in *Life* magazine, "*The Four Horsemen of the Apocalypse* is a living, breathing answer to those who still refuse to take motion pictures seriously. Its production lifts the silent drama to an artistic plane that it has never touched before." Mathis was involved in everything from writing the script, to casting, to editing the final product. It was her efforts in all these areas that introduced diversity in race, religion and sexuality to American audiences. Film historian

Thomas Slater comments on Mathis' risk, "Furthermore, Julio (Valentino) becomes a war hero, and American audiences would most likely want such a figure, even if he were in the French army, represented by an ethnically acceptable "white" actor. Mathis resisted or ignored all such pressures in casting Valentino. Her bold casting choice is where the quote that sums her talent in visual storytelling first came into existence, "I first notice the eyes. There I find what I call soul, and by this alone, I judge" (84). Mathis took motion pictures seriously, and she did so by refusing to obey Hollywood's whitewashed hiring and casting.

Out of the quartet of films, *Four Horseman* carries the most spiritual weight, for its plot is based on the Bible's final book of Revelation. The last scene between Julio's father and Tchernoff at the cemetery especially hones in on the Christian undertones. "When Julio's father asks if he knew his son, Tchernoff spreads his arms in a crucifixion pose and answers, "I knew them all." The final title states that only when love replaces hatred in men's hearts will the terrors of the four horsemen end. Such a transformation is possible through the guidance of spirituality'" (Slater 108). However spiritually inclined her films were, Mathis' movies were not entirely straightedge, Christian films. "When speaking of Christianity and film, Mathis would usually proclaim that she believed in clean comedy, finding European films 'vulgar.'" It seems in private Mathis felt differently, as she inserted clever comedic and scandalous bits into many of her films. In *Four Horseman,* she deliberately inserted a small bit of German soldiers cross-dressing" (282). Mathis was aware that this famous scene of the German soldiers parading in drag would jolt audiences. She told the *Los Angeles Times,* "'I had the German officers coming down the stairs with women's clothing on. To hundreds of people that meant no more than a masquerade party. To those who had lived and read, and who understood life, that scene stood out as one of the most terrific things in the picture'" (Slater 82). Just as one of her title cards in *Four Horseman* states:

> The world was dancing.
> Paris had succumbed to
> the mad rhythm of the
> Argentine tango.

America had succumbed to the mad rhythm of the Mathis movie.

Blood and Sand, another film with Valentino as the lead, is centered on Spain's most cherished sport, bull-fighting. The film tracks a toreador, Juan (Valentino) and his career as a bullfighter from boyhood to his demise. Mathis' titles are littered with spiritual proverbs such as, "Tall trees gather much wind." Additionally, the character of the Philosopher is meant to hit the audience over the head with the bittersweet realities of love and life. These quotes include: "Impure love is like a flame, when it is burnt out, there is nothing left but the embers of disgust and regret"; "Passion is a game which was invented by the devil at which only two can play" and "Happiness and prosperity that's built on cruelty and bloodshed cannot survive." The final line in the film, and arguably the biggest admonition is spoken directly by the Philosopher, "But out there is a beast with ten thousand heads." The Philosopher is referring to the audience in the bull-fighting arena (or perhaps the audience in the movie theatre) as the beast. In a broader sense, the audience represents society, who is the biggest beast and critic of them all. The them appears to be if we, the toreador, allow the beast to define and influence us, it will cause us to crumble, if not bring us to our death, just as they did to our toreador, Juan. Mathis' movies often leave the audience with a life application that's told through a Mathis metaphor.

The manifestation of mysticism in *Blood and Sand* went hand in hand with its murder of masculinity. Juan was not only crippled by society, but even more so by the women in his life. In the romantic balcony scene, the camera switches to Juan's wife Carmen's point of view and the audience stares at Juan through the bars of a balcony. The angle suggests that women imprison Juan. This notion is further supported in a title card that reads, "Woman was created for the happiness of man, but instead she destroyed the tranquility of the world." Thomas Slater argues, "More importantly, Mathis presented strong women who possessed the courage and values needed to reconstruct masculinity in a more positive fashion." Although women wearing the pants in the relationship can be considered strong and powerful, especially given the time period, Carmen and Doña Sol (Juan's lovers) rocked the tranquility of Juan's world to an incredible fault and at the expense of their own identities. Both women we're damned if they did love and damned if they did not. Carmen was punished for being a loyal wife and a delicate, spiritual woman. Her beauty sent Juan running and into the sharp fangs of the seductive Doña Sol who was referred to as "the serpent of Hell" keeping Juan from taking responsibility for his own adultery. Additionally, Juan's fellow matador asks him, "Are you more afraid of a woman than the wild beasts of the arena?" Yes, this question mocks Juan's masculinity as Slater suggests, but it also demeans woman. So while Carmen and Doña Sol carry significance in the film, they do so to the degree that makes the audience fear them and compare them to evil beasts. Slater's point is valid. Mathis' films did redefine masculinity, but that did not make them a complete victory for women. Carmen and Doña Sol did survive the battle on the big screen, but are they genuinely represented or respected? Because fear does not replace respect, the answer has to be no.

The Saphead provides Mathis' drama top-heavy filmography with comedic relief. It's one of a handful of comedies that she was involved in, despite her keen interest the genre. The film has more of a historical importance than anything as it was silent comedian star, Buster Keaton's feature length debut. *Saphead* is peppered with Keaton quirks. He is portrayed as a clumsy sap constantly tripping down stairs and taking his bullying at the stock exchange with a sourpuss pout. Today, Keaton fans criticize *Saphead* for not being close to the capers Keaton would later create, writing it off as slow and boring. However, it's vintage Keaton and it's likely that he, at beginning of his career, didn't have control over the story. It's highly likely Miss Mathis was in control. Despite the criticism, the climactic scene at the stock exchange gives the audience a taste of the physical gags Keaton would tickle audiences with for years to follow. Nora Sayre of the *New York Times* wrote, "The sublime somersaults and the stoicism enhance a hazing scene where men knock one another's hats off on the floor of the Stock Exchange—a refreshing view of that institution." It's a mystery whether Mathis had any say in this iconic somersault sensation. If she did, Keaton is yet another man to add to the list of those forever indebted to June Mathis.

Then there is *Camille*, a heartwrenching, melodramatic romance that would be remade and loved by Hollywood and audiences again and again. The film brought Valentino and his wife Natacha Rambova (art director) together. *Camille* stands out from the other four movies because the lead is a woman. Unfortunately, it's similar to the others in that she is a woman who strips a man of his masculinity, and does so in a way that ends up backfiring on her. The figurative castration of Armand (Valentino) does Camille's (Alla Nazimova) image more harm than good. Camille is a Parisian courtesan who is doomed when she falls for Armand and finally gives real love a chance. The film ends in Armand's favor, even after he humiliates Camille by throwing money at her in front of a room of elites at a casino party. Days later Camille falls ill and is sentenced to her deathbed. In modern parlance, the film is a sob story about a sick prostitute dying alone. However, Armand doesn't completely win the day either. As she did with *Blood and Sand*, Mathis reduced her characters to animals. In *Camille* Mathis connects men to dogs. Slater supports this idea, "Connecting characters to animals, seeps into Valentino's character as well. Mathis creates parallels via associations between men and animals and ones that ridicule men and traditional masculinity. For example, in *Camille*, "Armand tells her, 'I wish I were a relative—your servant—a dog—that I might care for you, nurse you—cure you'" (113). Armand performs this line on his knees, gaining extra sympathy points from the audience. While Camille stands high and mighty above him, she is portrayed as a low, wicked person for putting the poor Armand in such a compromising position.

Though *Camille* ended on a negative note, the film positively teased lines of sexuality. "Gavin Lambert, in his biography of Nazimova (Camille), claims that Mathis liked to put small unconventional sexual elements into her scripts. For example, in Nazimova's Camille, co-starring Valentino, the great actress fawns over the young Patsy Ruth Miller, playing a friend who stops by her apartment" (Slater 82). In the intimate, after party scene, Camille and Patsy's characters were very affectionate, holding each other in their arms and kissing frequently. Additionally, Camille was very protective of Patsy's character. She eventually tells a male friend to, "Take your hands off—she's too good for you!" Her words are followed up with a possessive glare. This was a small interaction, yet its taboo elements made a lasting impression. Imagine how many more barriers Mathis could have hurdled had she lived longer.

Some could argue that Mathis' adoration for adaptation compromised her ability to show a distinctive flair of her own, and that her work lacked originality. However, that opinion skips acknowledging that this woman was original in the risks she took to create these movies. Mathis had bite and wasn't afraid to use it. "Mathis was never one to be shy with the opposite sex. She enjoyed telling the story of a drunken leading man who tried to rape her in her dressing room. Mathis bit him on his shoulder and 'held on like a little bulldog' until he let her go" (Pickford 286). This woman wrote the original screen version of *Ben Hur* and eerie drama-thrillers, such as *Greed*. Additionally, Mathis wrote and produced action-packed, violent, "masculine" epics, a task largely left to male directors in today's gender-biased world. Whether the concepts were completely original or not, it is important to acknowledge it was a woman who was in charge of these scenarios. Today, women are largely absent from the action-adventure epics behind the camera and on screen. Even with female chairman Donna Langley as the face of Universal Pictures, a company celebrated for its blockbuster budget crunchers, women are still denied the opportunity to write, produce, or direct the next *Fast in the Furious* or *Transformers*. Time's up. It's time for modern June Mathis types to unleash their inner bulldogs.

Mathis' masterpieces, Mathis' movies, Mathis' metaphors—the empowering alliterations connected to this remarkable woman are endless. However, what is truly forever is the Mathis magic. Hollywood has come to a point to where who but a magician, could trick society into thinking a woman could be relied on, let alone given an opportunity, to write, cast, produce, edit and manage a film from scratch. If one matches Mathis' fearless and fierce determination and continues carrying the fiery torch she lit for women in the film industry, a torch that burns with race, religion, sexuality and gender bends, there is a possibility that her movie magic can be restored. When asked about censorship, Mathis firmly answered, "You can't portray life and obey the censor!" I wonder if she knew her exclamation would ring universally true a hundred years after it left her mouth? Mathis may have hung up her filmdom cap, but her legacy of ignoring the beasts lives on.

WORKS CITED

Ben Hur: A Tale of the Christ (1925). Screenplay. Wr: June Mathis. Dir. Fred Niblo, Metro-Goldwyn-Mayer, USA 142 mins.
Blood and Sand (1922). Wr: June Mathis, Dir: Fred Niblo, Paramount Pictures, USA 80 mins.
Camille (1921). Wr: June Mathis, Dir: Ray C. Smallwood, Metro, USA 72 mins.
The Four Horseman of the Apocalypse (1921). Wr: June Mathis, Dir: Rex Ingram, Metro Pictures Corporation, USA 150 mins.
Hardy, Gus. "June Mathis: Her Career." *Scenario Bulletin Digest* 4 Sept. 1924: 5–7. Web.
Rambova, Natacha, and Hala Pickford. "June Mathis Biography." *Rudolph Valentino: A Wife's Memories of an Icon*. Hollywood, CA: 1921 PVG Pub., 2009. 275–305.
The Saphead (1920). Wr: June Mathis, Dir: Herbert Blache and Winchell Smith, Metro, USA 77 mins.
Sayre, Nora. "Screen: 'The Saphead': Buster Keaton Shines in 1920 Feature The Cast." *New York Times*. Web. 28 Aug. 1974.
Slater, Thomas J. "June Mathis' Valentino Scripts: Images of Male 'Becoming' After the Great War." *Cinema Journal* 50.1 (2010): 99–120. Web.
Slater, Thomas J. "Moving the Margins to Mainstream: June Mathis's Work in American Silent Film." *International Journal of Humanities* (2007): 81–87.
Tildesley, Alice. "The Road to Fame." *Motion Picture Magazine*, April 1926:43, 94–95.

Writing Around Lois Weber

Chase Thompson

Receiving 118 writing credits, 137 directing credits, 102 acting credits, and 19 producing credits in one's lifetime should secure them a spot in film history. However, Lois Weber is seldom more than a footnote in the zeitgeist of early Hollywood. Like many underappreciated artists, Weber died penniless and alone with only her films to preserve her legacy. Unfortunately, many of Weber's films have not survived or been transferred for modern screening technology, making her impact on film history more difficult to process. Instead, much of the credit for pioneering early Hollywood is given to Weber's male contemporaries, D.W. Griffith and Cecil B. DeMille. Only recently have historians and researchers begun to truly see the impact Weber posed on the silent era of film. Weber's decision to focus on social issues rather than spectacle and physical comedy created milestones for Americans to measure how far they had come socially and, in many cases, how little things had changed. Now, 100 years removed from her earliest films, we can now see a bigger picture. With few clues to work with, historians must turn to her films, documented relationships, and articles to try to piece together her story. The following pages examine the life and work of Lois Weber while considering the conditions that led to her omission from Hollywood's opening chapter.

At the height of her career, "Weber would receive an annual salary amounting to $5,000 per week, making her the highest-paid director in Hollywood" (Stamp 148). So how did a modest girl from Allegheny, Pennsylvania become the highest paid director, male or female, in Hollywood? Like many successful creative people, their stories begin with an eventful childhood. Florence Lois Weber, born on the 13th of June 1879, was deeply inspired by her father. The stories he told Lois would have a lasting effect on her and, although she would go on to direct, produce, and act, at her core she was a writer. Stamp explains:

> Weber spoke of tremendous fondness about her father, an upholsterer and decorator who had worked on the Pittsburgh Opera House. "We were great pals," she said, recounting his talent for telling "fascinating fairy stories…" To him she credited her artistic temperament and her talent for writing stories. "I don't remember when I did not write," she said [11].

Weber's passion for writing stayed with her for the rest of her life and it was her desire to be in control of all aspects of filmmaking that allows audiences a clear view into her mind. Her love for writing could also be her reason for directing her own films. By playing the role of writer and director, there were fewer chances for Weber's message to be misinterpreted on screen.

Writer Lois Weber takes charge behind the camera, circa 1916. Silent film actress, screenwriter, producer and director, Weber is considered to be one of the most important female directors the American film industry has known (courtesy Cari Beauchamp).

Many women writers of the silent era, like Weber's life-long friend Frances Marion, found their way to writing through acting. In the early days of the silent era, a pretty face was a foot in the door for an aspiring actress. Although Weber acted for the stage in her teenage years and would go on to act in many of her own films, it was her writing that first brought her into making films. Biographer Shelley Stamp explains, "Like many other women of her generation, she first became interested in pictures by writing scenarios" (13). Because the film industry was so young and unorthodox, it offered many opportunities for people with drive and aspirations of storytelling. This included women. Film historian Cari Beauchamp sheds light on this period in Hollywood's history by explaining, "Women flocked to Hollywood, where they could flourish.... With few taking moviemaking very seriously as a business, the doors were wide open to women" (12). The conditions were right for anyone with vision and drive to break in to movie making. It was during this migration that Weber and Marion would first meet. Marc Norman's account of this meeting in his book *What Happens Next: A History of American Screenwriting* contrasts slightly with Beauchamp's. Speaking of Marion, Norman says, "Her good looks had landed her a job in Hollywood in the early 1910s as an actress.... A woman director, Lois Weber, noting her intelligence, assigned her to write dialogue for extras" (39). It should be noted that this is the only mention of Weber in his entire *History of Screenwriting* book.

Already having more than two-dozen credits to her name, Weber was well established when Marion entered the scene at Bosworth Studios in 1914. Beauchamp says, "Bosworth... owned the studio where Frances [Marion] was first hired as an actress and assistant to the director Lois Weber at fifteen dollars a week" (10). Both Beauchamp and Norman establish that Weber and Marion met during a filming at Bosworth Studios in the early to mid-1910s. However, Norman's tone and dismissal of Weber as a pioneer is one of the many contributing factors that leads to Weber's lack of recognition as a writer and director. Referring to her as "a woman director" and ignoring her for the rest of his text shows that he views her as an exception and not an important part in the history of writers and directors in early Hollywood.

Like her contemporaries, Weber was trying to make her audiences think. Griffith's follow up film to his historic *Birth of a Nation* (1915), *Intolerance: Love's Struggle Throughout the Ages* (1916) looked at four different timelines across 2,500 years. Griffith made this an issue film to examine human's intolerance over centuries. By mixing historical and modern storylines, Griffith forced the audience to decide where they stood. Thomas H. Ince also used American history to capitalize on public interest. In his films *The Battle of the Red Men* (1912) and *The Deserter* (1912), Ince uses the Native American's narrative in the same way Griffith used the Ku Klux Klan's to mold his story. DeMille would also use the historical approach and explored the Native American experience in *Squaw Man* (1914), a film he would remake as a talkie in 1931. The common denominator between each of these films is their use of historical events to critique both the past and modern society. Weber took a different approach. She used the present issues facing her times to boldly confront her audiences. For example, she explored themes such as sexual harassment in *Sunshine Molly* (1915), abortion in *Where Are My Children?* (1916), capital punishment in *The People Vs. John Doe* (1916), birth control in *The Hand That Rocks the Cradle* (1917), and infidelity in *Two Wise Wives* (1921). By putting these issues on-screen directly, Weber was not entertaining her audiences as much as she was holding a mirror in front of them.

By examining the present instead of looking at the past for inspiration, Weber was going against the grain of her fellow filmmakers. Her ability to address social issues showed great foresight as a filmmaker and distinguished her from many of her contemporaries. Stamp explains some of Weber's distinctions:

> When Weber disparaged happy endings in favor of more complicated plots, she was not simply rejecting filmmaking formulas; she was calling for a wholesale rethinking of tropes surrounding heterosexual romance.... When she advocated nuanced character development over action ... she was demanding that we rethink roles typically assigned to men and women on screen [30].

Choosing to take risks on controversial social issue films may have played into her fall from public interest in the 1920s and '30s. While this cannot be certain, one thing is clear from her films, Weber was there to deliver a message. Film historian Kay Sloan states, "Weber had always seen her film career as an opportunity to advance her moral convictions.... [Weber] confided to a journalist, 'The newspaper and the clergyman each do much good in their respective fields and I feel that, like them, I can, in this motion picture field, also deliver a message to the world'" (341). With the loose morals of the roaring '20s rapidly approaching, Weber's method of social introspection would be put to the test.

By 1914, Weber and then-husband Phillips Smalley were well established as writers and filmmakers. According to Stamp, "By 1914 Weber had already completed more than 200 pictures" (16). Many of these films and collaborations with Smalley took place during their tenure at Rex Motion Picture Company (Rex), an independent studio that would later fall under the Universal motion picture umbrella. Weber's early films at Rex began with *A Heroine of '76* (1911). In this piece of historical fiction, Weber plays the part of a woman who foils an assassination attempt on George Washington while losing her life in the process. Even from the very beginning, Weber was already exploring women's issues and gender roles. In the case of *A Heroine of '76*, Weber is asking the question, "What if one of our nation's greatest generals was saved by a woman? Would that change anything?" In Rex's first year, the independent studio released 56 films. While these films lacked the spectacle of a Griffith picture, they made up for it with provocation.

Within one year, Rex had tripled in size, and in January of 1912 the company began releasing two films per week. "We worked very hard," Weber recalled of her time at Rex. "I wrote the scenarios, Mr. Smalley selected the types, assisted in directing, and we both acted" (Stamp 16). During her time at Rex, Weber's catalog of films included *The Greater Christian* (1912), *The Power of Thought* (1912), *The Dragon's Breath* (1913), *His Sister* (1913), *Woman's Burden* (1914), *The Final Pardon* (1914), *The Spider and Her Web* (1914), and *On Suspicion* (1914). All of these films have strong female protagonists and could be considered "high-brow" because of their social commentary. The sheer volume of short films Weber and Smalley made at Rex allowed them to experiment and hone their craft, not only in writing but also in perfecting the visuals.

Weber's 1913 film *Suspense* is a great example of her innovations in visual storytelling. In the film, a hobo intruder cuts the telephone line as a frantic mother of a newborn calls her husband for help. All three of these scenes are depicted in a single composition. By using a triangle matte, Weber is able to have three different perspectives unfolding together in real-time. This effect has been copied numerous times by filmmakers in a variety of scenes but never to the extent as it was in the 2000 film *Time Code* where four stories unfold in real-time simultaneously across the entire feature-length film. While *Suspense* moves the audience through the will-he-get-there-in-time plot, it puts her typically strong female character in the passenger seat and lets the husband be the hero. For this reason, *Suspense* feels like it was written more by Smalley than Weber. If a viewer is familiar with her other works, they expect the female character to play a more active role and stand up to the intruding hobo, but she never does. *Suspense* also sticks out from her other work because the hobo has absolutely no motivation to harm the woman. This lack of motivation felt strange and uncharacteristic of Weber and further suggests that Smalley played a larger role in the writing of *Suspense*, while Weber focused her efforts on the visual storytelling.

Releasing two films each week at Rex allowed Weber and Smalley to explore themes that would directly contrast with the slapstick vaudevillian comedy that was popular at the time. While many writers and directors were aiming at the gut, Weber was aiming at the head. Weber and Smalley had outgrown Rex and would sign with Bosworth, Inc. This migration would align with the audiences' demands for longer films and Weber would make the leap into writing, producing and directing feature-length films.

While at Bosworth, Weber and Smalley would go on to make some of their most important and successful films. The titles created for Bosworth would explore similar themes and techniques used at Rex but on a much larger scale. *Hypocrites* (1915), for example, used complicated double exposures of a nude woman, which was considered very cutting edge at the time. According to Mahar, "While its negative cost was $18,000, it earned $119,000 in sales in the United States alone and made Weber a 'household name'" (96). Profit margins of this scale allowed Weber and Smalley to pursue whatever topic they wished with complete autonomy.

Weber and Smalley were adapting nicely to the making of feature films, and while their time at Bosworth was brief, they continued to build on their number of credits together. One of those credits included *Sunshine Molly*, their last film at Bosworth. This film revealed Weber's appreciation of a new character—the environment. Weber stayed away from close ups and preferred to compose her shots in wide and full-body shots, bringing attention to the environment. Using a location to suggest something about the characters' psychology may have been lost on the audience at the time. On many of her films at Bosworth, Weber stayed with her well-composed and well-lit compositions rather than close up images with quick cuts. This forced her characters to act more with their gestures and less with their facial expressions. Her failure to recognize the trend of close-ups and quicker editing early on could have factored into her losing touch with her audience in the coming decade.

Nineteen fifteen would be a landmark year for Weber. She would find herself mayor of Universal City and under an extremely lucrative, hands-off contract with Universal Studios. Andrea Richards of Bitch Magazine describes this time in Weber's life:

> At Universal, she had complete control over the subject matter of her films, using her freedom to take on taboo topics like abortion, capital punishment, and racial prejudice. Not only did she make some 16 features there, she also encouraged other women, including the actors Cleo Madison and Dorothy Davenport, to direct. Weber's influence at the studio extended even further: She was elected the mayor of Universal City, California, in 1915 [67].

Weber's time at Universal was brief but prolific. She would gain the trust and respect of Carl Laemmle who had complete faith in Weber. It must have been a difficult decision, but in 1917 Weber left her throne at Universal to start her own company. Because she was already working with little to no oversight at Universal, her decision to leave could have been perceived as a slap in the face. It is unknown what provoked this sea change. Richards explains, "Weber left Universal to found an independent company, Lois Weber Productions. This act was both a harbinger of things to come and a reflection of what was already in the air" (67). Weber's confidence and self-assurance that she would be able to be independent in Hollywood aligned with her audiences' preference towards longer, more complex stories.

During her time at Lois Weber Productions Weber made the work that would make her most proud. Over the next five years, Weber created a volume of work and brought several young women into stardom. Mildred Harris (later married to Charlie Chaplin) was one of these stars. In two years the duo cranked out *The Price of a Good Time* (1917), *The Doctor and the Woman* (1918), *For Husbands Only* (1918), *Borrowed Clothes* (1918), *When a Girl Loves* (1919), *Home* (1919) and *Forbidden* (1919). The popularity of Weber's films with Harris struck a long-ringing chord with her audiences. Weber credited her success to not being tied down to the bureaucracy of a convoluted studio system. Quoting Weber herself, Stamp explains:

> Enjoying "full authority," Weber found herself "free of that vacillation shattering of objectives from which many organizations now suffer where half a dozen executive heads must come to an agreement about their story, director and cast, on which subjects no two of them have the same idea" [147].

For any auteur, getting a single voice and vision to transcend all the obstacles is the greatest challenge. It is especially challenging in film because there are so many moving parts and opinions involved. In her films made at her own studio, Weber's voice was never clearer. Her final film under Lois Weber Productions would be what many fans and critics agree is her masterpiece, *The Blot* (1921).

Weber's control of cinematography, directing, and social commentary all culminate in her feature-length film *The Blot*. Technically, *The Blot* encompasses many styles that are visible in Weber's early work. The architecture of the lecture hall echoes her use of architecture as a psychological tool as it did in the cafeteria scenes in *Sunshine Molly*. Her title mattes are more evolved by the way they contain vignettes of moving images that pertain to the text on screen. For example, we see the text, "Professor Andrew Theodore Griggs whose reward for long and faithful service was less than a bare living wage." To the right of this text is Professor Griggs preparing to give his lecture. This image is not a freeze frame; it is footage of the man we are reading about. This effect is much more personal and communicates more of his character than if we were just reading a title card. Weber uses this technique to give the main characters more depth and instantly provide backstory to set up a more complex scene. Weber also used superimposed imagery and creative dissolves in *The Blot* to provide deeper insight into what each character is thinking. Similar to the way Weber superimposed the image of an "unwanted" angel child in *Where Are My Children?* to show us exactly what the woman is thinking, Weber makes the viewer aware of Phil West's admiration of Professor Griggs' daughter, Amelia, from his sketchbook. The drawings in his book are motivated and have been previously referred to earlier during the opening scene, but in the case of Amelia's drawing, the viewer sees a beautiful profile that slowly dissolves into the real Amelia. This transition works on many levels. The amount of care and detail put into Amelia's drawing is much higher than the previous drawings we have seen in Phil's sketchbook. When the shot begins to fade to Amelia working in the library, it not only naturally transports the viewer to her; it shows that Phil is thinking about her in a romantic way. It comes as no surprise when we see Phil arriving at the library counter to checkout a book and flirt with Amelia in the following scene.

While the visual techniques I have described from *The Blot* are effective and well crafted, the most important one is the use of point-of-view camerawork (POV). In the scene where Mrs. Griggs takes inventory of their home, we do not simply see that they are poor; we feel it. Mrs. Griggs is depressed and embarrassed about being poor and we feel this because of Weber's use of POV shots. As Mrs. Griggs looks around the rooms she sees that her upholstery is in shambles, the rug is wearing thin, grandmother is ill, and their guest has expensive shoes. All of this information is given without a title card. We are shown, not told—the essence of good writing and directing. What is so masterful in this approach is that Weber only uses the POV shots for Mrs. Griggs. This makes her character all the more important and literally lets us view the world from her perspective. Jennifer Parchesky discusses the significance of these POV shots in her article "Lois Weber's *The Blot*: Rewriting Melodrama, Reproducing the Middle Class."

> Feminist critics E. Ann Kaplan and Lisa Rudman have observed that the film's use of point-of-view cutting from the perspective of a female character (the professor's wife) is a radical departure from Hollywood practice and makes *The Blot*, like many of Weber's other films, a strikingly women-centered narrative [23].

Combining all of these techniques allows the audience to be more in-tune with the psychology of the characters and tell a deeper, more nuanced story.

The decision to tell a melodrama about a professor's struggle to make a living wage is odd in many ways. Why would a filmmaker that has tackled issues as bold as capital punishment and abortion want to add professors' salaries to her list? From her earliest films, Weber used the medium to spread her morals, messages, and beliefs with the greater public. One explanation for telling a story about professor salaries is that she merely wanted a large, middle-class audience. While Griffith and DeMille were speaking to their audience through spectacle and grandeur, which felt realistic to their audiences at the time, Weber was trying to tap into something that was more real. At one point in *The Blot*, Weber shows us a close-up of an article. Phil brings these articles to his father, the wealthiest college trustee, as evidence that professors are underpaid. While this is a ploy for the hand of Amelia, the articles were very real. Parchesky explains, "Weber makes use of 'documentary evidence' from the print media to establish the reality of the problem she addresses" (26). Using real published articles within her film helps anchor the truth of her claims and show that these issues existed and she was not pulling them out of thin air. Moreover, from a historical context, using print media of the time helps paint a better picture of the world in which Weber's films were made.

Why *The Blot* would be Weber's last film at her own studio is puzzling. There are speculations that her divorce from Smalley proved too devastating and that she was simply burned out from the constant process of making films for a decade. While these may have been contributing factors, they did not keep her from making films. The further away we get from 1922, the less we see the name Lois Weber. However, she was able to keep making films. Through her films up to this point, we see a consistent voice of strict morality on a wide range of social issues. Weber tried to adapt with the loose morals of the Roaring '20s. For example, several of Weber's 1920s Universal titles include *A Chapter in Her Life* (1923) and *Sensation Seekers* (1927). The scenarios from these films are much more melodramatic and feel far removed from the woman who brought us such controversial films as *Hypocrites* and *Where Are My Children?* In her final film, *White Heat* (1934), Weber returned to provocative subject matter addressing interracial relationships. In the film, a Hawaiian plantation owner becomes involved with a native woman and betrays their love by taking a white woman as his wife.

Understanding why Lois Weber is just recently starting to gain recognition for her contributions to filmmaking is as mysterious as it is intriguing. The answer is: there is no single answer. Many factors are responsible for her earlier omission. One reason is while many of her films, like *The Blot*, are in the public domain, they have yet to be made readily available to the masses. *The Blot* was released as part of a Library of Congress collection titled *The Origins of Film* (2001) and most recently released by Grapevine Video (2012). Due to the painstaking process of restoring films, these releases remain expensive and further prevent Weber's work from reaching the mainstream. We should be seeing her body of work live on in the digital era as we do with her male contemporaries. Weber's lack of a digital presence in the 21st century is certainly a major hurdle keeping her films from reaching a broader audience. By adding her public domain works to websites such as archive.org, Weber's films will continue to critique the past and present. Other reasons for Weber's limited acknowledgment include changes in the way major studios made movies, shifts in audience preference to celebrity actors instead of directors, and sexist historians that choose not to write about her. We want a single explanation for why such a prominent figure can so easily be dismissed, but there is not one. Omission from history is more complex than that.

If Weber's films become more readily available, the public will have an increased knowledge of the Hollywood pioneer and she will write herself back into the history books. The name Lois Weber will become more than a footnote, known not just as one of the few "women directors" of the time, but as a writer, producer, actor, activist, and director during Hollywood's infancy.

On December 3, 2015, Weber's film *Shoes* (1916) screened at the Linwood Dunn Theater in Hollywood, California. Weber's films have also appeared in the San Francisco Silent Film Festival (2011) and annually at the Lois Weber Film Festival in Grand Prairie, Texas. Weber addressed many social issues. As our country continues to have growing pains, we will be able to refer to her for guidance, inspiration and assurance that a determined voice can never be silenced.

Works Cited

Beauchamp, Cari. *Without Lying Down Frances Marion and the Powerful Women of Early Hollywood*. Berkeley: University Press of California, 1998.
Mahar, Karen Ward. *Women Filmmakers in Early Hollywood*. Baltimore: Johns Hopkins University Press, 2008.
Norman, Marc. *What Happens Next: A History of American Screenwriting*. New York: Harmony, 2007.
Parchesky, Jennifer. "Lois Weber's The Blot: Rewriting Melodrama, Reproducing the Middle Class." *Cinema Journal* 39:1 (Fall 1999).
Richards, Andrea. *Bitch Magazine: Feminist Response to Pop Culture*. Spring 2007, Issue 35, p. 67.
Sloan, Kay. "The Hand That Rocks the Cradle: An Introduction" *Film History* 1:4 (1987): 341–366.
Stamp, Shelley. *Lois Weber in Early Hollywood*. Oakland: University of California Press, 2015.

Gene Gauntier
Ascending by Drowning
Yasser Omar Shahin

A 21-year-old woman who risks her life for a life in motion pictures should not be called crazy, she should be called ambitious. Or she should be called Gene Gauntier (also known as Mrs. Jack Clark, or Genevieve G. Liggett), the screenwriter-director whose very first appearance in motion pictures came as an actress after she auditioned for the Biograph Studios in 1906. Gauntier was asked by director Sidney Olcott, who later became her business partner, to play the role of a drowning girl in a short film. In his book *The First Female Stars: Women of the Silent Era* David W. Menefee reports that after Gauntier explained that she could not swim, "Olcott soothed her worries with a promise she would only get her feet wet" (72). Gauntier agreed to play the stunt role for this picture and showed up the following morning at the South Beach. When the director of the film found out that Gauntier did not know how to swim, he was furious and "railed at Olcott for hiring the wrong girl for the job and threatened to call production to a halt for the day" (72). Though Gauntier came close to drowning while playing the part, that perseverance became a trademark to her successful career in early cinema. As an actress-writer, she remembered, "I was terrified at each daring thing I had to do ... but for some inexplicable reason, I continued to write them" (Wrathall). In the career she wrote for herself, Gauntier contributed to motion pictures as a writer, producer, director, and business owner.

When Gauntier's name is mentioned, it is commonly associated with great directors, companies, actresses, actors, producers, screenplays, and films. Gauntier was truly a pioneer in the motion picture world at its outset. According to Anne Ciecko in *Hollywood's "Scriptgirls"* Gauntier "wrote and performed all her own action stunts in the popular series *Adventures of a Girl Spy*. In addition, she tried her hand at directing" (230). Gauntier sailed through cinema from the port of the silent era. As an actress she played many roles both in and outside the United States, visiting several continents in her travels. She produced films ranging from shorts to feature length. She first co-directed and then solo directed. But most importantly, Gauntier was always a screenwriter.

Like many other writers, Gauntier started her career by adapting a book. Early on, Gauntier was asked to adapt *Ben-Hur* and "the work involved into the controversy that established the first copyright laws covering motion pictures" (Bisplinghoff). Gauntier did not know that this adaptation would start a battle in the courts, the results of which still affect the legal aspects of writing in the United States and the rest of the world. It began in 1907 when Frank J. Marion, who worked as a sales manager at the Mutoscope-Biograph, moved to join the Kalem Company, established by George Kleine, and Samuel Long.

This choice influenced Sidney Olcott to follow Marion. Olcott, in turn, convinced Gauntier to join him at the Kalem Company, which she did without hesitation. When Marion noticed what a brilliant writer Gauntier was, he "placed an urgent call to Gene to quickly adapt *Ben-Hur* for a quick picture to be made at the Sheepshead Park racetrack" (Menefee 73). Despite being a short film, with only sixteen scenes over a 1,000-foot reel, it made a big splash in the market. People watched the film repeatedly, including the Harper Brothers and General Lew Wallace, the publishers of the original book. They were not pleased that their work had made money for others without their being informed, let alone involved.

The Harpers and Wallace filed a suit against the Kalem Company, alleging that their copyright had been infringed (Menefee). Four years later the suit was settled in favor of the plaintiffs. The 1911 decision "cost the company twenty-five thousand dollars in damages and another twenty-five thousand dollars in legal fees, making the film the costliest one-reeler of the time" (Stempel 8). The case established new laws and rules for adaptation and screenwriting. Prior to this court action, many other scripts had been adapted into screenplays without the original writers' knowledge or permission. This supposition leads to some analytical questions: How many of the great films made during the silent era were similar to *Ben Hur* in this regard? How many scripts made it all the way to the top the same way as it was entirely possible for someone to adapt a foreign book during the silent era without informing the original writer?

Writer Gene Gauntier, circa 1919. A woman of great determination, Gauntier nearly drowned during her very first acting job in an effort to prove to the producer and director that she could play the scene realistically (Academy of Motion Picture Arts and Sciences' Margaret Herrick Library).

With the case behind them, Gauntier became known as the first "Kalem Girl" and the films she wrote and starred in revolutionized film locations: "In the early years of silent film, the Kalem Company made significant contributions to on-location filming, often going as far afield as Florida, Ireland and the Middle East" (Harner 1). Dr. Sara Ross, who teaches Women in Film, Film History, Narrative Video Production, and Screenwriting as an associate professor at Sacred Heart University, made it clear that the Kalem Company indeed pioneered taking a film crew across borders and over oceans to create a picture. "In 1910, the Kalem film company sent a small group of filmmakers from New York City to scenic County Cork, Ireland, where they shot the emigrant drama *The Lad From Old Ireland*, reportedly ... the first American fiction film made outside the Americas" (Ross 80–82). In a short time, Gauntier had become a pillar of the Kalem Company and part of this revolution:

> For four years I headed their foreign companies, writing every picture they produced abroad, Mr. Clark playing the leads,—in Ireland, England, Scotland, Germany, Italy, Madiera [sic], Gibralter [sic], Algiers, Egypt, and terminating with the taking of *From the Manger to the Cross* in Palestine. This masterpiece was also conceived, written and codirected by me as was *The Colleen Bawn, Arrah-na-Pogue, The Sharghraun, The Kerry Gow, The Wives of Jamestown,* and five hundreds [sic] others [Bisplinghoff par. 5].

Despite this body of work, Gauntier is largely unknown in texts on screenwriting used in major universities today. She does appear in Cari Beauchamp's *Without Lying Down: Frances Marion and the Powerful Women of Early Hollywood.* In an interview with Beauchamp, David Sterritt posits that "Men have largely run the film industry from the start, allowing little power or prestige to their female counterparts. Men have also dominated the film-history field, writing books that take male privilege in Hollywood for granted. Steritt quotes Beauchamp as noting, "Women are always in the footnotes" (Sterritt). Marc *Norman*, author of *What Happens Next: A History of American Screenwriting* did not bypass Gauntier in his book; however, he spoke of her sparingly, and did so disparagingly: "Gauntier became a screenwriter, as many did then, because somebody had to do it. An actress knocking around New York—Gauntier couldn't have been very good at it" (Norman 25). Though *What Happens Next* published in 2008, five years after Beauchamp's research proved there were as many if not more women writing silent films than men, Norman did *not* choose to focus on any female writers. Furthermore, Norman failed to include an equitable number of portraits of female writers in his book. In the sixteen-page selection of photographs Norman pointed out forty-seven male writers and only eleven female screenwriters. Similarly, reading through *The Encyclopedia of Hollywood*, it becomes clear that women screenwriters in the silent era were not given their due. Among numerous female screenwriters, only four were actually mentioned in the *Encyclopedia*.

This is quite a slight considering at the age of 27 Gauntier decided to create her own feature company. Near the end of 1912 "she left Kalem to form the Gene Gauntier Feature Players Company, a decision enthusiastically hailed by the *Moving Picture World*" (Bisplinghoff). Gauntier and her crew and cast had just come back from Ireland, where they had been filming *The Lad from Old Ireland* (1910). She then embarked on the making of *From the Manger to the Cross or Jesus of Nazareth* (1912), which was striking for a number of reasons, one of which was its length. The film reached seventy-one minutes at a times where films were typically less than thirty minutes and many under ten minutes long.

Manger is historically influential, significant, and important because it was the first telling of this foundational biblical story, because of its location shoot, length, script style, cast, and cost. It required 42 actors and cost $100,000, not to mention a cast of 100 natives and numerous camels (Loughney):

> *From the Manger to the Cross* is generally recognized today as a breakthrough in the achievement of realism on the early American screen. It is historically important specifically because of its length, subject matter, and the fact that it was filmed on location in Palestine with an international cast. It is

also of significance to the history of movie screenwriting because of the photoplay authored by Gene Gauntier, who played the role of Mary in the production [*Bisplinghoff*].

The whole shoot was done outside the United States—a virtually unheard-of step in those early days. In addition to being filmed in Palestine, the movie also filmed partly in Egypt. Another factor that made this film influential was its reliance on dialogue. Out of the twenty-nine-page script, twenty pages were dialogue alone. Analyzing this, it is ironic that only five pages out of the twenty-nine were action descriptions in a silent film.

Manger illustrates what a detail-oriented talent *Gauntier* brought to her work as a writer-producer:

> the format of Gauntier's text is more structured and better designed as a film production tool. Every aspect of the information provided by Gauntier is more detailed and balanced in the sense that it addresses the needs of all members of the production team: the director, camera operator, electrician, set designer, carpenter, prop master and cast [*Loughney*].

Gauntier clearly also had an eye for the pieces that touched the heart. Another film Gauntier wrote with passion and emotion was *His Mother* (1912). She not only wrote the film but she played the role of Miss Foster, a mother who gives all her savings so her son can pursue the music that he loves. Though the son neglects his mother, he realizes her worth in the end and recognizes the value of her love. This theme of ingratitude followed by redemption was common for Gauntier, an expert at portraying real-life situations in a way that pulled at people's heartstrings.

Gauntier's storylines often revolved around a single child, a single parent, love, the willingness to travel for a better life, and a romance in which a hero leaves or a hero comes back. According to Ken Brecher, former Executive Director of the Sundance Institute, "A good script is a script where either someone is leaving town, or a stranger is coming to town." This was a plot device used in many of Gauntier's scripts. In *His Mother* (1912), *Come Back to Erin* (1914), and *The Lad from Old Ireland* (1910) the main character leaves town, comes to town, or both.

Tom Stempel, author of *Framework: A History of Screenwriting in the American Film*, mentions that Gauntier "was born Genevieve G. Liggett in Texas sometime in the 1880s. A graduate of the Kansas City Academy of Elocution and Oratory, she had a 'loving, gloriously ambitious' mother who made her clothes while Gauntier toured as an actress in stage melodramas" (7). None of the sources cited have mentioned a word about Gauntier's father. This leads one to believe that Gauntier's sense of missing a parent in her scripts comes from her own experience in missing her father. The ambitious part clearly comes from her mother. Gauntier successfully carried that quality from her mother to herself and on to the scripts.

Gauntier was a prolific writer of screenplays; it's estimated that she wrote more than 300 scripts. Her filmography as an actress and screenwriter or possible screenwriter includes *Ben Hur* (1907), *Hulda's Lovers* (1908), *The Girl Spy* (1909), *The Further Adventures of the Girl Spy* (1910), *The Girl Spy Before Vicksburg* (1910), *The Lad from Old Ireland* (1910), and *When Lovers Part* (1910). She also directed or co-directed the film *The Grandmother* (1909). In 1911 alone she worked on several scripts and films, including *The Colleen Bawn*, *Her Chum's Brother*, *The Fiddle's Requiem*, *The Little Soldier of '64*, *Rory O'More*, *A Sawmill Hero*, *Special Messenger*, *Tangled Lives*, and *A War Time Escape*. The list goes on until 1920 when Gauntier exited Hollywood and the business of screenwriting. She "gracefully retired in the early 1920s and wrote her autobiography in 1928, appropriately titled *Blazing the Trail*" (Menefee 82). Back at her start, at the moment she felt she was going to drown as a stunt girl for Biograph, Gauntier could not know that she was going to be such a successful writer and filmmaker. She truly is an example of someone who hits the bottom only to bounce up and rise, presenting an inspiration to the many women writers who came after her.

Works Cited

Beauchamp, Cari, and Anita Loos. *Anita Loos Rediscovered: Film Treatments and Fiction*. Berkeley: University of California, 2003.

Bisplinghoff, Gretchen. "Gene Gauntier." *Women Film Pioneers Project,* edited by Jane Gaines, Radha Vatsal, and Monica Dall'Asta. Center for Digital Research and Scholarship. New York: Columbia University Libraries, 2013.

Brecker, Ken. Speech. Introductory Welcome Remarks to the Inaugural Class of the Stephens College MFA in TV and Screenwriting, Friday July 31, 2015.

Ciecko, Anne. "Hollywood's 'Scriptgirls.'" *Literature/Film Quarterly*, vol. 28, no. 3, 2000, p. 230.

Francke, Lizzie. *Script Girls: Women Screenwriters in Hollywood*. London: British Film Institute, 1994.

Harner, Gary W. "The Kalem Company, Travel and On-Location Filming: The Forging of an Identity." *Film History*, vol. 10, no. 2, 1998, pp. 188–207.

Loughney, Patrick. "From *Rip Van Winkle* to *Jesus of Nazareth*: Thoughts on the Origins of the American Screenplay." *Film History*, vol. 9, no. 3, 1997, pp. 277–289. *ProQuest*.

Mahar, Karen Ward. *Women Filmmakers in Early Hollywood*. Baltimore: Johns Hopkins University Press, 2006.

Menefee, David W. *The First Female Stars: Women of the Silent Era*. Westport, CT: Praeger, 2004.

Morgan, Kyna, and Aimee Dixon. "African-American Women in the Silent Film Industry." *Women Film Pioneers Project*, edited by Jane Gaines, Radha Vatsal, and Monica Dall'Asta. Center for Digital Research and Scholarship. New York: Columbia University Libraries, 2013. https://wfpp.cdrs.columbia.edu/essay/african-american-women-in-the-silent-film-industry/.

Norman, Marc. *What Happens Next: A History of American Screenwriting*. New York: Harmony Books, 2008.

Ross, Sara. "The O'Kalem Collection: 1910–1915 (2011)." *Film & History*, vol. 43, no. 1, 2013, pp. 80–82.

Siegel, Scott, Thomas L. Erskine, Barbara Siegel, and James Michael Welsh. *The Encyclopedia of Hollywood*. New York: Facts on File, 2004.

Stempel, Tom. *Framework: A History of Screenwriting in the American Film*. New York: Continuum, 1988.

Sterritt, David. "Author Takes Hollywood Women Out of Footnotes, into Main Story: Interview Cari Beauchamp." *Christian Science Monitor*, 29 May 1997. http://www.csmonitor.com/1997/0529/052997.feat.film.1.html.

Wrathall, John. *What Happens Next: A History of American Screenwriting*. Crown Archetype. Kindle Edition, 2008.

Lorna Moon
A Woman of a Certain Influence
Elizabeth Dwyer

Any number of "badly-behaved" women preceded Lorna Moon, and a great many more will follow her. As Laurel Thatcher Ulrich noted in her academic paper, published in the journal "American Quarterly" in 1976 (and often misattributed later on), *"Well-behaved women seldom make history."* In fact, with the exception of Frances Marion, most of the women who made it onto the pages of early cinematic history were on the unruly side of the coin. Lorna Moon (née Nora Helen Wilson Low) was no exception, and one might even say she was a standard bearer for audacious living. Her audacity would not only carry her far and wide, but also provide consistent fuel for her various writings.

Born in rural Strichen, Aberdeenshire, in northeast Scotland in 1886, Nora Low did not grow up in a typical farmstead household. Her father, Charles Low, was a well-traveled, well-educated socialist. Their garden hut in Strichen was referred to by locals as 10 Downing Street, the address of the Prime Minister's office in London, as a nod to the heated debates that took place inside (Norquay 27).

Her mother, Margaret Benzies, was known as a beauty and a forceful personality, which seem to be the primary traits that Nora/Lorna inherited from her mother. Her father's situation at birth offers a small amount of insight into what may have shaped an apparently unceremonious attitude toward having children. At birth, Charles Low was registered as the illegitimate son of Mary-Ann Low and Charles May, the butler of a family that employed Mary-Ann. Rumors implied that Charles's father may have actually been an aristocratic member of the household. To be sure, his lineage is shrouded in a certain amount of intrigue and "taboo" sexual behavior on the part of his parents. Charles Low also made no effort to keep the mysteries of life from his daughter, so Nora grew up with a certain awareness that was denied to most of her female peers (de Mille 140).

In order to free herself from the confines of rural farm life, Nora Low married William Hebditch, a traveler who stayed at the hotel owned by Nora's parents. He took her to Alberta, Canada, which presented its own set of early twentieth century hardships. While it's unclear whether or not she ever legally divorced Hebditch or merely left him, it was not long before Nora hitched her star to Walter Moon. He brought her to the slightly more cosmopolitan city of Winnipeg, where she was introduced to journalism and adopted her new name, Lorna Moon. They then moved on to Minneapolis, Minnesota, where Moon began her journalism career in earnest. The details of the anecdote vary, but a few remain consistent across the board: Moon wrote a rather scathing critique of the 1920 film *Male and Female* (which was based on a Scottish play), and then she went so far as to send it to the film's director, Cecil B. DeMille. In his reply, DeMille challenged her to come out to Hollywood and, if she knew so much about the movies, write something better. Moon's later writing career illustrates how ambiguous things could be in the early days of Hollywood. On the Internet Movie Database (IMDB.com), the modern world's more or less definitive source on movies, her credits are listed as follows:

- *La fruta amarga* (novel "Dark Star")
- 1930 *Min and Bill* (suggested from the book: "Dark Star")
- 1927 *Love* (adaptation—uncredited)
- 1927 *After Midnight*
- 1927 *Mr. Wu* (adaptation and continuity)
- 1927 *Women Love Diamonds*
- 1926 *Upstage* (scenario)
- 1922 *Her Husband's Trademark*
- 1922 *Too Much Wife* (story)
- 1921 *Don't Tell Everything* (story)

An over-the-shoulder publicity portrait of screenwriter Lorna Moon, circa 1920. Ever the progressive thinker, while being treated at a sanitarium in New Mexico for tuberculosis, Moon wrote to her publisher: "It is revolting to me that in a civilized world a woman's virtue rests entirely upon her hymen" (Academy of Motion Picture Arts and Sciences' Margaret Herrick Library).

There are several casual references to Moon's involvement in writing *The Affairs of Anatol* (1921), but the only official writing credit on that film is for Jeanie Macpherson, DeMille's long-time collaborator (alongside Arthur Schnitzler, who penned a play of the same name that "suggested" the story for the film). In the book *Cecil B. DeMille and American Culture: The Silent Era*, a list of DeMille's filmography includes the following details for *The Affairs of Anatol*: "Scenario by Jeanie Macpherson, Beulah Marie Dix, Lorna Moon, and Elmer Harris" (Higashi 208). Much like present-day Hollywood, silent era film writers could see a script go through several hands and only one name end up in the credits, though unlike today, there were silent films that did not credit any writers at all. Moon's most successful work is easily *Mr. Wu*, a 1927 film starring Lon Chaney that solidified his place in history as "the Man of a Thousand Faces." In the film, Chaney plays two roles, that of Mandarin Wu and his grandfather, and he also appears as these characters at different stages in their lives. Although there were exceptions, Chaney's appearance continued an unfortunate and proliferate practice of the era where Caucasian actors portrayed characters of different races.

Many of Moon's films are hard to find online, and information about her life and work is scattered and varied. Words such as neglected, overlooked, unknown, and phrases like "little attention" are used in reference to Moon and how she is treated by history, both in terms of her life and her work as a writer. Still, evidence does exist, and it paints a picture of a woman who did not fit the confines of her time. Married to two men and the mother of as many children plus one, Moon did not stay married to anyone nor did she raise any of her children. Her nomadic spirit kept her wandering and searching, without much evidence of ever finding fulfillment. In later years, when her grown children found each other, her daughter Mary (who initially worshipped the mythos of her mother, the glamorous Hollywood screenwriter), garnered a decent amount of success as a writer in her own right. She sent a newspaper clipping to her brother, Richard, highlighting "Unwanted Children Who Grew Up to Be Great" that cited Leonardo da Vinci, Elizabeth I, and Sir Isaac Newton, among others. At the bottom Mary wrote, "So *there*, Lorna!" (de Mille 108).

Moon's writing appears to be the most consistent facet of her life, yet even there she vacillates from a confident voice speaking on her own behalf to an artist struggling with doubts in her own abilities. To the former, in letters to her publishers at Bobbs-Merrill (excerpted from *The Collected Works of Lorna Moon*), Moon not only negotiates the terms of her contract to ensure they are to her liking, she also asserts herself as an authority on the characters and settings in her own writing. She patiently and firmly explains to Hewitt Hanson Howland, one of the publishers, why her story *Feckless Maggie Ann* must take place in the town of Rosehearty and not Drumorty (the story appears in a collection titled *Doorways in Drumorty*). Her reasons not only include the geographic (the sea being a key feature of the story and Rosehearty being a fishing town), but also character-driven, as "…the fishing people and the land people in Scotland don't mix, they are widely separated in their sympathies, even their blood isn't the same." She goes on to clarify that "Maggie Ann is a true Celtic" and a "Drumorty lass" would never behave as Maggie Ann does. Moon does not waiver in her authority on this subject, but speaks simply and matter-of-factly to illustrate her deep-seated knowledge of Scotland and its people (258).

Moon goes on to suggest that the publishers approach J.M. Barrie about writing a preface for *Doorways in Drumorty*, but "…not, for God sake, if you think somebody is going to say that I 'write like Barrie.' I once said that I'd always wanted to write 'as WELL as Barrie,' and of course 'well' became 'like.' I don't write at all like Barrie. Do I?" (259). This passage illustrates much about Moon. Her casual suggestion of approaching one of the most popular and successful writers of the time for a preface to her book, coupled with her reluctance to be compared to him (one can suppose in the interest of possessing her own unique voice), demonstrate a confidence and self-possession that women, quite simply, weren't supposed to have in 1925.

Four years later, in 1929, Moon wrote once again to one of her publishers at Bobbs-Merrill, this time to one Mr. Laurance Chambers, about her novel *Dark Star*, as she worked on collecting quotes for the book jacket. In regards to her novel's heroine, Nancy, it seems one reviewer asserted that she "…belongs to the Scottish heroines of literature and that Scott, Stevenson, Barrie would have understood her…" Moon asserts that this is decidedly not the case, and goes so far as to say that "Nancy is 1929. Barrie the dear old 'whimsical' bastard wouldn't understand her at all" (267). In addition to this delightful moment of candor, and in only slightly more than a page of text, this letter encapsulates much of Moon's outlook on the world. She closes by acknowledging that Nancy has "all the romance of bygone heroines" as well as the "clear thinking bravery of 1929 girlhood." It's this assertion that leads to her final thought for this letter, a highly advanced and modern outlook for a woman in 1929. "You know, that is what all this is leading us to—sin will cease to be a nasty baster—there wont [sic] be a 'fallen woman' anymore [sic] than there are 'fallen men.' It is revolting to me that in a civilized world a woman's virtue rests entirely upon her hymen." And finally, Moon acknowledged her own audacity by saying, "Excuse me I always get worked up over this" (268). It is worth noting how many women of the era very likely felt the same uppity, rabble rousing feelings, yet did not have the gumption to speak up with such veracity. Moon was a unique person arguably living ahead of her time.

Aside from her son Richard de Mille and his book, *My Secret Mother Lorna Moon*, the foremost Moon scholar is easily Glenda Norquay, a professor of Professional Arts and Social Studies and an authority on Scottish literature at John Moores University in Liverpool, England. Her paper on *"Transitory Thresholds": Geographic Imaginings of Adolescence in Women's Fiction from North-East Scotland* examines text from Moon's novel *Dark Star*. Norquay asserts that Moon is among a handful of Scottish authors whom, when they "address the movement between girlhood and a female sexuality their narratives are less concerned with clear demarcations of boundaries, as in the cinematic explorations of masculinity, but are repeatedly driven towards marginal spaces, undesignated territories, and the people who inhabit them: travelers, gypsies, tinkers, circus folk." For Moon specifically, Norquay finds that "…outsiders also carry the most significant associations with sexuality. In her novel *Dark Star*, it is the figure of Divot Meg—running the local disreputable boarding/doss house for vagrants, travelers, and fair people—whom the developing heroine Nancy turns to for insights into love." Keeping in stride with both her personal behavior and the limitations imposed on her by the society of her era, Moon's writing depicts female sexuality as vibrant, visceral, and also confined. Again in *Dark Star*,

> Nancy's earliest memory establishes an association between the marginal and the sexual: "Watching their meeting, an emotion blind of understanding but vivid as pain shot through her. Something was meant by that glow in the dark face that bent upon her mother's; something terrifying was meant by the glamour in her mother's face as she looked back at him … these two were set apart and deaf to any cry but the cry that clamoured in their blood" [83].

Dark Star was later adapted into the film *Min and Bill*, with the scenario and dialogue penned by Frances Marion and Marion Jackson. As noted in the Moon section of the Women Film Pioneers Project, "The story of how Frances Marion and Kate Corbaley tricked the studio executives into paying Lorna Moon seventy-five hundred dollars, while reviving Marie Dressler's career, should be a legend in the history of female networking in the motion picture business." By this time, Moon was in need of a rest stay at a sanitarium, the second in her young life, due to recurring tuberculosis. She needed money to try a new, costly facility in Albuquerque, New Mexico. Frances Marion pitched *Dark Star* as great material for a new script, but she adjusted Moon's sad story to present it as a comedic vehicle for Marie Dressler, thereby financially aiding two female colleagues. Once the studio went for the pitch, they ultimately gave Moon the seventy-five hundred dollars as payment for the cinematic rights to her source material. This tale supports the truism that women have always known: contrary to the supposed propensity that women have to pit themselves against one another, the opposite is, in this author's experience, far more often the case.

Especially in male-dominated fields like filmmaking, women not only band together in support of one another, they will also celebrate each other's successes and fight to help other women in need. Odds are high that the story of successfully pitching *Min and Bill,* and so providing much needed support to two women artists, is one of countless undocumented anecdotes of the same nature. What is documented are the women of early Hollywood who helped to champion and mentor other women who were interested in filmmaking, such as Lois Weber, the accomplished film director. Weber was known for her support of women, and she actively "encouraged actresses such as Gene Gauntier, Cleo Madison, and Dorothy Davenport to direct" (Beauchamp 35). Frances Marion once observed "I owe my greatest success to women. Contrary to the assertion that women do all in their power to hinder one another's progress, I have found that it has always been one of my own sex who has given me a helping hand when I needed it" (12). One need only look to the Geena Davis Institute on Gender in Media, or the collective efforts of the production company We Do It Together, to see this culture of support and advocacy among women alive in the Hollywood of today.

The value of the friendship of women was not lost on Moon. Not only did Marion and Corbaley help her pay for her sanitarium stay, Moon was also a frequent collaborator with other women writers in Hollywood. Again with Marion, a dear friend, she helped to adapt *Anna Karenina* into the silent film *Love*, starring Greta Garbo and John Gilbert. It is an abridged version of the Tolstoy tale, and was given added box office appeal when the studio offered the option of what may be cinema's first ever alternate ending. Marion penned a happy alternative to Tolstoy's tragic conclusion, and theaters were given the option of showing one or the other at the film's end. In a telling example of American proclivities, the East and West coasts opted for Tolstoy tragedy, while most places "in the middle" chose Marion's happy ending (http://www.silentfilm.org/archive/love).

For *Her Husband's Trademark* (1922), Moon adapted a story by Clara Beranger, an interesting pairing, considering that William de Mille (the father of Lorna's third child, Richard), ultimately left his first wife, Anna, to marry Beranger, with whom he was reportedly very much in love. It makes a person wish that one of those women had kept a diary that could have been published to offer their perspective.

In adjusting to the news that Moon was his mother, Richard de Mille very thoughtfully considered the atmosphere in Hollywood at the time. His mother had just finished working on the script for *The Affairs of Anatol*, which de Mille refers to as a "spicy boudoir comedy" and on the day the film opened, newspapers were splattered with the story of lovely Virginia Rappe's untimely death (as well as pictures of her corpse), at an orgy hosted by the wildly popular film comedian Fatty Arbuckle. Less than two weeks before Richard was born, a director at Paramount Studios was found murdered in a "pornococaine love nest" (de Mille, *Secret Mother* 57). Regardless of how his parents might have felt, de Mille surmises the climate around motion pictures at the time was such that a scandal such as his birth—fathered by a married man, born of a twice-divorced woman who had left two other children behind—would not do the de Mille family an ounce of good. On the contrary, they would be plagued with conjecture and gossip and no doubt the published lies of sensationalist newspapers of the yellow press.

While he is not wrong in this assessment, the reader still feels a pang of sympathy for this adult man striving to understand the decision made by his parents to put him up for adoption. De Mille's theory is supported by the researchers at the Women Film Pioneers Project, who affirm that "At a time when the Fatty Arbuckle trial and the William Desmond Taylor murder were still making headlines, public judgment would have been harsh, and thus cover-up was imperative" (https://wfpp.cdrs.columbia.edu/pioneer/ccp-lorna-moon/). They further describe the fascinating details of how Moon's pregnancy was covered up in the press. She was, after all, a successful screenwriter at the time. Moon's clippings file at the Margaret Herrick Library include the following press announcements:

> In October 1921, the *Morning Telegraph* reports that Moon is on "a four month's tour of foreign countries." In December it reports that she is "gathering material during her European trip for another original for Gloria Swanson," and in April 1922, the *Morning Telegraph* writes that Moon is back after six months of writing short stories in Scotland. In reality Moon was convalescing in Monrovia, just east of Pasadena, in the California tuberculosis sanitarium where baby Richard was born [de Mille 1998 212].

According to de Mille's book about his mother, the press spin on where he came from involved the de Mille family adopting him after he'd been left in a fancy car with a note to the effect of the abandoned baby's mother not being able to handle his care (de Mille 57).

It later comes to light that William C. de Mille approached his brother Cecil about adopting Moon's child once he was born, as the de Mille family had already adopted two other children. After discussing it with his wife, Constance, and agreeing to the matter, it was a condition of Cecil's that William and Moon have no official interaction with the child. Of course in William's case this proved to be impossible, as he was purportedly Richard's uncle, but all the same his interactions with Richard were sparse and limited. In the case of Moon, the condition held firm. Other than their brief encounter post-childbirth, she never met her son (de Mille 55).

Her second child, Mary, who preceded Richard as the daughter of Walter and Moon, was born to her parents in wedlock, but had ultimately been sent to England to be raised by her father's brother and his wife. Mary Moon spent much of her life idolizing her mother, believing that her father had cruelly and unjustly sent Mary away from her. Mary ultimately moved to Hollywood to meet people who had known her mother, and to work in the same industry (albeit not as successfully). As told from the parents' perspective, Walter and Moon could not adjust their lives to agreeably raise a child, so Mary was sent off to England. In fact, it was not long afterwards that Moon wrote to Cecil B. DeMille, critiquing his film and invoking his invitation to come to Hollywood and give screenwriting a shot. Though still married to Walter (for the time being), but now free of childcare issues, Moon packed up her bags and was off without a hitch.

Many years later, when Walter wanted to remarry, his intended bride Helen insisted that he see Moon first, as Helen said she wouldn't marry Walter until she found out "how you kids feel about each other now." Walter did as Helen asked, and while in Los Angeles he found a much changed woman, her spirit as vibrant as ever, but her body and energy were sapped by tuberculosis. When she needed to rest, Moon gave Walter a note that would grant him access to visit the studio lots. On his tour Walter stopped in to see Lon Chaney, who wouldn't receive him until Walter said it was "Mr. Lorna Moon" who had come to visit, at which point Chaney ran out to shake his hand, exclaiming, "Lorna made me a star!" (de Mille 87).

In a glowing article titled "Writers of the Day" that appears in a 1922 issue of *The*

Writer magazine ("A Monthly Magazine for Literary Workers") there is a charming account of Moon, including a mention of her arrival in the U.S. and insights into her burgeoning writing career:

> Lorna Moon, whose story, "Feckless Maggie Ann," came out in the April Century, Says she began to tell stories at an early age, and was rebuked for it because she told such sad stories that she made the other children cry. Miss Moon was born in Scotland, and grew up among the simple people of whom she writes. Her first short story, "Silk Both Sides," appeared in the December Century, and "Feckless Maggie Ann," which is her second story, grew out of the recollection of a man in her native village who, after his wife died, took to wheeling an empty barrow when he went out because he was "so lonesome like." Miss Moon says she is still so young that she enjoys sorrow, so "Feckless Maggie Ann" had to die. Ten years ago Miss Moon came to America, and at first was "sob sister" on various daily papers. Then she wrote syndicated editorials under the title, "Talking It Over with Lorna Moon," until she began writing for the moving pictures. She says she now earns her bread and butter and reasonable amount of jam writing moving pictures, but adds that it is not the jam alone that keeps her writing pictures; it is because she believes in the future of pictures, and that if she ever loses the belief that some day moving pictures will become art, the jam will not tempt her [Hills 77].

The quote from Moon about earning her "bread and butter and reasonable amount of jam writing moving pictures" alludes to a claim she once made that she only returned to writing films after her first bout with T.B. for the money. It is the follow up that shows perhaps her more genuine feelings: "…she believes in the future of pictures, and that if she ever loses the belief that some day moving pictures will become art, the jam will not tempt her."

In the spring of 1927, Moon had to return to the sanitarium, yet while there she continued to work on the rewrite of *Love,* as a studio secretary typed by her bedside. This picture, a sick woman so adamantly persisting in her creative endeavors, is one of a woman working for the sake of her work and her art, not for the paycheck alone. This was somewhat commonplace among the women of early Hollywood, adopting a casual, breezy almost flippant attitude toward their work. In her book *Without Lying Down*, Cari Beauchamp mentions Frances Marion's early life lesson that "women could go where their interests led them, as long as they outwardly appeared to behave themselves" (16). The cavalier attitude towards their work that Hollywood women presented was likely a mechanism of self-preservation. Even today, women in Hollywood (and to be sure, in life in particular), are expected to behave themselves and if a woman is seen as caring too much or presenting forceful, impassioned views, she runs the risk of being perceived as overly emotional or "difficult" or—as many headstrong women have been branded—a "bad influence."

Moon lived in a manner so contrary to women of her time, she has even drawn comparison to salacious, modern day pop icons. In her book *Why Scottish Literature Matters,* Carla Sassi suggests that "in her shifts of identity Moon, like contemporary media icon Madonna, impersonates and parodies contrasting and clichéd identities, challenging their 'essence' and exploring performativity" (Sassi 157).

A great number of people changed their name when entering work in Hollywood. Moon had made the change before she made the move. In his Foreword for *The Collected Works of Lorna Moon,* her son Richard outlines his mother's reasons behind her new name. First, "Mrs. William Hebditch" was fleeing her first husband (and leaving behind her four-year-old son Bill), and didn't want Mr. Hebditch to track her down. Second, in the early twentieth century, "custom required her to travel as a married woman." Lastly, and as Richard points out, "the most telling" reason, her childhood heroine was Lorna

Doone, a literary figure caught up in thrilling, tumultuous adventures and star crossed loves. Ms. Lorna Moon, née Helen Nora Wilson Low, did indeed indulge in a number of identity shifts beyond her name alone. In an author questionnaire that she filled out for her publishers, Lorna Moon listed her parents as "Chas. Ewen Donald Cameron, Laird of Fassefern, and Margaret Helen Cameron of Erracht." After reading a bit of correspondence between Moon and her publishers, it's evident that, at least in part, she was likely taking the proverbial piss out of Americans who knew nothing about Scotland and were easy suckers for anything sniffing of royalty. In an interview with *Moving Picture World*, Moon builds even more myth around herself, claiming to have grown up in "…a home which was built in the fourteenth century. She is 'pure Scotch' and until she was nine years old spoke nothing but Gaelic, learning English at a convent in Laon, France. She achieved considerable success on the Scottish stage" (*Moving Picture World* 906).

These false tales and embellished histories make tracking Moon's life somewhat of a challenge. The factual details that survive are almost entirely owed to her son Richard, and the research he did for his book, *My Secret Mother Lorna Moon*. It is this book along with *The Collected Works* that bring Moon a sliver of the recognition she deserves, and that highlight the potential that was thwarted by her early death in 1930.

Moon had a moderate amount of success as a screenwriter in early Hollywood, but what sets her apart are her short stories and the novel that she published. According to letters, at least two other novels were in the works at the time of her death. In spite of her fear of being too closely compared to novelist J.M. Barrie, Moon was able to carve out a voice and style of her own. The detective novelist Augustus Muir sent comments to Moon's publishers (and they to her) acknowledging Moon's ability to stand apart as a writer. He notes that Barrie's writing is full of charm and wistful tears, but realism "is not his forte; and it is here that Lorna Moon scores. She is a realist, and her book is a little storehouse of truth" (*Collected Works of Lorna Moon* xiii).

It is proven time and again that the choices we make throughout our lives influence the paths we take, the outcomes we face, and ultimately the fate that lies in wait for us. As difficult as it is to understand some of Moon's choices—in particular her complete abandonment of three children—these choices are also what led us to talking about her today. Without leaving behind the people she brought into the world, she may never have brought forth her talent as a writer and storyteller. In her propensity for "behaving badly," Moon made a name for herself and assured that her stories would survive long after she left this world. In a twist of irony that she certainly would have appreciated, it is largely thanks to one of those children she left behind, her third son Richard, that Moon's legacy lives on.

Works Cited

Beauchamp, Cari. *Without Lying Down: Frances Marion and the Powerful Women of Early Hollywood*. Berkeley: University of California Press, 1997.
de Mille, Richard. *My Secret Mother, Lorna Moon*. New York: Farrar, Straus & Giroux, 1998.
Hills, William Henry, and Robert Luce, eds. *The Writer* 1922: 77.
Love (1927). Wrs: Frances Marion, Marian Ainslee, Ruth Cummings and Lorna Moon. Dir: Edmund Goulding. MGM, USA 82 mins.
Moon, Lorna, and Glenda Norquay. *The Collected Works of Lorna Moon*. Edinburgh: Black & White Pub., 2002.
Norquay, Glenda. "The Far Side of Lorna Moon." *ScotLit* 27. Autumn (2002).
Norquay, Glenda. "'Transitory Thresholds': Geographic Imaginings of Adolescence in Women's Fiction from North-East Scotland." *Scottish Literary Review 3* No. 2. Autumn-Winter (2011): 81–99. *MLA International Bibliography*. Web. 11 Dec. 2015.<https://www.mla.org/Publications/MLA-International-Bibliography>.

Clara Beranger
The Unseen Laborer
AMANDA R. STOCKWELL

Screenwriter is not a term society cares much about, or so it seems. Screenwriters are known if they themselves are one, and thus surrounded by other screenwriters, or if they are in the media business in some other capacity and working directly with a screenwriter. Otherwise, screenwriters are among the names of those no one ever looks for in the credits. Audiences are there to see the actors and actresses in a story they can travel into and become a part of, rarely realizing the passion and intent put into the words that formed this unique world. To be a screenwriter means minimal credit; to be a female screenwriter means rare credit buried under years of condescension. Only in recent years have Silent Era women screenwriters been given a voice, and it must continue until credit is given its due:

> The history of American silent cinema is marked by a strong presence of women also in other areas of work such as editing, but to ignore the contributions of so many women to such an important phase of filmmaking as screenwriting erases a crucial historical fact from our discussions of this period, not only with respect to gender issues, but also with regard to a larger cultural understanding of the time [Callahan 289].

Clara Beranger is one among many prominent female screenwriters during the Silent Era of film. Like the other amazing women who wrote at least half of the films produced during that time, very little is known about her, and what information there is, is hard to find. "It is lamentable that so little is known about Clara Beranger. From the piles of film books, even those devoted to the screenwriter, her name is conspicuously absent" (Tibbetts 135).

Beranger was born Clara Strouse in Baltimore, Maryland, on January 14, 1886. Her parents owned a department store, which did well and later became part of Beranger's inheritance. When Beranger grew of age, she married Albert Berwanger and they had a daughter named Frances, who would grow up to be an actress, though not one featured in the films her mother wrote. Their marriage did not last. As they drifted apart and she began submitting her work for publication, she took the "w" out of her surname, thus changing it to Beranger. Though she married again, this one more influential to her career and life, she kept her name Beranger.

During the 1910s, Beranger lived in New York working as a journalist, writing stage

Writer Clara Beranger on set with William C. de Mille, circa 1925. Beranger was not only a screenwriter, but also a journalist, professor, lecturer at USC and novelist (Academy of Motion Picture Arts and Sciences' Margaret Herrick Library).

plays, and working as a freelance screenwriter. In 1921, however, Paramount commissioned her to move to Hollywood and write an adaptation for William de Mille. *Miss Lulu Bett* (1921) was their first collaboration together and it changed Beranger's life forever. Before leaving New York, "Clara's friend Rita warned her: 'When you get to Hollywood, watch out for the de Mille boys!'" (de Mille 180). Beranger did not heed this advice and seven years after first working with de Mille, they were married.

Beranger's professional career as screenwriter, scenarist, and adaptation writer was largely associated with Famous Players–Lasky Company, which later became Paramount Pictures. She stuck with the company and with de Mille for most of her professional life as a screenwriter. Her best-known work occurred in the late 1910s through the late 1920s. During this period, Beranger wrote an adaptation of Zona Gale's novel *Miss Lulu Bett*, an adaptation of *Dr. Jekyll and Mr. Hyde* (1920), and *The World's Applause* (1923) plus a multitude of other screenplays, original and adapted. Beranger's films resonate because of their humanity and realism. Watching a silent film in the 21st century can sometimes be a task, but Beranger wrote films that had an "iconoclastic tone that could pass for today's. *Men and Women*, a silent film written in 1925, has a distinctly easy style…. After the opening credits, the movie declares: There is no hero, no heroine, no villain in this story—the characters are just men and women" (McCreadie 7). Another forward thinking idea of Beranger's is that happy endings (the man and woman ending up together in regard to romantic comedies) were not a necessity. She believed the American audiences ultimately wished for this, but "if the ending is one that must inevitably be unhappy, the audience will accept it. But the characters and the development must all work to an inevitable unhappy ending if it is to seem natural and right" (Tibbetts 145). Again we see Beranger's determination that films reflect real life situations and emotions in order for the audience to relate.

Miss Lulu Bett was Beranger's first screenplay collaboration with de Mille. It was a huge success, much like the novel, and rightfully so. De Mille spoke a few lines of his and Beranger's process in a much longer interview. "I discuss the story with Miss Beranger, then she makes a rough draft and we discuss it again," said Mr. de Mille. "I am able to follow her script scene for scene when I make my picture. With a less capable writer I could not do this. While I am finishing our picture Miss Beranger is getting the scenario ready for my next one" (Long 1). *Miss Lulu Bett* shows that whatever collaboration they had managed to find for their first film worked. *Miss Lulu Bett* isn't filled with extravagance but rather a subtle, realistic view of a woman burdened with a cumbersome family. Beranger doesn't make the audience fall in love with the lead female character; we do so on our own. In this Cinderella story of a young woman turned into the maid of her family, Lulu is a quiet soul, forever giving in to the whims of her family that sees her only as a tool for their household. The head of the household, Dwight, Lulu's brother-in-law, is constantly nagging her about housework and providing dinner on time. Finally, Lulu meets Ninian, Dwight's brother, whom she agrees to marry. There is fondness, but the truth of the matter is she wishes to leave her dreadful life ... until she finds out Ninian is already married. Lulu is forced to come back to the family where she is confronted by a dirty house, piles of dishes, and Dwight that will not let her save face and admit to the townspeople that Ninian is a bigamist.

Lulu finally finds love in the local schoolteacher. Beranger gives us a man we could easily choose as a champion; he aids Lulu as the church members denounce her, he washes and dries dishes as the rest of the family languishes in the living room, and he loves her *and* respects her. Once Lulu's family sees she has another suitor, they are more concerned with losing her as a maid than guiding her through her situation: "Why, she's lettin' him make love to her—and us waitin' for our dinner." Lulu finally found the love she so longed for and only at the end was she able to embrace it. At this moment of revelation, Beranger creates a beautiful situation by using a prop rather than a title card. Our champion writes on his chalkboard, "Teacher loves Lulu. Does Lulu love me?" An interesting note regarding the ending of *Miss Lulu Bett* was that it had to be re-written to appease the audiences. In the novel, Lulu found the courage to go after the man she loved without fully knowing whether her marriage to Ninian was legal or not. The script, however, added a scene with a note sent from Ninian saying his wife was alive so his and Lulu's marriage wasn't real, basically giving Lulu permission to move on with her romantic life. Though this is an unnecessary change brought on by studio bosses afraid of dismissing church-going audiences, it is of no surprise that such a truthful, romantic film soared and Beranger was the writer that gave it wings.

Beranger continued to write, amassing 79 screenplays to her name. *Miss Lulu Bett* was not her only success, nor her only adaptation. Beranger, in a lecture at the University of Southern California, admitted to her own intelligence and writing gift by detailing the difficulties of adapting one writing medium to another. "It is not an easy thing to take what is meant to be read or something that is meant to be spoken, as a play, and transfer it to a medium in which you can only show action plus such supplementary reading matter as titles and sub-titles" (Tibbetts 139). Title cards are another area where Beranger succeeded in captivating the audience while moving the story along, showing her ingenuity in giving the audience a vital part of the story without spelling it out. In *Dr. Jekyll and Mr. Hyde* title cards are given an eeriness that lends to the genre of the film. For example, instead of simply saying clinic or hospital, the term "human repair shop" is used. In both *Miss Lulu Bett* and *Dr. Jekyll and Mr. Hyde* beautiful lines are delivered that move past entertaining and become thought provoking. As Dr. Jekyll argues against the need to succumb to his baser side, he says, "Isn't it by serving others that one develops oneself, Sir George?" While Beranger cannot be given credit for being the original writer of all the words that appeared onscreen in the films she adapted, she can be given credit for choosing the ones that appeared on screen with an eye toward enhancing the audiences' experiences.

In many of Beranger's films, the finishing touch is given to the woman. Beranger gave women a voice through her scenarios. In *Miss Lulu Bett* and *Bought and Paid For*, both Lulu and Virginia have the courage to leave the men in their lives that are dragging them down in order to embrace something or someone they actually loved. In *Clarence* (1922), Violet chooses to accept the title character in the end when she understands who he truly is. A decade later, in *His Double Life* (1933), Beranger creates a more modern situation. Alice, the female lead, is the head of the household. She ensnares Priam, the two marry, and she cares for him not only physically but financially. There is a line of dialogue where Alice is so distraught because, "I don't want you to have to worry about money." In an interview with Louella Parsons regarding *The World's Applause* and how Beranger came up with the idea, she says, "…the thought came to me, these women mixed up in these scandals can never wash their skirts clean…. Why not write a scenario showing how impossible it is for a girl to get back her standing once her precious name is headlined throughout the country" (Parsons 1). Beranger fought for women on the screen, but she also fought for them off screen by being one of many that helped film rise from its knees and become the industry it is today. "…the work of these screenwriters had an impact on society in general in the 1920s. These women played an essential role in the modernization of society, both through their presence in the film industry, in a very peculiar, and visible, work market, and through the types of stories they wrote" (Callahan 299).

Beranger and de Mille didn't jump into a relationship together. They worked together for seven years before they were married. Richard, the son William C. de Mille never acknowledged, wrote that his father once said, "a close bond should exist between writer and director" (de Mille 34). De Mille took it a step further. Beranger wasn't the only writer he shared both a professional and a private relationship. He had affairs all his life, but Beranger was the only woman that captured and held him for life. Beranger and de Mille fell in love amid a difficult familial situation; he was still married to Anna. In the year 1927, de Mille, Anna, and Beranger met to see how the situation could be resolved. When Beranger learned de Mille was still sleeping with his wife, she backed off and the two did not work together for a whole year. De Mille and Anna tried to make their marriage work one last time, but in the end, de Mille came back to Beranger and they were married a year later. One account regarding Beranger's personal life mentions that it was only three days after the divorce had been finalized that Beranger and de Mille were married on a train in New Mexico (Darr 2). The marriage wasn't without its faults. De Mille had not only cheated on Anna but would later cheat on Beranger. Just before Beranger and he were married, but still during a time when they were seeing each other, de Mille cheated on her with Lorna Moon. This affair produced a child, Richard, which Beranger never knew was William's. The child was raised as Cecil B. DeMille's son, and only after both William and Beranger had died was the fact that Richard was William's son introduced into the rest of the family.

Though de Mille cheated on Beranger at the start of their marriage, no other infidelities were ever documented. The two truly seemed to fit each other, to propel each other's careers forward, and keep a stable marriage along the way. When Beranger was only his business partner, she was his anchor, "the port in the storm" (de Mille 203). "In April, 1928, I had just finished 'Tenth Avenue,' my forty-fifth production and was working on 'Craig's Wife' with Clara Beranger, who had written the screen plays of all my pictures for seven years and continued to do so even after our marriage" (de Mille 268). Though very little is known about de Mille and Beranger's marriage, and love is very rarely mentioned in reports of their relationship, ironically the person best able to report the most about the feelings between the two was the son William de Mille never accepted. Richard writes, "Then William fell in love with Clara Beranger, and for the first time it wasn't just an affair. Clara was his refuge, understood him, brought him peace" (de Mille 35). The closest reference found coming from Beranger was that she enjoyed working with William so much she married him. None of this is conclusive as to whether the two were truly in love or just had a workable relationship, but it cannot be disregarded that de Mille depended heavily on Beranger for the rest of his life and Beranger doted on him, caring for him even after she learned of his infidelity.

A very interesting part about their time together, particularly the roller coaster of his ending things with Anna and the year Beranger did not work with him, none of this seems to have affected Beranger's work. She continued both writing and being a mother. Beranger knew what it meant to hold multiple responsibilities and not only survive but conquer those aspects of her life. When Beranger first moved to Hollywood, she was "thirty-five, separated from her husband, a mother, and a professional woman. She had come to work, not play" (de Mille 180). This same sentiment continued throughout her life as she transitioned from journalist to silent films title card writer to talkies screenwriter to professor to novelist, all the while being a wife and mother.

After Beranger's success during the Silent Era, talkies were a bit of a let-down. She continued writing during the early period of transition between silence and sound, but both hers and de Mille's film careers began to fade. It began when de Mille sunk into depression and Beranger fought him out of it. "Clara swallowed her pride and went to Cecil to beg for help…. Clara then arranged for William to be dean of drama at the University of Southern California," a position that Cecil had helped created through generous endowments (Callahan 299). Unfortunately, for Beranger and for most of the Silent Era female screenwriters, they were being removed and replaced with men. Beranger and the rest of these women had dug the trenches and lain in them; now the men came once the war had already been won.

Beranger showed her talent for transition from silent to talkies beginning with *This Mad World* (1930). Though the focus of Beranger's work was silent films, this reviewer also analyzed the talkie, *His Double Life* (1930), and found it had lost none of Beranger's charm and wit. Beranger was not afraid of the industry moving from silent to sound. She believed talkies could be just as successful as silent films. Beranger "points out that earlier audiences took the first movies 'bad as they were' and 'developed with them.' She believes the same will hold true of sound pictures" (*Sound Waves* 3). Beranger reasoned that everything she had learned during the Silent Era would be just as valuable in moving on to the talkies. Likely because of bias and bigotry, Beranger never had the chance to show just how right she was.

After her screenwriting career, Beranger also taught at the University of Southern California. In the book, *Introduction to the Photoplay* Tibbetts gives an account of a lecture Beranger gave to students regarding the movie industry. During this lecture and in her own book, *Writing for the Screen,* readers are shown Beranger's meticulousness in rules and strategies pertaining to what it takes to be part of this soul-twisting, heart-wrenching business. An article entitled "Preparing the Screenplay" sets the tone for her concern at the leveled of preparedness one needs to be as a writer. "If there is one truism above all others concerning the production of a motion picture, it is that proper preparation is the first requirement for good work" (Beranger 1). If Post-it notes had been invented, Beranger would have bought out the store. Her determination to capture the human spirit and portray it correctly on screen appears on nearly every page. Her advice is that "to achieve true characters, the author must be deeply and sincerely interested in human beings" (Beranger 1). Beranger believed in research to better her understanding of people, nature, places, and ideas she put in her writing. She was an intellectual who did not scoff at the idea that motion pictures contributed to society; her intelligence and diligence toward writing only bettered the films she created and made a lasting memory for her audiences.

Writing for the Screen is short, running at 198 pages, but this does not diminish the content. Beranger includes writing for different mediums, prerequisites for what she believes a writer needs to have to be successful, terms used in production, considerations for driving the action forward, and she ends with story scripts, treatments, and shooting scripts. Her helpful suggestions regarding the development of a story include the following:

1. What is my plot, the bones of my story?
2. What is my plan or purpose?
3. Do all of the elements,–character, action, dialogue—contribute toward a unified whole?
4. Are all the elements consistent to the kind of story I am telling?
5. Do the supplementary details of character, action and dialogue explain the motives, clarify the characters or advance the plot?
6. Are the characters truly drawn?
7. Does the dialogue seem natural and easy?
8. Does the story move forward continuously from start to finish? [Beranger 71].

These may seem like obvious questions, but one has to remember that Beranger and the other women often left behind in today's courses on screenwriting history, made, cultivated and grew these guidelines and they are still being used today. Her suggestions for making your characters believable are also still accurate to this day. "Know your people so intimately that you can think, feel, and act as they would. If you do this, your characters will be individuals, not stereotypes" (Beranger 91).

Beranger created a set of questions to apply to situations that help writers realize whether that situation should occur or if a change is necessary. This is a very valuable tool in moving the story along and keeping the audience intrigued without repetition or dullness:

1. Does it arouse interest?
2. Does it stimulate an emotional response?
3. Are its potentialities completely developed?
4. Is it composed of action or merely useless movement?
5. Does it lead naturally and smoothly to the next situation?
6. Is it so firmly a part of the structure of the whole that it could not be omitted without destroying the story's unity?
7. Does it help the story's progress toward the final climax? (Beranger 101).

These questions prepare the writer for more of an in-depth look at their scenes rather than merely asking the question, "Is this scene pertinent?" There is a list that helps drive the suspense of the story to a point where the audience is holding their breath in anticipation, and she also created a list of the "Don'ts of Dialogue." Easily accessible, Beranger's manual on screenwriting is manageable and timeless. She seemed to want her readers to succeed, even providing "Common Mistakes of Beginners" (Beranger 134).

Screenwriting isn't just a list of rules and guidelines, however. Beranger had what it took to manage the chaos of early Hollywood and the work ethic required. Hollywood may have quit her but she didn't quit Hollywood. As a teacher and lecturer at the University, she gave students the opportunity to work under one of the best. What an amazing experience it would have been to be instructed by Beranger and the rest of these pioneering women. Beranger could take any medium and make it her own. She started as a journalist, then wrote for the stage, then wrote screen plays, and later in life moved on to novels. One of them, *Peace Begins at Home* (1954), published by Unity School of Christianity in Lee's Summit, Missouri, begs the questions how Beranger was connected to the school and requires further research. Chapter XIV, "The Good Fight," starts out,

> A woman who lives a truly spiritual life said to me recently: "It seems to me that life is one long test of our power to overcome wrong impulses and habits. No sooner do I seem to have conquered one weakness when another rears its ugly head and I have to get to work on it. Why do you suppose we have to labor constantly to keep as good as we know we should be?"

Beranger replies, "What the Lord meant, I think, was that practice in overcoming weakness is necessary for the development of spiritual strength" (Beranger *Peace* 145). Perhaps this is where Beranger found her drive for life and her work ethic. Her spirituality isn't found in most of her other works, so there is a question of whether she separated the two or found religion later on in life.

"Although the development of critical discernment does not predicate success in screenwriting, it will raise the level of audience intelligence; and the higher the intelligence of audiences, the greater will be the demand for better and more significant pictures" (Beranger, *Writing for the Screen* 9). Beranger was continuously encouraging higher learning. This did not necessarily mean a Bachelor's degree or beyond. Her concern was that writers continue to improve their minds and situations to better themselves and the profession. Beranger believed in the power of writing to expand the minds of her audience members and provoke deeper thought.

I wish to be honest and say I was leery of studying Beranger because of the initial lack of flair in her life. But through research, ultimately, I believe I found someone whose work ethic was along the lines of my own. I cannot pretend that I have done or will do as much as she or that I will be as successful. I wish to be as aware of this world as I can in order to fully develop scripts that will leave audiences wanting more, not necessarily a search merely for knowledge but for something more in life.

William C. de Mille died at the age of seventy-six on March 5, 1955. "A few months after William died, his heartbroken widow died" (de Mille 54). It was September 10, 1956, and Clara Beranger died at the age of 70. She was de Mille's sounding post and in turn he was her companion and sweetheart. Beranger had subtly entered Hollywood by way of Paramount and had drastically changed both the company and the man she chose as co-writer and life partner for the better. Beranger was the workhorse of early Hollywood with an intellect that could rival any New Yorker's and the stamina and determination to keep going creatively even as she was forced away from the film industry. Whatever she did, it made an impact, and I believe that to be her greatest achievement. Beranger didn't shout her proclamations, her advice, or her achievements. Her life was full and though her name is barely uttered, she will be remembered among those that appreciate and aspire to inspire women as she did and continues to do.

Works Cited

Beranger, Clara. *Peace Begins at Home*. Lee's Summit: Unity School of Christianity, 1954.

_____. "University Film Producers Association." *SMPTE Motion Imaging Journal* 5.3 (1952): 1–4. *Preparing A Screenplay*. Web. 8 Dec. 2015.

_____. *Writing for the Screen (with Story, Picture Treatment, and Shooting Script)*. Dubuque: W.C. Brown, 1950.

Callahan, Vicki. "Clara, Ouida, Beulah, Et., Al." *Reclaiming the Archive Feminism and Film History*. Detroit: Wayne State University Press, 2010. 289–302.

de Mille, William C. *Hollywood Saga*. New York: E.P. Dutton & Co., 1939.

de Mille, Richard. *My Secret Mother, Lorna Moon*. New York: Farrar, Straus & Giroux, 1998.

McCreadie, Marsha. *Pioneers*. 1/2 ed. Vol. 46. 0. 12.

Parsons, Louella. "Clara Beranger Comments on "The World's Applause." *TAYLOROLOGY: A Continuing Exploration of the Life and Death of William Desmond Taylor*. New York Telegraph, 7 May 1922. Web. 8 Dec. 2015. <http://www.taylorology.com/issues/Taylor62.txt>.

"Sound Waves, Volume 1 Number 7: Periodicals, Books, and Pamphlets." *Sound Waves, Volume 1 Number 7: Periodicals, Books, and Pamphlets*. 15 Nov. 1928. Web. 7 Dec. 2015.

Tibbetts, John C. *Introduction to the Photoplay: 1929, a Contemporary Account of the Transition to Sound in Film*. Shawnee Mission, KS: National Film Society, 1977.

Ida May Park
Prolific Pioneer

Jackie Perez

Ida May Park began and ended her life and career in Los Angeles, California, credited as a writer of approximately five hundred scenarios and fifty features, having had a successful career as a director with fourteen films under her belt. Unfortunately, as a woman of early Hollywood, she falls into a category of women who were notable enough to have some of their work survive and be remembered, but not notable enough for many history books or archives to chronicle her career. Sadly, the majority of her films both written and directed have been lost to time. The little information that has survived about Park, not only a prolific and successful screenwriter, but one of the pioneering female directors in the industry during her time, is scattered to the four corners of the internet and various books. Only a few pieces of her work have been saved. Thanks to research, her hard work and perseverance in the motion picture industry will be remembered.

At the age of fifteen Park started her career as a stage actress. She met her future husband, actor Joseph De Grasse, in the theatre and spent her career working side by side with him in the burgeoning film business. When De Grasse joined the Pathé Company as an actor in 1909, Park came with him as a scenario writer. After Pathé, Park and her husband found work at the Universal Film Manufacturing Company where she would stay under contract until 1920 (Slide 57). In its early days, Universal marketed films under the subsidiary brands of companies that had merged or were acquired. Park began her motion picture writing career at the Rex Motion Picture Company and her films were marketed and sold branded as Rex dramas. Universal's leading writing-directing team Lois Weber and husband Phillips Smalley led the way at Rex when it joined Universal in 1914. Later that year, Park and De Grasse joined the ranks as another husband and wife, writing-directing team. Each of Universal's subsidiary brands consisted of tried and true actor/writer/director combinations. Park and De Grasse's films featured Pauline Bush and Lon Chaney (Cooper 53).

When Universal formed a new film label called Bluebird, Park's name was absent from the announcement in the July 25, 1914, issue of Universal Weekly, though credits on their films show she was Bluebird's primary scenario writer. Bluebird's production model differed from the other Universal brands and functioned more akin to a modern day first look deal. Bluebird used Universal actors and lot space, and films were distributed

Writer Ida May Park shooting on location, circa 1914. Park wrote for more than 50 films between 1914 and 1930, and directed 14 films between 1917 and 1920 (Academy of Motion Picture Arts and Sciences' Margaret Herrick Library).

under the Universal name, while all business flowed through Bluebird's general manager. The Bluebird films, dealing with womanly issues of the time like high society and the importance of marrying well, became the top grossing Universal brand in 1916. When Weber departed, Park maintained the established brand.

Though she wrote close to five hundred scenarios the Internet Movie Database (IMDb) list credits fifty written films by Park, but only six of her produced films are viewable today and of them, only one survives in full, *The Hidden Way* (1926). *Alas and Alack* (1915) is missing its final five minutes. Only reels one and two exist of *A Mother's Atonement* (1915); reels 2, 3 and 5 of *If My Country Should Call* (1916); reels 2–5 of *The Place Beyond the Winds* (1916); and reels 3 and 4 of *Bread* (1918).

Alas and Alack and *The Hidden Way* (1926) are available online and the rest are archived at the Library of Congress, viewable only in person at the site. No websites or books are solely dedicated to the life and works of Park, but one can follow the trail to her work by way of actor Lon Chaney who was the premier actor for Bluebird. Chaney appeared in forty-one films written by Park, beginning with *Her Bounty* in 1914 and ending with *Broadway Love* in 1918 (Mirsalis). Park goes uncredited as the writer in many of her earlier films from 1914 and 1915. It is unknown whether that was a personal or contractual choice.

The majority of Park's films feature a female lead who begins the story as poor, beaten, and/or single and receives a fairy tale ending. It happens to Eve, the poor flower girl in *Lights and Shadows* (1914); Nan, the tempted chorus girl in *When the Gods Played a Badger Game* (1915) and Rose, raised by a cruel hag in *Where the Forest Ends* (1915). The same tropes are then repeated in Jess, the wife of a poor fisherman in *Alas and Alack* (1915); Lucille, the wife of a rich but neglectful social parasite in *Tangled Hearts* (1916) and Bobbie, the daughter of an invalid widow in *Bobbie of the Ballet* (1916). Finally the experiences continue for Priscilla with the cruel father in *The Place Beyond the Winds* (1916); Helen the orphan in *The Price of Silence* (1916); Mary and Fannie with a dead mother and criminal father in *The Girl in the Checkered Coat* (1917) and Madge with the frail mother and alcoholic father in *Fires of Rebellion* (1917).

Also, the same basic situations occur again and again in Park's stories. In *The Grasp of Greed* (1916), *The Sin of Olga Brandt* (1916), *The Millionaire Paupers* (1915), and *Fires of Rebellion* (1917) a woman is forced into a less than desirable situation due to lack of money. Jealousy caused by or causing someone to have an affair appears in *The Pipes of Pan* (1914), *When the Gods Played a Badger Game* (1915), *Mountain Justice* (1915), *An Idyl of the Hills* (1915), *Lon of Lone Mountain* (1915), and *The Rescue* (1917). Forced marriages are found in *The Sin of Olga Brandt* (1916), *The Grind* (1915), *The Grip of Jealousy* (1916), *The Gilded Spider* (1916), *The Place Beyond the Winds* (1916), *Hell Morgan's Girl* (1917), *The Grand Passion* (1918), and *Broadway Love* (1918). Often her characters fall in love with married men, particularly in *Where the Forest Ends* (1915), *When the Gods Played a Badger Game* (1915), *Tangled Hearts* (1916), *Lights and Shadows* (1914). Finally, Park had a penchant for virtuous women turning bad men's lives around, as seen in *The Grind* (1915), *The Stronger Mind* (1915), *The Grand Passion* (1918).

Overall, despite the beginning horrible circumstances faced by her main female characters, the majority of the films end on a happy note with the leads nuzzling in each other's arms once all their problems are solved. It can be quite disconcerting to think about these films as a reflection of the times for women. Yet there are several of Park's Bluebird films that broke with the brand's traditional storylines, and are worth mentioning.

In the 1915 one-reel film, *All for Peggy*, a woman falls in love with a man of high social status whose family disapproves of the relationship. His disapproving father makes a bet with his son that if his horse wins at the races, his son will give up the girl. The son agrees but learns that the horse is a sure thing. He gets the jockey drunk to ensure the horse will lose, but knowing a lot of the family's money is riding on the horse winning, the girl poses as the jockey and rides the horse to victory. The father allows the marriage due to her tenacity (Mirsalis). *All for Peggy* is one of the few films that feature a strong female protagonist who takes action to get what she wants. While a love across the tracks type of story, the twist of the girl taking her fate into her own hands and sacrificing her own future to save her lover transforms her character into one that stands apart from other Bluebird leads.

In the one-reel film *Quits* (1915) a sheriff is saved from quicksand by a Frenchman on the run from the law for murdering his wife. The sheriff takes the Frenchman home and discovers the Frenchman's dead wife is his old sweetheart, the one that got away and that he never forgot. When the police arrive to tell the sheriff about the murder, he repays the Frenchman for saving his life by allowing the man a head start out of town. When the cops catch up, the man escapes their bullets and remains on the loose (Mirsalis). The film received one of the best reviews from Motion Picture News when it was released: "The picture ... is positively one of the strongest single reel dramas that we have ever seen. While void of a love story—in fact not one woman appears in the film—the subject is tremendously powerful because of its character delineations and its excellent treatment ... this is a real drama and deserves to be highly featured." Leaving the model of most of her scenarios, Park wrote a thriller centered around two men, which was well received by audiences.

In the drama *The Price of Silence* (1916) the orphan Helen is sent to live with a strict family in the forest as punishment. She falls in love with a man named Ralph and because they plan on marrying the next day, he convinces her to sleep with him. He dies in a lightning storm before they marry. Back at her normal home, living with her aunt and her cousin Emily, Helen discovers she is pregnant when planning to wed millionaire Oliver. Oliver leaves for an extended time and Helen gives birth to a son named Billy. She gives Billy to her nurse's daughter Jenny to care for, not wanting Oliver to know of the bastard child. When Oliver returns, he and Helen have a daughter named Arline. Helen's doctor, who delivered Billy and Arline, blackmails Helen in order to marry her daughter Arline. But Arline loves Billy and neither of them knows they are related to each other. The two elope and Oliver and the doctor go after them. When the doctor exposes Helen's history to Oliver, he attacks the doctor, crashes the car, and the doctor dies in the crash. Jenny the nurse reveals that Helen's real son died shortly after birth and in order to keep the monetary support flowing, she passed off her son as Helen's. Arline and Billy are allowed to marry and live happily ever after (Mirsalis).

This description is by far one of the most enjoyable yet also ridiculous plotlines of any of Park's films, but unfortunately the actual film stock has been lost to time. With so many twists and turns this film could even keep the interest of today's jaded audiences. Critics in 1916 were less than enthusiastic. Moving Picture World said "While it is a well-made production, [it] is unfortunately based on an unpleasant theme ... considerable is made in the production of bedroom and undress scenes; more in fact than would give the production a place among films for young people."

The Hidden Way (1926) was written late in Ida May Park's career and is the only five-reel feature written by Park that is viewable in its entirety. A copy of the film was found at the New Zealand Film Archive and was preserved thanks to a grant via the National Film Preservation Society in 2013. The story follows three recently released inmates who save a young woman named Mary from a runaway carriage heading straight for a train. The youngest inmate, Harry, is injured in the process and Mary takes them all to her mother's house where she also lives. The gracious mother invites them to stay not knowing their background. While eating dinner, Mary puts away her unused money and the biggest scoundrel of the three, pick pocket Mulligan, plots to rob the women of their nest egg.

At the top of act two, fast driving slick Sid goes over to take Mary out shopping and almost runs his ex-wife and child over on the road. When Mary discovers the money is missing she does not raise questions about its whereabouts. While, Harry, the youngest and also best looking jailbird helps with chores about the house to win Mary's appreciation, the other two men find a natural spring on the estate grounds and hatch a scheme to sell phony mineral water. When they pool their money together for the company the third inmate, Bill, discovers Mulligan has robbed him, too. Bill and Harry take to their new setting and Bill starts falling for Sid's ex-wife while Harry falls in love with Mary. Their newfound loves prevent them from following through with their scheme. Mulligan leaves and all the stolen money is returned to Mary and her mother.

Compared to summaries of her other scenarios, *The Hidden Way* has many similarities to her previous work: a story that revolves around a pretty young women pining for a better life and a multi-character dramatic plot, but the numerous characters and storylines began to overshadow each other by the final act. Mary's mother, while one of the most interesting, is the least developed character. In 68 minutes, the story and relationships are set up nicely but by act three there is so much going on it becomes hard to keep track or continue caring. *The Hidden Way* did not do well when released in 1926 and may not be the best sample of Park's work. Unfortunately for those interested in Park, other surviving work left for study is rare.

As a director Park could not have started at a better time at Universal. From 1912 to 1919, the studio held female directors in high regard and gave them as good a chance as any male artist to direct a successful film. "From its inception in 1912 through 1919 ... the studio credited eleven women with directing more than 170 films." Despite this record, the good times did not least and "...in 1919, Universal credited five feature films to women directors. The following year, for the first time in its history, it credited not a single title to a woman. With the sole exception of [Lois] Weber ... the studio did not name a woman director again until 1982, when Amy Heckerling made *Fast Times at Ridgemont High*" (Cooper 15). The reason for this dramatic shift well before sound is unknown. There are no recorded meetings, conversations, or decisions that pinpoint why Universal went from being a leader of female directors to not hiring a single female to direct one of their films for decades.

During her time at Universal, Park directed fourteen films in a time when female filmmakers were scarce. Of all the studios in town Universal employed the greatest number of female directors. In an interview with Frances Denton in Photoplay Magazine, Park tells the readers that directing wasn't something she naturally gravitated towards. "It was because directing seemed so utterly unsuited to a woman that I refused the first company offered me." Park received her own subsidiary company at Universal in 1917 the same year the Photoplay article was written ("Ready! Shoot!" *Photoplay* 1 December 1917).

Finally, Park became a mentor to other female filmmakers. In 1920 she wrote "The Motion-Picture Director" chapter for Boston Publishing House Houghton Mifflin's informational handbook *Careers for Women*, a book that outlined the qualities and responsibilities of numerous career options women could pursue in that year. This publication was printed just after her stint at Universal, which means she wrote it at the tail end of her time there. Although this is a book for women, Park opens by making a point that directing is a job that both men and women can perform equally.

> The vocation of the motion-picture director is one that commands so comprehensive a knowledge of the arts and sciences, economics and human nature that it is particularly difficult to describe. To the almost unlimited mental demands on the director is added the necessity of an invulnerable physique. Perhaps that is why the number of consistently successful directors, both male and female, is relatively so small. But having these things there is no one, man or woman, who might not take up the profession with a certain degree of confidence in his or her ultimate success [335].

Park wanted women to understand that while a "well-developed dramatic instinct" was absolutely necessary for success, with hard work, knowledge, and confidence one could set out on a path towards a successful directing career. She goes on to mention that a natural born instinct is more powerful than anything that can be learned in training. In the *Careers for Women* handbook, Park states:

> (I am now writing to women alone) it is her sense of dramatic value that imparts to, or withholds from, the pictures that indefinable something which can raise it to the ultimate peak of picture perfection or relegate it to the vast scrap-heap of "rubber-stamp" productions [335].

Park inspires women to be confident in their opinions! It is their personal touch that will elevate their film, something referred to today as an artist's individual voice. Don't be afraid to think outside the box or raise one's voice to be heard. That is what will set one apart.

The next section on "Opportunity for Advancement" is worthwhile to note and compare with the state of the industry then and now. Park assures, "Once in the game the aspirant to a directorship will find the opportunities limitless.... The perfect picture is still a thing of dreams. An industry can develop only as the intelligence which directs it develops" (Filene 336).

The same year that *Careers for Women* was published, Park's directing career effectively ended. She had fourteen films under her belt but the paradigm shift at Universal in 1920 saw a dearth of female directors for decades to come. All over the industry, less and less women were helming films, meaning Park's vision of limitless opportunities never came to fruition. Even today there has not been a steady climb towards equal directing numbers for men and women. Quite the contrary. An article on Deadline Hollywood announced that "6.4% of the 347 feature films released in 2013 and 2014 were directed by women, and only 3.1% of the 212 films with domestic box office grosses greater than $10 million were helmed by women" (Robb "DGA: Women Directed Only 6.4% of Feature Films in 2013 & 2014"). Warner Bros, Disney, Weinstein, and Open Road did not hire a single female director on any of their films during those two years. In the same article, DGA President Paris Barclay commented on the directing imbalance, "What this report does not reflect is what people who love film—even our culture as a whole—are missing when such a disproportionate percentage of films are directed by one gender or one ethnicity." I believe Park would agree. If more than half the population is shut out from participating because of gender or the color of their skin, than the path towards increased artistry in the medium will be slow and stagnant. We are in an age of the "male gaze" and until women and minorities fill more leadership positions in film as screenwriters, directors, producers, and studio executives, this disturbing pattern shows no signs of changing.

When *Careers for Women* was revised and republished in 1934, the "The Motion-Picture Director" chapter was not included (Slide 58). Park states in *Careers for Women*:

> The director must never lose her poise, must never betray the slightest annoyance unless she wishes to jeopardize the success of her picture.... As for the natural equipment of women for the role of director, the superiority of their emotional and imaginative faculties gives them a great advantage.... But unless you are hardy and determined, the director's role is not for you [337].

Did Park ever feel that she needed to be more "hardy and determined" than her male colleagues? Women have quietly experienced sexism for many years. Recently there has been a vocal outcry in Hollywood regarding the lack of gender parity and rampant sexism in the film and TV industry. In May 2015 the outcry rang so loudly that the A.C.L.U. demanded an investigation into the discrimination against female filmmakers in Hollywood (Buckley). In response, the federal Equal Employment Opportunities Commission launched a formal inquiry into the allegations in October 2015 (Robb "Feds Officially Probing Hollywood's Lack of Female Directors").

Ida May Park was a strong woman who accomplished much and paved the way for women working in the film industry during the early days of film. By recognizing her contributions to film, and taking the time to acknowledge her life, we are bringing life to women whom history has forgotten. Park is not only a pioneer but also an inspiration.

WORKS CITED

Buckley, Cara. "A.C.L.U., Citing Bias Against Women, Wants Inquiry Into Hollywood's Hiring Practices." *New York Times*. New York Times, 12 May 2015.
Cooper, Mark. "Ida May Park." *Women Film Pioneers Project*. Center for Digital Research and Scholarship, 27 Sept. 2013.
Cooper, Mark Garrett. *Universal Women Filmmaking and Institutional Change in Early Hollywood*. Urbana: University of Illinois Press, 2010.
Denton, Francis. "Ready! Shoot!" *Photoplay Magazine*. 1 Dec. 1917.
Filene, Catherine. "The Motion-Picture Director." *Careers for Women*. Boston: Houghton Mifflin, 1920. 335–337.
The Hidden Way. Dir. Joseph De Grasse. 1926.
Mirsalis, John. "The Films of Lon Chaney, Sr." *Lon Chaney Filmography*. 2008.
"PRESERVED FILMS." *National Film Preservation Foundation: The Hidden Way (1926)*.
Robb, David. "DGA: Women Directed Only 6.4% of Feature Films in 2013 & 2014." *Deadline*. 9 Dec. 2015.
_____. "Feds Officially Probing Hollywood's Lack of Female Directors." *Deadline*. 6 Oct. 2015.
Slide, Anthony. *The Silent Feminists: America's First Women Directors*. Lanham, MD: Scarecrow Press, 1996.

Frances Goodrich and Albert Hackett

The Most Beloved Couple in Hollywood

JULIE BERKOBIEN

Securing a writing partner in Hollywood that one can maintain longevity through various successes and failures is a unique find. Even more rare in Hollywood are monogamous and devoted marital partnerships. The brilliant and witty Frances Goodrich and Albert Hackett were blessed to find both in each other. "The Hacketts," as they were affectionately labeled for the majority of their careers, most often dismissed their extraordinary talent for good old-fashioned hard work. While the couple's humility was refreshing to many in the film industry, their contemporaries saw the situation a bit differently and praised the writing team accordingly.

Writer and director Garson Kanin referred to the Hacketts as "...an enchanting couple; they were the writers the producers and directors used to kill to get" (Goodrich 2). David Brown said they were "The ultimate class writing team of the Golden Age of Hollywood.... Virtually all their films were successful.... They were the epitome of elegance in writing" (Goodrich 167). Philip Dunne, while listing screenwriters he admired most, put Goodrich and Hackett first: "They are professionals whose name on the script is a guarantee of excellence" (Goodrich 97). "Film actors, it is said, liked to perform scripts by the Hacketts; for some reason they always ended up getting praised for the intelligence of their interpretations" (Hamilton 255). Famed in the industry for being kind, modest, decent people first, and gifted writers second, Frances Goodrich and Albert Hackett not only made a lasting impact on their peers but also on culture in America and the world.

Both Goodrich and Hackett started their careers as stage actors. Albert Hackett beginning at six years old, just after the death of his father. His then twenty-two-year-old mother had three children, no income to support them and was advised by many in her family to take the children to an orphanage. Hackett's mother listened to another suggestion instead: that she put the family on stage (Goodrich 21). Frances Goodrich, nine years Hackett's senior, had a more privileged upbringing and pursued the stage after graduating from Vassar. She performed with various companies, notably the North Hampton Massachusetts Players production of *Hamlet*. Cast as the Player Queen she

Frances Goodrich and Albert Hackett (Berkobien) 141

Writers Frances Goodrich and Albert Hackett in their office at MGM, circa 1930. Married for 54 years and writing partners for even longer, "the Hacketts" were revered by their contemporaries in Hollywood for both their talent and integrity (Academy of Motion Picture Arts and Sciences' Margaret Herrick Library).

shared the stage with William Powell, who played Horatio, and for whom she would one day write three films (Goodrich 7–10). Both Goodrich and Hackett acted on the stage with Humphrey Bogart during their careers as performers: Hackett in New York during a production of *Up the Ladder* and additionally in various vaudeville routines, and Goodrich in June of 1929 at the Lakewood Theatre in a performance of *Upstairs and Down*. Bogart carried her on stage, as he was then playing the charming playboy roles that preceded his tough guy screen image. "That was fun," Goodrich remembered with a smile years later (Goodrich 49).

By the time the couple first met, they were both aspiring playwrights and Goodrich asked Hackett for assistance on a play she was penning entitled *Such a Lady*. "He tore it to bits and destroyed it" Goodrich recalled, to which Hackett added, "It's a wonder we were still speaking after that" (Goodrich 37). "We began to write together. We were both trying to make some money writing; then we exchanged views on things; and then we started to rewrite each other's stuff. That's how we got involved, exchanging those dreadful comments" (Rowland 201). The two never worked alone or collaborated with others again, though Goodrich did have one unsuccessful attempt at collaborating with another female writer once while Hackett was away. "I had to be very polite so as not to hurt her feelings. I'd say, "My dear, this is just delightful … but don't you think it might be a little easier to speak if you wrote it a bit more colloquially?" It took so much time being polite that we got very little work done (Goodrich 37).

Politeness was not a staple in the working relationship between the Hacketts. Once when Hackett suggested a line Goodrich yelled, "over my dead body does that line go in!" so loudly that she lost her voice. Hackett recalled: "For three days, we couldn't work because I couldn't hear what she was saying" (Goodrich 38). Goodrich was quoted as saying, "Albert once said to me, which was a much crueler thing, 'If you think that's good, you should be scared.' You know, you couldn't say anything worse than that, could you? Quietly, he said it. Didn't lose his voice at all" (Rowland 203–204). The couple's writing process was so intense that when they finished a scene they were unable to lay claim upon original ideas, always graciously giving one another the credit but never truly knowing or caring.

Up Pops the Devil was their first hit, "…spiked by the sort of snappy dialogue and sly turn of wit that would eventually become their trademark" (Rowland 197). The show ran for 146 performances on Broadway and a West Coast production of the show in Los Angeles followed. Soon after, Paramount purchased the movie rights to the play and invited Hackett to come to Hollywood as the "dialogue director." All of these sudden life-changing opportunities nudged Goodrich and Hackett towards an important business decision. On the morning of February 7, 1931, a deputy clerk married them at city hall in Manhattan with only two city office workers in attendance as witnesses. The writing team tried their best to keep the ceremony a secret, but they were recognized and soon reporters and photographers crowded around the building to capture photos of the couple (Goodrich 52–53).

While Hackett was working in Hollywood he quickly realized that "dialogue director" was not a stable job. He decided to utilize his time on set studying the nuanced differences between stage and screen. He was offered a lucrative seven year acting contract but knowing that Goodrich was unhappy living in Los Angeles (his hours at the studio were long she had no other friends in the city) Hackett opted to return to New York. Back east and happy, the team penned a second successful stage comedy *The Bridal Wise*

(Rowland 197). Sometime later, the Hacketts received an offer from MGM to return to Hollywood as a writing team for $750 a week, an enticing offer during the Great Depression. They did their calculations and realized that they had spent almost a year writing and rewriting *The Bridal Wise* and had made roughly $3.50 a week, "so we were glad to go back to California and begin earning a salary that was very gratifying indeed" (Goodrich 58). "We put in a long stretch at Metro ... but we were never glamour; we were just very busy writers" (Wilk 216).

The birth of the Screen Writers Guild in 1933 brought with it new hope for overworked and underappreciated writers; the Hacketts quickly offered their free time to the effort. Both cared deeply about their fellow writers, believed in supporting underdogs and were already members of the Dramatist Guild and Actors Equity Union, which had successfully fought management back in New York. Goodrich volunteered as the Guild's secretary and Hackett served on the board (Goodrich 98–99). Goodrich recalled:

> The pressure at MGM was relentless ... the [studio] had influential people around all the time, day after day, talking to writers, particularly the young writers, the ones who are just starting.... So we proselytized, too. We walked around the lot, and so did Lilly Hellman, and we talked to the young kids ... but only on our lunch hour so that no one could ever say we had used studio time for union activities [Goodrich 101].

The efforts of the volunteers paid off and the Screen Writers Guild won the binding election for union membership through the National Labor Relations Board. In a newsletter mailed to members of the Academy, an article titled "In the Beginning" addressed to the members of the AMPAS Writer's Branch offered what seemed like a peace offering:

> Screenwriting has received little critical evaluation. Individual screenwriters have no fan-following. But every person who has been professionally engaged in any one of the motion picture arts or sciences knows the primary importance of story to a picture ... the script needs its interpreters and the interpreters need the script [McCall 2].

In 1934 MGM assigned the couple to adapt *The Thin Man*, a book by Dashiell Hammett. The Hacketts admittedly struggled with the story at first. Goodrich wrote to a friend: "Albert and I do not believe it's a good script or a good book or a good story." In a separate correspondence she wrote: "Still slaving away at *The Thin Man*, if it would only make me thin I could bear it" (Goodrich 76). Dramatics aside, the Hacketts finished the script in three weeks. *The Thin Man*, was a tremendous success and labeled "superlative cinema" (Goodrich 77). Hailed as one of the first happily married couples on the big screen, it was not hard to imagine the leads, Nick and Nora Charles, as "slightly idealized" versions of their screenwriters who were often dubbed "Hollywood's most playfully affectionate husband-and-wife team" (Goodrich 75). In his book, *Writers in Hollywood*, Ian Hamilton wrote:

> The banter between [Nick and Nora] is witty enough, line by line, but what makes it unusual is its deeply companionable spirit: the barbs and counterbarbs add up to a sort of ardently literate love talk, a sustaining of the relationship's vitality and edge—and it's equality.... The Nick and Nora Charles partnership was Dashiell Hammett's invention, but Albert and Frances Hackett knew it from within and added much that was their own [255].

The film bursts with witty banter and clever one-liners that still strike a nerve with modern day audiences. Mark Rowland wrote in "Frances Goodrich and Albert Hackett: Perfectionists": "Myrna Loy, who played Nora Charles in the film, lauded her character's 'gorgeous sense of humor. She appreciated the distinctive grace of her husband's wit and laughed at him and with him when he was funny'—comments that apply with equal felicity to the Hacketts themselves" (197). The film also featured a dog named Asta, used to liven up "necessary but potentially dull conversation" in the screenplay by having Nick and Nora talk while dog walking. Asta was as big of a hit with audiences when the film released; she was named "the best known dog in the nation" and became famous abroad (Goodrich 77–78).

The Hacketts worked for Hunt Stromberg while under contract at MGM and rarely interacted with Irving Thalberg. Under Stromberg the couple experienced a great deal of control over their work that contracted studio writers seldom enjoyed. In a 1972 interview, the couple recalled their appreciation for Stromberg:

> He listened ... not may writers could have that going with a producer... we could go off on a vacation and when we'd come back we'd say, "we found a beautiful actor in New York" and he'd say "Who? Who?" and we'd say "He's a young guy named Jimmy Stewart," and next thing you'd know, they'd signed him up, and he'd come out, and he ended up in one of our Thin Man pictures [Wilk 215].

Jimmy Stewart was cast in two of the Hackett's films at MGM after they discovered him. First in *Rose-Marie* (1936) and then in *After the Thin Man* (1936), both roles bolstered his career.

The success of *The Thin Man* (1934) led to plans for a sequel, and the series would eventually go on to feature six films with the Hacketts writing the screenplays for the first three. David L. Goodrich wrote in his book The Real Nick and Nora: "The couple intentionally closed all three of their screenplays with intimate, emotionally charged and funny final scenes. In the first they deftly caught the delicious, naughty, only us feeling of exciting sexual encounters—and did so without resorting to today's flesh shots and heavy breathing" (113). "Instead they wrote Asta covering his eyes while Nick joins Nora in her bunk for the night" (Van Dyke 1934). At the end of the second picture, *After the Thin Man* (1936) the Charleses are again in an intimate setting while they prepare for bed. Nora is knitting, after a few rounds of banter Nick mentions that her project "...looks like a baby sock" and Nora smiles. Realization hits; Nick's jaw drops and then Nora has a line that particularly pleased Goodrich, who remembered the joy of writing it: "And you call yourself a detective" (Goodrich 113). The Hacketts were growing sick of Nick and Nora and wrote them as expecting a child in hopes of ending their adventurous life and the possibility of yet another sequel. The baby was Goodrich and Hackett's second choice: "We wanted to kill both of them at the end of the second picture just to be sure ... but Hunt [Stromberg] wouldn't let us" (Goodrich 113–114). In 1939 the Hacketts finally wrote their last final scene for the Thin Man series. Goodrich and Hackett plagiarized from their own work to create it. True to form, the leads are once again in an intimate setting, dressing to go out with friends that they flat out ignore in an effort to spend the night in together instead (Van Dyke 1939). In its sexual tension, and the deadpan ignoring of interruptions, this scene is a close copy of the ending of *Up Pops the Devil* (Goodrich 131).

Robert Lord, a friend of the Hacketts, once gave a speech in which he called the film business in the 1930s: "...hectic, frenzied, hysterical, tough, exhausting, and man-killing and furthermore, most people in it suffered from battlefield nerves.... The men curse, the women weep. Both sexes develop luxuriant crops of stomach ulcers" (Goodrich 123). The majority of his words accurately described the Hacketts' Hollywood experience from 1936 to 1939, as David Goodrich wrote: "They worked far too hard; they did curse and weep; they did experience battlefield nerves; and in the end they were hit by a health problem—not ulcers, but something Frances called 'our lovely nervous breakdown'" (123).

The couple grew tired of their writing assignments, studio grind and friends, a time which Goodrich described as, "You get feeling so horribly dull out here and you see the same people and hear the same talk all the time" (Goodrich 134). Their crisis was mutual: "We had a nervous breakdown together—this is a real team!" They found themselves unable to write, when they did write something they hated it, Hackett lost a great deal of weight and they both felt "punch drunk, slaphappy and on the ropes." The couple packed up, left Los Angeles and headed home to Manhattan. Together they began a self-imposed sabbatical from the movies, vowing to never overwork themselves again, a promise they kept to one another until they took on the script for *The Diary of Anne Frank* (Goodrich 135).

For three years the Hacketts lived on the East Coast and returned to writing for the stage, reworking some of their old scripts for fun. Hackett returned to acting, the couple bought land in Vermont and spent time relaxing with family. In 1942 they returned to Hollywood when Paramount offered them a contract for $3,250 a week for six weeks to write the screenplay for Moss Hart's Broadway hit *Lady in the Dark*; the first work to dramatize psychoanalysis for a large scale audience. Paramount had purchased the movie rights to the play for an unprecedented sum of $285,000. The film did well at the box office but received many bad reviews, mainly due to the fact that Paramount felt that psychoanalysis would not appeal to mass audiences and rewrote a large portion of the Hacketts' script. Paramount replaced many of the Broadway show songs with new ones and took out thought-provoking elements in order to stress more elaborately costumed dream sequences instead. The changes both disappointed and infuriated Goodrich and Hackett. Amongst the poor reviews, one critic wrote: "The producers, and not Goodrich and Hackett, should be blamed for the superficiality ... their screenplay was inoffensively amusing and the interplay between Ginger Rogers and Ray Milland benefited from Goodrich and Hackett's dialogue, with its usual good-natured banter" (Goodrich 143).

In 1945 Frank Capra bought the story rights to *The Greatest Gift* (a short story printed on a Christmas card) for his newly formed Liberty Films. Dalton Trumbo, Clifford Odets and Marc Connolly had all drafted screenplays to no avail before the Hacketts were attached to the project (Goodrich 160). Goodrich said that those screenwriters "had gone off track ... they had gone off into stories of politics and other things.... But [basically], it was a simple story so we went back to the Christmas card" (Goodrich 161). The Hacketts kept some of the scenes created by Odets in their script, such as the young George Bailey being hit in the ear by the drunken druggist; George rescuing his drowning brother; and the moonlit walk taken by George and Mary; all iconic moments from the film. The process started out smoothly but while the Hacketts were moving the story for what was now renamed *It's a Wonderful Life*, someone told them Capra had hired Jo Swerling to work on the script with him. "Jo Swerling was a very close friend of ours and when we heard that he was working behind us all the time, which was supposed to be against the rules of the Screen Writers Guild, it was a very unpleasant feeling." Soon after, tensions worsened during a meeting when Capra condescendingly addressed Goodrich as "my dear woman" (Goodrich 161–162). The final straw for Goodrich was when Capra continued to pressure the Hacketts to finish the script quickly. In her words: "He couldn't wait to get writing on the script himself" (Rowland 210). When the Hacketts turned in their draft, Capra quickly began making changes but later, while the film was being shot, he reverted back to the simple, gentler scenes that Goodrich and Hackett had originally written (Goodrich 160–161). The couple could never bring themselves to see the film when it released due to their bitterness towards the project. In a 1983 interview, one year before Goodrich died, the couple confirmed that they had never seen the beloved film at all. Goodrich stated, "It's the only unpleasant experience we've ever had" (Rowland 210).

A comparison of the unpublished 1946 draft of *It's a Wonderful Life* to its unpublished draft of the Final Script as Shot: March 4, 1947, at the Margaret Herrick Library in Los Angeles confirms that Capra did in fact insert his own scenes into and add to the Hacketts' work, only to later drop those changes while filming. The 1946 draft contains scenes dated between January and May that read as though they might belong to the Hacketts, with new scenes inserted throughout the summer that say FRANK CAPRA at the top of pages in large bold letters. A quick comparison of these Capra scenes to the shooting script, both published and unpublished, and to the film itself is all that is needed to showcase how Capra was severely reaching for the one third writing credit he ended up sharing with Jo Swerling and the Hacketts (Capra 1947). Capra's largest scene in the unpublished draft of the script was added on August 5, 1946, and runs for five pages. The scene revolves around young George, Harry, Mary and the rest of their friends participating in some sort of Winter Olympics–like games while Potter watches. The boys tease Mary, Mary makes eyes at George and at the end of the scene George saves Harry when he falls through the ice. All but George's heroic moment was removed from the script prior to or during filming, and as previously mentioned, that plot point existed in Goodrich and Hackett's pass from the script as originated by Clifford Odets. Also noteworthy, the line "George Bailey, I'll love you till the day I die"—a fan favorite—is dated as being added to the script April 18, 1946, indicating that Goodrich and Hackett had something to do with its creation.

The Hacketts' next two scripts were musicals. First, they worked on *The Pirate* (1948) starring Judy Garland and Gene Kelly for four months and were paid $75,000 for it. It opened to excellent reviews but did poorly at the box office, losing over $2 million. The failure has been explained many ways: "the movie was almost too fine for huge commercial appeal, the merchandising was wrong and the picture was 20 years ahead of its time" (Goodrich 170). The following month, their film *Easter Parade* (1948) was released, also starring Judy Garland, and this time they pleased both the critics and the audiences. The film succeeded financially for MGM and has been called "one of Hollywood's most memorable musicals" (Goodrich 173). The Hacketts won two Screen Writers Guild Awards for their contributions: Best Written American Musical (Screenplay) and Best Written American Musical (Story); but unfortunately, once again, their work had been tampered with and Goodrich and Hackett were not happy. Arthur Freed thought the script was too harsh and brought in Sidney Sheldon to give it a lighter tone. Absolutely furious, the Hacketts refused to work for Freed ever again, turning down *Annie Get Your Gun* when he offered it to them (Goodrich 173–174).

Feeling a bit pigeonholed as writers of musicals, the Hacketts moved back to comedy in 1949. The team took on an adaptation of the best-selling book *Father of the Bride*, a comedy about a man whose heart breaks as he is about to lose his daughter to marriage. Released in 1950, directed by Vincent Minnelli, the film starred Spencer Tracy, Elizabeth Taylor, and Joan Bennett: "Sadness in reality—again, as in *It's a Wonderful Life*, Goodrich and Hackett helped to create a marvelous movie that has lasted not simply because of clever dialogue, but because it puts audiences in close touch with a likable, well-drawn character who's suffering in a way that's understandable and moving" (Goodrich 184). The success of the film lead to a sequel, *Father's Little Dividend* (1951). There were talks of a third film which worried Goodrich and Hackett, not wanting to get roped into yet another series. Serendipitously, an altercation between Joan Bennett, Jennings Lang—Bennett's lover—and Bennett's husband, Walter Wanger (that resulted in Lang being shot in the scrotum and Bennett's career in shambles) prevented the third film from happening. Always witty, Hackett was quoted as saying, "…that saved us…. He didn't kill him, but I imagine he ruined the affair" (Goodrich 186).

When MGM bought the rights to the novel *The Long, Long Trailer* they offered it to the Hacketts and director Vincent Minelli. The film was set to star Lucille Ball and Desi Arnaz, the hope being that they would lure television viewers back into the movie theaters. *The Long, Long Trailer* (1953) brought in a great deal of money for the studio and the Hacketts' screenplay was nominated for the Writers Guild of America's Best Written Comedy award (Goodrich 195).

In November of 1953, Goodrich and Hackett embarked upon a journey they would one-day call their most important and rewarding achievement. Kermit Bloomgarden reached out to the team about writing a play based on the book *The Diary of Anne Frank*. Lillian Hellman had been offered the job but had declined and suggested the Hacketts in her place saying, "If I did this it would run one night because it would be deeply depressing. You need someone who has a much lighter touch" (Goodrich 205–206). Less than a month later Goodrich, Hackett and Bloomgarden agreed to proceed forward with the play and the Hacketts asked their agent to secure them six months off from MGM. They turned their guest bedroom into an office and filled it with books on Holland, Jewish religion, Jewish holidays, Jewish history, teenagers, Jewish prayer books and hymnbooks, any and everything they could get their hands on to immerse themselves in Frank's culture. On January 21, 1954, Goodrich wrote in her journal: "Finished rough, very rough draft … started back at beginning. This is not like any other job we have done … terrible emotional impact, I cry all the time" (Goodrich 206–207).

On April 22, 1954, the Hacketts finished their third draft of the play and, feeling that the first 30 pages lacked direction, started again from the beginning. Frazzled by the process and defensive of their work, Goodrich found herself over explaining their project to film industry colleagues, even shouting "…if we wanted a picture job we could go get a picture job" at a Hollywood party given by Nunnally Johnson. Hackett noted: "When you're writing a play in New York, you're treated like a playwright. In Hollywood you're an unemployed screenwriter" (Goodrich 208). In May the couple finished their fourth draft of the play, only to have everyone involved dislike it. While traveling to New York, the Hacketts decided to stay there for the remainder of their rewrites and found themselves refreshed by the change of location (Goodrich 208–209). While in New York, Hellman provided Goodrich with "brilliant advice on construction" which lead to a completed sixth draft of the play in October 1954. The Hacketts asked for more time off from MGM and sent the script to Garson Kanin who agreed to direct and further collaborated with Goodrich and Hackett to make Frank's world as realistic and deep as possible. Kanin's contributions were so immense that Goodrich and Hackett wanted him listed as a collaborator on the script, but he declined. Unsatisfied, when Random House published the play the Hacketts dedicated the script to Kanin (Goodrich 212–213).

The production team went to Amsterdam to meet Otto Frank and see the Annex where his family and their friends hid for years. Goodrich wrote in her journal: "Very harrowing. Stood in Anne's room, stretched out my arms, touched walls on either side. This is the room she had to share with the crotchety dentist. Saw Garson looking at one of the photographs Anne had pasted on her wall. It was Ginger Rogers in a picture he had directed, *Tom, Dick and Harry*" (Goodrich 214).

Both inspired and emotionally destroyed by their visit to Amsterdam, the Hacketts went to London to work on their eighth rewrite of the play. Rehearsals of *The Diary of Anne Frank* began on August 22, 1955, at the Court Theater in New York City. Kanin addressed the cast giving a wonderful talk, as Goodrich recalled: "This is not a play in which you are going to make individual hits. You are real people living a thing that really happened." His message to the company was that this was a group effort and that they were all working for a singular noble cause. Goodrich wrote in her journal that she had never seen a company "so dedicated, united and selfless" (Goodrich 223).

On opening night, October 5, 1955, the Hacketts sat in the Court Theater's top gallery "with dry mouths and twitching bodies" waiting for the curtain to rise (Goodrich 228). When the curtain fell later that night there was "total stunned silence that lasted and lasted before, finally, hesitantly applause began and then grew and grew" (Goodrich 229). The New York production of *The Diary of Anne Frank* ran for almost two years, 717 performances and won all the major awards for 1955: The New York Drama Critics Circle Award for the Best New American Play, the Tony award for the Outstanding Play of the Year and the Pulitzer Prize. In the decade following the Broadway opening, the Hacketts' play spread its message around the world in hundreds of productions put on in dozens of countries and languages (Goodrich 229–230).

Twentieth Century–Fox purchased the movie rights to *The Diary of Anne Frank* and George Stevens was assigned as director and producer. Stevens pursued Audrey Hepburn for the role of Anne in the film and even elicited Otto Frank to help persuade her. When all attempts failed, Stevens stated that due to Hepburn's schedule and height, he had rethought the casting choice (Goodrich 243). In reality, Hepburn turned the role down repeatedly because the material was too traumatic given her own wartime experiences in the Netherlands.

Hepburn and Anne Frank were the exact same age, looked alike, and grew up in the same country. While Frank and her family were hiding in Amsterdam, Hepburn and her mother were living in the Nazi occupied town of Velp a mere 108 kilometers away. Frank's diary mentions the Germans executing a civilian named Otto during 1942; that man was Hepburn's uncle (Dottie 20). Hepburn and her mother suffered from extreme malnutrition during the Dutch Famine and survived by eating boiled tulips and grass; Anne Frank nearly survived long enough to be liberated, but ultimately died of malnourishment and illness (Dottie 20–21). Two years after the war ended, Hepburn read the manuscript of Anne Frank's diary and it shook her to the core, she said: "That child had written a complete account of what I had experienced and felt" (Dottie 21). Hepburn turned down the role, even after Otto Frank visited her home and asked her personally (she was his first choice), because she didn't feel she would be emotionally stable enough to handle the performance. Eventually Stevens offered the role to Millie Perkins (Goodrich 243).

The Hacketts only worked on one film following the adaptation of their award winning play, *Five Finger Exercise* (1962). The couple left Hollywood and spent the rest of their lives living in New York. They were "happier because they mostly kept their health, worked occasionally at their craft, stayed close to their families and friends, traveled, and enjoyed new experiences" (Goodrich 255). In 1977, after dinner with the Hacketts, who had then been married for 46 years, Hellman said to her escort Peter Fieldman: "Did you see Albert's face when Frances tripped? He turned white. He's more in love with her than he ever was. Imagine someone wanting you that long ... just imagine" (Goodrich 82).

Julius Epstein, another screenwriter of the era (best known for *Casablanca*), is quoted in David L. Goodrich's book, *The Real Nick and Nora*, saying that the Hacketts were the "greatest hosts in the world." His praise did not stop there: "Their dinner parties were the most coveted in town.... They gave parties every other Friday evening—or so it seemed.... Invitations were highly prized. Without exaggeration, they were the most beloved couple in Hollywood" (Goodrich 156). Frances Goodrich and Albert Hackett shared a love that was effortless, deep, playful and fun. In public, they weren't demonstrative—no handholding, no affectionate caresses—but when either spoke, the other concentrated intently (Goodrich 39). "The Hacketts" existed for nearly 54 years, as writing partners for even longer, always well respected in their talent, admired for their integrity and an inspiration to all they encountered in both private and professional circles.

WORKS CITED

After the Thin Man (1936). Wrs: Frances Goodrich, Albert Hackett, and Dashiell Hammett. Dir: Van Dyke W.S. Metro-Goldwyn-Mayer, USA 112 mins.
Dotti, Luca, and Luigi Spinola. *Audrey at Home: Memories of My Mother's Kitchen with Recipes, Photographs, and Personal Stories*. New York: Harper Design, 2015.
Goodrich, David L. *The Real Nick and Nora: Frances Goodrich and Albert Hackett, Writers of Stage and Screen Classics*. Carbondale: Southern Illinois University Press, 2001.
Goodrich, Frances, Albert Hackett, Jo Swerling, and Frank Capra. *It's a Wonderful Life*. 1946. MS, Unpublished Film Scripts. Margaret Herrick Library, Los Angeles.
Goodrich, Frances, Albert Hackett, Jo Swerling, and Frank Capra. *It's a Wonderful Life*. 1947. MS, Unpublished Film Scripts. Margaret Herrick Library, Los Angeles.
Hamilton, Ian. *Writers in Hollywood: 1915–1951*. New York: Harper & Row, 1990. Print.
It's a Wonderful Life. Dir. Frank Capra. Screenplay by Frances Goodrich and Albert Hackett. Perf. James Stewart, Donna Reed. Liberty Films, 1947.
McCall, Mary C., Jr. "In the Beginning." For Your Information: To the Members of the Academy of Motion Picture Arts and Sciences 3 (June 1947): 1–2.
Rowland, Mark. *Backstory: Interviews with Screenwriters of Hollywood's Golden Age*. Berkeley: University Press of California, 1986.
The Thin Man (1934). Wrs: Frances Goodrich and Albert Hackett, Dir: Van Dyke W.S. Metro-Goldwyn-Mayer, USA 91 mins.
Wilk, Max. *Schmucks with Underwoods: Conversations with Hollywood's Classic Screenwriters*. New York: Applause Theatre & Cinema, 2004.

In Defense of Lillian Hellman

KELLEY C. ZINGE

> History is made by masses of people. One man, or ten men, don't start the earthquakes and don't stop them either. Only hero worshipers and ignorant historians think they do.—Lillian Hellman

If it was possible for one woman to shake up a world, Lillian Hellman did it, and shook it till it raged back at her. When one goes about searching for information about Lillian Hellman, there is a never-ending bounty about her trials and tribulations, her accomplishments and failures, and most of all, about her personally. However, it is extremely hard to find anything wholly positive about her. Titles such as "Scandalous Women," "A Difficult Woman," "Stalin's Trollop" and "Lillian Hellman: Antagonist" abound in book lists the world over. It is very clear that Hellman made a name for herself, but what is also clear, is that she made a notoriously bad impression on so many.

Hellman once said, "Nobody outside of a baby carriage or a judge's chamber believes in an unprejudiced point of view" and for certain so many have seen her in a negative light, but why? Hellman, who always used "Miss" instead of "Ms." (she hated the title of Ms.), was an extremely talented writer; having written critically acclaimed plays, movies and memoirs. She was a force to be reckoned with against the HUAC (The House Un-American Activities Committee), and she was an incredibly loud voice in the fight for racial equality, yet, there can be no doubt of the controversy surrounding her.

Born in New Orleans on June 20, 1907, to salesman, Max, and mother, Julia, Hellman was a well to do only-child and a southern Jew who wasn't very religious, though after World War II she came to revere her Jewish heritage. After watching southern African Americans being treated like inferiors, she set off at a very young age to "right the wrongs of society" (Rollyson 8). She once took her African American guardian, Sephora, to the front of a streetcar, which caused an enormous scuffle, but Hellman prevailed. Hellman was also quite a character with a vivid imagination. Near the beginning of World War I, she and a friend started following two men they found suspicious because the girls felt they looked like spies, only to find out that they were a professor and a musician. Hellman started writing stories and poems at age 12 and once when she had the role of the villain in a school play, she took the unlucky happenstance of a stage door being stuck to stay on stage and enlarge her role. Clearly, Hellman came of age in the 1920s, likely influenced by its more liberal, flapper spirit, but as she aged, so too did the culture surrounding her. Hellman's lifestyle, writing, and personality seemed to have rubbed society the wrong way. What seems clear when researching her is that cultural differences and outright misogyny appear to be the logical culprits in her being so reviled, and in some cases, slandered. What is remarkable is that her estrangement from some people considered more well behaved has only grown stronger as the years have passed since her death in 1984.

Lillian Hellman's play (later a movie), *The Children's Hour* is a story about two teachers being accused of "lesbianism" and the fall-out from such a slanderous accusation. However, in the end we learn that one of the teachers does have romantic feelings for the other. Hellman is generally credited with putting onto the worlds' stage the idea of homosexuality before anyone else ever thought to do so. Her play was banned in Boston, London and Chicago, but it was so popular and so overwhelmingly well written that when she was denied the Pulitzer Prize in 1934, it is widely believed by film scholars that the New York Drama Circle Critics Award was later given to her as compensation. The play was adapted into a film with Hellman credited for the screenplay, but because of the Hays Code, the story was greatly changed from the lesbian themed *Children's Hour* to a story about a heterosexual love triangle called, *These Three*, starring Merle Oberon. Later, in 1961 another film adaptation to the play was written by John Michael Hayes and Lillian Hellman with the original title, and with the original idea and story.

Writer Lillian Hellman and producer Hal B. Wallis confer during pre-production of *The Searching Wind* (1946). Ever creative, Lillian Hellman had an imaginary friend even as an adult (Academy of Motion Picture Arts and Sciences' Margaret Herrick Library).

Despite this groundbreaking work, and most likely, because of it, Hellman has been criticized by religious groups and other writers. Indeed, in the play, *The Children's Hour* (and real life), "Hellman challenged traditional gender roles and sexuality. She presented a story about women who are part of a changing society, but also about lesbianism, which challenged proper sexuality" (Paradis 38). Hellman, herself was one of these women. According to Samantha Paradis, this transition is why women faced such criticism of their work and their lives. Paradis continues to quote Sexologist, Carroll Smith-Rosenberg, "by the 1920s, charges of lesbianism had become a common way to discredit women professionals, reformers, and educators" (Paradis 38). It must be noted that in her later memoirs, Hellman does mention bringing women home with Dashiell Hammett (her lover of over 30 years). Between that fact, her subject matter, her single status that lasted the rest of her life after her divorce from her only husband, Arthur Kober, and her truly independent style, she was accused more than once of being a lesbian herself.

Further, Hellman is before her time in that she condemns homosexuality for being treated as taboo. This is evident when she has her main character, Karen, tell Mary that she is guilty of nothing in this situation. Mary acknowledges her hidden feelings, though never does the word lesbian occur. Hellman's critics were not as understanding as her characters. "When the play was up for the Pulitzer Prize in 1935, *New Masses* confronted Hellman's use of the lesbianism taboo: "they [the Pulitzer Prize judges] were confronted with *Children's Hour*, with its inverted sex theme or with what was far worse: fine plays on social subject." Pulitzer Prize committee member Professor William Lyon Phelps refused to attend a performance because of the play's content" (Paradis 45).

Sadly, the modern era has brought forth no better understanding of the writer or her subjects from certain circles. John Zmirak of *Crisis Magazine* states, "Hellman's depiction of self-serving viciousness and callous lying might seem like the keen insight of a literary moralist—until we sat down next to Lillian on the divan and got to know her a little better..." (Zmirak). He bolsters his argument by quoting another writer, Rhoda Koenig of the *Independent*, who insults both Hellman's looks and morals:

> She was no beauty, even when young (when old, it was said she looked like George Washington, or Casey Stengel, the manager of the Mets baseball team), but never let that stop her from having plenty of men—rich men, successful men, men several decades younger. Well into her seventies she was the talk of Manhattan for not only purring huskily to young men at parties but flashing her silk knickers [Zmirak].

How often does misogyny rear its ugly head as attacks on physical attractiveness when it comes to women? How often does it condemn a woman's talent by accusing her of having low morals and subpar beauty? Clearly, as a woman of some substance, her success, as well as her openness about what was definitely taboo in those days (and still in some circles today) created a reason for men to dismiss her. Indeed, William J. Buckley "mocked" her greatness as a playwright by saying, "that was the same as talking about 'the downhill champion on the one-legged ski team'" (Corrigan).

Despite such attacks, Hellman continued to create successful plays and movies. Her next, *The Little Foxes,* started as a play which she then adapted into film nominated for 9 Academy Awards, including Best Picture, Best Screenplay, Best Actress in a lead role, Best Actress in a supporting role × 2 (Patricia Collinge and Teresa Wright), Best Director, Best Art Direction, Best Film Editing and Best Music, Scoring of a Dramatic picture. Still, in the '30s and '40s female writers were often accused of writing melodramas (which were considered a sign of poor writing). For example, George Jean Nathan wrote in the *American Mercury* in 1941, "Give her an emotion, whether tragic or comic, and she will stretch it, not only to its extreme limit, but beyond. I believe that the drama of most female playwrights, Miss Lillian [Hellman] among them, most often resolves itself willy-nilly into melodrama" (Viels 56). This highlights how most all women playwrights were viewed, never mind the greatest playwright of the 20th century, female or not.

Lillian Hellman put an abundance of female characters into her stories; strong, complex, interesting female characters, and truly can be credited with ushering in the modern age with regard to equalizing gender roles, onstage if nowhere else. Still, Hellman has received a healthy dose of internal misogyny from other female peers. When she was in her '70s, she turned on the television and saw Mary McCarthy (a fellow writer) on the *Dick Cavett Show* saying that Hellman, "is tremendously overrated, a bad writer, a dishonest writer, but she really belongs to the past." Cavett prodded her further about what was "overrated" about Hellman and McCarthy replied, "Everything. I once said in an interview that every word she writes is a lie, including 'and' and 'the'" (Ulrich). This prompted Hellman to accuse McCarthy of libel, and started an endless civil lawsuit that never saw a ruling, because Hellman died before the case could be settled.

From a legal standpoint, the court first had to conclude if the "language complained of was susceptible of the particular defamatory meaning ascribed to it" (Kornstein 33). The court concluded that the comments made were "reasonably susceptible of a defamatory connotation" (Kornstein 33). The court must then say whether or not Hellman was a "public figure" and in this case, they said she was not. It is questionable why the court would say she wasn't a public figure after Academy Award nominations and several bestselling memoirs. It seems to follow that many more women of not just nominal success but enormous notoriety have been written out of history and hidden from the rewards they so richly deserve. Another step in the civil suit process was to find out if the statement was meant to be opinion or fact. In this case, Justice Baer stated, "To call someone dishonest, to say to a national television audience that every word she writes is a lie, seems to fall on the actionable side of the line and does not clearly pass the test as an opinion" (Kornstein 34). Finally, to find fault there had to be malice involved and proven, and Justice Baer ruled as follows:

> Ms. McCarthy's remarks casting doubt on Ms. Hellman's honesty and veracity might rise to the level of reckless disregard and indifference. The record reflects that Ms. McCarthy had only limited exposure to the works of the prolific Ms. Hellman. Moreover, her repetition of the remark which appeared in the *Paris Metro* tends to negate innocent error and may evidence ill will, which, while not necessary to prove "actual malice," is some proof of it [Kornstein 35].

Then the judge made way for the jury to decide the final outcome.

There has been much speculation as to what started the bad blood between McCarthy and Hellman, but what can be said definitively is that there had been "malice" between them before *The Dick Cavett Show* ever aired. Apparently, they met each other years earlier at a party and had a disagreement over politics. It had also been rumored that Hellman had a brief dalliance with McCarthy's lover, Philip Rahv. It was most likely more professional than personal, however. Hellman had money, McCarthy had looks. It was as if each woman decided to take a bite out of the other rather than stand together against a world of men. Nora Ephron wrote a play about the rivalry between the two women and had her own notions of what caused the friction. She concluded: "Both wanted to be the only woman at the table" (Roiphe). A feminine competitiveness that at times seemed trite developed between them. Hellman once said in the *Paris Review*: "Miss McCarthy is often brilliant ... but she is a lady writer, a lady magazine writer." (Roiphe) It only went downhill from there, McCarthy once observed that Hellman's arms "looked shriveled and fatty at the same time ... as if she was a hundred years old." (Roiphe). The bitter fight raged on and ended when Hellman died in 1984. She felt she had to fight to protect her honor, truth was, after all, a theme in so much of what she'd written. The rest of the literary world took sides, Norman Mailer begged for them to stop. He stood up for Hellman calling any accusations of lying from her "blarney," but firmly believed she should stop a lawsuit that could cause infringements upon the very freedoms she had fought so hard to protect (NYT).

It seems likely that due to that comment made on *The Dick Cavett Show*, and the legal battle following, a sudden overall mistrust of Hellman began to grow. She had written three memoirs: *An Unfinished Woman*, *Pentimento* and *Scoundrel Time*, and many were starting to doubt the truth that she was writing. More controversy came up with regard to her memoir, *Pentimento*, and a story in it about a woman named Julia, which later became a film starring Vanessa Redgrave and Jane Fonda. *Julia* was purportedly based on someone that Hellman knew who went to Vienna to be analyzed by Freud and ended up marrying a man who was head of the Nazi resistance there. The problem arose when a woman named, Dr. Muriel Gardiner came forward with her memoir with that exact same story. Though to be fair, Hellman's character dies at the end of her story and Hellman brings her cremated remains back to the States. The comparison is uncanny, making many readers and critics think Hellman stole this story from an acquaintance. Various people demanded to know who the real Julia was and Hellman refused to say, saying it must be kept a secret based on the person's privacy. Here it is fairly plausible that she could have taken a story that she overheard and fictionalized it. As Ephron often said, "everything is copy." It is hard to say with any clarity whether or not she fabricated her Julia from an overheard conversation, or whether it was the truth, but it is also true that the Gardiner book came out after Hellman's story published.

Rhoda Koenig concludes that these memoirs were indeed "legendary, not only in the sense of the word "famous" but also the word "'fictional'" (Koenig). Clearly not a fan of Hellman's, perhaps due to these continued questions, Koenig continues, "What was particularly amusing that her invented life was not one of romance, but of rectitude; with one major exception, her stories of fighting for the helpless and defending the truth were fairytales" (Koenig). There is not one shred of evidence that this statement of Koenig's is true. Hellman's response to the House Un-American Activities Committee during the McCarthy era was as she said it was. In response to being called before the tribunal she wrote a letter that stated, "I cannot and will not cut my conscience to fit this year's fashions" (*NYT*). She said she would speak of herself, but not of others, because "to hurt innocent people whom I knew many years ago in order to save myself is, to me, inhuman and dishonorable" (*NYT*). Further, for several years after, she "...continued to push for civil liberties. She organized a group called the Committee for Public Justice that during the 1960s and 70s spoke out in favor of first amendment and other constitutional rights, and investigated FBI abuses, CIA invasions of privacy, and wiretapping violations by the government" (Kornstein 29).

Additionally, Hellman spoke in defense of Vanessa Redgrave when she attempted to sue the Boston symphony orchestra for cancelling her contract for political reasons. Hellman came forward and made what was to be her last public statement as testament to being blacklisted in the entertainment industry:

> I was shocked and angered by what happened to me. But my shock and anger was directed primarily against what I thought had been the people of my world. As I wrote in *Scoundrel Time*, "I had, up to the late 1940's believed that the educated, the intellectual, lived by what they claimed to believe: freedom of thought and speech, the right of each man to his own convictions, a more than implied promise, therefore, of aid to those who might be persecuted." It never occurred to me that I or anyone else could be punished for exercising my inherited rights; "certainly there could be no punishment for doing what I had been taught to do by teachers, books, American history. It was not

only my right, it was my duty to speak or act against what I thought was wrong or dangerous" [Kornstein].

Still so many came forward after her death to say that she lied about one thing or another of varying levels of importance. Some even chided her about her memories regarding Dashiell Hammett, including Gore Vidal who said, "Has anyone really ever seen him with her?" Hellman's relationship with "Dash," was a long and fruitful union that lasted over 30 years. The proof is in his poems about her, and the fact that he fashioned the Nora character after Hellman for *The Thin Man*. Myrna Loy recalls, "He told me that he'd fashioned Nora after his friend Lillian Hellman, which I found interesting.... As we talked that evening, Dash drank heavily and began turning a little green. He went on and on about Lillian..." (Soares). When asked if she over-romanticized their connection, Hellman answered, "Yes. Then sometimes I feel that I haven't romanticized it enough. It's very hard to tell, when a relationship is over, what you saw and what was fact. If by romantic one means invention, then I didn't invent it. If by romantic one means maybe time has dulled the bad parts, then I don't know" (Doudnan).

Hellman's long term relationship with Hammett, the fact that she never married him, the fact that he never divorced his first wife, and the fact that she had several affairs with different men probably did not endear her to a more conservative society. Even today women fight against the double standard. Once more, it is expected that due to her less than perfect physical aesthetic, she would not be revered for her flings with men in the same way as Marilyn Monroe was. It is one thing to be beautiful and loose, but you are the bottom of pile when you're considered homely. What is unexpected is that women so often carry on this double standard by turning on each other. Hellman once said, "Everyone hates women, especially women" (Feiblemen 29).

At either turn, it is clear that not all the events Hellman remembered happened quite the way she recorded them. Besides having emphysema (she was a lifelong chain smoker), Hellman had also begun to go blind towards the end of her life. She made her "growing blindness" a metaphor for her "memory of events that had become shadowy— like a light that was masked with an unknown fabric " (Rollyson 14). The other possibility is that this woman lived largely in her imagination. She was an artist, a visionary, why should her memoirs not be taken with the spirit in which they were given? As an only child, Lillian probably lived in a world of her creation much of the time. Peter Feibleman talks about Hellman having imaginary friends, "Mimsy" and "Nursy" in her old age (Feibleman 35). Whenever a writer tells a story, true or not, they tend to embellish to make it compelling, to make it fanciful. At the end of Nora Ephron's play about Lillian Hellman and Mary McCarthy, the last two lines of the play have the character of Mary saying "I believe in the truth" and the character of Lillian responding "I believe in the story" (Ephron, end of Act 3).

The world seemed less forgiving, however, to a woman who had caused so much controversy. For a woman who wrote about homosexuality, had sex with many men, made a life of her own, was a "Stalinist" (though she never signed on with the communist party), brought lawsuits against other people (she also sued the government for Nixon's Watergate files), her achievements were above all of those things if you can take her personal life out of the equation. In reality, Hellman was a complex, difficult person who could hold a grudge like no other. In the book, *Lily: Reminiscences of Lillian Hellman* this exchange beautifully sums up her persona: Lily says "I'm famous for my modesty. I'm famous for my humility too!" Then Peter says, "You are?" and Lily responds "I'd like to see the cock-sucker who says I'm not!"

Why is her personality held up to the strict judgment that others are not? "There are those who found her difficult, mercurial, nasty and unlikable, and some incidents in her life did show her to be prickly at times. But much the same could and has been said of male figures like Rousseau, Shelley, Marx and Nietzsche, whose personalities were often less than winning but whose work was important" (Kornstein, 42). Indeed, society doesn't quite hold those men to the same rules that they hold women like Hellman.

Hellman was an award winning playwright, Oscar nominated screenwriter, bestselling author, socially progressive, forward thinking, courageous, honorable person who did not take responsibility lightly, as evidence by her testimony for the HUAC). She fought her critics, her biographers and friends with equal aplomb, and held her head high in an age when most women were told to hide in the kitchen. But for all of her achievements and strengths, she is remembered for being "Stalin's Trollop," a "Difficult Woman" and part of several scandals. If she had been born later, and came into her own in these modern years, perhaps she would have been seen differently. It is difficult to say. Gender equality and those double standards have not diminished, only morphed. It seems that any time a successful woman opens her mouth and speaks out against something controversial, or makes huge strides in the movement of human progress, they are deemed "difficult," or worse, they are called "liars." Perhaps the truth, their truth, is just too honest to handle. As Hellman once said, "Truth made you a traitor as it often does in a time of scoundrels."

WORKS CITED

Corrigan, Maureen. "Lillian Hellman: A 'Difficult,' Vilified Woman." NPR. NPR, 16 Apr. 2012. Web. 6 May 2016. <http://www.npr.org/>.
Doudnan, Christine. "A Conversation with Lillian Hellman." *Rolling Stone*. 24 Feb. 1977. Web. 07 May 2016. <http://www.rollingstone.com/culture/features/a-still-unfinished-woman-19770224?page=5>.
Ephron, Nora. *Imaginary Friends*. New York: Vintage, 2003.
Feibleman, Peter S. *Lilly: Reminiscences of Lillian Hellman*. New York: Morrow, 1988.
Hirschorn, Joel. "Review: 'Selected Letters of Dashiell Hammett.'" *Variety*. 17 July 2001. Web. 07 May 2016. <http://variety.com/2001/more/reviews/selected-letters-of-dashiell-hammett-1200469089/>.
Koenig, Rhoda. "Lillian Hellman: Mother of Invention." *The Independent*. Independent Digital News and Media, 2 Oct. 2001. Web. 6 May 2016. <http://www.independent.co.uk/arts-entertainment/theatre-dance/features/lillian-hellman-the-mother-of-invention-9183208.html>.
Kornstein, Daniel J. *The Case Against Lillian Hellman*. Fordham Law Review, 1989.
"Lillian Hellman, Playwright, Author, and Rebel, Dies at 77." On This Day. *New York Times*, 1 July 1984. Web. 6 May 2016. <http://www.nytimes.com/learning/general/onthisday/bday/0620.html>.
Paradis, Samantha L. "Prolific Playwrights: Claude Odets and Lillian Hellman Expose the Thirties." University of Maine, 2012.
Roiphe, Katie. "Nora Ephron's Theory of Mary McCarthy vs. Lillian Hellman." *Slate Magazine*. 2002. Web. 6 May 2016. <http://www.slate.com/articles/arts/culturebox/2002/12/imagining_enemies.html>.
Rollyson, Carl E. *Lillian Hellman: Her Life and Legend*. New York: IUniverse, 2008.
Soares, Emily. "After the Thin Man." Turner Classic Movies. 12 June 2015. Web. 07 May 2016. <http://www.tcm.com/this-month/article.html?id=614562|27608>.
Ulrich, Laurel Thatcher. "Uncivil Wars: Lillian Hellman vs. Mary McCarthy and the Question of Julia." Scandalous Women. 12 Aug. 2008. Web. 6 May 2016. <http://scandalouswoman.blogspot.com/>.
Vials, Chris. *Realism for the Masses: Aesthetics, Popular Front Pluralism, and U.S. Culture, 1935–1947*. Jackson: University of Mississippi Press, 2009.
Zmirak, John. "Stalin's Trollop: The Envy of Lillian Hellman." Crisis Magazine—A Voice for the Faithful Catholic Laity. 25 Nov. 2009. Web. 6 May 2016. <http://www.crisismagazine.com/>.

The Intimately Unknowable Dorothy Parker
A Study of Her Life and Art

Elizabeth Dwyer

> Oh, life is a glorious cycle of song,
> A medley of extemporanea;
> And love is a thing that can never go wrong,
> And I am Marie of Romania.

The charming and sarcastic little poem seen above, "Comment," is the perfect introduction to Dorothy Parker for any teenage girl. Reading that poem in high school made me feel an instant affinity to Parker and her writing. The cleverness and wit tinged with underlying melancholy reflects the angst that is so poignant in one's youth. For Parker, it was both her signature style, and an illustration of who she was and how she lived.

As an adult woman, to reacquaint myself with Parker, I began by reading her poetry each morning over breakfast, with the collection of poems titled *Death and Taxes* (a true collection title, as there is no poem by the same name). There was no avoiding how often one can laugh at her witticisms in one moment, only to be struck with empathetic heartache in the next, as evidenced in the short, lonely stanza that serves as "Sanctuary."

> My land is bare of chattering folk;
>   The clouds are low along the ridges,
> And sweet's the air with curly smoke
>   From all my burning bridges.

Other poems were not set up with wit, such as "After Spanish Proverb," but instead portrayed a splendid and touching anguish. As noted by the biographer John Keats in his book *You Might as Well Live: The Life and Times of Dorothy Parker*, "Her poems were not one thing or another, and neither was she. She was cynical, fantastic, sour, comic, witty, and lonely … she saw quite clearly the comical aspects of every tragedy, and the tragical aspects of every jape." Getting to know Dorothy Parker seems to be as easy now as it was when she lived (i.e., not easy in the slightest), and in this author's opinion, still best done through her writing.

Of her childhood, Parker spoke very little. Born Dorothy Rothschild in 1893, her mother died when she was an infant. The woman her father remarried was never a mother or stepmother figure, and if Parker referred to her at all she called her "the housekeeper." Keats notes in his biography that "She could never speak of her father without horror" (Keats 18). Perhaps saddest of all was how much Dorothy Rothschild was deprived of typical childhood activities, and therefore "hated being a child … she never flew a kite in Central Park; she never went to a skating rink. Each day she would walk to a school where she had no place, and each afternoon she would return to a house that had no love for her" (Keats 19).

To know of the successful adult writer and her witticisms, it's easy to imagine a sassy, vibrant woman full of moxie. In truth she was small in voice and stature (standing just under five feet tall), and most of her clever barbs were muttered under her breath—a habit she developed early in life as a means of self-preservation. She spoke her most intelligent observations only to herself, as a young lady was to possess manners above all else (particularly above such useless traits as intelligence and cleverness). Dorothy Rothschild, however, was not long concerned with embodying society's ideal for young ladies. Her transformation into Dorothy Parker likely began with her admittance to Miss Dana's highly exclusive school for girls—both "a finishing school and a college-prepatory one, quite progressive for its time" (Keats 23). Unlike most finishing schools, Miss Dana's was concerned with nurturing the intelligence of the young women in attendance, and encouraging them to be effective in the world. In 1911, at the age of eighteen, Parker completed her education there, and set about living the rest of her unorthodox life.

Writer Dorothy Parker, circa 1939. Once charged by her fellow (male) writers during lunch at the Algonquin to use the word "horticulture" in a sentence, Parker quipped, "You can lead a horticulture, but you can't make her think" (Academy of Motion Picture Arts and Sciences' Margaret Herrick Library and MGM Production and Bio Photos).

The expectation, even for educated young ladies, was to finish school and then move back home to await the arrival of a husband. Feeling no connection or devotion to her family, this was not to be Parker's fate. She "…smoked cigarettes, wrote verses about love, had opinions of her own, and wanted her own apartment and a job. In Parker's youth, such girls were not only rare but were also viewed with alarm" (Keats 30). Needless to say, with her father's death in 1913, nothing prevented Parker from setting herself up in a boardinghouse and working on writing her "verses" (not poems, she was quite clear on the distinction). Her first verse to be purchased was bought in 1916 by Frank Crowninshield, for publication in a new magazine called *Vogue*. In 1917, Edwin Pond Parker II proposed, and she shed her maiden name once and for all, having never liked it much anyway.

Writing for *Vogue* and then *Vanity Fair* carried Parker through January of 1920, when she was unceremoniously fired, with the explanation that she'd upset one too many Broadway producers with her less than flattering reviews. In one such review—for Oscar Wilde's *An Ideal Husband*—she was quite complimentary of the production, but far less so for the attending audience: "'Oh the lines, the lines!' they sigh, one to another, quite as if they were the first to discover that this Oscar Wilde is really a very promising young writer; and they use the word "scintillating" as frequently and as proudly as if they had just coined it" (Parker & Fitzpatrick 37). In her review of the comedic play *Tillie*, Parker wrote, "To quote the only line of Gertrude Stein's which I have ever been able to understand, 'It is wonderful how I am not interested'" (Parker & Fitzpatrick 64).

Parker's dismissal illustrated the influence Broadway producers held at the time, for Crowninshield was quite clear about his choice of Parker for Theatre Critic: "Though she was full of prejudices, her perceptions were so sure, her judgement so unerring, that she always seemed certain to hit the center of the mark." When she was fired, Parker's two closest friends resigned in protest. The three of them, Parker, Robert Sherwood, and Robert Benchley, all retreated to the Algonquin Hotel for lunch and to laugh about the whole affair, because in the lighthearted era of the twenties, it was important to not be seen as taking anything too seriously.

The Algonquin, of course, is the now famous hotel where Parker and the two Roberts were known to lunch with a number of other sharp, clever, sardonic minds of the era. Among the thirty people acknowledged to have at one time or another been a part of the Algonquin Round Table (also known as the Vicious Circle, due to the sometimes scathing commentary on their peers), were novelists, playwrights, editors, journalists, producers, agents, actors, and so on, all of them seen as some of the brightest, most creative minds of the era. The complete list of "members" of the round table includes such notable names as Harpo Marx, George S. Kaufman, and Edna Ferber. Parker is considered to be a part of the "core group," along with Robert Benchley, George S. Kaufman, and fellow critic Alexander Woollcott.

Parker's first marriage proved unsuccessful, and she spent much of it separated from her husband. In 1928 they finally divorced, though Parker openly took lovers in the meantime. For her, love was not a flippant thing; she loved being in love, and even her more 'casual' romances often led to one-sided ardor on her part. Her attractiveness did not wane with age, and at thirty-eight she had a fling with a young actor in his twenties, a social climber named John McClain. He claims her attachment to him grew too intense, but regardless of why it fell apart, the affair illustrates Parker's affinity for handsome young men (Keats 158).

With the success of her writing and her money not tied up in stocks (she tended to spend it rather than save it), the Great Depression did not particularly impact Parker. She spent the late 1920s and early 1930s adventuring around New York and traveling to Europe for the second time. Her first visit was compelled by Ernest Hemingway's ardor for Paris and Parker's admiration of Hemingway, but her second trip had a more altruistic bent. Her dear friends the Murphys were in Switzerland, their son Patrick had contracted tuberculosis, and Parker spent almost all of 1930 there to help them and keep them company, though she would later confess to being bored out of her mind.

Returning to New York, the country was officially mired in the Depression, but not Parker. Having achieved her first financial success in 1926 with *Enough Rope*, a collection of poems, being both a frequent contributor to and subject of articles in publications like her friend Harold Ross' magazine *The New Yorker*, combined with her pervasive wit, charm, and magnetism, conspired to make Parker a figure of notoriety, especially in New York City. Hers was a zany, madcap existence, at least on the surface. Underneath every witticism and scheme was a thread of "…contempt for herself and others, and a quality of despair…" (Keats 87). In 1922, Parker became pregnant and had an abortion, and not long after she attempted suicide for the first time. She put in an order for food and when the waiter arrived he found her in the bathroom, her wrists slashed. On a night in 1925, she took an overdose of sleeping pills. Benchley and other friends found her in her apartment. Both of these occasions were met with the required light touch of wit demanded by the twenties. Benchley told her, "Dottie, if you don't stop this sort of thing you'll make yourself sick" (Gaines 116). In truth, the repeat attempt caused genuine alarm among her circle of close friends, and amplified the protective, caretaker feelings they all had for their little Dottie.

Those who knew her all had their own version of who she was, and none of them were wrong, for Parker enjoyed telling whatever version of a story of herself she felt in any given moment. In the early 1930s, one such story came about when she and a yet another handsome young actor, Alan Campbell, took off in the wee hours of the night to visit the Bowery, a destitute part of town. Parker decided it would be a lark to get tattooed. According to one of Parker's friends, she and Campbell each got a small dark blue star tattooed on the inside of their upper left arms. Ask another friend, and the tattoo was "a dark blue or black star on her right thigh." In the telling of yet another friend, Beatrice Ames Stewart, it was actually in Greenwich Village that Parker got the tattoo, and it was a small blue star on her left shoulder. Regardless of where the tattoo was, what color the star, and how she came about acquiring it, Campbell quickly became a favorite of Parker's, and in 1933, much to the astonishment of her friends (accustomed as they were to Dottie taking lovers, not husbands) they married. She was forty years old and Campbell was twenty-nine.

Love fueled Parker. In the early stages of love, life was always on an upswing. When Campbell's acting career as a juvenile lead stalled, and it was widely known that Hollywood was pilfering writing talent from New York whenever possible, he knew the studios would jump at the chance to hire his renowned, sought after wife. In the throes of love, Parker offered no resistance to the scheme. Campbell pitched them as a writing team. Not only did the studios bite, they bit hard. Metro-Goldwyn-Mayer hired the duo at $5,200 a week. It should be noted that whatever aspirations Campbell might have regarding his new wife, he was no John McClain. Parker and Campbell were generally seen as an excellent match, and it was clear to those who knew them that he genuinely loved her. Campbell took care of everything for Dorothy, from cooking to cleaning up after her dogs and giving "some point to her days." He had also "…shaken the cocktails, paid the bills, amused her, adored her, made love to her, got her to cut down on her drinking, otherwise created space and time in her life for her to write, and taken her to parties" (Keats 176). Perhaps this devotion to her is why Parker stayed on with him in Hollywood for so long, even though she rather detested it. Before marrying Campbell, she had had a brief stint working for MGM for three months, writing dialogue for *Madame X*. After she and Campbell became a writing team, however, Parker experienced a healthy dose of Hollywood.

Between 1933 and 1938, the writing team earned credit for writing fifteen films, the most memorable one being the original script for *A Star Is Born* (Keats 178). They also worked on "additional scenes and dialogue" for the film adaptation of Lillian Hellman's play *The Little Foxes*. As part of another writing team (alongside Peter Viertel and Joan Harrison), Parker helped pen the original screenplay for *Saboteur*, a 1942 Hitchcock film. Outside of these films, Parker's other contribution to Hollywood was her short stories, many of which were adapted into short films and TV movies, a fair number of them after her death in 1967. One such TV movie, is an adaptation of Parker's short story *Big Blonde*, which won the national O. Henry Prize for best short story published in 1929 (Keats 144). It is the story of a rather simple-minded, working class woman who has a job as a dress model and is a "good sport" about going to bed with the various men in her life, until she meets a man she particularly likes and marries him. The marriage falls apart, she takes to drinking whiskey and her life is a downward spiral from there. The fictional character Mrs. Morse was "a dumb blonde of the lower classes who associated with traveling salesmen in cheap bars while the real-life Mrs. Parker was "an intelligent little brunette of the upper classes who associated with fascinating men in expensive bars" (Keats 146). Nonetheless, there are twenty-eight specific attributes possessed by both Morse and Parker, which lends the story a heart-wrenching intimacy and familiarity between author and subject.

Big Blonde came before Campbell and the move to Hollywood, where Parker settled into a writing routine that she considered soul crushing. A consummate perfectionist, writing never came easily to her. Under the pressures of studio deadlines and the demands of producers, Parker wrote,

> Well, I found out, and I found out hard, and found out forever. Through the sweat and the tears I shed over my first script, I saw a great truth—one of those eternal, universal truths that serve to make you feel much worse than you did when you started. And that is that no writer, whether he writes from love or from money, can condescend to what he writes. What makes it harder in screenwriting is the money he gets. You see, it brings out the uncomfortable little thing called conscience. You aren't writing for the love of it or the art of it or whatever; you are doing a chore assigned to you by your employer and whether or not he might fire you if you did it slackly makes no matter. You've got yourself to face, and you have to live with yourself [Sterling 111].

Parker persuaded her husband that they should buy a farm in Bucks County, Pennsylvania as an antidote to her distaste of Hollywood. She had often made allusions to such a dream in New York, but of course all of her witty, intellectual friends took it as one of her jokes, since none of them could imagine Dorothy Parker: Domestic Housewife. When she and Campbell purchased the farm in 1934, it was meant as a means for Parker to escape and retreat whenever the banality of tinseltown overwhelmed her. Then it was revealed that the farm would serve a second purpose, for Parker was pregnant. For a brief moment in time, there emerged a picture of the gentle, maternal Parker. She knit baby clothes and talked emotionally of motherhood and children. She was very clear that the pregnancy was intentional, as both she and her husband wanted a child. However, being a woman of forty-two in 1935, carrying a baby to term was highly unlikely, and sure enough, Parker miscarried in the third month of her pregnancy (Keats 201).

Over the course of the next year, Parker and Campbell returned to 'life as usual,' which for them centered around writing scripts and attending parties and the like. They still traveled between Hollywood and the farm, but Parker's own writing all but stopped—no more poetry or prose came forth for quite some time. Her distaste for Hollywood combined with the disquiet stemming from the loss of her child and her affinity for the underdog, all of these forces united to lead her to an involvement in radical politics. She took up many causes while living in Hollywood, among them "…poverty and unemployment, the segregation of blacks in the United States, and the growing clamor of anti-semitism in Germany." She also banded together with her friend Lillian Hellman and Dashiell Hammett to act as principal organizers of the first union for screenwriters, the Screen Writers Guild. Hammett and Parker were not friends, per say. He "…disliked Parker for her "game of embrace-denounce" toward most people, (but) they shared their support of liberal causes" (Barranger 11).

Political work gave Parker a sense of purpose. Long suspicious of the wealthy, and ambivalent about her own financial success, radical politics gave expression to the sincere connection that Parker had always felt to underdogs, thanks to her personal struggles with the pain of living, as expressed through almost every line of her writing and creative work. Parker was also chairman of the Voice of Freedom, an organization that supported liberal radio commentators and was a supposed asset of the Communist Party. All in all, Parker was mentioned in *Red Channels* as a "…writer and versifier with nineteen pro–Communist credits, (and) she came to the attention of four investigative committees" (Barranger 7). Moreover, Parker's name was mentioned during the espionage trial of Judith Coplon, when an FBI document that named Parker and actor Edward G. Robinson as traitors was read into evidence. Then her name appeared on a list of "Hollywood Communists" recited by a witness during a House Un-American Activities Committee (HUAC) hearing, and it was common knowledge that to be named on such a list meant "certain blacklisting by the studios" (Barranger 12).

Thus ended Parker's stint in Hollywood, and with her divorce from Campbell in 1947, she packed up and headed back to New York to try her hand at writing plays. The marriage had soured somewhat unexpectedly, according to their friends, but it was known to everyone, including Parker, that her romantic proclivity was that she loved them until they loved her back. She had taken to turning her wit and cynicism on her husband, particularly in the company of other people, telling barbed stories about his mediocre acting career. As if disparaging remarks about his talent were not bad enough, she later went on to say that he was a homosexual (both in front and behind his back). Oddly, this was not considered to be news among her friends. They had all supposed she'd heard the rumors (that Alan was bisexual) before she married him. It was widely believed that her public assertions about his sexuality were yet another symptom of her new radical ideology. These were not times for "little, selfish, timid things" (Barranger 9). Anyone close to her who did not feel the same call to action was ultimately squeezed out, including Campbell. After their divorce in 1947, they briefly remarried in 1950, but their marriage was over for good a year later.

Ever the contradiction, Parker was on the one hand quite ardent in her political beliefs and activities—declaring herself a socialist, siding with the underdog, and participating in demonstration when called upon—and casual on the other hand. Sometimes she lived her life blithely as she chose, crossing picket lines to have a drink at one of her favorite spots, "21," with Harold Broun, who himself was the founder of a union, the

American Newspaper Guild. Caught there by their friend Robert Benchley, he chastised the pair for crossing a picket line, "the Left wing's cardinal sin." Their friendship forever rooted in sharp wit, he went on to advise Parker, "And don't blink those ingenue eyes at me." She batted her eyes at Mr. Broun, chirping, "What did he mean by saying I had ingenue eyes?" as Benchley chuckled and moved on (Keats 191). It is certain that Mrs. Parker's commitment to anti–Fascism was very real. She made impassioned speeches on behalf of the Anti-Nazi league, and after a trip to Spain in 1937 to report on the Loyalist side of the civil war there; she became a vehement anti–Franco activist. Also born out of this trip to Spain was the short story, "Soldiers of the Republic," which may or may not be fiction. Told in the first person, the story details an account of Parker and a Swedish friend visiting a cafe in Valencia where they met a handful of soldiers who drank and smoked and ate with them before heading off to their likely deaths. The tone of the story has a "...universal, timeless quality. In this writing, she did what Hemingway tried all his life to do: she created literature more true than fact" (Keats 220). A unique aspect of this story (differing from Parker's typical fare), is its affirmation. One might not go so far as to use the word 'hope,' but there is certainly an absence of Dorothy Parker's usual despair. As Keats puts it, it is "a report on the human condition" (Keats 220). Whether fiction or an account of her personal experience, Parker shares the truth of her perceptions about the Spanish civil war in "Soldiers of the Republic."

When the Second World War broke out, Parker attempted to become a war correspondent. However, the United States government had kept a close eye on its citizens, and Parker was identified as a premature anti–Fascist (PAF). Allowing her to be a war correspondent would put her in a position to learn military secrets. Her application for a passport was denied. Met with despair over her inability to participate in the war effort, Parker ultimately set to writing about it. In an article for *Vogue* titled "Who Is That Man," Parker addressed the women who awaited their husbands' homecomings:

> You know him as he was.... But what will he be, this stranger who comes back? How are you to throw a bridge across the gap that has separated you—and that is not the little gap of months and miles? He has seen the world aflame, he comes back to your new red dress.... There are pictures hanging in his memory that he can never show to you. Of this great part of his life, you have no share.... That is where you start, and from there you go on to make a friend out of that stranger from across the world [Childers 63].

This was the truth of her experience, having one husband away at war presently (their marriage already on shaky ground), and having had her first husband, Edwin Parker, come home to her from World War I a changed man. The milestone in 1945 for Dorothy Parker was not the end of the war, but the death of her closest friend—estranged from her by her intense political convictions–Robert Benchley. Parker's misery surfaced again, as she asked, "Isn't it a bit presumptuous for us to be alive, now that Mr. Benchley is dead?" (Keats 244). Her writing became sparse, and she utilized wit that was more sour than clever. She would never again publish another poem.

By the mid–1950s, Dorothy Parker had tried her hand at theater to varying degrees of success, ranging from poor to fair to middling. Nothing she wrote or co-wrote was ever a huge hit, and the New York she now lived in was not the New York of her carefree, Algonquin-fueled youth. Her last theatrical endeavor was to help write the lyrics for a musical comedy version of *Candide*, which proved to be as ambitious as it sounds, and the results were lukewarm at best. At the same time of this last non-triumph, in 1956, Parker once again heard from Campbell. It turns out there was a producer in Hollywood who wanted to hire the Parker-Campbell writing team (the Blacklist be damned), to work on a script called *The Good Soup* starring Marilyn Monroe. With the New York she once knew now so changed, and so many of her old friends dead and gone, Parker saw no reason to resist the pull of her former husband, even if it meant returning to Hollywood. She packed up and moved across the country to live and work with Campbell, though this time they had sense enough to not remarry.

Their life in California was only briefly tied up with screenwriting. Their script for *The Good Soup* was so overworked by the studio that it was never produced, and it became the last script Parker and Campbell worked on together. Without the pressures of the film industry, Parker seemed less disgusted by Hollywood living. She and Campbell relaxed into a comfortable, familiar (if at times strained) existence together, living off a combination of unemployment and Dorothy's royalties until she was hired to write book reviews for *Esquire* at $750 a month. The young editor who suggested hiring her admitted that "editing her was a terrifying experience," but also that meeting her was far from what he expected. Instead of a "wisecracking hotshot, a very old one," he found Parker to be "a genuinely warm woman with a sense of great dignity, an old-fashioned great lady" (Keats 276). For all her literary successes, Parker was still a perfectionist of the highest order, which sometimes resulted in typewriter paralysis. Even when there was work to be done, she could not bring herself to write for fear of failure or inadequacy. But of course when she could force herself to buckle down and get to it, she was "marvelously precise and witty—her voice was as true and distinctive as in her writing in the twenties" (Keats 278).

The 1960s ushered in an era where Parker was "not so much known as remembered" (Keats 279). Thankfully, a phonograph company called Verve asked her to do a recording, which resulted in the treasure of a record of Parker reading some of her own poems and stories. "The World of Dorothy Parker" allows for insight that only an author's voice can lend to her writing. Her intonations and emphasis enlighten the listener to her subtler and more intricate meanings, and provide a lifeline to a woman who might otherwise have lost some of her humanity in the process of becoming viewed as a literary icon. In June of 1963, after a night of not unusual drinking and some sleeping pills, Parker awoke to find Alan dead beside her. His death was ruled an accident, but Parker suffered a great deal to think that she'd been right next to him when he died, but not awake to do anything to prevent it. Four years later, also in June, Parker went the way of so many before her, dying of a heart attack alone in her hotel room in New York, at the age of seventy-three.

Dorothy Parker's artistic expressions of life's complexities are unique and unparalleled thanks to her firm grasp on both levity and despair. For Parker life and art were never one thing now, another thing next, and still another thing after that. Everything was inextricably linked—wit, gaiety, melancholy, snark, love, and despair—for Parker, none could exist without the other. Her body of work is delightfully comprehensive, from clever reviews to thoughtful articles, from droll and heartbreaking poetry and saccharine screenplays, to the truth stripped bare in her short stories.... Dorothy Parker remains not only one of the most quotable people who has ever lived, she remains, above all else, a fiercely talented writer.

WORKS CITED

"Algonquin Round Table." *Algonquin Round Table*. Accessed 07 May 2016. http://www.algonquinroundtable.org/

Barranger, Milly S. "Dorothy Parker and the Politics of McCarthyism." *Theatre History Studies* 1 Jan. 2006.

Childers, Thomas. *Soldier from the War Returning: The Greatest Generations Troubled Homecoming from World War II*. Boston: Houghton Mifflin Harcourt, 2009.
"Dorothy Parker Society." *Dorothy Parker Society*. Accessed 07 May 2016. http://www.dorothyparker.com/
Gaines, James R. *Wit's End: Days and Nights of the Algonquin Round Table*. San Diego: Harcourt Brace Jovanovich, 1977.
Keats, John. *You Might as Well Live: The Life and Times of Dorothy Parker*. New York: Simon & Schuster, 1970.
Parker, Dorothy. *The Collected Dorothy Parker*. London: Penguin, 1973.
Parker, Dorothy, and Edith Goodkind Rosenwald. *Death and Taxes*. New York: Viking, 1931.
Parker, Dorothy, and Kevin C. Fitzpatrick *Dorothy Parker: Complete Broadway, 1918–1923*. Bloomington, IN: iUniverse LLC, 2014.
Sterling, Anna Kate, ed. *Celebrity Articles from the Screen Guild Magazine*. London: The Scarecrow Press, 1987.
Weaver, Angela. "'Such a Congenial Little Circle': Dorothy Parker and the Early-Twentieth-Century Magazine Market." *WSQ: Women's Studies Quarterly WSQ* 38.2 (2010): 25–41.

Joan Harrison
Redefining Femininity in Film Noir and Hollywood

CHELSEA ANDES

The addition of sound to motion pictures brought about not only a change in the production methods of filmmaking but also a change in the types of stories being told. Melodrama dominated the silent era carrying over tropes from the stage, but with the advent of sound, writers could tell a more nuanced and fully realized story. Gangster and crime films quickly became one of the more popular genres. "In the sound era, crime films gained immense sensory appeal and enormous popularity—reproducing sirens, screams and gunfire while relying on tough, urbane dialogue" (Biesen, 18).

The genre stagnated in the 1930s under the weight of the Hays code and intense censorship, but societal factors during World War II coalesced with crime films to create a new genre in the 1940s known as Film Noir. As rationing became commonplace, Hollywood learned to work with darker sets and less lavish props. Lightweight cameras were developed for war photography but utilized by filmmakers of the time as well.

During this time period, women gained a unique opportunity to participate both as stronger characters within these stories and, perhaps more importantly, behind the scenes.

> Hollywood's "red meat" hard-boiled crime cycle during the war, seemingly targeted a masculine gendered audience. Yet, these films included surprisingly strong female femme fatale "love interest" characters who redefined "femininity," capitalizing on wartime easing of Production Code Administration (PCA) censorship to promote heightened erotic appeal [Biesen, 126].

One female screenwriter who took unique advantage of this was Joan Harrison, a former protégé and writing partner to Alfred Hitchcock, who became one of the only female producers of the era. When asked to comment on her achievement in such a role Harrison said "We women have to work twice as hard to be recognized in our own fields. But today there is more recognition of women's talents than ever before. Those women who want a career can certainly have one" (Unterburger 181).

Joan Mary Harrison was born in Guildford, England, in 1904, the daughter of a journalist. Her father served as managing director of the *Surrey Advertiser*. Though petite, with blonde hair and blue eyes, Harrison was never content to rest on her good looks.

Writer Joan Harrison sits for a publicity photograph in her office in 1943. Hedda Hopper described Joan Harrison as "a 33-year-old, golden haired ball of fire with a temper of a tarantula, the purring persuasiveness of a female arch-angel, the capacity for work of a family of beavers, and the sex appeal of a No. 1 glamour girl" (Academy of Motion Picture Arts and Sciences' Margaret Herrick Library).

"In a Chicago Tribune article on Harrison titled 'Glamour Galvanic' Hedda Hopper described her as 'a 33-year old, golden haired ball of fire with a temper of a tarantula, the purring persuasiveness of a female arch-angel, the capacity for work of a family of beavers, and the sex appeal of No 1 glamour girl'" (Snelson 116). Intending to follow in her father's footsteps, Harrison pursued journalistic ambitions initially but according to her obituary "after her editorial writer father discouraged her interest in journalism because there was too much drinking, smoking and swearing, she turned to film" (Oliver).

She attended Oxford University and then the Sorbonne in Paris where she studied classical and English Literature. While no doubt her formal education provided her with a foundation for her later career pursuits, Harrison also gained an education from a slightly less conventional source.

Harrison's uncle worked as a keeper at the Old Bailey, the central criminal court of England and Wales. Harrison attended trials and police line-ups while frequently visiting Scotland Yard and this certainly influenced her chosen path: "Harrison's mark was made in various types of crime films, particularly those which featured a woman in jeopardy. She had always been interested in criminal cases, and had followed many of England's more colorful examples through the courts of London" (Unterburger 180). While many female screenwriters of the time were pigeon holed into writing "women's films" Harrison was resolutely dedicated to working within a specific genre and referred to herself "as a 'specialist' in psychological crime narratives, explaining 'I don't want to make pictures with the Andrews sisters'" a singing boogie-woogie group of the era (Biesen 131). Harrison could not have found a better mentor for these pursuits and gained incomparable knowledge while working under one of the most renowned auteur filmmakers in history.

In typical historical tradition, there is far more written on the early life of Harrison's male mentor than on her own. Alfred Joseph Hitchcock was born in London's East End in 1899. Though World War I raged during his adolescence "the people of London developed, as people in war do everywhere, a habit of doleful but courageous insistence on trying to go on with life as normally as possible. For Hitchcock, this meant frequenting more often the local movie theaters" (Spoto 38). When Famous Players–Lasky opened a studio in London, they employed Hitchcock as a title-designer. In 1921 he met his future wife, Alma Lucy Reville, who worked as an editor and continuity supervisor at the Lasky office. They were married five years later in 1926 with Hitchcock proclaiming " I had wanted to become, first, a movie director ... and second, Alma's husband—not in order of emotional preference to be sure, but because I felt the bargaining power implicit in the first was necessary in obtaining the second" (Spoto 65). Though Alma continued to receive continuity credits on Hitchcock's films the true level to which she participated was somewhat questionable with some believing her credits were designed merely to increase Hitchcock's own salary. This was compounded by the 1935 film *The 39 Steps* in which Hitchcock insisted Alma receive credit and that her fee be worked into the budget though she attended none of the writing conferences between Hitchcock and Charles Bennett (Spoto 146).

It was for this same film that the fortuitous meeting of Hitchcock and Harrison occurred. In 1933, Hitchcock placed an ad in the London newspapers seeking a "young lady, high education qualifications, must be able to speak, read and write French and German fluently" (Spoto 147). He sought a secretary who could read and cover scripts as well as help with numerous production elements. Though Hitchcock turned away over one hundred applicants, Harrison was hired on the spot and asked to report the following morning to the set of *39 Steps*. According to Harrison, "I was probably the worst assistant Hitch ever had" (Unterburger 180) but this had nothing to do with her competence or work ethic and instead had to do with her drive to participate in every aspect of the filmmaking process.

Though she would rise in the ranks quickly, Harrison's early tenure with Hitchcock was notably challenging. Hitchcock was a notorious prankster, his tricks ranging from the harmlessly absurd, such as dyeing all the food at a dinner party blue, to borderline dangerous and humiliating, such as when he handcuffed a man to a camera for an entire evening after dosing his drink with a strong laxative (Spoto 111). "The schemes that allowed him to watch other people experience discomfort, were calculated, carefully controlled antisocial gestures ... smaller analogues of the appearance of chaos in a world gone suddenly mad—the chaotic world that Hitchcock was in lifelong fear of and that, in his mature work, he inflicted on his characters and on his viewers" (Spoto 112). In an effort to break Harrison's reserve down, Hitchcock called her into his office for a story meeting and proceeded to read, out loud, the graphic toilet scene from *Ulysses* in which Leopold Bloom's bowel movements are described in painful detail. Clearly, Harrison passed whatever test Hitchcock was administering with his inappropriate reading. She moved up to continuity assistant in 1936, then to script consultant in 1937, dialogue writer in 1938 and scenarist by 1939. Her first screenwriting credit came in 1939 with *Jamaica Inn*.

In 1938 Hitchcock was busy negotiating a contract with David O. Selznick while leaving Harrison to negotiate the option rights for Daphne Du Maurier's upcoming and much talked about novel, *Rebecca*. In the midst of this frenzy Harrison, along with Sidney Gilliat, was recruited to adapt Du Maurier's previous 1936 novel: *Jamaica Inn*. The script tells the story of Mary Yellan, a young woman who discovers a conspiracy of engineered shipwrecks for profit being run from inside the Jamaica Inn and featured Maureen O'Hara in her first starring role. The film was notably different from the novel, much to Du Maurier's distress, and opened to generally disappointed reviews with the *New York Herald Tribune* calling the film "singularly dull and uninspired" (Spoto 185). But amidst *Jamaica Inn*'s disappointing release Hitchcock had secured his contract with Selznick, even arranging a weekly salary of $125 for Harrison. Perhaps more importantly during this time Du Maurier sold the rights to *Rebecca* to Selznick. So in March of 1939 the Hitchcocks and Harrison set out on a sojourn to Hollywood with Harrison working daily on the treatment of *Rebecca*.

Like *Jamaica Inn*, the original screenplay for *Rebecca* was radically different from the novel and Selznick set out on a campaign for a rewrite:

> Comparisons of the original and final scenarios confirm the statement of Charles Bennett, who was in close contact with Selznick and Hitchcock at the time, that the screenplay is "ninety percent the work of Michael Hogan, although some rewrites were done by Joan, very little at the end was contributed by the one who is most famous and therefore most credited. [Robert] Sherwood" [Spoto 214].

The film, released in 1940, tells the story of a young woman, played by Joan Fontaine who, while on holiday in Monte Carlo is swept up in a whirlwind romance with the wealthy widower Maxim De Winter. After a brief courtship, Maxim proposes, whisking his young bride back to his lavish estate: Manderley. The honeymoon glow fades quite quickly for Fontaine's character, who's only name in the film is Madam De Winter, as she discovers the memory of Maxim's deceased wife Rebecca hangs heavy on the entire estate. With Maxim away for lengthy periods of time, the new Madam De Winter is left alone with the terrifying Mrs. Danvers, who keeps all of Rebecca's things as a sort of shrine to her. *Rebecca* draws heavily from gothic tropes, particularly those of Charlotte Bronte's *Jane Eyre*. In both stories a young woman of low status is drawn into the intrigue of a much wealthier man cursed with the shadow of a previous marriage. Both stories also see the grand manors burned, either by or in the name of the first wife.

In *Jane Eyre* Rochester's mad wife, Bertha Mason, actually inhabits the attic of

Thornfield Hall, and though Rebecca never actually appears in the film, Hitchcock never lets the characters, or the audience for that matter forget her presence. "During the memorable confession scene, while Maxim tells the heroine how his first wife taunted him on the last night of her life, the camera follows the invisible Rebecca around the boathouse, giving her, according to one critic, a 'spectral presence' that cannot be easily eradicated" (Wheatley). The confession to which Wheatley refers is Maxim explaining to his new wife that he never loved Rebecca and the night they fought, she was accidentally killed. He feared he'd be blamed and covered up her death. This is a radical departure from the novel but curiously enough did not result from efforts by Hitchcock or Harrison. Instead this change was forced from the outside. In Du Maurier's novel Maxim did kill Rebecca in his hatred of her and as a result of her wicked nature. The Hays Code, the censorship bureau of the time, dictated that Maxim De Winter could not go unpunished for the murder: "It would be necessary, the Hays Office insisted, to attribute Rebecca's death to an accident, or, to otherwise alter the situation so that the happy ending, when Maxim and his new wife face a brighter future, did not depend on the cavalier dismissal of a capital offense" (Spoto 214).

Though *Rebecca* won Hitchcock his first and only Best Picture Academy Award and earned a screenplay nomination for Harrison and Sherwood, Hitchcock has this to say of his first American film: "Well it's not a Hitchcock picture; it's a novelette, really. The story is old fashioned; there was a whole school of feminine literature at the period and though I'm not against it, the fact is that the story is lacking in humor" (Wheatley). Despite Hitchcock's consideration that the film is "feminine" it actually proves problematic from a feminist perspective most glaringly in the main character's lack of identity, she's literally known only by her husband's married name. This detail though does mirror the original text. In addition to defining herself by Maxim's name, Fontaine's character also lets her moral compass be dictated by his feelings toward her. The biggest revelation for her during the boathouse confession has nothing to do with the manner of Rebecca's death, but instead focuses on the fact that her husband hated his first wife and is not harboring romantic feelings for her. "Perhaps most threateningly, Maxim overlaps with Rebecca, a seepage reinforced by Olivier's almost startling beauty. Neither are what they seem, and the heroine responds to both of them masochistically" (Wheatley).

Perhaps most problematic is the decision to shift the perspective in the third act away from Fontaine and toward Lawrence Olivier's Maxim:

> Regardless, some would say that any power that the heroine gains is negated by the fact that the woman's perspective—in which we see through the Fontaine character's eyes—vanishes toward the end of the movie: unlike in the novel, which concludes with the heroine accompanying Maxim to question Rebecca's doctor, in the movie she is left behind while Maxim and three other male characters travel to London [Wheatley].

Removing the second Madam De Winter from a large portion of the third act further reduces her to a passive bystander and though she does escape the fire in the end, viewers are denied the adventure and heroics of such an endeavor.

As production on *Rebecca* drew to a close, Harrison and Hitchcock set to work revising another adaptation, this time of Vincent Sheean's political memoir *Personal History*, which recounted his time as a journalist overseas during the 1920s and 1930s:

> [Charles Bennett] and Hitchcock, with Joan Harrison helping in the rearrangement of scenes and continuity, closeted themselves for eight hours daily the entire month of February. They began with

little more than the Sheean title and the book's setting in Holland, but they agreed that the ingredients for success must be the ingredients of the most popular film they had done together, *The 39 Steps* [Spoto 227].

Eventually this would become *Foreign Correspondent,* which would earn Harrison her second screenplay Academy Award nomination in one year. *Rebecca* was nominated in the Writing (Screenplay) category and *Foreign Correspondent* was nominated in the Writing (Original Screenplay) category. *Foreign Correspondent* also earned a Best Picture nomination, a Supporting Actor nomination for Albert Basserman and three production nominations.

Foreign Correspondent tells the story of a cynical American journalist most concerned with having an expense account sent overseas as Europe stands on the precipice of World War II. Once there, he becomes embroiled in the assassination/kidnapping plot of a Dutch diplomat. This is further complicated when he becomes romantically entangled with a British heiress whose father happens to be behind the plot. The film features an iconic scene in which Joel McCrea's character observes a windmill spinning against the wind which leads him to the first piece of a much larger puzzle. It also features a climactic plane crash in the third act.

Perhaps most notable about the film is that, in stark contrast to most of the films Hitchcock and Harrison worked on together, the final cut of *Foreign Correspondent* ended up playing like a message movie. In the original draft the film was supposed to end with George Sanders' and McCrea's discussing the plane crash with Sanders declaring "Documents will undoubtedly be found, old boy, proving that it is a British trawler disguised as a German battleship and the whole thing has been organized by the pirate, Churchill, to drag America into the war" (Spoto 235). However, Hitchcock and Harrison were touring London in the summer on 1940 and rumors of an inevitable bombing seemed to be everywhere. As a result a new ending was crafted. In the final version, the film ends with a scene in which McCrea's character broadcasts a radio show from a London building as bombs begin falling outside. The camera shakes and rubble falls around him as he gives an impassioned speech to American listeners while the national anthem plays behind him. "There was no doubt that it was a hastily added scene, dramatically unjustified, out of character and out of line with everything that had preceded" (Spoto 234). According to Spoto this new scene was filmed on July 5, 1940, five days before the Germans dropped the first bombs on England.

Like *Casablanca,* history caught up to fiction during the script development and this led to certain inconsistencies throughout the film:

> It is interesting that in the first half of the screenplay nowhere are those plotting against Van Meer clearly identified as Nazis. They even speak a strange, made-up language. But in the second half of the film the villains are clearly identified. This results from the fact that the screenplay was started before the war and then was revised after the outbreak of hostilities in September 1939. The final revisions on the scene where Marshall is revealed to be a traitor are dated April 9, 1940, by which time the Germans had not only conquered Poland but had attacked Denmark and Norway in western Europe [Rossi].

In 1941 Hitchcock and Harrison would again unite with Fontaine to tell the story of a woman swept up in a whirlwind romance only to discover that her husband has far more secrets than she imagined. Adapted from a British novel originally titled *Before the Fact* the screenplay went through many iterations and challenges before finally being released under the title *Suspicion* in 1941. In the novel Lina Aysgarth, a wealthy heiress, discovers her new socialite husband is actually poor, suffering from a gambling addiction and as the story progresses she comes to suspect he is guilty of far worse. She first discovers he has murdered his friend and business partner and later grows wise to a plot on her own life in order to claim insurance money. The novel ends with the female protagonist succumbing to her own murder by poisoning after she discovers she's pregnant, convinced her husband should never reproduce. The film ends with something of a hatchet job. Johnnie Aysgarth takes his wife on a harrowing drive through a winding road, even going so far as to open the passenger door during a sharp curve before reconsidering and pulling the car over. The two reconcile and drive away into the sunset together.

There are many accounts as to why the film ended in this fashion instead of using the novel's ending. The first was the idea that Harrison, working with both Alma and Alfred Hitchcock, had set out to tell a more subtle story about the nature of suspicion in which the husband's crimes are imagined and exaggerated within Lina's mind:

> The first complete screenplay for *Before the Fact*, dated December 28, 1940 ends with the husband's innocence affirmed and the couple reconciled.... Nevertheless, dissatisfaction with the script obviously persisted since Reville and Harrison tinkered with assorted scenes during production and then wrote a new ending after the summer previews [Worland].

The idea of the psychological thriller fits with themes seen in *Rebecca* in which Fontaine is haunted by her predecessor's memory, but there may have also been more practical and less artistic reasons for the shift from the novel's ending.

Cary Grant was cast as the charming Johnnie Aysgarth. At the time Grant was known primarily for his romantic roles such as the role of Walter Burns in *His Girl Friday*. "The most commonly repeated explanation for the movie's abrupt and unsatisfying ending, one Hitchcock encouraged, is that either RKO would not allow Cary Grant to play a murderer or Grant himself refused to risk compromising his romantic screen persona" (Worland). Some stories state that reshoots of the ending were ordered while Hitchcock was out of town solely to preserve Grant's status. Grant's star power and gravitas also transformed the character from what should have been a manipulative, emotionally abusive thief to something of a charming rogue, incorrigible but impossible not to love.

The film also represents what was surely an uphill battle against the Hays Code. Had Lina actually gone through with accepting the poison and killing her unborn child, she would have essentially been giving herself an abortion, something the Hays office surely would not have been able to abide. Also Johnnie's punishment for the murder would need to be shown onscreen, he could not get away with it in the same way Maxim could not in *Rebecca*. But there was another element that did not make it onto the screen in any way and that was an overt lesbian relationship:

> Since the Isobel-Phyllis relationship originally written so clearly flaunted the PCA's prohibition against "sexual perversion," this may have been one of those instances, often alleged but hard to prove, of screenwriters deliberately inserting into early drafts provocative material that they knew would not get past the censors to create "bargaining chips" for more sincerely desired story elements [Worland].

This technique was common of writers at the time, a sort of red herring to draw the eyes of the censor away from other, less objectionable but still questionable, choices.

Regardless of the piecemeal ending, the film earned another Best Picture nomination for Hitchcock and a Best Actress win for Joan Fontaine. Unlike Madam de Winter, this Fontaine character commands the screen throughout the entire film. The film only shifts to Grant's Johnnie for a single scene after Lina's father's death in which he toasts the old man's portrait. This portrait seems an homage to other gothic traditions, hanging heavy and watchful over both characters throughout most of the film.

Harrison's last partnerships with Hitchcock was a return to the war film in 1942's *Saboteur*, which tells the story of an innocent man framed for an act of terror and trying to clear his name. Harrison's first feature without Hitchcock was *Dark Waters*, in which she wrote and served as associate producer. In the film a woman, recovering from a boating accident, in which she was the sole survivor, seeks refuge from relatives but finds there is an insidious plot to murder her for her inheritance. After this, Harrison found little more success as a writer with her scripts being bought but never produced. "In a February 1944 interview with the *Los Angeles Times* Harrison described herself as a 'thwarted writer.' She explained that her scripts had been so butchered that she had requested to have her name removed from the credits and became a producer to gain greater creative authority" (Biesen 129).

Perhaps her most important work came next, though, with *Phantom Lady*, on which Harrison served as executive producer. It was during the mid 1940s, when Film Noir seemed to morph again, this time into outright horror including an increased fascination with the paranormal and occult. "This revival in occult rituals was not attributed to a desire for escapism; rather, it was understood as an attempt to engage with the emotional and epistemological uncertainties of wartime" (Snelson 91). Those most affected by this desire were those on the domestic front: women. During this time period women had more options to join the workforce due to the vacancies left by male soldiers. This caused a change in their social situations granting them more disposable income and independence. With this growing market also came a growing need for female expertise in reaching this market, which correlates directly with Harrison's work on *Phantom Lady* in 1943. When discussing her switch from writer to producer Harrison said: "I think very few women make good directors but producing is different. Directors must at times be able to shout in a way women can't or shouldn't. But no production which does not satisfy the feminine point of view is a success" (Oliver). Though the first part of her statement does prove quite problematic and is certainly incorrect, she makes her point in the end and Harrison proves it all the more with the strength of *Phantom Lady*.

The film tells the story of Carol "Kansas" Richman, a secretary who sets out to clear her boss's name after he is charged with the murder of his wife. Kansas is hunting for his alibi, a mysterious lady who no one seems to be able to identify. Kansas utilizes every resource at her disposal including her sexuality in her quest for information. However rather than playing into gender stereotypes, *Phantom Lady* actually turns many of them on end. "What's more, her emotional strength is contrasted to that of [her boss] Scott, who is shown crying in despair. In fact, Kansas reveals that she loves Scott for 'how soft he really is'; the film therefore explicitly subverts traditional gender expectations'" (Snelson 116). Kansas is neither femme fatale nor is she a passive or virginal victim, often the only two options for women in film noir. Instead she's a strong, independent woman setting out to save a male victim.

Harrison worked hard for Kansas' character to be defined from within rather than from her exterior explaining to her lead actress, Ella Raines, that " 'the nature of her character would not permit her to be beautiful. That her clothes would be ordinary, some of them downright shabby.' The actress responded 'I didn't work so hard for years and years just to be pretty'" (Snelson 115). The film was mostly considered a sleeper hit but

Harrison was praised extensively for it, with one review saying, "the pupil equals, perhaps even outdistances, the master" (Snelson 112). The master of course refers to Hitchcock. Harrison was never truly able to escape the shadow cast by her former mentor, with most of her success being attributed to his tutelage.

Harrison's time, along with that of other women in the workforce during World War II, was to be short lived. Harrison's next feature in 1945 was called *The Strange Affair of Uncle Harry* and proved problematic on several levels. A war between Harrison and the Hays office delayed the release of the film for so long and caused such conflict between Harris and Universal that it marked the end of her employment there. The final cut of the film included an abrupt and surprise ending that negated most of the second half of the film as dream sequence. Harrison was furious. Ultimately the film was poorly reviewed as a result of this ending. But the ending did not simply represent a poor choice on the part of the studio; it also represented a lack of respect for Harrison's authority as producer. "The film, particularly its much-maligned "tacked-on ending," indicates the postwar direction of industry policy in relation to women and horror production that helped motivate the end of the female monster cycle" (Snelson 125).

In 1947 as men returned home from war and back to their jobs the opportunities for women dried up rapidly with women relegated back to domestic life. Harrison went on to produce several more features without much success. Ultimately Harrison returned to her roots and worked as a producer on the television series "Alfred Hitchcock Presents": "'It was Hitchcock's way of paying her for her earlier loyalty,' according to one writer 'but as time went on she became rather proprietary about Hitchcock—she wanted people to know she had a certain power and control over his affairs" (Spoto 370).

In 1958 she married the crime writer Eric Ambler, a union that lasted until her death in 1994 at the age of 87.

World War II was a unique time in Hollywood's history. Crime stories and a fascination with darkness birthed the new genre of Film Noir at the same time that men were being called away to serve their country. As a result of this, women were afforded a brief and unique opportunity to form their own stories and images. Joan Harrison was a woman who capitalized on this opportunity, learning what she could from one of the greats and synthesizing his knowledge into her own talents. Pushing back against stigmas about her own appearance, Harrison helped to redefine the image of her entire gender.

Works Cited

Biesen, Sheri Chinen. *Blackout World War II and the Origins of Film Noir*. Baltimore: Johns Hopkins University Press, 2005. Print.
Nelmes, Jill, and Jule Selbo, eds. *Women Screenwriters: An International Guide*. N.p.: Springer, 2015.
Oliver, Myrna. "Joan Harrison, 83; Producer, Writer for Alfred Hitchcock." *Los Angeles Times* 24 Aug. 1994, Online ed., Collections: n. pag. Print. Obituary.
Rossi, John. "Hitchcock's Foreign Correspondent (1940)." *Film & History (03603695)* 12.2 (1982): 25–35. *Communication & Mass Media Complete*. Web. 30 Apr. 2016.
Snelson, Tim. *Phantom Ladies: Hollywood Horror and the Home Front*. New Brunswick, NJ: Rutgers University Press, 2014. eBook Collection (EBSCOhost). Web. 30 Apr. 2016.
Spoto, Donald. *The Dark Side of Genius: The Life of Alfred Hitchcock*. First Edition ed. Boston, Toronto: Little, Brown, 1983.
Unterburger, Amy L. *The St. James Women Filmmakers Encyclopedia: Women on the Other Side of the Camera*. Detroit: Visible Ink, 1999.
Wheatley, Kim. "Gender Politics and the Gothic in Alfred Hitchcock's *Rebecca*." *Gothic Studies* 4.2 (2002): 133. *Humanities International Complete*. Web. 30 Apr. 2016.
Worland, Rick. "Before and After the Fact: Writing and Reading Hitchcock's Suspicion." *Cinema Journal* 41.4 (2002): 3. Art & Architecture Complete. Web. 30 Apr. 2016.

The Six Degrees of Sarah Y. Mason and Victor Heerman

Pamela L. Scott

To begin by being perfectly blunt, the original conclusion of this research led to disappointment that Sarah Yeiser Mason, though she won an early Academy Award for writing, does not have enough verifiable information readily available on either her professional or personal life to give her name recognition in film history purely on its own. Comparing some of the random and different versions of mentions of her by other Hollywood autobiographies and the popular cultural trend of The Six Degrees of Kevin Bacon sparked the idea to mimic the game claiming anyone can be connected to the actor by just six short introductions to other people. What if this concept of the *Six Degrees of Separation*, originating from Hungarian author Frigyes Karinthy's 1929 short story, was applied to the seemingly incongruent puzzle pieces of data about Sarah Y. Mason? Perhaps a more thorough understanding of her life might be drawn.

The vast majority of information about her early professional life is derived and interpreted from the sixty-five page untitled manuscript of an oral history given by her husband and sometimes professional writing partner, Victor Eugene Heerman, in 1976. On the surface, even those stories reveal very little about her. Heerman's recollection became the starting point or baseline, which propelled research on every single subject in search of further connections, enlightening new details and perhaps timelines of their professional and personal lives. Some details can be confirmed, some are questioned, and others invite further searches by future scholars, leading ever closer to the fuller picture Mason deserves to have painted about her life and work.

An example of easily confirmed data despite the multitude of misprinted numbers, both Mason and Heerman died at the age of 84 in Los Angeles, Heerman on November 3, 1977, and Mason on November 28, 1980. Only Heerman left behind manuscripts, interviews, notes, and various documents for future reading. The Heerman papers are available in the Special Collections section of the Academy of Motion Picture Arts and Sciences Margaret Herrick Library. Anthony Slide conducted the oral history interview May 17, 19, 24, and 26, 1976, just four years before Mason died. On the one hand, her husband knew her best, yet his memory at eighty years old of what they did fifty years or more earlier, is the predominate evidence of Mason's existence. One cannot completely reconcile the discrepancies between his account and the few documented facts from other sources. The complete picture of Mason's contributions to film history is likely gone forever, however, with patience, creativity, and time, enough can be derived to see that Mason clearly warrants her name to be known individually as well as paired with Heerman.

An early example of conflicting answers surrounds the year Mason and Heerman married. Between IMDb, Wikipedia, Women Film Pioneers Project, Heerman's Oral History, and *The Morning Telegraph* to name a few, it was either 1920 or 1921. Heerman said it was 1920, but without having access to the actual marriage license, the correct answer most likely comes from an article in New York city's *The Morning Telegraph* since it published during the period. The May 1, 1921, article reads: "Sarah Mason weds Victor Heerman. The two were married last Wednesday in Pasadena, with Mrs. ZaSu Pitts Gallery, Sarah's pal, and Tom Gallery as their supporting cast at the wedding." The year of publication supports the idea that 1921 is the best answer when compared to the credibility and likelihood of mistakes published in other sources. The lesson learned by this emerging scholar is that researching with the goal of establishing factual history of who, what, when, where, and why is a serious responsibility and details cannot be taken for granted.

The longer litany of errors begins at the end, with one of Heerman's obituaries, published by *Variety* November 7, 1977. *Film Pioneer Victor Heerman Dies* reads,

Writer Sarah Y. Mason, circa 1930. Mason was one of the first people in Hollywood to specialize in script supervision and film continuity when the industry switched from silent film to talkies (Academy of Motion Picture Arts and Sciences' Margaret Herrick Library).

His wife, the former Sarah Mason, shared his *Little Women* writing chores and the Oscar. She survives, along with two sons. Heerman was born in Surrey, England, Aug 17, 1893, but grew up in New York, and became involved in showbiz as a child actor. His interest in films dated almost from the beginning of the industry, starting with Kinemacolor. He later started directing for Mack Sennett, and went on to work with David O. Selznick, First National and Famous Players, RKO and others. Among Heerman's original scripts were *My Boy* for Jackie Coogan, the Owen Moore farces for Selznick, *John Smith* and *Personality*. He directed *The Poor Simp*, *The Confidence Man* and the Marx Brothers *Animal Crackers* and others. No services will be held for Victor E. Heerman, 84 who won an Academy Award for his part in a 1933 collaboration on the screenplay, *Little Women*. He died last Thursday at the Motion Picture & TV Hospital in Woodland Hills. Heerman was a film industry pioneer whose career started in 1914, and who remained active—working as producer, writer, and director—until 1954. During that period, he worked at all major studios.

Among the errors in this obituary is the fact that he was born August 27, 1893, not the 17th, and Heerman had a daughter and a son, not two sons. It is also worth noting that the obituary writer failed to mention his collaborator on the Academy Award-winning *Little Women*, which continued the work of erasing Mason from history.

Three years later, December 2, 1980, *Variety* also published Mason's obituary. *Sarah Heerman* reads: "Sarah Heerman 85, widow of writer-director, Victor Heerman, died Nov 28 at the Motion Picture & Television Country Home in Woodland Hills. She is survived by a son and a daughter. No services." Error number one is that she had been born on March 31, 1896, and died at the age of 84, not 85. More importantly, this obituary finds her relationship to a man more worthy of mention than her own shared Academy Award win with that man as an equal collaborator. Clearly there's something to be said for comparing the contrasting both content and length of the obituaries. Assuming they are strictly known as a writing team, why would one person warrant more attention than the other? Part of the problem comes from the transformation of the film industry from a ragtag collection of independents into an assembly line production model. "The beginning of the studio system can be traced to the formation of MGM in 1924. Although women had made successful films, their contributions were not recognized and they were bypassed in the development of the studio system." (Seger 13).

By being a team, however, Mason and Heerman, seemed to share publicity during their working years. Reporters relished both their professional and private lives. For example, *The Morning Telegraph* (NY) report of April 17, 1921: "Sarah Y. Mason has returned to Hollywood after a year in New York as a leading lady in the Selznick scenario department. She has just completed an original story for screen purposes and has orders for several continuities. However, Mason contrives to divide her time equally between screen and society." Again, *The Morning Telegraph* reports March 19, 1922,

> Correction note—Re: it recorded that the heiress to the talents and fortunes of Mr. and Mrs. Victor Heerman (Sarah Y. Mason y'know) has been christened Katherine Auliss Heerman, and it is not spelled with a K as at first announced. We have this news direct from the little lady's popular mother, who admits she is so proud of the tiny daughter that she "is just delirious!" But then the Selznick director is just as proud in his fatherly way, so baby Katherine is to be congratulated on having chosen such doting parents.

One final example of their shared publicity also comes from *The Morning Telegraph*, December 2, 1923,

> Mrs. Heerman Heerman (Sarah Y. Mason, y'know) was hostess at luncheon today at the Writer's Club. She gave the affair to say good-by to a group of her friends, among them ZaSu Pitts, Julianne Johnston, Carmelita Geraghty, Emma Drury Mason, Violet Clark Freeman, Nell Newman and ye scribe. The Heermans are leaving Thursday for New York where, by special arrangement with Joseph Schenck, to whom he was under contract, Mr. Heerman is to direct the next two Thomas Meighan productions for Paramount.

Mason is described playfully and lovingly in these examples intertwining both sides of her life just as Heerman is mentioned with the same lighthearted tone. So when considered as a couple, they gain matching attention in the press. It is when asked about their careers in later years that Heerman takes precedence, perhaps because he turned to directing and film historians have a penchant for considering directors the *auteurs* of their films.

In the oral history done by Slide, he questioned Heerman about when he met Mason, but Heerman began the story with his professional experience as a director. In 1920 Heerman signed on to direct *The Poor Simp* starring Owen Moore and produced by the

Selznick Pictures Corporation. "I'll tell you how. I was working for Selznick—I mean I was working for the Owen Moore Company, and I was making a picture. It was called *The Poor Simp*." Immediately the six-degree-of-separation connections lead to a complicated and intertwined web of relationships that finally connected Heerman to Mason.

Loosely, Lewis J. Selznick originally founded a distribution company in Fort Lee, New Jersey around 1914 and through various partnerships, dissolutions, successes and failures stayed involved with films on the East Coast until sometime around 1920 when he moved to Hollywood. Considered a pioneer of film, he was the father of David O. Selznick, Oscar winning producer of *Gone with the Wind* (1939). Leading up to *The Poor Simp* (1920), Owen Moore starred in numerous Selznick films beginning with *Piccadilly Jim* (1919). After the project, Moore starred in *Love Is an Awful Thing* (1922) written and directed by Heerman which was the only film produced by the Owen Moore Film Corporation. Moore was the leading man with Mary Pickford as the leading lady in numerous films between 1911 and 1914, their first being *Their First Misunderstanding* directed by Thomas Ince produced by Independent Moving Pictures Company of America (IMP) in 1911. Moore and Pickford were privately married in 1911 and divorced in 1920 even though Pickford had long before left Moore for Douglas Fairbanks. *The Little Princess* (1917) starring Mary Pickford, adapted by Frances Marion, directed by Marshall Neilan and produced by the Mary Pickford Company also includes ZaSu Pitts in the cast.

Preparing for the film, Heerman heard that they were also searching for a comedy writer for Moore and pursuing Agnes Christine Johnston, writer of *23 ½ Hours Leave* (1919), the first of several collaborations produced by the Thomas H. Ince Corporation. Agnes previously adapted *Daddy-Long-Legs* (1919) starring Pickford, directed by Marshall Neilan, and produced by the Mary Pickford Company. Thomas Harper Ince's oldest brother John Edward Ince directed a film *Held in Trust* (1920) with Mason credited for the adaptation. Unavailable for the job, Johnston said, "I know just the girl for you. She writes for ZaSu Pitts" (Slide 25). Johnston recommended Mason. Already credited for continuity on *Arizona* (1918), Mason also had writing credits for *Bright Skies* (1920) and *Heart of Twenty* (1920), starring ZaSu Pitts, directed by Henry Kolker, and produced by Brentwood Film Corporation. The Brentwood Film Corporation produced only six films. *Better Times* (1919), the first film included Julianne Johnstone in the cast along with ZaSu Pitts. *The Morning Telegraph* mentioned their names earlier as friends of Mason. Also, the first three Brentwood films were directed by King Wallis Vidor in 1919.

Mason was hired, put on a train Sunday June 12, 1919, headed for Fort Lee, where she met Heerman for the first time. According to Heerman, they had a rocky start since the group split up during the journey. As Heerman remembered it, "I'd only just met the girl, so nobody paid any attention to her, and she's wandering around. So she said, 'They're not gentlemen anyway.' So she had a very poor opinion of us." Each person made his own way to the destination before being reunited for the current project.

According to Heerman, Mason told him during one of their first conversations that while in Arizona, Fairbanks and Dwan saw her at a theatre, introduced themselves to her mother, and offered Mason with an opportunity to act in films. He also remembered asking, "What stories did you write?" She said, "Well I never really finished, only the one for ZaSu Pitts." Well, I said, "That was two years before. Didn't any of those stories..." She replied, "No."

Did she become an actress on the side, as several female screenwriters did in order to enter the business? *Sarah* Y. Mason has no acting credits, however, *Sara* Mason does.

Fairbanks and Dwan collaborated on many projects beginning in 1916 sometimes sharing credits as director and writer. Later, Sic 'Em Sam (1918) stars Fairbanks and *Sara* Mason. Paramount Pictures produced the short film as a fund raising effort for the U.S. Liberty Loan Drive for World War I. Sic 'Em Sam (1918) was produced just prior to *Arizona* (1918).

Arizona (1918) is mentioned in nearly every variation of stories found about Mason's entrance into the industry and in some versions of where and how she met Heerman. Filmed in Tucson, Arizona, the credits include producer/director/writer/actor Fairbanks, writers Dwan, Albert Parker, Theodore Reed, Augustus E. Thomas (Play), and Mason, for continuity. Mason is considered the first person with a continuity credit, which meant she was in charge of the storyline following in an understandable way. According to IMDB.com, "The very first continuity girl. She suggested the position to Allan Dwan, who accepted the idea for his film *Arizona* (1918)." The modern day position is script supervisor. It certainly seems logical the idea of a brand new position being approved by a seasoned writer and director would come from someone they know rather than a stranger. Heerman's story continues claiming Mason had a fear of the camera. "The minute the camera would start, she would go and hide behind something." So she said, "I'd rather be a script clerk" (Slide).

Putting it all together, given that Heerman's memory at eighty years old is not 100 percent accurate, it's reasonable to assume Mason met Fairbanks and Dwan in her native state of Arizona, acted in one small role alongside Fairbanks, established a favorable relationship, then worked in continuity alongside writers Fairbanks, Dwan and others. Perhaps through their connections with Pickford Mason moved on to write two complete scripts for star Pitts, and finally adapted the novel *Held in Trust* (1920) by George Kibbe Turner for the screen, directed by John E. Ince, produced by Metro Pictures Incorporated, before ever meeting her future husband. *Sic 'Em Sam* was the perfect test for a newcomer using the alternative name spelling as assurance of anonymity. Perhaps it cannot be proven, but the coincidence between the spellings of *Sarah* Mason and *Sara* Mason at this precise time is too much to ignore. For whatever reason, Mason did not continue acting, but the door was open for other opportunities and she became an established writer for the screen. Conclusion? Everyone knows someone who knows someone else that leads you to someone else. Perhaps Kevin Bacon and the Six Degrees of Separation is not that ridiculous a concept when it comes to research. For example, Mason knew Douglas and Dwan, who knew Moore and Pickford, who knew Pitts and Johnston who knew Thomas Ince who was brothers with John Ince who knew Pitts and Mason.

According to Heerman's oral history, once the two met Mason offered to write a new story for Keystone, but Heerman replied, "The way we do it at the Keystone, we get an idea, and then we get the characters we're going to tell that idea with." Mason replied, "I never did it that way." "Well" he said, "That's the way we're going to have to do it." The two decided to collaborate with their first two scripts together, *The Chicken in the Case* (1921) and *A Divorce of Convenience* (1921) satisfying Heerman's two-picture agreement with Selznick Pictures Corporation. With that move, Mason and Heerman established themselves as an effective writing team. As to their relationship, Heerman recalled, "So wasting time and not working on anything, we went out and got married, and ZaSu and Jack Pickford were the best man and maid of honor." Eventually, they had one daughter and one son and remained married until Heerman's death.

Linda Seger, author of *When Women Call the Shots*, offers this thought about female screenwriters in this era. "By the 1920's the careers of almost every woman director and producer and many women writers was over" (Seger 11). "The lack of opportunity in most jobs did not prevent women from continuing to have influence in the film industry, but their influence was largely behind the scenes" (Seger 17). Since Heerman was born into the industry, it's plausible the vast multitude of connections he mentioned in the oral history far outweigh Mason's even though she was obviously talented. Perhaps Mason fit nicely behind the scenes during their marriage, choosing to split her time between writer, mother, wife, and society figure. Yet Mason wrote more as a solo writer than Heerman did so scholars of screenwriting should have delved into her career further. Mason has over a dozen writing credits in these years and Heerman has only seven. Heerman spent most of his time as director with about twenty directing credits up until 1931. As a team, from the time of their marriage in 1921 up to their Oscar winning adaptation of Louisa May Alcott's *Little Women* (1933) followed by *Magnificent Obsession* (1935), they are only credited with one other joint effort.

In many ways, *Little Women* was the peak of both their individual and collaborative careers, which may explain why Mason is little known today. In *History of the American Cinema* Tino Balio wrote,

> RKO's *Little Women* (George Cukor) was considered the first picture of the decade based on a literary classic to be turned into an artistic and commercial success.... *Variety* described the picture as a superb "human document, somber in tone, stately slow in movement, but always eloquent in its interpretations.... There doesn't occur a picture in recent film history produced with so uncompromising a degree of sincerity, or one that so wholeheartedly aims at an honest realization of a significant novel of another era." Earning $800,000 in profits, *Little Women* became one of RKO's biggest hits of the decade. Nominated for an Academy Award for best picture and ranked number five on *Film Daily*' Top ten list of 1934 [Ballo 187].

The biographical information published by RKO Radio listed each writer separately, beginning with Mason:

> Writers (Adaptation)—
> Sarah Y. Mason
> "Little Women"
> (RKO-Radio)
> Born in Pima, Arizona, on March 31, 1896.
> Educated in public schools, Tucson, Arizona.
> Entered motion pictures in 1918 with the Douglas Fairbanks company,
> and sold first original to Robertson-Cole company (now defunct).
> Has written originals and screen plays for MGM, Paramount, Columbia
> and RKO-Radio. "Alias Jimmy Valentine," "Broadway Melody," "Shopworn,"
> "Age of Consent," and many others in collaboration with Victor Heerman.
> Victor Heerman
> "Little Women"
> (RKO-Radio)
> Born in London, England.
> Educated in public schools, New York.
> Comes from family of theatrical costumers. Directed first picture in 1914,
> and has written and directed for practically all the major producing companies,
> dating as far back as the old Thanhauser company in 1911.
> All screen work in collaboration with Miss Mason, who is his wife in private life.

The Toronto Film Society screened *Little Women* (1933) along with another film December 18, 1983. The program states,

George Cukor's 1933 film of *Little Women* is actually its second filmization [sp], a silent version having been released in 1918. In the early 1930's, David O. Selznick, then at RKO became fascinated with Alcott's novel of a middle-class New England Family, living frugally but tastefully in the 1860's, believing in old-fashioned virtues, dreaming attainable dreams, and being grateful for what they had. Through Selznick's efforts, the husband and wife team of Victor Heerman and Sarah Y. Mason took over an existing unsatisfactory screen treatment of one of their favourite novels and acted out all the parts (Heerman played all four daughters) while writing their fresh and largely unsentimental script.... *Little Women* was nominated for three Academy Awards: Best Picture, Best Director, and Best Screenplay Adaptation. The Heermans won the last category: Katharine Hepburn, who has been so rightly called the spine of the film, was named Best Actress of 1934 at the Cannes International Film Festival [*Little Women*. Programme 4].

As far as their second collaboration, "Hollywood knows that love and sex sell. But many of its greatest films are not about sex, but about romance. The slow developing relationship. About love. Falling in love. Being in love. Falling out of love. Falling in love again" (Seger 125). *Magnificent Obsession* (1935) is one such movie. Irene Dunne's biographer, Bodeen DeWitt, felt,

> The Lloyd C. Douglas novel Magnificent Obsession was on the fiction best seller lists for several years during the days of the Great Depression. It did not come to the screen until the last few days of 1935 because it had been regarded as a well-needed fictional sermon, a treatise on righteousness and the true rewards of brotherly love. Yet there was a definite audience for the cinema version when it was presented at the Radio City Music Hall. It was a good tear-jerker, sensitively presented and tenderly acted by a first rate cast.... Box-office receipts and book sales have shown that in times of stress, book and cinema audiences have been drawn to any theme that is basically spiritual. Although the country was out of the worst part of the Depression which might have destroyed it had Franklin D. Roosevelt not become the type of presidential leader that he was, it was crippled anew by a recession during the 1935–1936 period, and again people were seeking spiritual salvation, so they were ready for the message contained in the Douglas novel [DeWitt].

On 31 December 1935, Variety reported the film, "...presents a spiritual theme with delicacy, beauty, and power in terms of human, moving drama along the lines of popular entertainment."

Not all other reviews were as glowing. One of the New York reviews published in *The Hollywood Reporter* 9 January 1936 by *Mirror* reads, "The story will appeal more keenly to the feminine film fans than to the male ones." *Journal* gave the backhanded compliment, "the production is impressively mounted, and Director John M. Stahl has handled the tear-inducing sequences with thoughtful dignity."

In the world of entertainment and big money, clearly relationships and connections play an important part of anyone's career. Sadly, this paper only scratches the surface of Sarah Y. Mason's talent, contributions, and accomplishments to the early film days. Both Mason and Heerman were talented writers together and separately, but unless things are rewritten, she will mostly be remembered as the wife of an early husband and wife writing team.

Works Cited

Balio, Tino. *History of the American Cinema*. New York: Charles Scribner's Sons. 1993.
Beauchamp, Cari. *Without Lying Down: Frances Marion and the Powerful Women of Early Hollywood*. Berkeley: University of California Press, 1998.
Bennett, Carl. Silentera.com. Progressive Silent Film List. 1999. Web. 6 May 2016. http://www.silentera.com/PSFL/index.html.
DeWitt, Bodeen. *The Best of Irene Dunne*. Magill's Survey of Cinema. The Margaret Herrick Library—Academy of Motion Picture Arts and Sciences.

Francke, Lizzie. *Script Girls*. London: British Film Institute, 1994.
Heerman, Victor. *Heerman Papers*. Special Collections, The Margaret Herrick Library—Academy of Motion Picture Arts and Sciences.
Herrick Library—Academy of Motion Picture Arts and Sciences. 5 Dec. 1986.
Little Women (1933). Wrs: Sarah Y. Mason & Victor Heerman, Dir. George Cukor. Warner Bros., USA 115 mins.
Little Women. Programme 4. Toronto Film Society. The Margaret Herrick Library—Academy of Motion Picture Arts and Sciences. 18 Dec. 1983.
Menefee, David W. *The First Female Stars: Women of the Silent Era*. West Port, CT: Greenwood Publishing Group, Inc., 2004.
Needham, Col. IMDB.com, http://www.imdb.com. An amazon.com company. 1990. Web. 6 May 2016.
Norman, Marc. *What Happens Next: A History of American Screenwriting*. New York: Three Rivers Press, 2007.
Obituary. "Film Pioneer Victor Heerman Dies." *Variety*. The Margaret Herrick Library—Academy of Motion Picture Arts and Sciences.7 Nov. 1977.
Obituary. "Mason Heerman." *Variety*. The Margaret Herrick Library—Academy of Motion Picture Arts and Sciences. 2 Dec. 1980.
Russell, Tony, Allen Brizee, and Elizabeth Angeli. "MLA Formatting and Style Guide." *The Purdue OWL*. Purdue University Writing Lab, 4 Apr. 2010. Web. 20 Jul 2010.
"Mason Mason Arrives." *The Morning Telegraph*. The Margaret Herrick Library—Academy of Motion Picture Arts and Sciences. 17 Apr 1921.
"Mason Mason Gives Good Bye Luncheon." *The Morning Telegraph*. The Margaret Herrick Library—Academy of Motion Picture Arts and Sciences. 2 Dec. 1923.
"Mason Mason Weds Victor Heerman." *The Morning Telegraph*. The Margaret Herrick Library—Academy of Motion Picture Arts and Sciences. 1 May 1921.
Scripophily.com. http://scripophily.net/secode19.html. The Gift of History, Quality Service Since 1880. Web. 6 May 2016.
Seger, Linda. *When Women Call the Shots*. New York: Henry Holt and Company, Inc. 1996.
"She's Catherine—Not Katherine." *The Morning Telegraph*. The Margaret Herrick Library—Academy of Motion Picture Arts and Sciences. 19 Mar 1922.
Slide, Anthony. "Unedited Transcript of an Oral History with Victor Heerman," Heerman Papers, Special Collections, The Margaret Herrick Library—Academy of Motion Picture Arts and Sciences. 17 May 1976, 19 May 1976, 24 May 1976, 26 May 1976.
Stempel, Tom. *Framework: A History of Screenwriting in the American Film*. New York: Continuum, 1991.
Sturtevant, Victoria. "Mason Y. Mason" Jane Gaines, Radha Vatsal, and Monica Dall'Asta, eds. *Women Film Pioneers Project*. Center for Digital Research and Scholarship. New York: Columbia University Libraries, 2013. Web. September 27, 2013. https://wfpp.cdrs.columbia.edu/pioneer/ccp-sarah-y-mason/#bibliography.
Welch, Roseanne. "Re: Article." Message to the author. 3 May 2016. Email.

Zoë Akins
A Quiet Rebellion
SARAH AMBLE WHORTON

Zoë Akins is described as "a perplexing figure in the history of American theatre" by historian Yvonne Shafer (58). Akins was a poet, novelist, playwright, and screenwriter. Despite many successful publications, productions, films, and a Pulitzer Prize, she is not considered an obvious success. In creative fields dominated by the male perspective, her female-centric work failed to find acclaim with critics. By contrast, women, starved for fictional counterparts, filled theaters and cinema houses for the chance to encounter an Akins' leading lady. Artistic tastes fluctuated with the changing times, but Akins rebelled by never straying from her primary query. Her work contemplates how the modern woman can discover her true self within the social, political, and financial restraints remaining from a bygone era.

On October 30, 1886, Zoë Akins was born in Humansville, Missouri, to Thomas Jasper Akins and Sarah Elizabeth Green Akins. Zoë had two siblings, but little information exists about them. When Thomas Akins received the position of postmaster, the family moved to St. Louis, Missouri. Deeply embedded in the political scene, he served on the Republican State Committee and held the position of United States Sub-Treasurer under President Theodore Roosevelt. Financially secure, Thomas and Sarah Elizabeth catered to their children's artistic whims, but climbing the social ladder meant boarding school for the young Akins.

Akins was enrolled at Monticello Seminary in Godfrey, Illinois. A creative child longing for new challenges, she blossomed in the pristine surroundings. Later in life, she reflected, "I really didn't come alive, it seems to me, until I went to Monticello Seminary..." (Cranmer 253). Miss Alden, the English teacher, saw great potential in Akins' essays and encouraged her intensive study of drama. The girls' school was the perfect environment to meet like-minded confidantes. Sara Teasdale, a former student, founded a group called "The Potters," self-described as a "women's art and literature collective." Akins wanted to join the club, but never received an invitation. When The Potters disbanded, Teasdale was forced to turn her attention and friendship to Akins.

Teasdale was an accomplished poet, having first published in 1907. Despite being isolated due to illness Teasdale was confident in her abilities. Akins said Teasdale would "sometimes be a trying friend. But there was no one more honest, more intelligently captious, nor rarer" (*Others Than Myself* 47). The Missourians had opposing personalities.

Writers Charles Brackett and Zoë Akins at a dinner party, circa 1949. Originally from Missouri, when Akins moved to Los Angeles to be a screenwriter she bought a pink stucco house and remained in California until her death in 1958 (Academy of Motion Picture Arts and Sciences' Margaret Herrick Library).

Teasdale was rigid in her beliefs while Akins was easily swayed by new experiences. Teasdale was righteously devoted to her endeavors while Akins only worked when distractions were not available. Teasdale sought to improve Akins, but Akins accepted Teasdale without reservation. Akins admitted, "[Teasdale] was always trying to redeem me from what she considered my worldliness, and which was somehow entwined with my passion for the theatre … [but] I never took the fault finding of my intimates too seriously. Probably not seriously enough" (*OTM* 50). Despite these differences, Akins and Teasdale found common ground in poetry.

Spurred by Teasdale's unofficial mentoring and with the assistance of publisher William Marion Reedy, Akins' first volume of poetry, *Interpretations,* was printed in 1912. Recognition from the literary community brought Akins fame and criticism. Her gender and female centered tales placed her at odds with her male peers. "Poetry and playwriting became the last bastions of the literary male's control. Literary criticism became a way to perpetuate male domination by developing standards that degraded methods and topics considered "feminine" (Kreizenbeck 30). The most egregious offense was Ernest Hemingway's "The Lady Poets with Foot Notes." He attacked the private lives of six female poets, including Akins. This form of lambasting became popular among male writers, each releasing their own version. "Lady poets" might have been deterred in continuing their careers if not for the bonds created by enduring such discrimination. "…nearly all of the support for Akins' poetry came from women, and that nearly all of the criticism of her dramas—criticism written almost entirely by men—focuses on what they considered her excessive emotionalism" (Kreizenbeck 30). Throughout her career, Akins treasured the company of creative associates, often resulting in lifetime relationships.

Poetry presented new opportunities and secured Akins a new mentor. After receiving a rejection letter from S.S. McClure, Akins arrived unannounced at his office, looking for guidance. The meeting with McClure was fruitless, but Willa Cather, McClure's assistant, took note of Akins' work. New to poetry, Akins often mimicked other poets in style and tone. Cather encouraged Akins' to hone her own voice and develop her natural proficiency for writing drama. Mentoring morphed into friendship. "For all of Zoë's superficial smartness and theatricality, Willa took her seriously enough to talk to her about her own work. She also knew her own life would be much drabber with Zoë Akins in it" (Robinson 184). Cather knew Akins was a talented poet but suggested she explore another avenue, theatre.

Akins loved the stage after a quick flirtation with acting. Teasdale, like Cather, coaxed Akins to consider writing plays. When Akins vetted the idea to Teasdale, "Sara said: "But you *are* a dramatist!" and thinking it over, Zoë realized that she was" (Cranmer 255). Akins threw herself into the study of successful plays, reading everything about the New York theatrical season. Actress Julie Marlowe noticed her eagerness and introduced her to several producers. In 1916, *The Magical City*, a one-act play, was produced in New York and Akins' trajectory was forever changed. "Everybody wanted to know who she was and where she came from" (Shafer 60). With the taste of success, Akins turned her attention to Broadway, but the theatre would prove to be a temperamental arena.

After five years of wavering support and finances, Akins' first play, *Papa*, was produced in Los Angeles (November 1916) and New York (April 1919). The response was favorable and Akins was considered a "promising" talent. George Jean Nathan, the American drama critic, wrote, "…[*Papa*] is the perhaps the best thing of its eccentric kind in the theatrical writing of our day. I know nothing in Europe equal to it…" (Shafer 61). Akins' intensive research of published plays inspired her to experiment with the rules of storytelling. In an article for *The Drama* magazine, Akins described her approach for developing new material,

> [With *Papa*], I tried to break away from all the formalities of the theatre and to fly straight in the teeth of all the prejudices and taboos of traditional drama. I set out to write a play that was penetrating and sophisticated but neither flippant nor cynical. Sometimes I think I made the mistake of making it too realistic ["The Writing of a Play" 191].

Papa was Akins' attempt to air her grievances against single-minded producers. When they demanded a "well made play," she gave them a rebellious masterpiece that mocked the establishment. The avant-garde structure earned *Papa* praise as a literary triumph, but the intellectually stimulating material did not fill theaters. Poor ticket sales impacted the gap years between the Los Angeles production and the New York production. Project longevity required paying customers.

Akins' upbringing influenced her hesitation to find common ground with mass audiences. Hailing from Southern nobility, Sarah Elizabeth Akins took pride in upholding the family name. By adopting the social graces of her parents, Akins easily maneuvered into the lives of the crème de la crème. "[Akins] had been told her whole life, and had come to believe that her ideas, education, and standards made her superior person. She wanted the company of her equals" (Kreizenbeck 71). The desire to infiltrate high society is evident in Akins' work. She favors the socialite over the working girl, the titled earl over the common man. When questioned about this pattern, Akins responded, "Some of the New York critics have made light of what they call my fondness for writing plays about the English aristocracy from the point of view of St. Louis. Well, that's all right. It happens that many of my best friends are English people" (Cranmer 259–260). Apparent by the response, Akins was willing to laugh at herself.

Thomas and Sarah Elizabeth Akins never discouraged Zoë's artistic expressions, but they did not take a vested interest in her writing. During the early years, Akins tried to involve her parents in her creative endeavors. Encouraged by her beloved Miss Alden of Monticello Seminary, Akins shared a well-received original play with them. Believing the reading to be unimportant, teasing followed the presentation. This incident severely damaged Akins' connection to her parents. She wrote, "My failure to hold their attention that night caused an estrangement between my parents and me that was a psychic abyss which, in spite of a great natural affection and my admiration and love for them, we were never able to cross" (*OTM* 8). Released from her parents' emotional support, Akins redirected her devotion.

Narrative storytelling allowed Akins to explore topics never expressed in her household. Sarah Elizabeth Akins believed in the values of civility, instructing Zoë to "<u>never refer to anything unpleasant. Never ask a personal question. Never notice a blemish. Never complain or explain</u>" (underlining is Akins') (*OTM* 5). Akins defied her mother's rules when crafting her tales. Her enterprising characters admitted money could influence the path to self-actualization:

> Akins' women suffer like men: they can admit to pain, but not its painfulness; can recognize the immanent approach of destruction, but not admit to it's possibility; can suffer great loss, but count only what has been gained. Adding to their complexity is an articulated self awareness: they realize the gravity of their actions and share their insights with the audience [Kreizenbeck 107].

Despite the emotional intelligence of these characters, conventional beliefs hamper their personal resolutions. The protagonist finds passionate love and monetary security in a heterosexual martial relationship. "[Akins] does not argue for a return to traditional solutions; rather, she argues that the new, "modern" ones are equally inadequate" (Kreizenbeck xiii). Akins wrote women who defied her mother's social code of conduct, but, even as an author, she could never escape the traditional views instilled by her background.

Akins' self-imposed belief in societal standards impacted her creative choices. She wanted to be successful, but was discouraged from admitting that truth. "Women writers were expected to give the impression that they were gifted amateurs who could offhandedly compose a brilliant sonnet, no matter how hard they had actually worked to perfect it" (Kreizenbeck 33). Without an outlet to express her ambition, Akins had a habit of showing off in her plays.

Witty comments would distract from the dialogue and structural twists would complicate the act break. Akins knew these additions mutated the story from realistic to implausible. By ending all narrative conflicts with satisfactory conclusions, she knew audiences would accept her foibles.

As Akins attempted to prove the legitimacy of her work, the need for commercial success could not be ignored. Like her characters, Akins had to secure her own economic future. While her parents lived a comfortable life, they did not support her fiscally. Such restraints meant setting aside the high-minded rebellion of *Papa*. She needed to fill theatre seats, so she had to fulfill specific story requirements. Akins wrote, "...I longed for the freedom which money alone could buy" (*OTM* 127). She used that declaration as the foundation for her next work.

In 1919, *Déclassée* brought success to Akins and Ethel Barrymore. Lady Helen Haden (Barrymore) achieves sexual independence outside the bounds of marriage but remains financially dependent on her husband. The play is quintessential Akins. Socially buoyant characters, speaking in a literary tone, ponder if romance, love, and sex can exist simultaneously. The difference between *Papa* and *Déclassée* occurs in leading lady's disposition. When Lady Helen Haden laughs at herself, she appeals to the masses and the public responded favorably. Barrymore revived her career and Akins earned around $300,000 and renewed hope for true creative latitude.

Success introduced a new set of challenges for Akins. Critics equated mass appeal with "artistic corruption." With playwrights migrating to Hollywood, theatre stalwarts became fearful their most talented would leave New York. Akins had never expressed a desire to maneuver into motion pictures, but *Déclassée*'s popularity caused speculation from former allies. George Jean Nathan, an early supporter, was particularly harsh. He wrote,

> Let this Akins girl remain the independent artist of *Papa*, the artist uncontaminated by the devastating boll-weevils of Broadway and she will produce work of a quality uncommon to our stage. Let her become inflamed with the success of *Déclassée* and pursue the more popular species of writing ... and she will ruin as engaging a potentiality as the curtain of an American Stage has lifted upon [Schultheiss 14].

Like the foray into poetry, Akins found criticism overshadowing the quality of her work.

Akins disregarded the negative feedback and wrote her most shocking work to date: a sex comedy. *The Greeks Had a Word for It* is about three morally bankrupt golddiggers. They are willing to chase any man and manipulate any situation to secure a wealthy husband. The risqué play featured near-nudity and heaving petting. What elevates the subject matter is the relationship between the three female protagonists. They have no scruples when obtaining the ideal mate, but the bond between them is sacred. *The Greeks Had a Word for It* was a hit with Depression era Americans. Beginning in 1930, the play ran for an astonishing 253 performances.

The public's delight in *The Greeks Had A Word for It* was a response to a cultural shift. Women were gaining societal agency. They were creating an ulterior life in the workplace and began expressing sexual desire in the bedroom. This coincides, or perhaps propels, the rise of female comedy teams in cinema. Marie Dressler and Polly Moran, ZaSu Pitts and Thelma Todd, and Joan Blondell and Glenda Farrell ushered in a new kind of protagonist. In these films, mostly two reels, the friends struggle to cross the intersection between marriage and career. Single women were expected to work until the wedding. Then, life outside the home ceased to exist.

> The female-centred communities created in these films exist at the edges of married life. The majority of team comedies are set in one of two worlds, either the world of the working girl, the young, unmarried woman living alone, or more commonly, with a female room-mate, or in the world of the widow [Karnick 79].

Anita Loos, Frances Marion, Zelda Sears and Akins were frequent writers for this genre.

This new facet of comedy attracted female spectators, an important strategy by the film industry. The untapped market proved a viable investment. "By the 1920s, some industry estimates set the percentage of the female audience anywhere from sixty to eighty-three percent" (Karnick 81). Proving to be worthy consumers, women filled cinema houses to watch female-driven comedies. By the 1930s, external pressures halted progress. Economic restraints brought daughters back home to live with their parents. Screenplays mirrored this change. Stories began revolving around the home life, often lead by the patriarch.

Women were still buying tickets and they sought role models on the big screen. Opportunities on Broadway were fading for Akins, so she headed west to Hollywood. Her mastery of language and her creation of vibrant female characters made her valuable in motion pictures. The rights to *The Greeks Had a Word for It* were bought for $80,000, although Akins never verified that number. She sold another play, *The Moonflower*, for a reported $8,000. The first adaption of *The Greeks Had a Word for It* occurred in 1932, released by United Artists. The original title was considered too suggestive so the producers changed it to *The Greeks Had a Word for Them*. The most popular adaptation is *How to Marry a Millionaire* released in 1953. Twentieth Century–Fox combined Akins' play with Dale Eunson and Katherine Albert's play, *Loco*. Earning an estimated $8 million worldwide, *How to Marry a Millionaire* was the fourth highest grossing film of that year.

Actresses, looking to raise their profile, sought out Akins' work. The adaption of Akins' play *Morning Glory* (1933), benefited from an extraordinary talent. Katharine Hepburn won her first Academy Award playing Eva Lovelace, a small town performer hoping to make it big on Broadway. The screenplay for *Camille* (1936) was written by James Hilton, Frances Marion, and Akins. The film brought a New York Critics Best Actress win and an Oscar nomination to Greta Garbo. Ruth Chatterton benefited most from the Akins touch, starring in five of her films, and received positive reviews for each performance.

Chatterton introduced Akins to a powerful ally. Dorothy Arzner was a successful director, one of the few women to work continuously in that role. In contrast, Akins' had only achieved minimal acclaim as a screenwriter. Her original plays had been adapted by male peers, with Akins not receiving an offer of participation. Her sense of story was indisputable, but she lacked the opportunity to prove her talent. Working with Arzner altered Akins' course in Hollywood. The Arzner directed *Sarah and Son* (1930) starred Chatterton, with Akins adapting a novel by Timothy Shea. The film did well at the box office and Chatterton became known as "The First Lady of the Screen." The trio reunited for the unsuccessful *Anybody's Woman* (1930). For *Working Girls* (1931), Arzner directed the picture with Akins writing the screenplay, based on the play *Blind Mice* by Vera Caspary and Winifred Leniham.

Like the relationships with Teasdale, Cather, and Marlowe, Akins become fast friends with Arzner. Arzner's personal life was constant fodder for the gossip magazines because she favored "man-tailored suits" and pursued friendships with women. Akins, unafraid of additional scrutiny, welcomed Arzner's association. Such relationships were forged with more than friendly acquaintance in mind,

> Important industry figures, the women worked for the major movie studios on big-budget pictures, earning large salaries that enabled them to dine at exclusive nightspots. They forged friendships, attended and hosted parties, and built a community of like-minded women in Hollywood [Abrams 72].

The group sought to strengthen the female perspective in cinema.

Malice toward these women arrived in allegations of lesbian affairs, effecting public perception and subsequent job offers. The comments were meant to shock and were never followed by proof. Akins' deep connection with other women and her fondness for crafting rebellious characters made her a target. Historian Alan Kreizenbeck refutes the scandalous claims on Akins' reasons for belonging to this community:

> It is easy to understand, given the open hostility of many male writers, why a woman writer would search out and establish friendships with other women. It is also understandable that a young woman writer, given the climate created by male writers, would want to know and emulate successful artists of her own gender. But it is not necessary to justify any of Akins' choices or even to be overly concerned about what they were. It is evident that she had close, productive friendships with women throughout her life, just as it is evident that the main characters in poems and plays are women because it was their conflict that interested her [37].

Despite the negative press, Akins continued to pursue such relationships and actively looked for opportunities to work with her friends.

Arzner and Akins' last collaboration arrived with *Christopher Strong* (1933). David Selznick acquired the rights to the Gilbert Frankau novel and his first step was to hire Arzner. Katharine Hepburn, in her second on-screen role, was hired to play the title character, Lady Cynthia Darrington. Selznick completed the trifecta by hiring Akins to write the script. From the first day, Arzner, Hepburn, and Akins disagreed about the creative direction. Selznick spent most his time negotiating personality clashes. While not a monetary windfall, *Christopher Strong* brought each woman critical praise. Hepburn began shaping her persona as an autonomous performer. The *New York Times* review was complimentary of Arzner and Akins. Mordaunt Hall wrote,

> … Zoë Akins, who is responsible for the script, and Dorothy Arzner, the director, have accomplished their respective tasks … with marked intelligence and also they have dodged shrewdly the usual stereotyped ideas, with the result that the unexpected often happens ["Katharine Hepburn and Colin Clive in a Film of a Gilbert Frankau Novel"].

Arzner, Hepburn, and Akins never worked together again, choosing to follow different paths within the movie industry.

The creative disagreements on *Christopher Strong* highlighted Akins' Achilles heel. She did not believe in compromising her vision. During her early days on Broadway, she would withdraw from a project rather than change her script. Concerning the production of *The Learned Lady*, Akins wrote,

> But after four week of rewriting in attempt to meet half way the muddled demands of the producer and the star, I tore up the manuscript and returned home. It was a victory after all, I suppose, for I determined to write what pleased me whether it pleased anyone else or not ["The Writing of a Play" 191].

In Los Angeles, the treatment of screenwriters turned her stomach. In her unpublished memoir, she wrote, "…I had found the circumstances in which the writer is expected to work in the Hollywood studios strange, irritating and humiliating" (*OTM* 240). Success in the film industry meant Akins had obtained "the kind of freedom only money can buy," but the endeavor left her uninspired.

Adapting *The Old Maid* exemplifies Akins' struggle with collaborators. Edith Wharton, the novelist, was interested in transforming her novella, *Old Maids: The Fifties*, into a play. Akins was an obvious choice. She was well known in the theatre community and had experience adapting novels for film. The partnership seemed like a natural fit. Wharton's work is about upper class women struggling to establish themselves outside the bounds of societal expectations. Akins was eager to approach the challenge and make her return to the theatre. In the initial stages, trust was so absolute that Wharton never read the script. As the production neared opening night, the women ardently disagreed about the direction of the project. In the past, Akins would have deferred to her elder peer. Now an experienced screenwriter, she was confident in her decision-making. Although the issues were resolved, the memory of these confrontations would later become ammunition against Akins.

Akins' wrote a steadfast interruption of Wharton's story. Judith Anderson, as Delia, reveled in the role of a lifetime. All the pieces were in place for a hit show, but the response was lukewarm. A critic for the *New York Sun* wrote, "…a pretty water-color of yesteryear with an aura of wistfulness and sentiment which is affecting, but the play is more tableau than drama" (Shafer 72). One issue was the subtle source material. In the novel, the protagonists are insular and rarely react with action. Externalizing internal emotions was challenging and did not easily translate to the stage. Another problem was cultural context. Many wondered if the characters, and their creators, were too old-fashioned. A woman hiding her illegitimate child in order to marry seemed out of touch with modern times. The straightforward version of Wharton's novella may have cost Akins critical acclaim.

The Old Maid did not impress insiders, but, due to the reputation of Wharton and Akins, the play made the short-list for the 1935 Pulitzer Prize. Lillian Hellman's *The Children's Hour* was the favorite to win, according to Burns Mantle of *The Daily News*. He failed to consider two important facts. First, the Pulitzer Prize committee believed the award was cumulative and, therefore, rarely given to young talent. At the time, Akins was 50 years old and Hellman was 29 years old. Secondly, *The Old Maid* received the Theatre Club's gold medal. The club was "one of the leading organizations of women theatergoers in [New York City]" (Kreizenbeck 180). The group did not have a deciding vote in the Pulitzer Prize, but their influence cannot be overlooked. When Akins won the coveted award, the reaction from the theatre community was mutiny. The Pulitzer Prize committee was attacked by directors and producers, declaring the judges had "lost their critical standards." Criticized by other playwrights, Akins' disagreements with Wharton became public, with most blaming Akins for the play's failure. Akins was deeply hurt by the response. Since the days of *Papa*, she had devoted herself to playwriting. Receiving the greatest honor of her career was bittersweet.

The Pulitzer Prize controversy gave *The Old Maid* new life, running for an impressive 305 performances. The award also raised Akins' reputation in Hollywood, allowing her to escape the firestorm of Broadway. Akins had not yet transformed her own play into a feature film, but wanted to accomplish that feat with *The Old Maid*. She proposed a unique opportunity for the studios. They would buy the rights to the script and she, as the attached writer, would not require payment up front. Rather, she would take a percentage of the profits. Akins felt sure the movie would be as successful as the play and she would receive a hefty check. The plan was risky, but showed her understanding of how Hollywood operated. In 1935, Akins set the price tag for *The Old Maid* at $100,000. Paramount, MGM, and Warner Brothers passed outright on the property. Akins even toyed with the idea of self-financing the production. Eventually, Paramount bought the script for $40,000 without a supplemental contract for Akins. The purchase occurred in

1936. The studio shelved the project for three years, finally selling the rights to Warner Brothers. In the end, Akins' gamble had not paid off.

Despite Akins' qualifications, Casey Robinson received the job as screenwriter of *The Old Maid*. Arriving in 1939, the public rushed to the cinema, hyped by the civil war it caused in New York City. They bought tickets to join the cultural conversation, but they stayed for deeply moving story. Frank S. Nugent of the *New York Times* admits the drama's inherent attraction,

> Whether Zoë Akins's "The Old Maid" was a good play ... is of less consequence today than the point upon which they all were agreed: that it was a tremendously popular show of predominantly feminine appeal ... dramatically it is vital, engrossing and a little terrifying. That is a compliment to Miss Akins... ["Zoe Akins's 'The Old Maid' Reaches the Strand as a Mature, Engrossing and Poignant Drama"].

Nugent continues by comparing Akins' *The Old Maid* to Emily Brontë's *Wuthering Heights*. In both stories, the tense conflict bubbles just below the surface. He concludes by stating, "No drama can be as tepid as "sentimental" implies when it is built on the cone of such an emotional volcano." In the midst of great professional tragedy, Akins' work was starting to be understood.

With an observant mind, a sharp sense of humor, and an unrelenting passion for storytelling, Zoë Akins staged a quiet rebellion against the status quo. She translated her talent into poems, plays, novels, essays and screenplays. Unwilling to compromise her creations to the whims of peers, critics, or audiences, she wrote strong woman grappling to find their voice in a society determined to silence it. When her dissenters refused to take her seriously or when they regulated her to "feminine" genres, she rebelled by ignoring their comments. She wrote about topics that pleased her and topics that worried her. Female patrons connected to Akins' characters because they could express what the American public was discouraged from asking: how can a woman obtain personal freedom within the hardened boundaries of social, economic, and political restrictions? Akins never dared to provide a definitive answer, finding the possible solutions to be as troubling as the current reality.

Works Cited

Abrams, Brett. "Latitude in Mass-Produced Culture's Capital: New Women and Other Players in Hollywood, 1920–1941." *Frontiers: A Journal of Women Studies* 25.2 (2004): 65–95.
Akins, Zoë. *Interpretations*. New York: Mitchell Kennerley, 1912.
_____. *Other Than Myself*. Zoë Akins Collection.
_____. "The Writing of a Play." *The Drama*. Mar. 1922: 191–192.
Cranmer, Katharine. "Little Visits with Literary Missourians, Zoë Akins." *Missouri Historical Review*, Jan. 1926: 252–261. Print.
Hall, Mordaunt. "Katharine Hepburn, Douglas Fairbanks, Jr., and Adolphe Menjou in 'Morning Glory.'" *New York Times*, 18 Aug. 1933. Web. 1 Feb. 2016.
Karnick, Kristine Brunovska. "Community of Unruly Women: Female Comedy Teams in the Early Sound Era." *Continuum* 13.1 (1999): 77–95.
Kreizenbeck, Alan. *Zoë Akins: Broadway Playwright*. Westport, CT: Praeger, 2004.
Nugent, Frank S. "Zoë Akins's 'The Old Maid' Reaches the Strand as a Mature, Engrossing and Poignant Drama." *New York Times*, 12 Aug. 1939. Web. 1 Feb. 2016.
Robinson, Phyllis C. *Willa, the Life of Willa Cather*. Garden City, NY: Doubleday, 1983.
Schultheiss, John. "George Jean Nathan and the Dramatist in Hollywood." *Literature/Film Quarterly* 4.1 (Winter 1976): 13–23.
Shafer, Yvonne. *American Women Playwrights, 1900–1950*. New York: Peter Lang, 1995.

Marriage of Words
Bella and Sam Spewack

LAURA KIRK

Writers with a body of work spanning decades and exercising both serious influence and excellent entertainment value, Bella and Sam Spewack were a married writing couple who shared dozens of theatre and film credits. The quality of their stories warranted multiple versions from theatre to film to remakes and adaptations. Their musicals were award-winning and a collaboration with Cole Porter contributed timeless classic lyrics to matching memorable melodies. Prior to writing for stage and film they served as foreign correspondents in Berlin and Moscow bringing depth to their worldview.

Married at age nineteen and together until Sam's death, their marriage fed the comedic portrayals of the mishaps of women and men as they fall head over heels for each other and rage against the other. More of a writing partnership than romantic in some ways, as a team the Spewacks conquered Hollywood during a turbulent time when their peers were being sacrificed by producers to a government blacklist fueled by fear of Communism. Their films had a signature style with rapier-sharp dialogue, international intrigue, and lively romantic comedy. Individually they contributed socially and politically to America and beyond. Shaped by early life struggle, global worldview, the war, and most certainly marriage, their work both informs and entertains the golden era of filmmaking with legendary depth and precision.

Bella and Sam Spewack were both born in Eastern Europe, Bella Cohen in Transylvania, and Sam Spewack in Ukraine. Much detail of Bella's early life is known from her memoir *Streets*, written at age twenty-three, published posthumously. Bella's single mother brought her to America in 1902 to the Lower East Side of New York City already dense with many other immigrants. The memoir is clearly a painful examination of early beginnings. Each chapter is the name of a different street where the family lived. The first street is where she "learned to fear people" (3). Later she discovers she "liked to make people laugh" (6). Her first connections to theater were to imitate actors and actresses as she ran errands for them. Early childhood was filled with predators threatening her, her mother and the orphans that surrounded them. Entertaining others brought her peace. Noting her difference as a Jew she wanted to be a "Krisht." In her eyes, the characters in her beloved books were all "Krishts" and her observations of the women around her considered ladylike in manner and dress were all "Krishts" (29).

Escaping the streets in books via the great social leveling institution of the public library brought Bella solace. By age 12 she felt "acutely conscious of the sordidness of the life around her" (66). In public school, the bible was read aloud and she describes not wanting to skip the conversation or exposure to dialogue. After her mother's second husband left they faced rats peering at them while in bed and revolving boarders. Long hard days were spent caretaking her younger siblings while others died around them. Her mother was determined Bella stay in school and be a lady, though many around them suggested the girl needed to work to help support the family. Eventually Bella began punishing labor for a few dollars a week.

Bella met Sam in the early 1920s as she began her career as a reporter. She describes the long walks they took when they were nineteen and her proposal they become partners, which Sam "misconstrued" and proposed marriage (Richards 3). Bella said he "fell in love with her writing" (Hevesi). Married in 1922, they worked as foreign correspondents in Berlin and Moscow from 1922 to 1926. Afterward, their collaboration as playwrights began, though their contributions as reporters continued

An undated publicity photograph of writer Bella Spewack. Spewack co-wrote with her husband Sam Spewack, but it is widely accepted that Sam created the plot and action while Bella wrote most of the dialogue (Academy of Motion Picture Arts and Sciences' Margaret Herrick Library).

throughout their careers. In 1923, as a contributing writer for the *New York Times*, Bella wrote about what Europeans thought of Americans from her time spent there. When posing the question "Do they like us?" she answered, "Some do. Lots don't." Europeans' dismissal of American contribution to the arts equals "minus zero" ("What They Think"). In another article for the *Times*, "The Women of Red Russia-Observations and Classifications, from Commissars' Wives to Tram Conductors," Bella observed and wrote characters with exquisite detail much like in her memoir (Cohen).

This willingness and curiosity to go into the unfamiliar world and crack the code of humanity in individuals would resonate in the Spewacks' work throughout their career. Bella even noted that Russian women were portrayed in American films and plays as slinky, swearing, screeching and fainting. They plotted and were mysterious. In Bella's actual encounters she found them to be "all shades, red, pink and white and all of them desperately blue—divulging everything" leaving no mystery whatsoever. She noted none wore slinky gowns but were quite modest in dress. The article goes on to describe different types of women but notes their desperate working conditions perhaps due to equal rights in the eyes of the men. The Russian men tell her women would have to be treated like men to share rights. She closed with a quote from a premiere ballerina, "Russia's salvation lies with her women" and added, "Perhaps" (Cohen). Later, the Spewacks would go on to correct stereotypical characterizations in their own plays and films.

One of her most celebrated articles was about the rumored Czarina, Anastasia, who claimed to be the daughter of the late Czar of Russia. Refusing to fully corroborate that it was indeed the real Anastasia, Bella lost money on the story choosing to publish her balanced account rather than take larger sums to confirm or deny whether the young woman was in fact, Anastasia. Bella's involvement and access as the only foreign reporter to visit this mysterious girl distinguished her as witness to one of the great mysteries of the world. Bella noted Anastasia's scars from guns and bayonets and thought her hand looked aristocratic. Anastasia's nurse confirmed her scars and physical likeness matched the child she had known. Bella questioned her inability to speak English and Russian as all children of the royal household were taught to do. All sides of the controversy are presented in the article along with Bella's own first-hand impressions ('Europe's Deepest Mystery").

After their time overseas the couple began to write for the theater. Bella defied agents and tackled theatrical offices herself leading to their triumph as playwrights. Sam often directed their plays (Richards). In the early 1930s there was an influx of playwrights from the East coast to Hollywood to assist with dialogue as silent films transitioned to "talkies" and writers began to become more important to the medium. Verbal sparring and word play were the result of clever writing. Rapid fire dialogue helped stay ahead of the Hays Code imposed in response to the Catholic Church exercising power against the feared horrible influence of Hollywood pictures over youth and culture. The Spewacks were known for rapid storytelling in plays such as *Clear All Wires* (1932) as noted by famed critic Brooks Atkinson in his review calling it "brisk, noisy, extravagant and funny" (Atkinson). The play became a film one year later, then evolved into a musical version called *Leave It to Me* (1938), which introduced Mary Martin to her coming stardom with the famous song "My Heart Belongs to Daddy" and featured a new dancer. Gene Kelly played the inevitable end of boy getting girl or in this case girl getting boy (Richards). Historical, political and romantic angles can all be found in this film. As written into the play the Spewacks' experience as journalists and Russophiles is evident in the opening lines with reporters asking, "Why bother to spell those tricky names when the paper is only read by dames ... who only care for the society page" (Richards).

The Spewacks are best known today for their musicals and collaboration with Cole Porter. Author Stanley Richards dedicates Volume 2 of his *Great Musicals of the American Theatre* to Bella Spewack. American musicals were big business and the Spewacks proved to be bankable so it was no surprise Hollywood invited them to the party. Musicals had a reach that stretched perhaps even deeper than film at the time via touring companies and regional theaters following their Broadway runs. The Spewacks won a Pulitzer in 1930 for *Dialogue for a Horse*. Later in 1949 their musical *Kiss Me, Kate* won the first Tony awarded to a musical, was performed in over 22 countries, and adapted into the successful film version in 1953. Unforgettable lyrics and melody in songs like "Too Darn Hot" seared audiences. Their boy meets girl meets "Shakespearean *Taming of the Shrew*" show within a show formula, peppered with their own insights of show business and marriage, proved both entertaining and profitable.

Though the film industry experienced upheaval in the 1930s, regarding their sojourn to Hollywood Sam felt the studios imported vast quantities from Broadway then tried to flatten them out by "teaching them gimmicks and tricks." Believing films could not "keep up with literature," his disdain for Hollywood grew because "[they] stamp it into a mold that they think will sell." Sam also derided playwrights who went to Hollywood as having nothing more to say in the theater. Qualifying himself and Bella apart from the fray he felt they "went to Hollywood at the height of their career but they never stayed very long." Sam called the Hays code "the stupidest thing ever foisted [because] Catholics didn't approve of divorce" and went on to suggest the motion picture industry invited censorship and accepted it because it was scared to fight for free expression since "it hadn't grown up" (S. Spewack). A common frustrating producer ploy would be to put screenwriters under contract but never have them write. During a two-year period when they were kept under contract to do nothing the writers were so upset that gave the studio a free outline (S. Spewack).

At the end of the day their talent prevailed, with critic Pauline Kael arguing that their presence "assured" production of "lively" movies that producers would otherwise make "mediocre" (MacMillan 154). The hit *My Favorite Wife* (1940) starring Cary Grant and Irene Dunne, which was nominated for an Academy Award for best story, demonstrates this with its screwball storyline of a wife missing for seven years and presumed dead who returns home on the day of her husband's second marriage. In a feminist twist the wife has a hunky man she hides from her husband. Alone on the island during her time away they nicknamed themselves Adam and Eve ... and her husband doesn't want to imagine any more. Always one-upping the other the farce plays out with both fury and love. The film was remade into *Move Over Darling* in 1963 with actual homage reference lines to the 1940 original delivered by Doris Day. Masquerading as a Swedish masseuse, she gives a massage to her husband's new wife while describing a movie she saw as a little girl in Sweden—a movie starring Cary Grant and Irene Dunne. The new wife asks, "When were movies ever like real life?"

The film *Rendezvous* (1935) starring William Powell as William Gordon and Rosalind Russell as socialite Carol Carter, is based on the memoirs of Herbert Yardley. The Spewacks' facility with war stories cross-pollinated with their signature screwball romance style makes this film about a former newspaperman turned codebreaker a charming combination. Diabolical mistresses and corrupt Germans threaten the new romance between socialite Carol and newly enlisted soldier William. Carol continually pulls strings with her powerful uncle to keep William stateside much to his consternation, then the plot thickens. When Carol is imprisoned as leverage she jealously believes it is only a cover by men William controls while he's with the mistress spy Olivia. In the end girl gets boy once again, which leads directly into the title for their next film.

Based on their play, *Boy Meets Girl* (1938) satirizes Hollywood film studios. Called "a perfect example of a depression era farce" by the Wall Street Journal (Wilson) it involves screenwriters who proclaim the perfect formula for a film: boy meets girl, boy loses girl, boy gets girl, a formula applied not only to this movie, but to most romantic themed films. In this particular work the Spewacks interweave the satire with story, then with classic chaos and obstacles. It could be posited that in several of their stories Bella seems to have tweaked the formula with a feminist bent of the girl getting the boy.

During World War II Sam received sole credits for two documentaries, *A Welcome to Britain* (1943) and *The World at War* (1942) sandwiched in between much lighter fare such as *My Favorite Wife* (1940) and *Weekend at the Waldorf* (1945). Commissioned by the U.S. Office of War Information these films were created as propaganda for use at home and abroad. A few short years in existence the Office of War Information hit many roadblocks to its goals. At home, it was dedicated to the "strategy of truth," sought to convey to the American people the purposes of the war (Winkler 47). During this time Sam both wrote and produced *The World at War* (1942) containing a bigger picture of the events that led up to why America was at war with the Axis powers. One of the first documentaries of its type *World at War*, with its vivid accurate footage not available for average viewers became the precursor to director Frank Capra's *Why We Fight* (1942–1945) campaign.

As might be expected from a musical theater writer, *A Welcome to Britain* (1943) opens with the strains of the famous perennially patriotic popular song "Over There" by George M. Cohan. The Ministry of Information commissioned *Welcome*, which stars Burgess Meredith as the everyman soldier who takes the audience on a tour of foreign British culture. In the 38-minute film, Sam uses comedy to train soldiers to be less abrasive as Americans when they encounter their allied countrymen and women. Even Bob Hope appears to play a prank on Meredith. There is literal winking, wit and a confessional bent to entering the world young soldiers would visit. In signature Spewack style a lovely woman on a bicycle frequently rides by which amorously distracts the soldier narrator. Starting in a pub, since that would be a certain stop for off-duty soldiers, there are explanations of pub culture to Americans from beer that is not cold to the practice of both men and women gathering together after a long day at work. Sam's dialogue further enlightens the audience that the pub patrons of all ages drink "not just to drink but for the company." The narrator further advises that English people are a little more reserved than Americans, but if you take your time they will come around.

A poignant moment involves explaining how there are less social restrictions in England regarding African American soldiers, though Meredith refers to the soldier as a "colored boy" (the military term of the day). He advises all new soldiers that though he knows that might not happen at home, "we're not at home." Then General Lee from Kansas, whose family fought for the Confederacy, appears. The African American soldier joins in on the conversation as Meredith stands by his side and asks General Lee how he feels about "him and me." The General answers by saying, "America has promised the Negro real citizenship and a fair chance to make the best of himself … the army takes Negroes along with Whites. Everyone's treated the same when it comes to dying." The General goes on to say "the promise of treating each other with respect is our patriotic duty and an America worth fighting for." At the end, he adds, "it's not a bad time to learn to respect each other both ways" (*Welcome*).

After the separation caused by war, another threat to the Spewacks and their peers was the blacklisting of communists in Hollywood. Due to the Spewacks' first-hand experience in Russia, the couple candidly voiced their opinions about the era when Dalton Trumbo and others lost work and financial security in their oral history at Columbia University. The Spewacks found the existence of the Communist party "highly exaggerated and mostly social. People felt guilty for getting money for shoddy work." There was a practice of "underpaying the stenographers who were the steady workers but overpaying everyone else." Sam thought infiltrations the communists achieved could be explained by Hollywood being a lonely "city of homes," and due to "newspapers (being) ghastly" and because unlike New York, there was "no culture." Though they regarded themselves as anti-communist they were on a "gray" list for "fostering exchanges between Russia and U.S. films" which bemused them since that was their job, and for contributing to the Spanish loyalist party.

During this turbulent time, Bella wrote incendiary speeches for politician Wendell Wilkie and actresses Katharine Hepburn and Ingrid Bergman, which could have further caused suspicion. Sam called the inquisition "absolute hysteria and stupidity." He further quipped, "If a man were a communist what earthly difference does it make if he wrote a musical?" He went on to admit the House Un-American Activities Committee seemed to be after "do-gooders" and "do-gooders covers an awful lot of people." Sam observed peers such as Larry Adler, Leo McCarey and Sam Wood being hurt during this hunt. Summing up attitudes of the time Sam pointed out ideas about income tax being "a source of all evil" and that President Roosevelt was a communist due to his support of both labor unions and income tax. Both producers and studios were opposed to the Writers Guild and tried to break it not from Communist fears but in fear of the loss of their profits (S. Spewak).

The Spewacks' attitude toward the powers that be, whether producers or studio heads, is one that people who know their own worth often display. Bella's friend Lois Elias writes in her afterword in Bella's memoir that Bella's "belief in herself as a writer was unshakable." Bella "did not hesitate to place a monetary value on her skills." There were further stories of Bella demanding her agreed upon fair wage from powerful producers if necessary. Sam groused about the pressure to socialize with those who could dole out work while in Hollywood and felt the push to entertain producers in their private home was not something they practiced. "We never entertained anybody, except people we liked and we never liked producers" (S. Spewack).

One of the last Spewack credits is for when David Mamet adapted their play *My Three Angels* (1953) into the film *We're No Angels* (1989) starring Robert DeNiro and Sean Penn with early supporting work from John C. Reilly. The Spewacks' signature mistaken identity farce works because of the comedic rule Roger Ebert pointed out in his review, "the heroes be funny no matter who people think they are and that the other characters be funny even despite the mistakes they're making" (Ebert).

After their deaths, Aaron Frankel wrote a play called *A Letter from Sam to Bella* "revealing their private side." The Spewacks donated their entire private collection of correspondence, manuscripts, photographs, and memorabilia to Columbia University's Rare Book and Manuscript Library's Theatre collection. Frankel used the collection to research their 50-year marriage, much of which was spent apart; their success in competitive fields of theatre and film; and their marital problems, which caused a split for a time (Marshall). In an April 2016 phone conversation with Mr. Frankel (then 94 years old) he could not say where a copy of the play might be at this time but expressed fondness for the subject and wished this writer luck on my research (Frankel). Columbia University could not locate a copy in their collection but with more time, the 150 boxes donated to the collection could reveal the play and more about their marriage and careers.

It is notable that Bella never pursued publishing her memoir. In Ruth Limmer's introduction, she ponders Bella's tackling of the extended narrative of a "real writer" and whether it was the one genre where Bella lacked comfort (ix). Her memoir and the pain it contained was a part of her life she shut away, though it overshadowed much of her behavior throughout her life. In the afterword, Bella's dear friend, Lois Elias, suggests that perhaps her fear of poverty caused her to turn off a light whenever she left a room and hindered her from ever relaxing since she kept writing up until the death of her husband Sam in 1971 (172). Substantiated by Bella is her own assessment of charity: "I do not know whether I can make it understood how the thought I was a 'charity case' was always with me—how it never left me" (135). It was a wrenching exercise both to write and perhaps to consider revisiting the painful memories in order to publish.

In closing, Bella speaks of how reliving the death of her beloved younger brother Herschey "pain[ed] her to want to rush through the writing but also sought to have others understand." Her mother was so bereft at his passing that Bella as a very young woman was saddled with arranging the burial. It is a heartbreaking work for which its existence is appreciated in order to examine how her early life influenced her writing life. Bella and Sam never had children but they did found the Ilan Sport Center for the disabled in Ramat-Gan, Israel. Perhaps Bella had her handicapped younger brother in mind. Additionally, in 1938 Bella helped found the New York Girls' Scholarship fund and claimed to invent "that heinous, heinous thing the Girlscout cookie" (ix).

Bella Spewack auspiciously added a subtitle to her memoir that the publishers chose to use, "Why I Wrote Comedy" (159), referencing another successful formula—tragedy plus time equals comedy. In a rare drama offering, *Spring Song* (1934), Bella wrote, "When people came out of the theater in tears, I would say, 'Don't cry, it's only a play'" (Richards). The Spewacks' characterizations refuted the commonly held stereotypes and misconceptions of foreigners and instead explored the commonalities during wartime when fear clouded perception. Foreshadowing the need to combat unconscious bias they would give a character "the last name of Shapiro instead of Jones or Smith and establish them in a landscape all over the country doing all sorts of jobs" (S. Spewak).

Bella and Sam's working method was described in the *Los Angeles Times* as talking out a story, then going into separate rooms and writing. When finished they would blend the individual efforts together, take the best elements from each and fit it all together (Carleton). Their marriage provided emotional depth to their depictions of men and women in long time partnerships. Their fifty-year partnership gave them a special breadth of knowledge about the hardships and comforts of married life: their art reflected the shared decades of two gifted, worldly wits with a wealth of inside jokes and memories writing about the culture they had lived. As portrayed by their many characters, marriage was a complex relationship that could flare up in white-hot anger bred by familiarity and stoked by complicated history. Yet the foundation of marriage was true love, the very thing that sustained them through the years, allowing Sam and Bella to work and live together. It was a love that left audiences with a rich legacy of theatre and film.

Works Cited

Atkinson, B. "Satire and Melodrama in a Newspaper Play Entitled 'Clear All Wires.'" (1932, September 15). NYTimes.com Web 26 Apr. 2016
Calta, L. "Comedy Outlook Saddens Spewak." (1960, March 5). NYTimes.com Web 26 Apr. 2016
Carleton, J. "Ideas Flow Best When." (1923, September 27). LATimes.com Web 26 Apr. 2016
Cohen, Bella. "The Women of Red Russia; Observations and Classifications, From Commissars' Wives to Tram Conductors." *New York Times Magazine*, Page SM4, November 25, 1923.
Ebert, R. *We're No Angels*. (1989, December 15). Rogerebert.com. Web 26 Apr. 2016.
Frankel, Aaron. Personal Interview.
Hevesi, D. "Bella Spewack, Author, 91, Dies; 'Kiss Me, Kate' Is One of Her Hits." (1990, April 29). NYTimes.com Web 12 Mar. 2016
H.H.T. "'We're No Angels' Bowa." (1955, July 8). NYTimes.com Web 26 Apr. 2016.
MacMillan, R. "Hollywood in the 1930's: A Discussion of Pauline Kael." (1981). Historical Journal of Film, Radio and Television, 154.
Marshall, L. "From the Rare Book and Manuscript Library's Archives to the Stage." (2000, June 16) Columbia News. Columbia.edu. Web 12 Mar. 2016.
Richards, S. (1976). *Great Musicals of the American Theatre Volume Two*. Radnor, PA: Chilton Book Company.

Spewack, Bella. "'Anastasia' Is Europe's Deepest Mystery." (1926, March 28). NYTimes.com Web 26 Apr. 2016.
Spewack, Bella. *Streets: A Memoir of the Lower East Side*. New York: The Feminist Press at the City University of New York. (1995).
Spewak, Bella. "What They Think of Us." (1923, October 28). NYTimes.com Web 26 Apr. 2016.
Spewak, S. *Reminiscences of Samuel Loebel and Bella Cohen Spewack*. Columbia Rare Book Library/ Special Collections. New York: Columbia University. (1958).
A Welcome to Britain (1943). Wr: Sam Spewack, Dir: Anthony Asquith, USA 60 mins.
The World at War (1942). Wr: Sam Spewack, Dir: Lowell Mellett, USA 66 mins.
Wilson, E. "Laughs From Days Long Gone." Wall Street Journal. (1976, April 15). Wsj.com Web. 26 Apr. 2016.
Winkler, Allan Michael. *The Politics of Propaganda: The Office of War Information, 1942–1945*. New Haven, CT: Yale University Press, 1974.

The Forgettable Ms. Murfin

AMY L. BANKS

Jane Murfin has been lost somewhere in Hollywood history like nitrate film, the Vitascope and most other female screenwriters. Let us strive to relieve her of her obscurity. Murfin (née Macklem) was born October 27, 1884, in Quincy, Michigan and lived 70 years, dying August 10, 1955. Between these dates she wrote plays, films and was a director, animal trainer and founding member of the Screenwriter's Guild. Murfin is best remembered for her successful collaborations, including an Academy Award nomination in the category of Best Story for *What Price Hollywood?* (1932), which she co-wrote with Adela Rogers St. Johns (they lost to Frances Marion, who won for *The Champ*). Murfin is also remembered for her collaboration on *Brawn of the North* (1922) which she co-directed with her then-husband, Laurence Trimble, and which helped dog-actor (and her personal pet) Strongheart catapult to fame. Shared writing credit with Jane Cowl on the World War I melodramas *Smilin' Through* (1919) and *Lilac Time* (1917), and others under pen name Langdon Martin, were feathers in her cap. Over the course of her illustrious Hollywood career, Murfin earned writing credit on 65 films, produced three films, and directed two, yet as previously mentioned, has been mostly forgotten by time.

Murfin had an ordinary upbringing in a typical middle-class home. She attended public school and went to college at Michigan State Normal School where she trained as a teacher. She did not, however, pursue a job in education, focusing instead on acting. Her fateful first role was in a touring production of comedian David Warfield's *The Music Master* (1904). During this endeavor she met her lifelong friend and collaborator, Jane Cowl, also in the play. Rumors that the two had a sexual relationship as well as a close personal friendship followed, but there is, no proof outside of the circumstantial points that the two are buried side by side at Valhalla Memorial Park in North Hollywood and neither Murfin nor Cowl bore any children. Cowl had been married to a dramatic critic of the *New York Times*, theatrical producer and manager, Adolph Edward Klauber, from 1906 to 1930 and Murfin married three times. In an undated typed letter Cowl describes Murfin as, "the best friend any person could hope to have" (Cowl Papers, Box 2, Folder 8).

In 1907 the 23-year-old married James Orin Murfin, an attorney, a former state senator and a judge in Wayne County, Michigan. During their brief marriage, the new Mrs. Murfin organized a women's drama club and began her playwright collaboration with Cowl. The Murfin marriage lasted less than five years but Murfin kept her first husband's last name for her entire career and next two marriages.

Writer Jane Murfin at RKO Pictures in 1934. Murfin wrote and co-wrote more than 60 produced films, lobbied for strong female roles as a producer and had a Hollywood career spanning over three decades. She is one of the most prolific but least known writers of the 1920s and '30s (Academy of Motion Picture Arts and Sciences' Margaret Herrick Library).

After her divorce, Murfin and Cowl moved to New York City where Murfin landed a job as a script editor at Vitagraph Studios in Brooklyn. In 1917 Murfin and Cowl had their first theatrical collaboration hit with *Lilac Time*. Riding the wave of success, the duo had three more successful plays over the following three years: *Daybreak* (1918), *Information Please* (1919), and *Smilin' Through* (1920), all of which were melodramas with a World War I theme. The duo released the plays under the pen name Alan Langdon Martin, possibly feeling that a man would have better success than two female writers. Murfin regretted that decision later in life after she became a successful screenwriter.

Around 1920, Murfin may or may not have married Laurence Trimble, whom she had met in New York many years prior. Trimble was a dog trainer, actor and early director for Vitagraph Studios. There is no public record of their marriage, but a daughter from his previous union claimed that by 1921, the couple was residing together in Hollywood. Jan Trimble is sometimes listed as Murfin's daughter, but evidence proves she was actually born from the marriage of Laurence and opera singer Louise Trenton. Reportedly Murfin broke up that marriage by following Trimble to Europe, where he had moved to direct films and train animals. When Murfin and Trimble moved to Hollywood, Cowl followed.

Whatever the case may be, Murfin and Trimble formed Trimble-Murfin Productions together, allowing them to produce films for her pet German shepherd, Strongheart. The Strongheart pictures are what Murfin is perhaps best remembered for and Strongheart grew to such stardom he inspired both a dog food named after him and bearing his likeness and a published book of fan letters. As the couple explained, Trimble bought Strongheart (at the time named Etzel von Oringer) while visiting Germany at the end of World War I. The attack dog had been trained in Berlin police kennels and had served the Red Cross in the war. Though it is unclear if the dog was purchased as a gift for Murfin or as a personal pet for Trimble, Murfin was listed as Strongheart's sole owner for the duration of his life. Thanks to their collaboration, Strongheart became the first canine film star; his success predated the famous Rin Tin Tin by two years. Trimble-Murfin produced six Strongheart films, most of which are sadly lost to time. During this time Murfin made her directorial debut with the 1922 Strongheart film *Brawn of the North*. The next piece she directed was the 1924 film *Flapper Wives*, in which Strongheart made an appearance. *Flapper Wives* was an adaption of a play she had written with Cowl, in which Cowl was to play the lead. Cowl, who was still a stage actor at this time, became popular in Shakespearean productions so the play's debut had to be postponed. Because of this, *Flapper Wives* became a film before it debuted on Broadway.

In an article appearing in the June 17, 1923, edition of the *New York Times* titled, *Writing for a Dog Star*, Murfin discussed the many challenges a writer faces when trying to script an animal's actions. "So you must know your dog well—as well as you know your child or your husband or your best friend—and you must observe him carefully, and when one day you see him in a particular engaging attitude, with a certain expression in his wonderful dog eyes, find out what stimulus is making him feel that way." It would seem that Murfin was the master not just of Strongheart the dog, but also of Strongheart the actor, as his nuanced performances earned him a star on the Hollywood Walk of Fame. Sadly, a tumor he developed after being burned from falling on a klieg light cut his acting career short. The end of Strongheart's career also signaled the end of Murfin and Trimble's professional partnership and personal relationship. Trimble immediately moved on to female screenwriter Bradley King (who is even more obscure than Murfin) and Murfin remained close to Cowl. Strongheart died at home, at the age of 13. on June 24, 1929.

During the Trimble-Murfin years, Murfin also worked with Cowl adapting their plays into films at other studios. The duo gained success through this collaboration, with their adaptations being picked up by several studios. *Smilin' Through* (1932) was their most successful adaptation. Joseph M. Schenck purchased it as a starring vehicle for his wife, actress Norma Talmadge. As well as starring in the World War I dramatic film, Talmadge also produced it. Though Murfin and Cowl had released the play under the joint pen name Alan Langdon Martin, they decided to share screenwriting credit in their real names. Luckily the pair had the business savvy to retain the rights to the story as it became a seminal favorite with audiences and was re-made as a talkie in 1934 by MGM, starring Norma Shearer, Fredrick March and Leslie Howard, and again in 1941 with Jeanette McDonald and Gene Raymond.

Murfin celebrated many successful collaborations over the years, with some of her most acclaimed films as a result. She paired with Anita Loos for the 1939 classic *The Women*, which she also garnered a screenwriting credit for in 2008 when the film was re-made by Diane English. Loos called Murfin one of the most reliable screenwriters in

Hollywood along with Frances Marion, Bess Meredith, Sonya Levien and Vicki Baum in her 1974 tell-all *Kiss Hollywood Good-By*. It should be noted that Murfin and Loos took over writing *The Women* from F. Scott Fitzgerald, who had originally been given the job by Hunt Stromberg. It was an adaptation of a play by the same name penned by Clare Boothe; Fitzgerald passed it off to Murfin and Loos, who turned it into a hit (Hamilton 154). In 1940 Murfin collaborated with famous British novelist Aldous Huxley for *Pride and Prejudice* for MGM. Huxley was fresh off his failure of adapting *Madame Curie*, but the collaboration seemed to suit them both (Hamilton, 138). The film that really established Murfin's career, however, was the 1931 hit *Way Back Home*. She penned the original story as well as the script. The movie is best remembered as one of Bette Davis' first films.

In 1932, Murfin wed for a third time, this time to British-born actor Donald Crisp. Crisp was a renowned character actor, often playing the role of devoted, aging codger-father in such films as *Lassie Come Home* (1943) and *National Velvet* (1944) (Hamilton 138). The marriage coincided with her collaboration with director George Cukor on *What Price Hollywood* starring Constance Bennett. The writers garnered an Academy Award nomination for the film and led to further collaboration with Cukor for dialogue in *Little Women* (though Murfin did not receive credit) and *The Women*. Murfin and Crisp stayed together until 1944 when his health began to decline. He moved back to his hometown and Murfin stayed on in Hollywood; he died two years later.

Murfin had a fruitful career starting as a silent film scenarist and lasting well into the talkies. She wrote many films of note, many of which had major star power such as Katharine Hepburn (*Spitfire*, *The Little Minister* and *Alice Adams*); Irene Dunn, Fred Astaire and Ginger Rogers (*Roberta*); Joan Crawford (*The Shining Hour*, which Murfin co-wrote with Ogden Nash) and as previously mentioned, Greer Garson and Lawrence Olivier (*Pride and Prejudice*, co-written with Aldous Huxley). In the 1940s Murfin's career tapered off. The last film she wrote, an adaptation of Pearl S. Buck's *Dragon Seed*, starred Katharine Hepburn.

Over the course of her Hollywood tenure, Murfin garnered 65 screenwriting credits, but that's not all she accomplished. In 1921, she became one of the founding members of the Screenwriter's Guild. When the Guild was re-formed as the Writers' Guild of America in 1933, Murfin's friends Francis Marion, Anita Loos and Bess Meredith asked her to write the original rules and guidelines (Beauchamp, 307). She also served on the Board of Directors for the Academy of Motion Picture Arts and Sciences, and became RKO's first female supervisor as well as a producer at MGM. She died five years after her lifelong best friend Jane Cowl, and as mentioned, the two are buried side by side.

Perhaps Jane Murfin is mostly forgotten because she was plain, did not create scandals and worked hard. She may not have had the style and panache of Anita Loos or the nurturing patience of Frances Marion, but she was a force of nature in the screenwriting business. She had skill, longevity and enviable friendships. Whatever the reason Murfin has been lost to history. It is truly a pity that she is not lauded as the creative filmmaker she was.

Works Cited

Beauchamp, Cari. *Without Lying Down: Frances Marion and the Powerful Women of Early Hollywood*. Berkeley: University of California Press. 1997.
Brownlow, Kevin. *Obituary: Jan Zilliacus*. Independent. Pub. Monday, May 31, 1999. Retrieved April 20, 2016. <http://www.independent.co.uk/arts-entertainment/obituary-jan-zilliacus-1097376.html>.
Buck, Julie. "Jane Murfin." In Jane Gaines, Radha Vatsal, and Monica Dall'Asta, eds. Women Film Pioneers

Project. Center for Digital Research and Scholarship. New York: Columbia University Libraries, 2013. Web. September 27, 2013. <https://wfpp.cdrs.columbia.edu/pioneer/ccp-jane-murfin/>

Hamilton, Ian. *Writers in Hollywood: 1915–1951*. New York: Harper and Row. 1990.

"Jane Murfin Crisp; Film Writer, Taken by Death." Obit. *Los Angeles Times* (11 Aug. 1955). Retrieved 16 April 2016.

Kear, Lynn, and King, James. *Evelyn Brent: The Life and Films of Hollywood's Lady Crook*. EBSCO eBook academic collection. Jefferson, NC: McFarland, 2009. Retrieved April 1, 2016.

Loos, Anita. *Kiss Hollywood Good-By*. The Viking Press. July 8, 1974.

Moss, Marilyn Ann. *Giant: George Stevens, A Life on Film*. Madison: University of Wisconsin Press, 2004, pp. 38–39.

Murfin, Patrick. "Celebrating Screenwriting Pioneer Jane Murfin." Heretic, Rebel, a Thing to Flout. May 6, 2012. Web. Retrieved April 20, 2016. <http://patrickmurfin.blogspot.com/2012/05/celebrating-screenwriting-pioneer-jane.html>

Parrill, Sue. *Jane Austen on Film and Television: A Critical Study of the Adaptations*. EBSCO eBook academic collection. Jefferson, NC: McFarland, 2002. Retrieved April 3, 2016.

"Strongheart Gets Last Cue." *Los Angeles Times* (25 June 1929). Retrieved 20 April 2016.

"Writing for a Dog Star." *New York Times* (17 June 1923). Retrieved 16 April 2016.

A Team in Passionate Action
Ruth Gordon and Garson Kanin

Rosanne Welch

AMANDA
Listen Adam. I know that deep down you agree
with me with all I believe and want and hope for.
We couldn't be so close if you didn't. If I didn't feel you did.
—From *Adam's Rib* by Ruth Gordon and Garson Kanin, 55

From the start Ruth Gordon and Garson Kanin had a writing career like few other writers in the Hollywood of the 1940s and 1950s. Their career earned them praise as "probably the greatest pure screenwriting collaboration in all Hollywood history" (McGilligan 90). They wrote all four of their films as original screenplays on speculation, not under the auspices of a particular studio producer, and the same personal friend, George Cukor, directed all four films. This resulted in the fact that none of their films underwent major studio rewrites by other writers. Gordon and Kanin were involved in the production of each film beginning in pre-production and all the way through filming and post-production periods; a privilege not granted many screenwriters then or now.

In the introduction to his interview with Kanin in 1991, Patrick McGilligan claims, "The films the Kanins wrote together signaled, to a large extent, the high tide of American sophisticated comedy. No films were (are) more admired by other Hollywood comedy writers—few films play as well today, without embarrassing concessions to yesteryear's artificialities" (McGilligan 90). His words are backed up by the fact that three of the four films—*A Double Life* (1947), *Adam's Rib* (1949), and *Pat and Mike* (1952)—earned Academy Award nominations for Best Original Screenplay. Only one can be considered in the genre of traditional boy-meets-girl romantic comedy (*Pat and Mike*) while one (*A Double Life*), fills the genre of Broadway-based film in that it concerns the life of an actor overwhelmed by his role as *Othello*. Two of the four films delve deeply into the study of marriage, *Adam's Rib* and *The Marrying Kind* (1952). One a comedy, one a drama, yet both deal with the gender politics of the day. The diversity of the films in tone and genre shows that the Gordon/Kanins were given rare privileges by the studio system in a period when most Hollywood artists—writers, directors, and actors—were typecast in one genre or another for the duration of their careers.

Though the Gordon/Kanins escaped typecasting, they could not avoid the other

Screenwriter Ruth Gordon and her partner, Garson Kanin, during production of *Pat and Mike*, 1952. They wrote four films together—three of which earned nominations for Best Original Screenplay—before returning to acting and directing. They remained married for the rest of Ruth's life (Academy of Motion Picture Arts and Sciences' Margaret Herrick Library).

fate that befell other writers in the studio system, having the credit for some of their best work granted to the director of their films in reviews and film history books, a fact that irked Kanin all his life. "You can imagine how I feel when I pick up, say, the *New Yorker* magazine and in the front are all the listings of the revival pictures. And they always refer to it as "George Cukor's *Adam's Rib*" (McGilligan 97). This may be one of the reasons Kanin left writing after the four films he did with Gordon and returned to directing.

While they only wrote four films together, the Gordon/Kanins continued to collaborate on each other's individual creative efforts without taking formal credit for the rest of their careers. Kanin's obituary in the *New York Times* notes the intense intimacy they shared:

> For most of his life, Mr. Kanin and his first wife, the actress Ruth Gordon, were a team. They were feisty, argumentative collaborators as playwrights and strikingly close as man and wife for 43 years. They became something of a fixture at the Russian Tea Room—first booth on the left—where they had lunch together almost every day. After Miss Gordon died in 1985, he said: "I'm half dead. If you understand what it's like to be a team, with Ruth no longer here I feel half alive, that's all. I don't feel completely with it" [Berger].

The Gordon/Kanin scripts also helped invent Katharine Hepburn's popular culture reputation for female empowerment. Upon Gordon's death in 1985 *New York Times* writer Mel Gussow wrote in his appreciation of her work: "Every time you enjoy Spencer Tracy and Katharine Hepburn sparring in *Adam's Rib* and *Pat and Mike*, remember who created their characters and wrote their witty dialogue. Ruth Gordon and Garson Kanin's contribution to the symbiosis of the Tracy-Hepburn team is inestimable" (Gussow). Biographers and critics of Hepburn often claimed that she based her independent women persona and characters on a combination of her mother and of Eleanor Roosevelt. I contend that Hepburn was also, even if subconsciously, basing the women in her Tracy/Hepburn films on Ruth Gordon. As actress and writer Elaine May once observed to Kanin about his wife, "She really is about the only person who gives you the feeling that maybe it *could* be a woman's world" (Ware 129).

Gordon and Kanin clearly had a feminist agenda at work in their films, one that focuses on the need for both members of a marriage to understand the inherent equality of the sexes and to respect the equal intellectual capacity of wives. When summarizing Kanin's screenwriting career author Richard Corliss says: "Because of Kanin's close collaboration with his wife on scripts written for another, very close couple—Tracy and Katharine Hepburn—the 'marriages' portrayed in ADAM'S RIB and PAT AND MIKE have a sense of natural familiarity and mutual respect rare in Hollywood domestic comedies" (Corliss 18). In fact, the Gordon/Kanin marriage proved so intrinsic to the work and the work to the marriage that once the work infringed on the marriage, the couple chose to end the working partnership in order to save the marital partnership. Decisiveness and determination seemed to be in their individual DNA from the beginning of their separate careers.

Almost anyone who worked with Gordon over the course of her career wrote with admiration for her determination to succeed as an actor despite not being considered a beautiful woman. In a 1936 letter to his friend Sibyl Colefax, playwright Thornton Wilder, one of Gordon's close personal friends, once wrote: "Every year sees the approach to final triumph of intelligence, will and character over a host of disadvantages. The disadvantages were voice, appearance, lack of a sense of "dress," undependable taste arising from her environment when a girl, and the heart-wrenching and career-blocking association with Jed [Harris—Broadway producer with whom Gordon had an open affair and a child out of wedlock]. All New York giggled fifteen years ago when she forced a doctor to break her knees in order to straighten her legs; well, it's a sample, anyway, of the incredible determination" (Wilder and Bryer 308).

Gordon was born Ruth Gordon Jones on October 30, 1896, in Quincy, Massachusetts. As an only child, she enjoyed the attention of both her parents, Annie and Clinton Jones and benefited from their prosperity by being able to finish a full twelve years of school at Quincy High, an experience not all American women were yet having. Though her father's profession as a sea captain seemed steeped in the past, she convinced him to let her be a woman of the new century by moving to New York as a single nineteen-year-old to study acting. When she first began writing plays many years later, she immortalized the moment of her father's consent in her play *Years Ago* (1947) and later in the film adaptation *The Actress* (1953). Clearly, the moment she gained her father's permission to leave home stood as a defining moment in her life, but also as proof that she had no qualms about putting her personal life on paper for an audience to experience.

Gordon's first sojourn into theatre earned mixed results. Cut from her class at the American Academy for the Arts for lack of talent, she gained the role of Nibs in a Broadway production of *Peter Pan* starring Maude Adams. In three separate memoirs, Gordon repeatedly mentions the review given her by Alexander Woollcott, famed theatre critic, member of the Algonquin Round Table and later a close personal friend. "Ruth Gordon was ever so gay as Nibs" (Gordon *My Side* 17). That small recognition bolstered her through a succession of failures and illustrates her understanding of the importance and power of words.

Gordon became a successful actress and companion and friend to several famed male writers and artists of the day, among them Woollcott, Thornton Wilder and Harpo Marx. While rumors were that both Woollcott and Wilder proposed to her at various points in their friendships, in 1921 Gordon married fellow actor Gregory Kelly, whom she met three years earlier when they co-starred in Booth Tarkington's *Seventeen* on Broadway. When Kelly died of heart disease at the age of 36 in 1927, Gordon became involved with married Broadway producer Jed Harris. In her autobiography she explains that while she aborted their first unplanned pregnancy, she chose to carry a second one to term, though an out of wedlock birth was still socially unacceptable, even in the world of the theatre (Gottfried 92).

Gordon gave birth on October 16, 1929, in Paris, France, far from the attention of the New York newspapers and originally offered to let Harris adopt the child they named Jones, in honor of Gordon's family. When she caught Harris having an affair shortly after the birth, she changed her mind and Jones Harris became Jones Kelly on his birth certificate. Her anger was short lived, however, as she and Harris continued their relationship when they moved back to New York (Gordon *My Side* 233–249 and Gottfried 106–114).

As a writer Gordon reflected on her complex young adulthood in her 1981 novel *Shady Lady,* which is the story of a showgirl who has an affair with famed producer Florence Ziegfeld. The copy on the book jacket uses italics to infer that *Shady Lady* is a fiction. "Fiction, *of course*, but *Shady Lady* is also a knowing, authentic portrait of the life and times of an insouciant showgirl, and of the whole bygone … more's the pity … era that made her possible." Earlier in the jacket text the lead character, Winona, is described as having "burst into flapper glory on Flo Ziegfeld's stage—as well as in his private hotel suite." It does not take much to make the jump from a fictional flapper girl becoming the mistress of the greatest dance spectacular producer of the day to the real actress that Gordon once was becoming the mistress of the greatest Broadway producer of her day. Furthermore, the rich man's father offers to adopt his heir if the actress mother will swear off any further part in raising the child, the same deal Harris originally made with Gordon. As the novel demonstrates, Gordon continued to write long after she and Kanin ended their screenwriting collaboration, yet writing had only become a consideration in her life after she married Kanin. Her sister-in-law, writer Fay Kanin, gave all the credit for Gordon's interest in writing to Kanin. "I don't think she would have written if she hadn't married Gar, but I think that impelled her" (Beauchamp "Woman of the Years" 17).

As a man, Kanin was so unlike Harris that it caught her inner circle by surprise when the couple came together. "Several of Kanin's postwar films paid unusually sympathetic attention to the aspirations of women as they challenged conventional sex roles" (Smith 249). In the Introduction to his book on famous Hollywood acting teams Kanin wrote: "Consider that even in some of our celebrated He-She Chemistries—the female is sometimes the He and the male the She. Just like in real life—if there is a real life" (Kanin *Together* 7). Clearly, Kanin's comfort with strong, independent women showed through much of his work.

Born Gershon Labe in Rochester, New York, on November 24, 1912, Kanin and his family later moved to Brooklyn, New York. Like Gordon, he attended the American Academy of Dramatic Arts but unlike her, he succeeded in the program. When the call went out for an actor with red hair for George Abbott's new play, *Ladies' Money*, Kanin dyed his hair and impressed Abbott enough with his determination and talent that he won the part (Berger). Soon after Kanin found his talents better suited the offstage aspects of the theatre. Abbott put Kanin in charge of directing the road companies of his productions. His work for Abbott drew the attention of independent film producer Sam Goldwyn for whom Kanin worked as an assistant for a year. When Goldwyn refused to let him progress to directing, Kanin moved to RKO Studios and began a string a successful directing assignments including *A Man to Remember* (1934), *Bachelor Mother* (1939), *My Favorite Wife* (1940), and *They Knew What They Wanted* (1940).

Only the advent of a Second World War could part Kanin from his career trajectory. Drafted into the U.S. Army Signal Corps in late 1941, he later co-directed *The True Glory* with Carol Reed. A feature-length documentary about Gen. Dwight D. Eisenhower's preparations for D-Day, the film won an Academy Award. After the war Kanin returned to Broadway with a play he had written during down time in the army. *Born Yesterday* (1946) became his first and only solo writing success.

On the verge of being drafted, Kanin met Gordon and began the personal relationship that would grow into a professional partnership. In *My Side* Gordon wrote:

> One night after [*Evening Sun*] rehearsal, Elia [Kazan] and I and some others went over to Sardi's. At another table sat Garson Kanin. We'd met once at Radio City Music Hall, the opening of his film *They Knew What They Wanted*, Charles Laughton and Carole Lombard the stars.... The second time I met Garson was dinner at George Cukor's. George and I, Garson Kanin and Katharine Hepburn. Neither time struck sparks; the third time we meshed. At least we knew we were going to. Leonard Lyons and I and Garson Kanin and Simone Simon at the Copa.
>
> At Sardi's, Garson came over to the table and asked if I could go Sunday night to *Candida*. Katherine Cornell was playing it one week for a benefit, Guthrie had directed it. It was at the Shubert and sold out, of course. Now Garson invited me. I looked at Elia. He'd told us to make no plans for Sunday, rehearse Sunday night.
> "It's important to me," I said.
> "Go. We'll rehearse around you." The words began my new life.
> I was in love again. For life [426].

Despite the fact that Gordon was 16 years older than Kanin they married in 1942 they remained together until her death in 1985. They were, in fact, in love for life.

In each of her three memoirs Gordon recalls that the idea of writing with Kanin came to her merely because she wanted to spend more of her days with him when he entered the military. When Kanin was stationed in Washington, D.C. Gordon moved there and came up with the idea for the play *Over Twenty-One*, based on their lives as artists suddenly thrust into military life. When she told Kanin her idea for a play "about us" he originally dismissed it as "not a play." After several friends disagreed with his opinion, Kanin recanted and they talked through her daily work on it. While it was their first experience writing together, only Gordon's name appeared as author (Gordon *My Side* 440).

The experience of working together on *Over Twenty-One* taught the Gordon/Kanins that they enjoyed sharing both their personal and their private lives. Kanin lovingly describes Gordon during a moment of striking creativity:

> A look I have come to know appeared on my wife's face. It is an expression that usually heralds the birth of an idea for a line, a character, a play, an effect, a theme, a matchmaking scheme, whatever. This look is generally followed by a beeline to the nearest pad and pencil where she may scribble a note, or sit for three hours surrounded by the invisible, impenetrable walls of her most private retreat [Kanin *Tracy* 262].

According to Gordon, she wrote alone during the day while Kanin worked with his military unit. At the end of his work day they would have what Gordon describes as an early dinner (considering theatre performers were used to eating after a show) and then they would walk to and from Lafayette Park talking about the play. When they returned home Gordon would show him what she'd written that day. Kanin would offer her stories he planned to use in a play sometime but hadn't yet, with the phrase, "I was going to use it, but you take it." Kanin seemed to understand that his wife preferred story fodder to gifts of flowers and candy. Gordon claims Kanin came up with the title *Over Twenty-One* since he heard her give that as her age once and liked the wit of it (Gordon *My Side* 441). She describes his assistance on her first play by saying, "When a playwright needs help, it's beautiful to be married to another playwright!" (Gordon *My Side* 449). This comment illustrates the importance of their relationship to both the craft and the content of the product they created.

Gordon's potential contribution to Kanin's first writing experience, *Born Yesterday*, is not documented. He wrote it while in the army after they had been married for a few years and directed it for three years to full houses on Broadway, from 1946 to 1949 (Berger). It is significant that each of their individual first writing experiences came from writing Broadway plays since the writer's power in that medium is equal to, if not stronger, than that of a director. It may be one of the reasons they were more comfortable writing speculative scripts in Hollywood rather than working under a studio contract. When Columbia bought the film rights of *Born Yesterday* in 1950, the studio hired George Cukor to direct. The Gordon/Kanins were comfortable with that choice. They had come to know Cukor after Gordon had written him a complimentary letter on how well he directed Katharine Hepburn in *The Philadelphia Story* (1940). In response to the letter, Cukor asked MGM casting director Billy Grady to hire Gordon for his next film assignment, *Two Faced Woman* (1941). This complimentary letter of Gordon's was no mere nicety. The Gordon/Kanins were known for their business acumen as much as for their other talents. Cukor would later joke about being "infected with the Kanins' shameless mania for publicity" (Levy 345). The Gordon/Kanins maintained the combination of business acumen and artistic control throughout their professional careers.

After their two separate successes on Broadway, Gordon and Kanin collaborated fully on their first speculative screenplay, *A Double Life*, which starred Raymond Massey and became such a hit that Hollywood wanted more work by the team. "We were trapped by success," Mr. Kanin said. "The studio wanted us to write together or not at all" (Berger).

As no new events in their own lives yet inspired them, Gordon told Kanin the story of Massey's wife, Dorothy Ludington Massey, and her first husband, which influenced the creation of *Adam's Rib*. When Massey and his first wife divorced, a married set of lawyers represented them individually. After earning the divorce decree the married lawyers also divorced and then each married their former client, leaving Ludington with Massey as her second husband while her former husband married Massey's former wife. According to film historian David Kimmel this gave them the idea of a movie about married lawyers on different sides of a case.

Gordon and Kanin wrote what became *Adam's Rib* with their friends Katharine Hepburn and Spencer Tracy in mind to play the married lawyers. The male lawyer, Adam, is assigned by his firm to prosecute a woman for shooting at her philandering husband as the female lawyer, Amanda, takes up the defense of the accused shooter. "Their original title "Man and Wife" highlighted the battle of the sexes theme of the story and it was purchased by MGM, not the usual way business was done in the late forties/early fifties" (Gordon *Open Book* 360 and Kimmel 82–84.) Studio executives thought the title too risqué, hence the change, but they loved the script. Studio producer Lawrence Weingarten said in an interview later in life, "It was the first time in thirty years that the studio had seen a screenplay that was ready to shoot immediately, without changes" (Kimmel 84).

Stanley Cavell in *Pursuits of Happiness: The Hollywood Comedy of Remarriage* believes the equality represented in the fictional marriage was essential to why the film worked

> The sense of participation or partnership in their intimacy is essential to the way the film works, because it is exactly this intimacy that the woman puts on trial in taking her marriage to court. We will not understand her bravery (nor, hence, the man's) unless we know that for her their intimacy, their privacy, their home at home, is almost everything [192].

Orit Kamir notes the gender transcendence in the piece when he writes,

> The ancient notion of "couple" takes on a new dimension when, in the context of Hollywood's conventions, the viewer is invited to identify with a symbiotic pair of male-female heroes. Gender roles—both on and off screen—are transcended when the man-woman couple is posed as the fundamental unity reconciling contradictory myths [Kamir 6].

Discussing which films he chose to analyze for his book on great romantic comedies, Kimmel calls *Adam's Rib* "arguably the best of the Spencer Tracy / Katharine Hepburn matchups," where, as married lawyers on opposing sides of a case, the question of sexism (a word not yet coined) could be addressed within in the conventions of a traditional "battle of the sexes" (Kimmel 6). Later, in a chapter dedicated to the film, Kimmel reiterates that the film never became dated because the argument put forth by Hepburn's character still exists. Amanda's idea that there ought not to be a double standard for men and women

> is born of not only Hepburn's (and Ruth Gordon's) [Kimmel includes Gordon here, not this author] independence and feistiness, but the dawning of a new attitude about women's roles after they had contributed so greatly to the recent war effort.... Amanda's case that women should be subjected to the same expectations as men anticipates the debates that would take place in the 1960s and 1970s.

Finally, Kimmel insists the major reason this particular battle of the sexes stays contemporary is because, "this is a couple deeply in love, and part of their fun comes from their playful contention" (Kimmel 92).

Several critics and film historians claim that the natural charisma between Hepburn and Tracy helped make the films they made together, including Gordon and Kanin films, so successful, and this certainly contributed. Kanin himself contributed to that idea in his own biography of the couple, *Tracy and Hepburn: an Intimate Memoir* (1970). The next collaborator considered in discussions of *Adam's Rib* has generally been Cukor, who directed all four of the original Gordon/Kanin screenplays and insured the couple's continued control over content. The trio shared an equal creative relationship. According to Cukor,

> It was a very happy and very equal collaboration. Ruth and Garson worked very closely together—no question of a writer trying to get his wife a job. Garson was a brilliant playwright and screenwriter and had the enormous advantage of knowing his *métier* very well—he'd already directed some successful comedies. Many of the lovely directorial touches in our films together were in the script [Lambert *Cukor* 192].

This mutual understanding of what constituted an equal marriage was evident from the beginning of the screenplay for *Adam's Rib*. In 1972 the screenplay was published in book form as part of the *MGM's Library of Film Scripts* series for Viking Press. A note at the beginning explains that it was the original script with square brackets denoting parts that were not filmed and footnotes showing additions made during filming, while Gordon and Kanin were present on the set. In the opening scene of this original screenplay a New York City doorman approaches the door of the Bonner apartment and drops off two newspapers, not one to share, but two, representing the fact that each member of the marriage has a professional need to know the news of the day and their respect for each other extends to spending the extra money required to give them each their own copy. Then Amanda Bonner is introduced in the action lines by a full assortment of names: "Meet Amanda. Amanda Faring Bonner. Also known as Mrs. Bonner (to neighbors, doormen and headwaiters). As Amanda Faring to others (of Boyd, Karsh, Faring and Wellman). As Miss Faring (to the staff there). As Madoo (to close friends), and as Pinkie (to her husband)." From this the audience learns the many faces of Amanda, the fact that she only uses her married name socially but not as a partner in her law firm, though in the film, perhaps because it would have consumed too much dialogue to explain, her office door reads "Law Office of Amanda Bonner."

The issue of the equality of the genders appears often in the script in small moments and large. They open the first courtroom scene on the exterior of the façade of the Court of General Sessions "featuring the chiseled Jefferson Inscription" which reads "Equal and exact justice to all men of whatever state or persuasion." Here both the word equality and the word men appear prominently and in juxtaposition. Why not all women? The phrase seems to mock the very argument Amanda has prepared to make. Also, noticeable in the stage directions is the fact that of Adam's three assistants at his counsel table, one is a woman. This is not a cast note that often appeared in law films of that era. Her appearance suggests Amanda's career trajectory. The largest moment involving equality comes when Amanda brings in a collection of women from generally male fields—chemistry, foreman, and weight lifter—and asks the court to "be fair to the Fair Sex" (75–81).

Once *Adam's Rib* solidified Gordon and Kanin's reputation as a reliable writing team, they wrote *Pat and Mike* and offered it to Cukor to direct. *Pat and Mike* functions as more of a classic romantic comedy as it is about the coming together of two distinct opposites; a female athlete fashioned in the mold of Babe Didrikson Zaharias, played again by Hepburn and her rough and gruff manager, played by Tracy. The success of *Pat and Mike* gave the writing team the chance to do something more challenging.

By the time Gordon and Kanin began work on *The Marrying Kind* in 1951, the tension that writing together placed on their marriage became unbearable. Years later, when interviewed about their working collaboration, Kanin said,

> When we wrote together, I would say a line and laugh hysterically, and she would look at me stonily and say, "What's funny about that?" Sometimes we'd compromise, which never satisfied either of us. Sometimes, because I was much more experienced than Ruth in directing, she would defer to me. But I wasn't always right, you see. Or I'd hold back my opinion because she's very sensitive. She could always tell anyway. So we stopped collaborating [Levin].

He repeats that story with more intensity in the introduction to *My Side*, where he explains how they stopped writing together in order to save their marriage:

> The writing side of her was fiercely disciplined, exhaustingly thorough, keep-out private, and maddeningly stubborn. I was divorced from this one [he's referring to the writing side of Gordon] many years ago, after writing four successful original screenplays with her. We quarreled on each of them with increasing intensity and decided to go our separate ways. After which, a return to Eden—for the most part [Gordon *My Side* Introduction].

Perhaps not coincidentally, rather than writing a comedy about a professional working marriage to wrap up their professional collaboration, they wrote a drama about a working class marriage in its death throes. *The Marrying Kind* became the last project where they would share writers credit in that era. Twenty-eight years later, in 1980, they shared their last writing credit on the script for a television movie, *Hardhat and Legs*, about a professor who falls in love with a construction worker (Roberts 279).

Many critics believe *The Marrying Kind* illustrated a more realistic portrayal of marriage in America than previously seen on film. Brandon French in *On the Verge of Revolt: Women in American Films of the Fifties* wrote that the end of the film, where the couple promises to try again, but do not promise unrealistically to change, is the "beginning of the public re-conception by Americans of marriage in general." French quotes the line, "The kind of love they got in books and movies, that's not for people. You've got to be more realistic" and considered this moment emblematic of the way Gordon and Kanin captured the "central paradox of the American bourgeois marriage—She stays at home, bored and lonely, while he works 'for her'" (French 27–32).

The 1952 *New York Times* review of the film felt its potential impact from the start:

> *The Marrying Kind* is not so funny when tragedy strikes the little home and a good bit of mutual understanding and sacrifice are required. And it is in this phase of the story that Miss Gordon and Mr. Kanin have conveyed the poignancy of frustrations that make marriage so challenging. It is here that they prove their moral—that the natural and ever-hopeful chase after glittering, material ambitions is a wistful and endless dream [Crowther].

While analyzing the portrayal of democracy in post–World War II Judith Smith placed *The Marrying Kind* in a new genre of her own creation, postwar married realism. This new genre created alternative representations of courtship and marriage "focusing on love and intimacy, these stories featured men and women creating new kinds of marriage" (Smith 244–245). Smith claims that the writers in this new genre, including Gordon and Kanin, had Communist sympathies and so they created stories "shaped by writers who observed at first hand the unsteady boundaries between working-class ethnic cultures and cosmopolitan sexual modernism. A "modern marriage" promised the security of middle-class inclusion and romantic intimacy, along with freedoms not available to those in a "traditional" marriage embedded in obligations to kin and community" (Smith 246). Smith notes that many male writers in the post-war period had wives who worked for wages and relished the deeper intellectual relationships that shared knowledge of the work world created. She also considers the fact that these writers, men and women, came of age in the 1930s and 1940s, when sexual emotional intimacy and pleasure filled the worlds of advertising and music. All of these descriptions suit the Gordon/Kanins' lives.

The characters learn that knowing that a marriage can so easily be broken helps because they can now treasure their family all the more. In this way the near loss of Florence and Chet's marriage mirrors Gordon and Kanin learning how close they came to letting work issues destroy something more important. At the end of the film, Florence and Chet watch the bailiff erase their case number and names from the next day's list—as Gordon and Kanin essentially erased their names from sharing credit on any future scripts.

Even though they stopped sharing credit on projects, Gordon/Kanin never stopped working together. Kanin discussed Gordon's influence when he was writing *A Name for Herself* (renamed *It Should Happen to You*) in 1954. Kanin wanted a Danny Kaye type male lead but Gordon told him it would only work with a female lead. Gordon then suggested one of their favorite actresses and personal friend Judy Holliday for the part. Kanin took his wife's advice (Kanin *Hollywood* 198–199). Then, in 1955 Kanin gained great critical acclaim for directing *The Diary of Anne Frank*, written by Frances and Albert Hackett.

Actress Susan Strasberg, cast as the young Anne Frank, wrote that Gordon came to the theatre constantly during the pre-production period of the play,

> advising and lending moral support. She was delightful, as was Gar, but he was cerebral, exacting, thorough, whereas Ruth was spontaneous, warm, outgoing, the kind of person everyone should have on his side. She had put some of her own money into the show.... During rehearsals, whenever I was having difficulty interpreting a reflective passage or timing a laugh line, she'd come to my room and talk to me about her struggles when she was a young actress. I'd realize her stories always pertained to the problem I was having [Strasberg 68].

The fact that Gordon helped finance the production illustrates the fact that the play frightened some financial backers, but that Gordon believed in Kanin's ability to make the tragic story accessible to the average Broadway audience. Both the cast and the critics agreed. As Walter Kerr writes, Kanin "had not so much directed the play with love, as orchestrated it" (Schildkraut 236).

The Gordon/Kanins continued their professional collaborations into the sixties according to this letter from Thornton Wilder:

> I saw the Kanins in Boston. They're working at an awful pitch of tension, shaping and reshaping that vast project [*Do Re Mi*—Comden and Green musical for which Kanin wrote the book and directed and Gordon took no formal credit]. I believe it will be a success, but at what a cost. I get downright mad at the extent to which it has removed Ruth and Gar from all other interests, from all other exercise of their gifts, from their friends [Wilder and Bryer 576].

Clearly the act of professional collaboration fed their personal relationship. According to Kanin in his Introduction to Gordon's third memoir, published posthumously, Gordon needed writing as much as she needed acting:

She explained that her two professions were closely related—that her acting fed her writing and the other way around…. She was on the verge of beginning Act Two of a new play when she died. She was eighty-eight years old and I had the indescribably great fortune of sharing precisely half of that wondrous life. Three days before her death, she said, "I'm in love with the past, but I'm having a love affair with the future" [Gordon 3].

Kanin, who never retired, became president of the Authors League of America in the wake of Gordon's death. Five years later, he married Broadway actress Marion Seldes, whom he had once directed in a play, though they never wrote together. He died in 1999 at the age of 86. *Adam's Rib* lives on in perpetual reruns on television, at film festivals across the country, and in gender studies classes around the world.

Works Cited

Beauchamp, Cari. "Woman of the Years." *Written by Magazine* Vol. 5, issue 8 (September 2001): 12–19.
Berger, Marilyn. "Garson Kanin, a Writer and Director of Classic Movies and Plays, Is Dead at 86." *New York Times*, 14 March 1999: Accessed: July 17, 2009.
Cavell, Stanley. *Pursuits of Happiness: The Hollywood Comedy of Remarriage*. Cambridge: Harvard University Press, 1981.
Corliss, Richard. Editor. *The Hollywood Screenwriters: A Film Comment Book*. New York: The Hearst Corporation/Avon Books, 1970.
Crowther, Bosley. "The Screen: Two New Films on Local Scene; 'The Marrying Kind,' with Judy Holliday and Aldo Ray, Has Premiere at Victoria British Film, 'Marry Me,' Comes to Art Theatre—Patrick Holt and Susan Shaw in Cast." *New York Times*, 14 March 1952.
French, Brandon. *On the Verge of Revolt: Women in American Films of the Fifties*. New York: Frederick Ungar Publishing Co., 1978.
Gordon, Ruth. *My Side: The Autobiography of Ruth Gordon*. New York: Primus/Donald I. Fine, Inc, 1976.
_____. *Ruth Gordon: An Open Book*. Garden City: Doubleday & Company, Inc., 1980.
Gordon, Ruth, and Garson Kanin, *Adam's Rib: MGM's Library of Film Scripts* (New York: Viking Press, 1972), 55.
Gottfried, Martin. *Jed Harris: The Curse of Genius*. Boston: Little Brown and Company, 1984.
Gussow, Mel. "Grit And Wit Made Ruth Gordon a Star," *New York Times* 8 September 1985: Accessed July 22, 2009.
Kamir, Orit. *Framed: Women in Law and Film*. Durham: Duke University Press, 2006.
Kanin, Garson. *Together Again! The Stories of the Great Hollywood Teams*. New York: Doubleday and Company, Inc., 1981.
_____. *Tracy and Hepburn: An Intimate Memoir*. New York: Viking Press, 1970.
Kimmel, Daniel M. *I'll Have What She's Having: Behind the Scenes of the Great Romantic Comedies*. Chicago: Ivan R. Dee, 2008.
Lambert, Gavin. *On Cukor*. New York: G.P. Putnam's Sons, 1972.
Levin, Eric. "Garson Kanin and Ruth Gordon Agree That Disagreeing Keeps Them Together as Man and Wife." *People Magazine* 14, no. 15 (October 13, 1980) http://www.people.com/people/archive/article/0,,20077614,00.html. Accessed: July 17, 2009.
Levy, Emmanual. *George Cukor: Master of Elegance*. New York: William Morrow and Company, 1994.
McGilligan, Patrick. *Backstory: Interviews with Screenwriters of the 1940s and 1950s*. Oakland: University of California Press, 1991.
Roberts, Jerry. *The Great American Playwrights on the Screen*. New York: Applause Theatre and Cinema Books, 2003.
Schildkraut, Joseph. *My Father and I*. New York: Viking Press, 1959.
Smith, Judith E. *Visions of Belonging: Family Stories, Popular Culture and Post-War Democracy, 1940–1960*. New York: Columbia University Press, 2004.
Strasberg, Susan. *Bittersweet*. New York: G.P. Putnam's Sons, 1980.
Ware, Susan. *Letter to the World: Seven Women Who Shaped the American Century*. New York: W.W. Norton and Company, 1998.
Wilder, Robin G., and Jackson R. Bryer. *The Selected Letters of Thornton Wilder*. New York: HarperCollins, 2008.

About the Contributors

Chelsea **Andes** joined the inaugural class of the Stephens College MFA in TV and Screenwriting. She graduated with honors in May 2017. Her lifelong interest in TV and film led to her first attempt at screenwriting. She joined The Foundry, a subsidiary of Time Inc. and The Meredith Corporation, as a production asssistant in 2018.

Amy L. **Banks** graduated from the inaugural class of the Stephens College MFA in TV and screenwriting in 2017. She is an adjunct professor of English at State Fair Community College in Missouri where she also teaches adult education. Her screenplays, *Red Road Rastas* and *Rezpocalypse*, focus on giving a voice to the elderly and Native American women.

Julie **Berkobien** graduated from Stephens College with her MFA in TV and screenwriting in the spring of 2017. Her interests include the stage, post-production and screenwriting. She works as a researcher for award-winning historian, documentary filmmaker and author, Cari Beauchamp. She also served as photograph editor to this volume.

Mikayla **Daniels** earned her MFA in TV and screenwriting from Stephens College. She is an Emmy-winning video editor, as well as an on-camera host and writer for KSPS Saturday Night Cinema in Spokane, Washington. She has written several feature screenplays set in her home state of Alaska.

Elizabeth **Dwyer** earned her MFA in TV and screenwriting from Stephens College in 2017. She wrote and co-produced two award-winning short films, *Imagining Vera* and *Pinky Promise*, and she writes feminist erotic fiction for Bellesa.co. Her scripts have placed in several competitions, from the Austin Film Festival to the George R.R. Martin Screenwriting Grant.

Khanisha **Foster** is the recipient of the 2017 Fox Foundation Resident Actor Fellowship. She is also the associate artistic director of the podcast *2nd Story* and was a featured storyteller on NPR's *The Dinner Party*. Her story *Dance Outside Yourself* was published in *A Mixtape of Words*. She hosts the podcast *How I Wrote That* on women writing in Hollywood.

Sydney **Haven** is a graduate of the inaugural class of the Stephens College MFA in TV and screenwriting. She is also a writer whose interests include creating inclusive content that accurately reflects the diversity of everyday life.

Toni Anita **Hull** is a writer and comedian with an MFA in TV and screenwriting from Stephens College. She has performed stand-up in New York, Pennsylvania, and Los Angeles, including the world famous Comedy Store.

Laura **Kirk** is an award-winning filmmaker with credits including Cannes films *American Honey* and *Lisa Picard Is Famous*, which she co-wrote, and was a contributor to *Fast, Cheap and Under Control*. Kirk co-founded the mentoring program Women of Lawrence Film and is a full-time lecturer at the University of Kansas in both theater and film.

About the Contributors

Jackie **Perez** has been an MIT engineer, a Naval Officer and is now a screenwriter. She worked as an assistant in Hollywood for several years, and graduated from the Stephen College MFA in TV and screenwriting in 2017. Her interests include watching and writing horror films.

Amelia **Phillips** is a writer, actress, and producer. She earned her MFA in TV and screenwriting from Stephens College. She writes about the female identity, Judaism, social justice and family. She wrote and starred in the play *Grow a Pair of ... Wings* (The Lounge Theatre). She is the literary manager of LA–based theater company FRESH PRODUCE'd LA.

Sarah **Phillips** is a director, producer and award-winning screenwriter. She runs Phileon Productions, a production company that focuses on increasing the number of women in front of and behind the camera. The company produces films, VR content, web series, commercials, and theatre. She holds her MFA in TV and screenwriting from Stephens College.

Pamela L. **Scott** is a former helicopter pilot serving in both the U.S. Army and Alaska Air National Guard. She completed her second masters' degree with the inaugural class of the Stephens College MFA in TV and screenwriting.

Yasser Omar **Shahin** is a screenwriter and earned his MFA in TV and screenwriting from Stephens College. He works as a screenwriting lecturer at Eastern Washington University and is now a Middle East writing consultant for Hollywood's show runners and writers.

Lauren Elizabeth **Smith** graduated with an MFA from Stephens College in 2017. In 2016, her spec screenplay for *Orange Is the New Black* was a finalist in Scriptapoolza. She advocates for young women and LGBTQ youth in her writing.

Amanda R. **Stockwell** is a writer and teacher who has had the opportunity to experience other places and cultures due to being a military wife. Her interests include writing animation scripts, science fiction and fantasy.

Chase **Thompson** is an assistant professor of digital filmmaking at Stephens College. His love of film and story led him to screenwriting and research where he aims to reestablish forgotten voices while promoting new ones.

Rosanne **Welch** earned her Ph.D. from Claremont Graduate University in California. She teaches the history of screenwriting for the Stephens College MFA in TV and screenwriting. Her professional writing credits include *Beverly Hills 90210* and *Touched by an Angel*, among others. Some of her publications include *Why the Monkees Matter*, *Women in American History*, and *America's Forgotten Founding Father: Filippo Mazzei*.

Sarah Amble **Whorton** earned her MFA in TV and screenwriting from Stephens College in 2017. She was chosen to present her paper on Adela Rogers St. Johns at the 2016 Citizen Jane Film Festival. The panel "When Women Ran Hollywood" was part of the festival's "Film School." She is a strategic communications associate for Mizzou Online at the University of Missouri.

Kelley C. **Zinge** is a playwright, performer and professional vocalist. She earned her MFA in TV and screenwriting at Stephens College. She has written many musical revues and programs on the LGBTQ experience in World War II and Native American Trickster tales. She has performed her Patsy Cline revue to sold out audiences across Colorado and New Mexico.

Index

Academy Awards 2, 9, 15, 17, 58, 61, 153, 175, 177, 180–181, 188, 205, 209
Academy of Motion Picture Arts and Sciences 5–6, 25, 58
The Actress 208
Adam's Rib 9, 205–207, 211–212, 215
After the Thin Man 144
Akins, Zoë 9, 183–191
Alas and Alack 134
Alcott, Louisa May 9
Algonquin Round Table 18, 159, 208
All for Peggy 135
Anastasia, Czarina 194
Angle Shooter 14
Arizona 179
Arzner, Dorothy 14, 188
Astor, Mary 61

Back in Circulation 14
Ball, Lucille 147
Barrymore, Ethel 187
Barrymore, John 60–62, 73
Barrymore, Lionel 15
Beauchamp, Cari 1, 4–5, 32, 40, 105–106, 114
Belasco, David 81–82
Ben-Hur (1924) 7, 57–58, 60–61, 102, 112–113
Beranger, Clara 8, 121, 125–132
Bergman, Ingrid 197
The Big House 2
Biograph Studios 24, 38, 56–57, 113
Blaché, Alice Guy 6, 33, 47–55
Blaché, Herbert 47, 52, 54
Blacklist 8, 67, 164, 192
Blood and Sand 7, 97, 99–101
The Blot 109
Bogart, Humphrey 142
Born Yesterday 209=210
Bow, Clara 7, 65–67, 80–81, 84, 89
Boy Meets Girl 195
Brackett, Charles 184
Brawn of the North 202

The Cabbage Fairy 51
Camille (1921) 7, 99, 101–102, 188
Campbell, Alan 160–164

Capra, Frank 145–146, 196
Captain January (1924) 84
Careers for Women 137–138
Casablanca 58, 149, 171
Cather, Willa 185
The Cat's Meow 90
The Champ 2, 18, 200
Chaney, Lon 80, 83, 118, 122, 133–134
Chaplin, Charlie 5, 71, 74, 91, 99
Chatterton, Ruth 188
The Cheat 28, 30–32
The Children's Hour 8, 151
Christopher Strong 189
Cleopatra (1934) 25
The Consequences of Feminism 53
Corbaley, Kate 2, 120
Crawford, Joan 11
Cukor, George 17, 44–45, 180–181, 203, 205–206, 209, 212
Curtiz, Michael 58–60

Dance Madness 65
Dark Star 8, 120
Davenport, Dorothy 14, 121
Davies, Marion 2, 41, 91
Davis, Bette 203
Death and Taxes 157
DeMille, Cecil B. 1–2, 6, 20, 24–31, 65, 81, 83, 104, 110, 118, 122, 129
de Mille, Richard 120–122, 128–129
de Mille, William C. 8, 65, 71–72, 81, 121–122, 126–127
Dialogue for a Horse 194
The Diary of Anne Frank 8, 145, 147–148, 214
Dr. Jekyll and Mr. Hyde (1920) 126, 128
Don Juan 61
Doorways in Drumorty 8, 119
A Double Life 205
The Dramatists Guild 143
Dressler, Marie 2, 13, 120, 187
The Drunken Mattress 51
Dynamite 31–32

Earhart, Amelia 12
Easter Parade 146
Edison, Thomas Alva 50

Edison Company 20, 24
Emerson, John 28, 39–40, 43–45
Enough Rope 160
Ephron, Nora 154–155
Epstein, Julius 149
Esquire Magazine 164

Fairbanks, Douglas 1, 5, 27, 38, 40, 178–179
Fairfax, Marion 7, 69–79
Famous Players Lasky 25–26, 70–71, 76, 80, 82–83, 89, 126, 168, 176
Father of the Bride (1949) 146
Father's Little Dividend (1951) 146
Ferber, Edna 159
Final Verdict 15
First National 72, 74–75, 176
Fitzgerald, F. Scott 9, 43, 203
Fonda, Jane 154
Fontaine, Joan 169–170, 172
The Fool and His Money 53
Foreign Correspondent 171
Four Horsemen of the Apocalypse 1, 7, 98–100
Free Soul 15
From the Manger to the Cross 8, 114

Garbo, Greta 2, 15, 58, 61, 121, 188
Garland, Judy 146
Gaumont, Léon 6, 48–49, 51–52
Gaumont Company 50–51, 54
Gauntier, Gene 8, 112–116, 121
Gentlemen Prefer Blondes 1, 6, 35, 42–43, 65
A Girl Like I 37, 42, 45
Gish, Lillian 2, 37
Glyn, Elinor 7, 88–94
The Godless Girl 30
Goodrich, Frances 8, 140–150
Gordon, Ruth 9, 205–216
Grable, Betty 67
Grant, Cary 172, 195
The Great Moment 88
The Greeks Had a Word for It 187–188
Griffith, D.W. 5, 20, 24, 37–39, 51, 56, 83, 104, 106–107, 110

220 Index

Hackett, Albert 8, 140–150
Hammett, Dashiell 143, 152, 155, 162
The Hand That Rocks 106
Harlow, Jean 1, 44
Harrison, Joan 9, 161, 166–174
Hart, Moss 145
Hayakawa, Sessue 71
Hayes, Helen 45
Hays Code 44, 61, 151, 172, 194–195
Hearst, William Randolph 12–13, 90–91
Heckerling, Amy 137
Heerman, Victor 9, 175–182
Hellman, Lillian 8–9, 147, 149, 151–156, 161–162, 190
Hepburn, Audrey 148
Hepburn, Katharine 8, 181, 188–189, 197, 203, 207, 209, 211
The Hidden Way 134, 136–137
His Double Life (1930) 129
His Girl Friday 12, 172
His Picture in the Papers 39
Hitchcock, Alfred 9, 82, 161, 166, 168–169, 171–172, 174
The Honeycomb 12, 16, 18
Hopper, Hedda 2, 166–167
House Un-American Activities Committee (HUAC) 8, 150, 154, 156, 162, 197
How to Marry a Millionaire 188

Ince, Thomas 38, 90, 106, 178
Interpretations 184
Intolerance 39, 106
It 66, 88, 91
It's a Wonderful Life 8, 145–146

Jamaica Inn 169
Johnson, Nunnally 147
Julia 154

Kalem Company 113
Kanin, Garson 9, 140, 147–148, 205–216
Keaton, Buster 101
Kelly, Gene 146, 194
Kennedy, John F. 27
The Kid 99
The King of Kings 20, 26
Kiss Hollywood Good-by 45
Kiss Me, Kate 194

Lady in the Dark 145
Lady of the Night 15
Laemmle, Carl 65, 108
Lasky, Jesse 82, 88
Leave It to Me 194
Lilies of the Field 75
The Little American 30
The Little Foxes 8, 152, 161
Little Women (1933) 9, 176–177, 180–181
Lois Weber Productions 108–109
The Long, Long Trailer 147
Loos, Anita 1, 3, 5–6, 35–45, 65, 67, 89, 97, 188, 202
Los Angeles Times 20, 33, 173

The Lost World 73, 75
Love, Laughter, and Tears: My Hollywood Story 11, 16, 18
Loy, Myrna 143, 155
Luce, Clare Booth 44
The Lying Truth 73–74

Maas, Ernest 66
Maas, Frederica Sagor 7, 63–68, 84
Macpherson, Jeanie 1, 6, 20–33, 57–58, 97, 118
Madame's Cravings 51
Male and Female 28, 30, 32, 118
Marion, Frances 1–5, 16–18, 40, 88, 91, 97, 105–106, 120–121, 123, 178, 188, 200, 203
Marion Fairfax Production 72, 74
The Marrying Kind 205, 213–214
Marshall Neilan Productions 72–73
The Marx Brothers 9
Mason, Sarah Y. 9, 175–182
Mathis, June 1, 7, 95–103
May, Elaine 207
Mayer, Louis B. 2, 5
The Medicine Man 85
Mencken, H.L. 41, 43
Meredyth, Bess 7, 25, 56–62, 203
Metro-Goldwyn-Mayer (MGM) 1–2, 25, 43, 57–58, 60, 88, 142, 147, 160–161, 177, 190, 202–203, 210–212
Min and Bill 120–121
Minelli, Vincent 146–147
Minter, Mary Miles 27
Miss Fane's Baby Is Stolen 14
Miss Lulu Bett 126–127
Moon, Lorna 8, 117–124
Murfin, Jane 9, 17, 200–204
Murray, Mae 66
My Favorite Wife 195
My Side 209, 213
Mystery of the Leaping Fish 39

Neilan, Marshall 74, 178
The New York Hat 37
New York Times 14, 35, 95, 193, 200, 202, 207, 213
The New Yorker 160, 206
Noah's Ark 58
Normand, Mabel 11, 16

Old Love for New 14
The Old Maid 190
Old Wives for New 31
Only a Fireman's Bride 38
Over Twenty-One 210

Paramount Studios 26, 66, 71, 80, 121, 142, 145, 190
Park, Ida May 8, 77, 133–139
Parker, Dorothy 9, 157–165
Parsons, Louella 128
Pat and Mike 205–207, 212–213
Pathé 25, 133
Phantom Lady 173
The Philadelphia Story 210
Photoplay 1, 3, 13, 22–23, 39, 137

Pickford, Mary 2, 5, 25, 27, 30, 37, 73, 80, 82, 88, 97, 178
The Pirate 146
Pitts, ZaSu 2, 178–179, 187
The Plastic Age 65, 81, 84
Poor Little Rich Girl 2
The Poor Simp 177–178
Powell, William 140, 195
The Price of Silence 136
Pulitzer Prize 8–9, 18, 148, 151–152, 183, 190, 194

The Reason Why 92, 94
Rebecca 169, 172
Red Headed Woman 43–44
Redgrave, Vanessa 154
Reid, Wallace 14
Rex Motion Picture Company 133
RKO Pictures 172, 176, 180–181, 201, 203, 209
The Roaring Road 71, 73
Rogers, Ginger 145, 148, 203
Rolled Stockings 66
Rosemary's Baby 9
Russell, Rosalind 13

Saboteur 173
St. Johns, Adela Rogers 2, 5–6, 9, 11–18, 67, 98, 200
Samson and Delilah 63
San Francisco 45
The Saphead 101
Schulberg, B.P. 65, 80, 83–84
Screen Writers Guild 1, 143, 145–146, 162, 203
The Sea Beast 60
Selznick, David O. 17, 169, 176, 178, 181, 189
Sennett, Mack 38, 176
Shady Lady 208
Shearer, Norma 15, 66–67, 202
Sherlock Holmes 73
The Shocking Miss Pilgrim 66–67
The Single Standard 15
The Skyrocket 17–18
Smalley, Phillip 106, 133
Smart Woman 15
Smilin' Through 202
Solax Studios 52, 54
Some Are Born Great 18
Spewack, Bella 9, 192–199
Spewack, Sam 9, 192–199
A Star Is Born (1937) 9, 18, 161
Stevens, George 148
Stewart, Jimmy 144
Stromberg, Hunt 144, 203
Strongheart 9, 200, 202
Such Men Are Dangerous 90
Suspense 107
Suspicion 171–172
Swanson, Gloria 13, 28, 30, 32

Talmadge, Constance 41
Talmadge, Norma 202
Tarzan's Romance 57
Taylor, William Desmond 11
The Ten Commandments (1923) 20, 26

Thalberg, Irving 1–2, 43–44, 58, 61, 66, 144
The Thin Man 8, 143–144, 155
The 39 Steps 168
Three Weeks 88, 92
Tiffany Pictures 66
Tony Award 194
Triangle Films 38
The True Glory 209
Twentieth Century-Fox 148

United Artists 5
Universal Studios 20, 24–25, 57, 107–108, 133–134, 137
Unsell, Eve 7, 77, 80–87
Up Pops the Devil 142, 144

Valentino, Rudolph 1, 60, 97–98, 100
Variety 17, 74, 82, 176–177, 180–181
Vidor, King 88, 178
Vitagraph 201

Walt Disney Studios 138
Warner, Jack 5
Warner Bros. Studios 138, 190
Weber, Lois 2–3, 8, 104–111, 133–134
A Welcome to Britain 195–196
Wharton, Edith 189–190
What Price Hollywood? 9, 17, 200, 203
The Whispering Chorus 29
Wilder, Thornton 207–208, 214
Wilson, Carey 65
Winchell, Walter 12
A Woman of Affairs 58, 61
The Women 44, 45, 202–203
Wonder of Women 58
Woollcott, Alexander 159, 208
Writers Guild of America 7, 65, 71, 84, 147, 203
Writing for the Screen 130–131

yellow peril 7, 83

Zukor, Adolph 27, 82

www.ingramcontent.com/pod-product-compliance
Lightning Source LLC
Chambersburg PA
CBHW081554300426
44116CB00015B/2881